Shakespeare, Plautus and the Humanist Tradition

IN MEMORIAM
WOLFGANG CLEMEN

SHAKESPEARE, PLAUTUS
AND THE
HUMANIST TRADITION

Wolfgang Riehle

D. S. BREWER

First published 1990 by D. S. Brewer, Cambridge

D. S. Brewer is an imprint of Boydell & Brewer Ltd
PO Box 9, Woodbridge, Suffolk IP12 3DF
and of Boydell & Brewer Inc.
PO Box 41026, Rochester, NY 14604, USA

ISBN 0 85991 305 8

British Library Cataloguing in Publication Data
Riehle, Wolfgang
  Shakespeare, Plautus and the humanist tradition.
  1. Drama in English. Shakespeare, William, *1564-1616*
  I. Title
  822.33
  ISBN 0-85991-305-8

Library of Congress Cataloging-in-Publication Data
Riehle, Wolfgang, 1937 –
  Shakespeare, Plautus, and the humanist tradition /
Wolfgang Riehle.
      p.   cm.
  Includes bibliographical references (p.   ) and index.
  ISBN 0-85991-305-8 (hard : alk. paper)
  1. Shakespeare, William, 1564 – 1616. Comedy of errors.
2. Shakespeare, William, 1564 – 1616—Knowledge—
literature. 3. Plautus, Titus Maccius—Influence—
Shakespeare. 4. English drama (Comedy)—Roman
influences. 5. Humanists. I. Shakespeare, William, 1564 –
1616. Comedy of errors. 1990. II. Plautus, Titus Maccius.
Menaechmi. English. 1990. III. Title.
PR2804.R54   1990
822.3'3—dc20   90-2225

This publication is printed on acid-free paper

Printed in Great Britain by
St Edmundsbury Press, Bury St Edmunds, Suffolk

Contents

List of Illustrations

Abbreviations

AJPh	*American Journal of Philology*
Archiv	*Archiv für das Studium der Neueren Sprachen und Literaturen*
CD	*Comparative Drama*
CE	*College English*
CJ	*The Classical Journal*
CL	*Comparative Literature*
CP	*Classical Philology*
CQ	*Classical Quarterly*
EA	*Etudes Anglaises*
EC	*Essays in Criticism*
EETS	Early English Text Society
ELH	*English Literary History*
ELR	*English Literary Renaissance*
ES	*English Studies*
E&S	*Essays and Studies*
HLQ	*Huntington Library Quarterly*
JEGP	*Journal of English and Germanic Philology*
JMRS	*Journal of Medieval and Renaissance Studies*
MLR	*Modern Language Review*
MP	*Modern Philology*
NLH	*New Literary History*
NM	*Neuphilologische Mitteilungen*
N&Q	*Notes and Queries*
PMLA	*Publications of the Modern Language Association*
RD	*Renaissance Drama*
REL	*Review of English Literature*
RenQ	*Renaissance Quarterly*
RhM	*Rheinisches Museum*
SEL	*Studies in English Literature*
ShJ	*Shakespeare Jahrbuch*
ShJW	*Shakespeare Jahrbuch West*
ShS	*Shakespeare Survey*
SP	*Studies in Philology*
SQ	*Shakespeare Quarterly*
SR	*Sewanee Review*
UTQ	*University of Toronto Quarterly*

Preface

The idea of this book was first suggested to me by my experience of directing Shakespeare's *Comedy of Errors* and the Plautine *Menaechmi*. In the course of rehearsals over several months, I became more thoroughly familiar with these playtexts and their dramaturgic conditions as well as their interconnections than would have been possible by merely working at the scholar's desk. I soon realized that the impact of Plautus on Shakespeare was far greater than is generally assumed. When I began my critical studies I noticed that Shakespeare's interest in the brilliant Plautine *Amphitruo*, which has continued to inspire dramatists down to the present day, has been grossly under-estimated. The next step I had to take was to examine both the New Comedy tradition as well as the humanist context in which it was received during the Renaissance.

By combining the approaches of dramaturgic, comparative and historical criticism, an attempt has been made to avoid the mere rehashing of well-established facts. Some ideas in this book have been presented in lectures given at the Universities of Salzburg, Tübingen and East Berlin. Editorial problems concerning *The Comedy of Errors* which arose during my studies were presented to a seminar at the Shakespeare World Congress in Berlin in 1986.

My special thanks are due to my colleagues J. Dalfen, G. Petersmann and W. Pötscher of the Departments of Classical Studies at Salzburg and Graz for their kind advice as well as to P. Bierbaumer for his comments on linguistic problems. I am particularly grateful to G.K. Hunter for discussing with me important aspects of the present study.

I further have to thank the Austrian Ministry of Education for a sabbatical and the Styrian Provincial Government for a travel grant for work at the Horace Howard Furness Library at Philadelphia, where I received kind help from Ms. Georgianna Ziegler. My thanks are also due to the British Library, Cambridge University Library, the InterLibrary Loans department of Graz University and to the Shakespeare Bibliothek at the University of Munich, where Dr. I. Boltz always lent a patient ear to my requests.

Furthermore I am indebted to Ms. G. Politz and in particular to Mr. G. Whitehead for providing my English version with greater readability. In addition, I profited from Mr. Whitehead's valuable suggestions on matters of content. My warm thanks are also due to Dr. M. Reiter for her careful proofreading and for preparing the index as well as to Dr. H. Keiper for his valuable comments. The errors that remain are, of course, my own. I also want to thank Ms. R. Griesenhofer and especially Ms. K. Palzer for carefully typing the manuscript and for their unflinching patience. My greatest debt of gratitude is to Professor Wolfgang Clemen, a great critic and humanist, to whom this book was to have been presented. Sadly, he died before its completion, in March 1990; the book is now dedicated to his memory.

Graz, March 1990   W.R.

Introduction

In his novel *The Unfortunate Traveller* Thomas Nashe narrates how Jack Wilton and the Earl of Surrey, on their journey through Germany, come to Wittenberg, where they arrive just in time to attend 'a very scholastical entertainment' arranged by the Duke of Saxony. The festivity reaches its climax with the appearance of the magician Cornelius Agrippa, who is asked to conjure up famous figures from antiquity. The 'Doctors of *Wittenberg*' first wish to see 'pleasant *Plautus* [. . .] in what habit he went, and with what countenaunce he lookt when he ground corne in the mil'.[1] This episode nicely documents the great esteem that Plautus enjoyed during the Renaissance.

Shakespeare was intensely attracted by the dramatic qualities of this playwright, whom he had begun to study at school. Through his grammar school education he must have acquired enough knowledge of Latin to enable him to read and study the Plautine plays in the original. No doubt he read them from a humanist perspective. The humanists received Roman comedies not only as literary texts but also as plays intended for the stage; there were even performances by the schoolboys, and occasionally the humanists directed the plays themselves.

So far critics have failed to pay sufficiently close attention to Shakespeare's interest in Plautus and in the tradition of New Comedy in general. Whereas Molière's indebtedness to the Roman playwright was examined in a detailed study published about twenty years ago,[2] no such book yet exists on Shakespeare's relationship to Plautus. Clearly this is in part because both Shakespeare's humanist education and the extent of his knowledge of the classical tradition are still underestimated in many quarters. We still seem to be influenced by the Jonsonian formula of his 'small Latine and lesse Greeke'. Baldwin, many years ago,[3] tried to show that Shakespeare's knowledge of the classics was not at all small by any modern standards, and we now know that in the early stages of his career he was in fact occupied with classical authors, themes and dramatic traditions. It was Peter Alexander who pointed out that Shakespeare's early plays are such as a 'quondam schoolmaster' might have

---

[1] *The Unfortunate Traveller*, in: *The Works of Thomas Nashe*, ed. R.B. McKerrow, re-ed. by F.P. Wilson (Oxford, 1958), II, 252.

[2] W. Salzmann, *Molière und die lateinische Komödie. Ein Stil- und Strukturvergleich* (Heidelberg, 1969).

[3] T.W. Baldwin, *Shakspere's Small Latine and Lesse Greeke*, 2 vols. (Urbana, 1944).

written.[4] We think, for example, of the Senecan aspects of *Richard III* and *Titus Andronicus*, the latter also including some Ovidian themes. Ovid must have particularly captured Shakespeare's imagination because it was from Ovid that he drew the impulse for his poems *Venus and Adonis* and *The Rape of Lucrece*.[5]

Among his early works *The Comedy of Errors* enjoys a special position because it is based on two classical plays, the Plautine *Menaechmi* and *Amphitruo*. We are thus given the singular opportunity to examine in detail how Shakespeare studied classical texts, how they influenced him and how he transformed them in his own work. This chance has, however, been insufficiently exploited, because critical interest has centred much more on the classical, particularly the Senecan.roots of Shakespearean *tragedy*.[6] In the 1960s a remarkable shift of emphasis took place in Shakespeare criticism: the influence of Senecan tragedy came to be generally regarded as far less important than the native popular tradition. On the other hand, over the last few years, the pendulum has swung back again towards a renewed interest in Shakespeare's classical models. The importance of Seneca has been rediscovered,[7] and recent scholarship has raised the question of whether Shakespeare may even have been familiar with classical Greek tragedy.[8]

However, critical interest in Shakespeare's reception of classical comedy has been far less penetrating. There have been very few major studies of Shakespeare's relationship to the classical comic tradition. In his seminal book *Shakespearean Comedy*, H.B. Charlton concerned himself with the question of the origins of the comedies, and he seems to have been the first to recognize the importance of the classical influence, pointing out that, by studying Plautus, Shakespeare submitted himself to a 'salutary apprenticeship to the mechanics of play-building'.[9] Some critics have, it is true, analysed individual structural aspects, such as Shakespeare's transformation of the plots and characters he found in his sources[10] – and Harold F. Brooks's fine essay is

---

[4] P. Alexander, 'The Early Plays of the Schoolmaster from the Country', in: *Shakespeare Problems* III, ed. A.W. Pollard and J.D. Wilson (Cambridge, 1929), p.117–143.

[5] S. Clark Hulse, ' ''A Piece of Skilful Painting'' in Shakespeare's ''Lucrece'' ', *ShS*, 31 (1978), 13–22.

[6] The structural influence of the Senecan dramatic speech on Elizabethan tragedy has been perceptively analyzed by W. Clemen (*English Tragedy before Shakespeare* [London, 1961]).

[7] Cf., for example, the recent book by G. Braden, *Renaissance Tragedy and the Senecan Tradition: Anger's Priviledge* (New Haven, 1985).

[8] Cf., for example, P. Alexander, *Hamlet, Father and Son* (Oxford, 1955) and the recent book by A. Poole, *Tragedy. Shakespeare and the Greek Example* (London, 1987).

[9] H.B. Charlton, *Shakespearean Comedy* (London, 1938), p.4.

[10] Cf., for example, the two articles by E.M. Gill, 'A Comparison of the Characters in *The Comedy of Errors* with those in the *Menaechmi*' and 'The Plot-Structure of *The Comedy of Errors* in Relation to its Sources', *University of Texas Bulletin. Studies in English*, 5 (1925), 79–95 and 10 (1930), 13–65.

especially significant in this connection[11] – yet no comprehensive study of Shakespeare's reception of Plautus has so far been attempted. Even Leo Salingar's most useful book *Shakespeare and the Traditions of Comedy*[12] confines itself to a few aspects of Plautus's influence, such as the use of disguise, the trickster figure and the motif of Fortune.

There are a number of reasons for the general neglect of the wide-ranging influence which Roman, particularly Plautine comedy had on Shakespeare, and especially on his *Comedy of Errors*. As the plot is made up of a long series of confusions of identity, the play has, more often than not, been regarded as merely a farce; even Salingar shares this approach, quoting Coleridge, for whom the play was 'the only specimen of *poetical* farce in our language'.[13] We shall soon have to return to this definition, which has proved to be a great hindrance to the study of *Errors*; first, however, we have to discuss the second and more complicated reason for the almost incredible neglect of the impact of Plautine comedy on Shakespeare. His principal interest has been seen to lie in 'romantic' comedy, and so his remodelling of a classical Plautine comedy has been, and sometimes still is, considered as a more or less insignificant exception. Yet we would do well to recall Doran's wise suggestion that 'new light can be thrown on English romantic comedy from an attempt to understand what the Renaissance found in Terence and Plautus'.[14] As we shall see, for the Elizabethans themselves there would certainly not have been a fundamental difference between New Comedy and romantic comedy. It is wrong to make an artificial distinction between comedy and romance and thus to turn a blind eye to the fact that the romance element is fully at home even in some of Plautus's very best comedies. Salingar, who draws this distinction, starts from the assumption that Shakespeare began his dramatic career under the powerful impression of the medieval romance tradition and then turned to Plautus for various plot elements.[15] I believe that this view is incorrect, and one of the major objectives of the present book will be to demonstrate that Shakespeare in fact made a close study of the classical tradition and that, therefore, it is quite wrong to look primarily or exclusively at the medieval romance tradition, although I would not, of course, wish to deny that this too had a decisive impact on the shaping of Shakespeare's comedies.

A further, related reason for the comparatively slight interest of most critics in classical comedy is that they have tended to focus strongly on the links between Shakespeare's plays and the *native* popular dramatic tradition. Yet we

[11] H.F. Brooks's article 'Themes and Structure in *The Comedy of Errors*', in: J.R. Brown and B. Harris, eds., *Early Shakespeare*, Stratford-upon-Avon Studies, 3 (1961), p.54 – 71.
[12] L. Salingar, *Shakespeare and the Traditions of Comedy* (Cambridge, 1975).
[13] Quoted from Salingar, op. cit., p.59.
[14] M. Doran, *Endeavors of Art. A Study of Form in Elizabethan Drama* (Madison, 1954), p.14 and 152.
[15] Salingar, op. cit., p.66 – 67.

shall soon see that there is a strong popular element in the classical comedies of Plautus as well. I believe that it is time to ask whether we might not sometimes be too rash in attributing popular elements, such as puns and quibbles, solely to the native tradition without seeing that these elements were very familiar to the Elizabethan dramatists through Roman comedy. This popular character of Plautine comedy is a major reason why both traditions were able to merge so smoothly into the new form of Elizabethan comedy. At any rate, the humanist authors of Elizabethan comic plays were well aware of the ease with which elements of the native and the classical popular traditions could be fused together.

When Shakespeare decided to write a comedy based on two Roman plays, he did so because he must have felt the challenge to outdo this powerful tradition with a masterpiece of his own, which amalgamated *Menaechmi* and the very fine *Amphitruo*. Indeed, Shakespeare's reception of Plautus is markedly different from that of other Renaissance dramatists because in no other contemporary play is the classical model so clearly recognizable and yet at the same time so skilfully transformed.

If most Shakespeare critics, instead of considering the overall dramatic art of Plautus, have been content merely to compare the plot and characters of the Plautine *Menaechmi* with those of *Errors*, then this neglect reflects an age-old critical reserve towards the Roman comic playwright. For a long time Plautus has enjoyed a markedly mixed reception. On the one hand, he is recognized as the father of European comedy who launched a long tradition of plays making use of his plots, characters, and dramatic devices; yet, on the other hand, there has been a long-held prejudice against him based on the assumption that his works are not original texts but in the main adaptations of lost Greek plays of the 'Nea', the New Comedy. Furthermore, the tenor of his plays was for a long time considered to be notoriously immoral. Even fairly recently he has been criticized on the grounds of lightness and moral 'cynicism'.[16] However, objections like these oversimplify the facts because, in one respect, Plautus's plays are an important continuation of the New Comedy tradition. It may suffice in this context to refer to the interest which the young Montaigne took in the world of Plautine comedy.[17]

Today it is no longer possible to deny Plautus the qualities of a great comic playwright. As early as the twenties, E. Fraenkel,[18] the eminent classical scholar, was able to show that Plautus's plays, far from being mere translations, in fact contain many features which must be considered as his

[16] B.O. Bonazza, *Shakespeare's Early Comedies. A Structural Analysis* (London, 1966), p.23.

[17] S. Zweig, *Europäisches Erbe* (Frankfurt/M., 1981), p.34; H. Friedrich, *Montaigne* (Bern, München, ²1967), p.49.

[18] E. Fraenkel, *Plautinisches im Plautus* (Berlin, 1922); rev. ed. *Elementi Plautini in Plauto*, trans. F. Munari (Firenze, 1961).

own original additions, the most important undoubtedly being the characteristically Plautine comic play with language. At the time when Fraenkel wrote,
not a single complete comedy by Menander had been found: only fragments
were known. By a happy coincidence, the complete text of the Menandrian
comedy *Dyskolos* (*The Grouch*) was discovered in 1958. Scholars were surprised
to find that it did not abound in specifically comic elements to the same degree
that we find in Plautus. Unfortunately, this comedy was not the original for
any of the plays of Plautus that have come down to us. However, in 1969
E.W. Handley published 42 lines from a papyrus which contains 13 fragments
of Menander's *Dis Exapaton* (*The Double Deceiver*).[19] As this is the play Plautus
adapted in his *Bacchides*, it was now possible to compare Plautus's comic
method with the dramaturgy of his model. The comparison has shown beyond
any doubt that Plautus wrote with a much better knowledge of the
requirements of theatre than Menander had done.[20] The specifically comic
and 'theatrical' qualities of the Plautine plays are therefore clearly the
achievement of the Roman author himself. Modern research has likewise
shown that the structural ingenuity of Plautine comedy repays close study. By
regarding Plautus as an important dramatist in his own right and by making
extensive use of recent classical studies, we shall try to show that a close
comparison of Shakespeare's *Errors* with Roman comedy can throw new light
on an essential aspect of intertextuality. As the Elizabethans were not familiar
with the Greek authors of New Comedy, it is mainly Plautus on whose works
we shall focus our close attention.

In his perceptive study, Niall W. Slater has recently demonstrated that 'Far
from being the hack translator [. . .] Plautus is a superb comic craftsman who
remakes his genre in many ways'.[21] Slater interprets some of the comedies as
'play scripts', and arrives at most interesting conclusions. He shows that the
character of these texts is thoroughly 'performative',[22] that they come fully to
life only during a stage performance. Their 'dramatic self-consciousness'[23] is
especially noticeable in the many instances of 'games-playing',[24] where the
metatheatrical element comes to the fore. These plays draw part of their
theatrical impact from the frequent use of improvisation, triggered off by a
particular situation in which a character spontaneously assumes a different
role.

Slater is surely right in focusing on the metatheatrical aspect of
improvisation in Plautus and in pointing out correspondences with the

[19] E.W. Handley, *Menander and Plautus. A Study in Comparison* (London, 1968).
[20] V. Pöschl, *Die neuen Menanderpapyri und die Originalität des Plautus* (Heidelberg, 1973),
p.8 – 9.
[21] N.W. Slater, *Plautus in Performance. The Theatre of the Mind* (Princeton/N.J., 1985),
p.18.
[22] Ibid., p.16 and passim.
[23] Ibid., p.4.
[24] Ibid., p.17 and passim.

Elizabethan 'ability and willingness to play a role, to transform oneself, if only for a brief period and with mental reservation, into another.'[25] Slater adds that these conditions are 'implicit in Plautus' theatrical background – but not that of the Romans at large'.[26] As Plautus knew how to avail himself of the traditions of the Mimus and Atellana,[27] the printed text of his plays reflects only part of the total theatrical experience because the element of mime has to be supplied by the actors. All this, *mutatis mutandis*, applies to Shakespeare's art as well.

As he himself acknowledges, Slater has been influenced by Erich Segal's important book *Roman Laughter*,[28] which in turn is indebted to Northrop Frye and C.L. Barber,[29] who opened up an entirely new view of Shakespearean comedy. As is well known, these two critics re-interpreted the significance of comedy in terms of spring rites and holiday customs respectively, so that its function is seen to lie in a release of vital energy and in a temporary suspension of the established social order. What we find is a saturnalian inversion of the everyday world which serves to confirm and to regenerate the existing norms and values. While C.L. Barber explained the saturnalian perspective in Shakespearean comedy, Segal succeeded in demonstrating how this is also an essential element in the comedies of Plautus and how Latin comedy is deeply rooted in the holiday customs and folk festivities of ancient Rome. He shows that, although these plays, by their vitality and panache, tend to mock the ruling system of values, they by no means overturn it. Nor does Plautus advocate sexual libertinism, as we might expect from the roles of the courtesans in his plays.

It has recently become fashionable to extend Bakhtin's theory of comedy to the plays of Shakespeare, and to argue that they contain an element of carnival which does not merely temporarily suspend the established order, but rather represents a revolutionary or at least subversive force.[30] In a sense, the recent popularity of Bakhtin in Shakespearean criticism has grown out of Robert Weimann's analysis of the native popular tradition in the plays of Shakespeare.[31] While we must be grateful for his careful analysis of the ways in which Shakespeare extended the popular traditions in his own work, it now

---

[25] S. Greenblatt, *Renaissance Self-Fashioning: From More to Shakespeare* (Chicago, 1980), quoted from Slater, p.17, note.

[26] Slater, ibid.

[27] G.E. Duckworth, *The Nature of Roman Comedy* (Princeton/N.J., 1952), p.10ff.

[28] E. Segal, *Roman Laughter. The Comedy of Plautus* (Cambridge, Mass., 1969).

[29] C.L. Barber, *Shakespeare's Festive Comedy. A Study of Dramatic Form and its Relation to Social Custom* (Princeton, 1959).

[30] On this approach cf. M.D. Bristol, *Carnival and Theatre: Plebejan Culture and the Structure of Authority in Renaissance England* (New York/London, 1985) and M. Pfister, 'Comic Subversion: A Bakhtinian View of the Comic in Shakespeare', *ShJW* (1987), 27 – 43.

[31] R. Weimann, *Shakespeare and the Popular Tradition in the Theatre* (Baltimore/London, 1978).

seems that he establishes too sharp a contrast between the native comic tradition culminating in Shakespeare and the comic concept of New Comedy. He claims that 'In the largely neo-classical tradition of Menander, Jonson, Molière [. . .], the audience, if indeed it laughs at all, definitely laughs *at* and never *with* the comic figure'.[32] He thus finds that laughter in New Comedy is achieved by a critical exposure of a character and 'by a critical view of the contradictions between the norms of society and the unconventional standards of comic *characters*, be they the dupes or intriguers, the cheats or butts of society'.[33] Weimann illustrates his theory with reference to Speed and Launce in *The Two Gentlemen of Verona*, who with their superb comic play do indeed laugh *with* the audience. Launce's quibbling speech in III,i draws from Speed the comment: 'Well, your old vice still: mistake the word' (284).[34] Basing himself on this exchange, Weimann suggests that when the two characters enjoy their subjectivity and laugh with the audience, we see the legacy of the Vice figure of the Moralities and an element of the English comic tradition.[35]

I am not fully convinced that Weimann is justified in making this association; I do not think that, wherever words like 'Satan', 'Hell' or 'Vice' appear in an Elizabethan dramatic context, we are meant to think of the Mystery or Morality Plays. Considering that these are basic Christian themes, we should see the absurdity in always immediately recalling the Mysteries and Moralities. More importantly, the dramatic context of the passage quoted from *Two Gentlemen* leaves no doubt that 'to mistake the word' is indeed the 'vice' of Launce, whereas the traditional Vice figure did not so much himself 'mistake the word' as use words in a double sense so that *others* were deceived into mistaking them.

Yet even if Shakespeare did intend a subtle allusion to the Vice tradition, Weimann's line of argument is still unconvincing because he does not give an accurate account of what we find in New Comedy, and especially in Plautine

---

[32] R. Weimann, 'Laughing with the Audience: "The Two Gentlemen of Verona" and the Popular Tradition of Comedy', *ShS*, 22 (1969), 35.

[33] Weimann, 'Laughing with the Audience', p.36.

[34] All Shakespeare quotations, except those from the *Comedy of Errors*, are from *The Riverside Shakespeare*, ed. G. Blakemore Evans (Boston, 1974).

[35] In his comparative study of the ancient mime tradition and Shakespearean theatre, Weimann works with a similar misunderstanding of the genuine dramaturgic qualities of Plautus. He admits that Plautus's plays have been influenced by the ancient Mimus and thus not only preserve Menandrian dramaturgy but also differ from it; yet he fails to recognize that Plautus extended, transformed and highly individualized the qualities of wit and spontaneous theatricality which he found in the Mimus so that his individual art contributed at least as much to the shaping of Shakespearean dramaturgy as the mimetic tradition itself. ('Antiker Mimus und Shakespeare-Theater. Vergleichbare Strukturen ihrer Dramaturgie und Narren-Komik' in: *Lebende Antike. Symposion für Rudolf Sühnel*, ed. H. Meller and H.-J. Zimmermann [Berlin, 1967], p.181 – 196, esp. p.189).

Comedy: plays that *abound* in situations provoking laughter, and among them a good many in which the audience certainly laughs *with* the comic characters. Most often, there are cunning slaves who, like Pseudolus, not merely delight in devising a comic intrigue, but also enjoy their own cleverness in wittily dominating the scene by their splendid ability at game-playing, so that they have the audience as their confederates, much like the medieval Vice figure. It is therefore quite wrong to claim this as a distinctive feature unique to the English tradition. If Greenblatt is right that the element of 'theatricality' is the very prerequisite for the subversive quality of Elizabethan theatre,[36] then the great theatrical potential of Plautus's comedies and the way in which it was used by the humanists had a considerable share in establishing the theatricality of the Elizabethan dramatists.

The humanists looked favourably upon the popular and saturnalian elements in comedy, on which Lucian, regarded as a great authority in humanist circles, wrote his interesting essay *Saturnalia*.[37] At the same time the humanists recognized that classical comedy could be used for educational purposes. This was also the view of the authors of Elizabethan comedy, many of whom, indeed, either were humanists themselves or else had had a humanist school education. It is highly significant that Shakespeare based one of his first comedies on a close study of two Plautine plays and that he presented it at Gray's Inn. As the contemporary report of the performance of *Errors* at Gray's Inn on December 28, 1594 shows, the play's saturnalian elements, which had been taken over from the Plautine *Menaechmi*, were at once responded to by the audience; they remained in a carnival mood long after the performance had finished, and they went on to celebrate a 'night of errors'.[38] Gray's Inn authors in particular had been very active in composing plays which tried to fuse the native tradition with classical models, and Shakespeare set himself a similar task in his *Errors*. The play thus seems to be situated firmly within the humanist reception of classical drama.

This view is supported by a further consideration. If Shakespeare, as there is no reason to doubt, read Plautine comedy in the original Latin, he will also have become familiar with the prefaces, dedicatory epistles and castigations of the humanist editions of Terence and to a lesser degree of Plautus, and so his

---

[36] 'Invisible Bullets: Renaissance Authority and its Subversion' in: *Shakespeare's 'Rough Magic'. Renaissance Essays in Honor of C.L. Barber*, ed. P. Erickson and C. Kahn (Newark/London/Toronto, 1985), p.297.

[37] In: *Lucian*, ed. M.D. MacLeod (Cambridge, Mass./London, 1961), VI. There is a perceptive introduction to Renaissance humanism by J. Martindale who, by the way, points out C.S. Lewis's misunderstanding of this movement (*English Humanism. Wyatt to Cowley* [London, 1985], 17 – 51).

[38] W.W. Greg, *Gesta Grayorum 1688*. Malone Society Reprints (London, 1914), p.20 – 24; cf. also D.S. Bland, 'The "Night of Errors" and Gray's Inn 1594', *N&Q*, 211 (1966), 127 – 8.

reception of the classical 'comedy of identity' will in important respects have been influenced by that of the humanists themselves. We can no longer be content merely to maintain that Shakespeare composed his plays with the humanist understanding of art as 'mimesis'. The connections between Shakespearean and humanist comedy are much closer. We shall see in particular how close Shakespeare sometimes comes to Erasmian thought. The only point where he is strongly opposed to Erasmus is his marked preference for Plautus over Terence, which he shares with many contemporary English dramatists.

Certainly, Plautus is the more 'farcical' author of the two, yet in the Renaissance even Plautus was not considered as an author of farces. A major reason why the real significance of *Errors* has not been recognized is the fact, already mentioned, that critics have very often thought of it as a farce, while no one, to my knowledge, has asked the necessary question whether the Renaissance had the same understanding of farce as we have today.

There is in fact not a single Shakespearean play which could properly be called a farce, not even the 'farcical' *Merry Wives of Windsor*.[39] With regard to this problem, most Shakespeareans have always argued as 'new critics', almost completely neglecting the historical perspective. But it is from the humanist circles that we learn the answer to our question. First, many Renaissance editions of Terence and some of Plautus contain an introductory Essay *De Fabula*, consisting of excerpts from Evanthius. This essay offers surprisingly detailed information on the varieties of classical comedy; we read that comedy has 'multas species',[40] that there is the *comedia palliata*, the Roman Atellana and the Mimus tradition. Thus, a certain distinction is made between high and low comedy, low comedy being mimus performances by low characters and having laughter as its sole aim. This the humanists would have called the realm of farce, although the term actually occurs very rarely. We find something similar, however, in the *Art Poétique Françoys* (1555) of the French humanist Thomas Sébillet. For him, farces are 'simple' and they consist merely of 'badineries' and 'nigauderies', that is, of practical jokes and tomfooleries, and their sole purpose is to move the audience 'a ris & plaisir'.[41] Interestingly enough, Sébillet then goes on to distinguish farce from the New Comedy tradition, and the reason he gives for this is worth quoting in full: 'Le subjet de la Comedie Greque & Latine estoit tout autre: car il y auoit plus de Moral que de ris, & bien souent autant de vérite que de fable'.[42] The plays of

---

[39] J.A. Roberts, *Shakespeare's English Comedy. The Merry Wives of Windsor in Context* (Lincoln/Nebr./London, 1979).

[40] Cf., for example, the edition *P. Terentii Afri Comoediae ex D. Erasmi et Jo. Rivii Attendoriensis Castigationibus* (Cologne, 1934).

[41] Thomas Sébillet, *Art Poétique Françoys* (Génève, 1972), p.64.

[42] Ibid.

the New Comedy tradition are thus entirely different from farces because the latter are 'Mimes ou Priapées'. Here, then, is a Renaissance author telling us that a play like *Menaechmi*, which, to us, appears to be a farce, was by no means seen in the farcical tradition in Shakespeare's time;[43] if the humanists had been asked to define the character of, say, the *Menaechmi*, they would have referred to the tripartite Evanthian subdivision of comedy into 'comoedia stataria, comoedia motoria and comoedia mixta'; what we habitually call a farce, was to them nothing else than a 'comoedia motoria'.[44]

The reason why the Renaissance regarded a play like *Menaechmi* as much more than a 'farce' is that the prevailing medieval conception of comedy as a form which should possess the quality of 'utilitas' was still alive.[45] This goes back to Horace, of course, and, above all, to the famous Ciceronian definition of comedy as 'imitatio vitae, imago veritatis, speculum consuetudinis'.[46] Thus, comedy was seen as a mimetic representation of human life which could be used as a 'speculum' for the audience or reader in order to improve their lives, and this is why Sébillet, in the passage quoted above, states that comedy must contain 'plus de Moral que de ris'. Even a 'farcical' play like the *Menaechmi* fulfilled this function. When I examined Renaissance editions for marks and traces left by early readers, I found, for example, in an edition of the comedies of Plautus in the Stadtbibliothek in Ulm, that the play in which sentences were most frequently marked and underlined as important was none other than the *Menaechmi*.[47] When Sébillet in the quotation given above claims that comedies contain 'vérité', although their plots are 'fable', he is exactly rendering the general view of the humanists, who agreed with Evanthius that, unlike tragedy, comedy does not represent 'life-realism' by dramatizing the lives of historical characters, but rather by showing fictional characters and their private affairs. Yet the fictional world of fable in comedy was seen to be 'real' and to contain 'vérité' in the sense that it was considered as *true to life* and reflecting a 'likeness of truth'.[48] Thus even comedies could possess 'utilitas'.

---

[43] R.B. Heilman is wide of the mark when he claims that *Menaechmi* is 'virtually a Platonic ideal of farce' ('Shakespeare's Variations of Farcical Style', in: *Shakespeare's Stagecraft. Eight Lectures*, ed. P.H. Highfill, Jr. (Carbondale/Edwardsville, 1982), p.47.

[44] In *Aeli Donati Commentum Terenti*, ed. P. Wessner (Stuttgart, 1962), I, 22.

[45] On this point cf. J. Suchomski's important book *'Delectatio' und 'Utilitas'* (Bern/ München, 1975), p.49. My attention was drawn to this study by G. Whitehead.

[46] Cf., for example, M.T. Herrick, *Comic Theory in the Sixteenth Century* (Urbana, 1950), p.60.

[47] Duckworth had already noticed that 'Plautus is equally rich in aphorisms [as Terence] − a fact that is seldom realized, perhaps because the farcical nature of his plays tends to obscure the value of many of his more sententious phrases' (op. cit., p.339).

[48] Cf. H. Hawkins's study *Likenesses of Truth in Elizabethan and Restoration Drama* (Oxford, 1972), e.g. p.31ff.

This approach, as we have said, corresponds to the medieval view of the function of comedy; in his famous *Etymologiae*, Isidor of Sevilla (using a definition of St Augustine) says that the subjects of the comedies of Plautus and Terence are not 'res factae' but 'res fictae'.[49] However, as they are meant to be interpreted in such a way as to improve manners and morals, they have, according to Isidor, to be true in a general sense.

It is, I think, very interesting in this context that, on the one hand, *Errors* greatly reinforces the fictional elements in its Plautine sources by doubling the twins and thus multiplying the improbable confusions, while on the other hand a strong note of 'realism' is introduced. Unlike the *Menaechmi* or *Amphitruo*, the play starts without a Prologue and immediately 'compels' the audience to identify with the world of the play. Moreover, this 'realism' even has a distinctly contemporary, Elizabethan quality. There is also a grim reality (and a 'corrective' purpose) behind the comic confusions between the Antipholi and the Dromios. These servants have good cause to fear that their masters may 'break' their 'pates',[50] because, as Thomas Platter observed: 'England is the servants' prison, because their masters and mistresses are so severe.'[51] The Elizabethan physician Dr Napier mentions in his notebooks the tragic misfortune of a servant whose 'pate' was indeed broken by his master, whereupon he fell into a state of madness from which he never again recovered.[52]

Once thoroughly familiar with a play like *Menaechmi*, one is surprised to find that even from a modern point of view, it is not appropriately described by the term 'farce'. There is a kind of seriousness behind the *Menaechmi*, and it is only because of Plautus's 'blinding comic skill'[53] that we have failed to recognize it. My own impression, when I prepared a stage performance of this comedy, was indeed that it contains and presents a 'humane vision'.[54] It makes us laugh in a pleasing and 'liberating' way, because it frees us for a short while from the all-too-human weaknesses of humankind. The situations which it develops are common human problems and concerns, such as a marriage crisis arising from everyday routine, a case of marital infidelity, and the

---

[49] Quoted from Suchomski, op. cit., p.86.

[50] All quotations from *The Comedy of Errors* are from the New Arden Edition by R.A. Foakes (London, 1962).

[51] Quoted from R. Wilson, ' "Is this a Holiday?" Shakespeare's Roman Carnival', *ELH*, 54 (1987), 35; the ultimate reason for this violence against servants seems to be the extreme political and social conservatism as represented above all by the Protestant William Tyndale who held that like an ox or a horse, a servant is part of a man's possessions (cf. L. Borinski, 'Der englische Humanismus' in: L. Borinski and C. Uhlig, *Literatur der Renaissance* [Düsseldorf, 1975], p.23).

[52] M. McDonald, *Mystical Bedlam. Madness, Anxiety, and Healing in Seventeenth-Century England* (Cambridge, 1981), p.87.

[53] Cf. D. Haberman, 'Menaechmi: A Serious Comedy', *Ramus*, 10 (1981), 129 – 139.

[54] Ibid., p.139.

human desire for topsyturvydom. However, what we are interested in in the present study is not so much Plautus's possible original intention, which must remain a matter for speculation, but rather the way in which he was received by the Renaissance humanists and by Shakespeare in particular; and this can be assessed quite precisely. There can be no doubt that the humanists saw even in the *Menaechmi* a mirror of human life and manners: the experience of the traveller Menaechmus with the Courtesan could be employed as a warning against the temptations to lust and the same applies when the other twin receives a kind of punishment for his illicit love. As an examination of the Renaissance editions shows very clearly, this theme formed a major item in the humanist education of young men. Shakespeare, although he writes plays which are so overwhelmingly dramatic and which are usually (but not always) remarkably free from direct didacticism, nevertheless shares the humanist concern with the problem of identity; to a considerable extent, his comedies are 'comedies of identity'. It appears, then, that in order to assess the real importance of Shakespeare's reception of Plautine comedy it is indispensable to combine the dramaturgic *and* the historical approaches.

In trying to examine Shakespeare's reception of Plautus, I am, of course, aware of the fact that Plautine comedy exerted both a direct and an indirect influence on Elizabethan drama, the latter coming through the Italian *commedia erudita*. Yet this does not preclude an assessment of what Shakespeare owes *directly* to Plautus. A detailed study of this problem has shown that the plot of *Errors* does not resemble the plots of Italian *commedia erudita* in any essential respects.[55] What Shakespeare may have adopted from Gascoigne's English version of Ariosto's *I Suppositi* is the motif of the enmity between the two cities Syracuse and Ephesus.[56] All the other resemblances that have been claimed, such as the element of pathos, the 'hint of tragedy', the motifs of providence, sorcery and madness and finally the 'weaving of multiple sources into a newly complicated pattern of errors'[57] which occur in Elizabethan comedies, are far from providing sufficient proof of the influence of Italian comedy: far from being a new Italian element, the emphasis on providence and fortune, for example, can be found, as we shall see, in the New Comedy tradition itself, and the same applies to the other motifs as well as to the occasional pathos and the hints of tragedy in the native comedies. As Salingar and others have argued, it seems, however, that the double plot structure in Elizabethan comedies derived mainly from Italian models.[58] Yet it is wrong to place *Errors* in this context because it has no double (love) plot but only one

[55] L.G. Clubb, 'Italian Comedy and *The Comedy of Errors*', *CL*, 19 (1967), 240 – 251.
[56] T.W. Baldwin, *Shakspere's Five-Act Structure* (Urbana, 1947), p.665, 685, and Salingar, *Shakespeare and the Traditions of Comedy*, p.207.
[57] Clubb, op. cit., p.251.
[58] Salingar, op. cit., p.207.

love scene which, as we shall see, strongly resists being interpreted in terms of a second plot.[59]

It is, of course, true that there are a number of points of contact between Plautine and Terentian comedy, so that the individual impact of the one or the other playwright seems impossible to ascertain. Are we then justified in concentrating our studies on Plautus? I think that there are indeed very good reasons for this: first, Shakespeare based one of his comedies on two Plautine plays, whereas no comedy by Terence is known to have exerted a comparable influence; and, secondly, for most Elizabethan playwrights, Plautus was a far more attractive dramatist than Terence. The fact that Shakespeare wrote for the popular theatre precludes the possibility of his having been too profoundly influenced by Terence,[60] whose plays, avoiding major theatrical effects and appealing to the taste of an intellectual coterie audience, were recognized even by Terence's own contemporaries as running the danger of lacking structural variety and dramatic vitality (cf. the Prologue to his comedy *Phormio*, 5). His plays, which are masterpieces in their own right, consist of 'pura oratio' (*Heautontimoroumenos*, 46), of merely verbal discourse. Plautus's comic vision was recognized as having far greater dramatic intensity, linguistic variety and wit. Moreover, the humanism of Terentian comedy can to a considerable extent be found in Plautus, too, especially in his best plays. – We shall, therefore, on the one hand focus on *Errors*, but we shall conclude our study by a detailed examination of the ways in which Plautus and the New Comedy tradition as a whole, as received by the humanists, contributed to the shaping of Shakespeare's comedies as well as of the so-called romances. However, it has to be emphasized that we are not trying to deny the importance of the native popular tradition. If we are not concerned with it in detail, this is because so much has already been written about it. What we do want to show is that by concentrating on English popular drama, it has too often been forgotten that the classical comic tradition and in particular the theatrical vitality of Plautus had a comparably important share in the making of Elizabethan drama.

[59] It is correct to assume that the Italian double plots seem to have been anticipated by Terentian comedy, although the double plot in Terence is like 'the two sides of a coin', rather than a doubling of situations (R. Hosley, 'The Formal Influence of Plautus and Terence', in: J.R. Brown and B. Harris, eds., *Elizabethan Theatre*, Stratford-upon-Avon Studies, 9 [London, 1966], 133); cf. also W. Görler, 'Doppelhandlung, Intrige und Anagnorismos bei Terenz', *Poetica*, 5 (1972), 164 – 180.

[60] The evidence assembled by Baldwin for the influence of Terence on Shakespeare is rather slight (*Shakspere's Five-Act Structure*, p.547ff.).

I

The Elizabethan Reception of Plautus

1. The preference for Plautus over Terence

The extent to which Plautus was studied by the English humanists and the degree to which he influenced Renaissance comedy are still moot points. If we study the introductions and prefaces of the Renaissance editions afresh, we realize that, throughout the Renaissance, opinion was divided as to whether preference should be given to Terence or Plautus; in fact, two opposing camps were established and each corroborated its view by referring to classical authorities. The supporters of Terence believed that the function of comedy, defined by Cicero as *speculum consuetudinis* (rendering the Aristotelian '*ηϑη*'), was best fulfilled by the comedies of Terence.[1] A number of humanists, above all Erasmus and Melanchthon,[2] praised these plays for their moral inoffensiveness and didactic value. As Terentian comedies were thought to be of considerable educational importance, the Christian humanists even sought to establish a 'Terentius Christianus' by dramatizing Christian themes such as the parable of the Prodigal Son.[3] Terentian comedies were further admired for their tightly-knit plots and their overall artistic unity, particularly for their classical style with its eloquence and urbanity.[4] Erasmus, who in his study of classical Latin was influenced by Lorenzo Valla's attempt to reawaken interest in the elegant Latin of the classics,[5] had high praise for the comedies of Terence; he published editions of them and also edited Plautus's plays.[6] Other Renaissance editions of Terence usually quoted Erasmus, according to whom there was more judgement and artistic skill in one of Terence's comedies than

---

[1] Cf., for example, the edition *In P. Terentii Comoediae Sex*, ed. S. Riccius (Leipzig, 1575), f. IVff.

[2] Cf., for example, the particularly interesting edition *P. Terentii Afri Comoediae ex D. Erasmi et Jo. Rivii Attendoriensis Castigationibus* (Cologne, 1534).

[3] On the Prodigal Son Plays cf. A.R. Young, *The English Prodigal Son Plays. A Theatrical Fashion of the Sixteenth and Seventeenth Centuries* (Salzburg, 1979).

[4] Cf., for example, the preface to the edition *P. Terentii Afri Comoediae* (Strasbourg, 1548).

[5] His important work is entitled *De Linguae Latinae Elegantia Libri Sex*.

[6] Cologne, Gymnicus 1530; cf. J.-C. Margolin, *Opera Omnia Desiderii Erasmi Roterodami* (Amsterdam, 1971), I,ii,116, n.2.

in the whole canon of Plautus: 'Plus exacti iudicii in una comoedia Terentiana quam in Plautinis omnibus'.[7]

By contrast, the other camp saw Plautus as the foremost comic playwright. They gave pride of place to him because of the brilliance and elegance of his language.[8] In praising Plautus's poetic style, they could claim to be following a very old tradition.[9] Aelius Stilo, the teacher of the great Varro and one of the first Plautine philologists, if not the very first, goes so far as to say that 'if the Muses themselves had spoken Latin, they would have done it in the language of Plautus'. Quintilian, quoting Varro, refers to this judgement by Aelius Stilo. Varro himself adds his famous classification of the three Latin comic playwrights Caecilius, Plautus and Terence: 'In argumentis [= plot] Caecilius poscit palmam, in ethesin [= character drawing] Terentius, in sermonibus [= language] Plautus'. Then there is Cicero's high praise for Plautus's heightened language and refined humour. His characterization of the Plautine comic art as 'elegans' and 'urbanum' was frequently repeated in the Renaissance: 'Duplex omnino est iocandi genus: unum illiberale, flagitiosum, obscenum, alterum elegans, urbanum, ingeniosum, facetum'. Although the comedies of Plautus were not to the taste of Horace, he was nevertheless ready to admit that Plautus had greatly enriched the lexical variety of the Latin language. Aulus Gellius, in his famous *Noctes Atticae*, is enthusiastic about the Plautine 'elegantia'; indeed, to him Plautus is 'uerborum Latinorum elegantissimus', and 'homo linguae atque elegantiae in uerbis Latinae princeps'. The Grammarian Diomedes likewise emphasizes the Plautine 'eloquentia' and 'elegantia'.[10]

As regards the reception of Plautus in the Renaissance, we find some continental humanists, such as, for example, Fabricius, who refer to the classical and post-classical authorities and, similarly, extol Plautus as 'linguae Romanae principem, elegantissimum antiquorum'.[11] These admirers of Plautus, a considerable number of whom can, by the way, be found in Italy, included, for example, Martin Luther, who disagreed with the usual view of the comedies as frivolous and immoral, and therefore unsuitable for teaching purposes, on the grounds that the same argument could be put forward against reading the Old Testament, which contained many 'immoral' stories.

---

[7] We find this in Erasmus's prefatory letter to his edition of Terence in 1532; the statement is then frequently repeated in later Renaissance editions.

[8] Cf., for example, the very interesting edition *Plautus Poeta Comicus*, ed. Io. Ad. Mulingus (Strasbourg, 1508), f.II[v].

[9] Here I follow closely the excellent survey by I. Fischer, 'Encore sur le Caractère de la langue de Plaute', *Studii Clasice*, 13 (1971), 59 – 78.

[10] Quintilian, *Institutio Oratoria*, X,99; Varro, *Saturae Menippeae*, 399B; Cicero, *De Officiis* I. 29, 104; Horace, *Ars Poetica*, 5357; Aulus Gellius, *Noctes Atticae*, I, 7, 17, 4; Diomedes, in Keil, *Grammatici Latini* I, 382, 15.

[11] In the edition *Elegantiarum ex Plauto et Terentio Lib. II* (Leipzig, 1554), f.II[v]; or in the edition of Terence (Strasbourg, 1548), he expressly praises the excellencies of Plautus (f.IVf.).

Luther, who owned two books – an edition of Plautus and of Vergil – when he entered the Augustinian monastery at Erfurt, maintained that, on the contrary, the Plautine plays were of great use for young students because they could serve as a warning against a wicked life, and as a mirror of Man's morality.[12] Others, too, had very favourable things to say about the rich variety of Plautus as compared to Terence. The followers of Plautus claimed that he had already anticipated the Renaissance ideal of *copia*.[13] As they gave priority to this stylistic ideal, they were ready to overlook the fact that his plots frequently did not exhibit the artistic unity for which Terence was famous. It is very interesting to note that these humanists often quoted a certain Volcatius Sedigitus, who had made a list of ten Roman comedy writers in which he gave second place to Plautus, whereas he put Terence in sixth position.[14] He even gave the criterion for this evaluation: he ranked the authors according to their mimic and comedic qualities. To the Terentians among the humanists, Volcatius's low opinion of Terence was, of course, scandalous, and they strongly rejected this classical authority.[15] Yet it is very significant that many editions of Terence first quoted Volcatius in full and then even went on to add Varro's praise of Plautus's linguistic superiority.

It cannot be denied that, among the humanists, the supporters of Terence were in the majority. The preference for his classicism was, so to speak, 'orthodox mainstream', a fact also reflected in the curricula of the Grammar Schools. Baldwin quotes many examples of school regulations in which Terence is preferred and Plautus comes second. Yet it is evident that in English schools Plautus, too, was a highly respected author. If we look, for example, at the full list of Grammar School texts published in London in 1581, we read that the boys 'legunt Plauti Amphitryonem: Epidicum: Menaechmos: Pseudolum: Stichum . . .'[16] From this we may perhaps infer that, at his own school, Shakespeare would have read more plays by Plautus than just the *Menaechmi* and *Amphitruo*. He would have studied them with the same care as the comedies of Terence. Madeleine Doran is surely right in concluding that 'whenever Plautus was studied he must have been subjected to the same

---

[12] Quoted in H. Kindermann, *Theatergeschichte Europas* (Salzburg, 1959), II, 307. Boccaccio praises Plautus's plays in the following enthusiastic manner: 'Their number and workmanship is such that the laurel of victory, the special decoration of triumphant emperors, was not too proud a distinction to encircle his brow', *The Genealogy of the Gods*, Book XIV, in: *Boccaccio on Poetry*, ed. C.G. Osgood (Princeton, 1930), p.27.

[13] Cf. the edition *Plautus Poeta Comicus* (Strasbourg, 1508), f.III. This edition also refers to Macrobius's praise of Plautus (ibid.) and S. Charpentier's edition mentions St Jerome's and Eusebius's preference for Plautus (Paris, 1512, f.3ʳ).

[14] Quoted, for example, in *P. Terentii Afri Comoediae*, ed. J. Rivius (Strasbourg, 1548), f. VIIIff. The list of Volcatius has come down to us through Aulus Gellius, *Noctes Atticae* (XV, 24).

[15] Cf. *Publii Terentii Afri Comoediae Sex* (Frankfurt/M., 1562), f.IX.

[16] Baldwin, *Small Latine and Lesse Greeke*, I, 436.

treatment [as Terence], for the method of rhetorical analysis and imitation was the general method of education.'[17]

In England, the humanist Nicholas Udall edited a famous collection of elegant Latin phrases drawn from Terence, entitled: *Flowers for Latin-Speaking, Selected and Gathered out of Terence and the same translated to Englysshe*. Roger Ascham introduced a subtle distinction: with general regard to language, he claimed, Terence is 'more pure and proper', while on the other hand, 'For word and speech, Plautus is more plentiful'[18], that is, *Plautus excels in linguistic variety*. And in his famous *Palladis Tamia*, Francis Meres had the highest praise for Plautus's language; in support of his view he cites our quotation from Aelius Stilo, but he confounds the name of Varro's teacher: 'Epius Stolo said that the Muses would speake with Plautus tongue if they would speak Latin',[19] and Ben Jonson repeated the same reference.[20] The function of improving the teaching of Latin, which had been assigned to Terence both on the Continent and in England by Udall and Ascham, is here transferred to his 'rival', Plautus. Interestingly enough, Plautus's moral 'laxness' is defended in England by the famous humanist Sir Thomas Elyot; his *The Book Named the Governor* (1531) contains the first English definition of comedy:

> . . . comedies, which they suppose to be a doctrinal of ribaldry, they
> be undoubtedly a picture or as it were a mirror of man's life [. . .] to
> the intent that men beholding the promptness of youth unto vice, the
> snares of harlots and bawds laid for young minds [. . .] the chances of
> fortune contrary to men's expectation, they being therof warned may
> prepare themself to resist or prevent occasion. [. . .] And if the vices
> in them expressed should be cause that minds of the readers should be
> corrupted, then by the same argument not only interludes in English,
> but also sermons, wherein some vice is declared, should be to the
> beholders and hearers like occasion to increase sinners.[21]

Elyot argues that scenes of sexual licence cannot be considered harmful because this objection would then also have to be raised against stage plays and religious texts in which vices are presented in order to warn against them. Elyot here seems to be making the same point as Martin Luther, who, as we have seen, had defended Plautus in similar terms. In his famous *Defence of Poesy*, Sidney tends towards the Terentian camp, since he pleads in favour of moral and aesthetic purity. He criticizes contemporary comedies for showing

---

[17] *Endeavors of Art*, p.151.
[18] *The Schoolmaster*, ed. L.V. Ryan (Ithaca, 1967), p.143.
[19] Reprinted in G. Smith, *Elizabethan Critical Essays* (Oxford, 1904), II, 318.
[20] *Ben Jonson*, ed. C.H. Herford and P. and E. Simpson (Oxford, 1954), VIII, 641.
[21] Ed. S.E. Lehmberg, Everyman's Library (London/New York, 1962), p.47-8; on Sir Thomas Elyot cf. also J.M. Major, *Sir Thomas Elyot and Renaissance Humanism* (Lincoln, Nebr., 1964).

on stage 'sinful things', 'unworthy of any chaste ears'.[22] Objections of this kind were often put forward against Plautus. However, the charge that comedy, and poetry in general, 'abuseth men's wit' is mentioned by Sidney with considerable restraint,[23] and unlike Elyot, Luther and Heinrich Bebel, the author of another continental *Defence of Poesy*,[24] Sidney does not refer to the many 'amoral' Old Testament stories in order to disprove the traditional argument. It is further remarkable that in his plea for classical purity of the genres, Sidney goes beyond even Erasmus. Erasmus, who had a sense of folk customs and folk-lore, would not have objected so strongly to the juxtaposition of the serious and the comic, the contrasting of high and low, the 'mingling of kings and clowns'[25] in the same work, as Sidney did. After all, Erasmus, in *The Praise of Folly*, had taken delight in showing the *ubiquity* of Folly, independent of people's social status. Erasmus's method is characterized by a mixture of irony, satire and understanding humour resulting in a tone of comic lightness which is absent from Sidney's *Defence*, even though he refers there directly to *The Praise of Folly*.[26] Sidney gives a precise description of the genre of New Comedy when he claims that 'Comedy is an imitation of the common errors of our life',[27] yet by neglecting the tragicomedies and by merely stating that comedy has to be 'full of delight' and that its function is simply 'delightful teaching',[28] he shirks a detailed discussion of comic theory.

As Sidney criticized the use of the native popular element in drama, he was certainly not too pleased with the popular mime contained in Plautine comedy. Yet there can be no doubt that it is through this popular quality that the English *playwrights* were attracted much rather to Plautus than to Terence. The plays of Plautus were frequently performed in England: according to Boas, during the years 1549 – 1583 plays written by Plautus were acted 17 times and works by Terence only 5 times in Oxford, while Cambridge saw 20 performances of Plautus and only 6 of Terence.[29] Whereas there are strikingly few plays in English Renaissance drama which reveal a direct Terentian

---

[22] G. Shepherd, ed., *Sir Philip Sidney. An Apology for Poetry or the Defence of Poesy* (Manchester/New York, 1973), p.137, 136.

[23] Ibid., p.125.

[24] Heinrich Bebel, *Comoedia de optimo studio iuvenum. Über die beste Art des Studiums für junge Leute*, ed. and trans. by W. Bamer (Stuttgart, 1982), p.57. Here it is mentioned that Bebel also wrote an *Apologia et defensio poeticae et oratoriae majestatis*, in which he tried to justify poetry and rhetoric.

[25] Sidney, op. cit., p.135.

[26] Ibid., p.121.

[27] Ibid., p.117.

[28] Ibid., p.136, 137.

[29] F.S. Boas, *University Drama in the Tudor Age* (Oxford, 1914), p.386 – 9; R. Hosley, referring to research by G.C. Moore, states that 'Plautus, in the seed-time of Elizabethan Comedy, was performed at Cambridge more than three times as frequently as Terence' ('The Formal Influence of Plautus and Shakespeare', *Elizabethan Theatre* [1966], p.131).

influence, the impact of Plautine comedy is overwhelming. Most probably the humanist authors recognized that, unlike Terence, Plautus provided an admirable opportunity to fuse elements of classical comedy with the native tradition. The first instances of this fusion can be found in the Morality plays; and we have to bear in mind this fact when we so often merely concentrate on the English tradition. Even in *Misogonus*, one of the Prodigal Son plays with a more Terentian structure, we find typically Plautine parasites and elements of native comedy.[30] *Jack Juggler* is well-known for its attempt to reshape part of the Plautine *Amphitruo* and at the same time to meet the needs of popular theatre.[31]

In this context we need to say a word about the interlude *Cambises*, with its crude mixing of the tragic and the comic. Its major dramatic elements are derived from the native tradition. However, for its main plot it also adopts suggestions from Senecan tragedy. The low comedy scenes, too, are indebted to the classical tradition: they introduce a markedly Plautine tone with the appearance of the 'Meretrix', the 'obligatory' courtesan, who becomes involved in a quarrel with three ruffianly soldiers. This does not come as a surprise to us if we have the European context in mind. In Italian comedies, for example in Cardinal Bibbiena's *La Calandria*,[32] the meretrix has a firm place in the comic world. By making her part of the *dramatis personae*, the author of *Cambises* clearly wants, as it were, to 'legitimize' the element of sexual release which he includes in his comedy. When the Meretrix first enters the stage, 'with a staff on her shoulder' (note the sexual symbolism), she articulates her sexual services in a language that is more outspoken even than anything in Plautus:

> Meretrix. What! is there no lads here that hath a lust
> To have a passing trul to help at their need?[33]

The appearance of the Meretrix brings the subplot to an effective dramatic climax. Two of the ruffians, who delight in the names Huf, Ruf and Snuf, start a quarrel about who is to enjoy her during the night. Ambidexter and one of the ruffians flee, the Meretrix defeats the remaining ruffian and thus proves to be in full command of the situation, a feature so typical of the Plautine meretrix. This linking of the popular characters with an element of classical comedy is very remarkable and anticipates later developments. It is, however, not specifically English: this popular element provides contrast in the comedy

---

[30] D.M. Bevington, *From Mankind to Marlowe. Growth of Structure in the Popular Drama of the Tudor Age* (Cambridge, Mass., 1962), p.64; cf. also Duckworth, op. cit., p.410.

[31] *Jack Juggler* in: *Early English Dramatists. Anonymous Plays.* 3rd series, ed. J.S. Farmer (London, 1906).

[32] P. Fossati, ed., Bibbiena, *La Calandria* (Torino, 4 1967).

[33] *Cambises* in: *Chief Pre-Shakespearean Dramas*, ed. J.Q. Adams (Cambridge, Mass., 1924), p.645.

of Aretino as well: in his *Il Filosofo*, for example, apart from the 'meretrice', we also find a 'ruffiano'.[34]

It is interesting that Nicholas Udall turned to Terence when looking for examples of first-rate Latin, and to Plautus when he set himself the task of writing a specifically English 'Roman' comedy. What the English dramatists learnt from a close study of Plautus was a number of dramaturgic aspects, such as the advantage of Act division, the economical organization of the plot, the dramatic use of the unities of time and place and the motivation of entrances and exits. It is significant that the Prologue to *Ralph Roister Doister*, which is so different in character from a Plautine Prologue, tries very hard to defend the play against those humanists who condemned Plautine comedy because of its alleged sexual freedom; by contrast, the author's aim is 'Avoiding such mirth wherein is abuse'.[35] The character of Roister Doister himself is modelled much rather on the Plautine *miles gloriosus* than on the more 'flat' Thraso in the *Eunuchus* of Terence, a fact which Baldwin totally ignored.[36] And the love motif, which already occurs in *Miles Gloriosus*, is enlarged and transformed. Finally, the Parasite Matthew Merrygreek is an interesting mixture of the Plautine parasite and native traits of comic character portrayal.

In Shakespeare's own time, Francis Meres, in his *Palladis Tamia*, gives the palm to Plautus by calling him 'the best for Comedy [. . .] among the Latines'.[37] Even the classically oriented Ben Jonson prefers Plautus to Terence; he finds that in Plautine comedy dramatic 'Oeconomy, and disposition' is 'better observed than in Terence'.[38] Like other authors, Ben Jonson imitates the Plautine cunning slaves. He had intended to adapt the Plautine *Amphitruo*, as the anonymous play *The Birth of Hercules*[39] and Thomas Heywood had done in his *The Silver Age*, but he gave up the plan on the grounds that there were no identical twins available to perform the play. His *The Alchemist* is vaguely reminiscent of the Plautine *Mostellaria*,[40] and for his play *The Case is Altered* he drew some suggestions from *Aulularia* and *Captivi*. Like Shakespeare in his *Errors*, Jonson here uses two Plautine plays in order to create a plot of a new kind. However, Anne Barton has shown that, unlike Shakespeare, Jonson 'constantly interrupts or obscures his story line'.[41] Lyly's

[34] G.B. De Sanctis, ed., Pietro Aretino, *Tutte le commedie* (Milano, ³1973).

[35] *Ralph Roister Doister* in: *Chief Pre-Shakespearean Dramas*, p.424.

[36] Baldwin, *Shakspere's Small Latine and Lesse Greeke*, p.380ff.

[37] Reprinted in Smith, *Elizabethan Critical Essays*, II, 317 – 18.

[38] *Ben Jonson*, VIII, 618.

[39] Cf. Hosley, 'The Formal Influence of Plautus and Shakespeare', p.132.

[40] Cf. A. Barton, *Ben Jonson Dramatist* (Cambridge, 1984), p.146.

[41] Ibid., p.32. In her discussion of *Every Man in his Humour* Barton notes that 'vestiges of a Roman comedy plot involving the outwitting of the Senex, a stolen marriage and the frolics of young men and their clever slaves do manifest themselves in Jonson's play' (p.51). Cf. also R. McDonald, *Shakespeare and Jonson. Jonson and Shakespeare* (Brighton, 1988), p.20 – 21.

Mother Bombie, a play that exerted some influence on *Errors*, is not Terentian in form and spirit, as Foakes has claimed,[42] but primarily a 'Plautine' play. Lyly's dramatic and comic use of language is closely related to that of Plautus; both playwrights use language with a wide stylistic range, including the conversational as well as the rhetorical level and subtle word-play.[43]

Here we come to a further reason for the Elizabethan preference for Plautus: the quality of 'wit' in which the dramatic language of Plautus excels. Thus the Prologue to *Jack Juggler* directly mentions the 'great wit' of Plautus.[44] Ben Jonson, too, contrasts 'witty Plautus' with 'neat Terence',[45] and he praises the wisdom of 'the witty *comick Poet*' Plautus.[46] What these quotations refer to is obviously the fact that Plautus's witty and playful command of language was felt to be suited to the Elizabethan delight in 'wit' and 'conceit'. There is no doubt that the *Menaechmi* is a particularly effective and *witty* comedy, not least because the idea of the mistaking of the twins is in itself an intellectual 'conceit'. This is referred to in the long and elaborate title of Warner's English translation: 'A pleasant and fine conceited Comædie, taken out of the most excellent wittie poet Plautus . . .'[47] As we shall see, Shakespeare, in his own *Errors*, has in many ways further increased the 'wit' and 'conceit' of the original.

We know some interesting details of how the plays of Roman comedy were performed by the Elizabethans. They were played in the Halls of the Inns of Court, and they were also acted on the so-called Terentian stage.[48] It seems that we can now be fairly certain how, for example, *Errors* was performed in the Great Hall of Gray's Inn in 1594, because the explanation offered by T.S. Dorsch is convincing and would suggest itself naturally to anyone having to stage the play there. The west end of the Great Hall, which has now been restored, has five wooden doors, all of which will have been used in an actual performance: 'the three inner doors [. . .] would have served admirably as the entrances to the houses of Antipholus and the Courtesan, and to the priory'.[49] 'The two outer doors could well have been left open to represent the ways leading to the port and the city [. . .] The gallery would, in 3.i, allow Luce

---

[42] In his edition of *The Comedy of Errors*, p.xxxiii.
[43] Further examples of Plautine adaptations have been given by R. Hosley, op. cit., p.131.
[44] *Jack Juggler*, op. cit., p.5.
[45] In *The Norton Facsimile of the First Folio of Shakespeare*, prepared by C. Hinman (New York, 1968), p.10.
[46] *Ben Jonson*, VIII, 575 (italics original).
[47] Reprinted in Bullough, *Narrative and Dramatic Sources of Shakespeare* (London, 1957), I, 12.
[48] Cf. C. Kernodle, *From Art to Theatre. Form and Creation in the Renaissance* (Chicago, 1944), p.160 – 164.
[49] T.S. Dorsch, ed., *The Comedy of Errors*, The New Cambridge Shakespeare (1988), p.24.

and Adriana to appear (*above*) . . .'[50] The Terentian theatre used several houses at the back of the stage, and the woodcut illustrations dating from 1493 suggest what the houses were like. They had front curtains instead of doors, and the bare stage facilitated abrupt changes of locality. On the frieze above the curtains the Lyon illustrations indicate the names of the *characters* to whom the individual houses belong, whereas Shakespeare gives special names to the *houses* of Antipholus ('Phoenix') and the Courtesan ('Porpentine'). We find this rarer practice, for example, in the Netherlands, where the houses are given individual names written on signs attached to or protruding from them.[51]

The houses of the Terentian stage of the Renaissance were a theatrical detail which, like other elements, may have been derived from the comedies of Plautus or Terence. What these houses were like in the time of Plautus is not known, but we may draw some inferences from a Phylax drawing.[52] Just as in the public theatres of Shakespeare's time, the comedies of Plautus were, of course, performed during daylight and without the use of detailed scenery; female roles were taken by male actors. Whether or not the actors wore masks is still a vexed question.[53] It is, however, irrelevant for our purpose because the texts themselves contain frequent references to the facial expression of a character. What the Elizabethans could further derive from the texts of Plautus or of Terence was the fact that they used a large bare platform stage protruding into the audience surrounding it: the plays contain many situations in which two actions take place simultaneously, and where the one character must not be able to notice what the other is saying or doing; frequently, close contact is established between the actors and the audience by means of soliloquy and aside. All this, and the fact that Plautus aims at building up an illusion and then suddenly suspending it, must have especially appealed to the Elizabethans because it closely corresponded to their own concept and practice of drama.

Furthermore, some of Plautus's Prologues, as well as some of Terence's, contain detailed information which reads almost like a description of the Elizabethan popular theatre. We learn that the audience was composed of all the different social strata of ancient Rome. The Prologue to *Poenulus* tells us that the maintaining of discipline during a performance was not always easy; the speaker therefore asks the audience to conduct themselves appropriately: 'Let no well-ripened wanton take seat upon the stage, nor lictor murmur, or his rods, nor usher ramble around in front, or show a seat, while an actor is on the boards.' ('scortum exoletum ne quis in proscaenio / sedeat, neu lictor verbum aut virgae muttiant, / neu dissignator praeter os obambulet / neu

---

[50] Ibid.
[51] Cf. H. Kindermann, *Theatergeschichte Europas* (Salzburg, 1959), II, 237.
[52] Cf., e.g. W. Beare, *The Roman Stage* (London, ³1964), p.335ff.
[53] Cf., for example, Beare, op. cit., p.192 – 194.

sessum ducat,dum histrio in scaena siet.' IV, 17 – 20).[54] As this passage suggests, even the Elizabethan custom of having some spectators sit on the stage was anticipated in the theatre of Plautus. We are further reminded of the situation in England by the fact that there were other kinds of entertainment which offered competition to the theatre so that it had to make great efforts to maintain its appeal to the public. The Prologue to the Terentian *Hecyra* tells us that its first performance was a complete failure because 'the vaunting of pugilists, the gatherings of their claque, the din, the clamour of the ladies, drove me prematurely from the boards.' ('quom primum eam agere coepi, pugilum gloria, / comitum conventus, strepitus, clamor mulierum, / fecere ut ante tempus exirem foras.' II, 33 – 35). Can we be surprised that the Roman comedies, and especially those of Plautus, written for a theatre so similar to their own, particularly appealed to the Elizabethans? What we find here is one of those very interesting cultural analogies which sometimes occur in history; we are reminded of the famous parallel between the culture of Athens in the 5th century B.C. and Italian culture in the 15th and 16th centuries.[55] The similarity in theatrical practice is well brought out in a medieval illumination of a French Terence manuscript and a woodcut in Roigny's Paris edition of Terence (1552), where we see the platform stage protruding into the audience and surrounded by them on three sides – much as it does later in the Elizabethan popular stage.

2. *The universe of Plautine comedy*

The connections between Plautus and Shakespeare are indeed numerous. They begin with the fact that, like Shakespeare, Plautus composed his play-texts for a performance on stage; he, too, was most probably an actor-poet who knew the conditions of acting from his personal experience. It may even be that he acted in some of his own plays,[56] as did Shakespeare. It is to the nature of these plays that we must now turn our attention.

In examining the comedies of Plautus, we are confronted with both New Comedy and Plautine dramaturgy: plays such as *Stichus* or *Mercator* are close Latin adaptations of Greek originals, whereas many others reveal in addition Plautus's own comic stagecraft. These have an improvisational quality that is easily forgotten when they are merely read. So essential is the dimension of improvisation that only 'the dynamics of performance will reveal the comic

---

[54] All quotations from Plautus are from P. Nixon, ed. and transl., *Plautus*, The Loeb Classical Library (Cambridge, Mass./London, 1916 – 1938), 5 vols.; all quotations from Terence are from J. Sargeant, ed. and transl., *Terence*, The Loeb Classical Library (Cambridge, Mass./London, 1912), 2 vols. The Roman numbers are volume references.

[55] Cf. P. Burke, *Die Renaissance in Italien* (München, 1988), p.339.

[56] Cf., e.g., Beare, op. cit., p.45; he may have acted the part of the Clown in the Atellan farces (Duckworth, op. cit., p.50).

1 Title-page woodcut of J. de Roigny's
Paris edition of *Terence* (1552)

appeal of these plays'.[57] Hence the characters of Plautus are often aware of
play-acting, of playing roles and being part of a drama which, therefore, has a
distinctly metatheatrical quality. For example, Epidicus, the main character in
the play to which he gives his name, is an improvising player who talks himself
into the role of the cunning slave.[58] Furthermore, we sometimes find in these
plays an implicit 'theatrical director',[59] or even a character who acts the part of
the 'playwright' of a comedy. In *Bacchides*, the slave Chrysalus teaches Senex,
the stock character, what he should say in a certain situation, and, in so doing,
he does indeed create his role for him, just as a playwright would.[60] In
Pseudolus, we have 'a play about the Plautine process of play-making'; the
'major activity' of Pseudolus 'is, in fact, play-writing',[61] and he even
comments on his acting style which he calls magnificent ('magnufice') (IV,
702).[62] It is here already that the Plautine and Shakespearean dramatic styles
reveal a considerable affinity. We find the motif of the implied stage director
manipulating the play from within, as is well known, with a number of
outstanding Shakespearean characters, for instance Oberon in *A Midsummer
Night's Dream* or Duke Vincentio in *Measure for Measure*; some of these figures
create a role for one or more of their fellow-characters in the manner of a
playwright. This is true, for instance, of Gloucester, who will become Richard
III, and of Iago: Gloucester instructs Buckingham how he is to influence and
manipulate the citizens so that they will press for Gloucester to be crowned

[57] Slater, *Plautus in Performance*, p.4.
[58] Slater, op. cit., especially p. 27 – 36.
[59] Cf. Slater, op. cit., p.135.
[60] Slater, op. cit., p.108.
[61] Slater, op. cit., p.144.
[62] Slater, op. cit., p.134.

2 From the French manuscript, second half of the fifteenth century,
MS GKS 1994 f.1r

King (III, v, 72ff.), and Iago, in his first two famous soliloquies, hatches his plot against Othello just as a poet might sketch the outline of the plot of a play.

Among the various character types of Plautine comedy, many of whom belong to the tradition of New Comedy, the slave is, of course, the best known, in both the running and the cunning varieties (*servus currens, servus callidus*). Other important stock characters are the young lover (*iuvenis*), the angry old man (*senex*), the voracious parasite, the shameless sycophant, the greedy pander (*leno*), the good housewife (*matrona, mulier*) and the sly courtesan (*meretrix*).[63] Plautus, although he does not aim at psychological realism, nevertheless knows how to use realistic details in order to characterize a person successfully and in order to produce comic effects. Occasionally Plautus contrasts high and low with a parodic intention, as when in the *Curculio* the comic infatuation of the master is ridiculed by the loquacious slave, a technique that was fully developed by Shakespeare in his great scenes of comic juxtaposition. The Shakespearean fools, too, have dramatic antecedents in the Plautine slaves and parasites. Let us again take *Curculio* as an example: the dramatic centre of this play is a parasite who is as sensual as he is witty, who praises the pleasures of the stomach and nevertheless prefers for himself the delights of the spirit. His comic language is remarkably dialectical in a manner anticipating certain aspects of the Shakespearean Fool, although, as a rule, the Fool is not involved in an intrigue.[64]

Plautus's plays present an impressive variety of dramatic forms, and therefore it is impossible to apply a simple formula when trying to characterize them. We find the rough knock-about farcial comedy (e.g. *Asinaria*), the burlesque about the gods of classical mythology (*Amphitruo*), the comedy of character (*Aulularia*) and the comedy which is at the same time near-tragedy (*Captivi*). But quite different distinctions are also possible: thus della Corte divides the plays into 'la commedia della beffa' (*Asinaria, Persa, Casina*), 'la commedia del Romanzesco' (*Mercator, Stichus, Mostellaria, Trinummus*), 'la commedia dell' agnizione' (*Cistellaria, Poenulus, Curculio, Epidicus*), 'la commedia della caricatura' (*Pseudolus, Truculentus, Miles Gloriosus*), 'la commedia composita' (*Aulularia, Captivi, Rudens*).[65] When studying these comedies, one may be surprised to find that they contain situations of feeling and emotion as well. They have, for example, a strong lyrical element, which manifests itself mainly in the soliloquies, which were not spoken, but sung as *cantica*. There are more than 60 songs in the comedies of Plautus, and to a certain extent they can be compared to operatic arias. Except for some iambic passages in the dialogues, the entire comedy was accompanied by music, and the overall effect

---

[63] For the following survey I am heavily indebted to the excellent essay by B. Blänsdorf, 'Plautus', in: *Das römische Drama*, ed. E. Lefèvre (Darmstadt, 1978), p.135 – 219.

[64] Richard Mellein in *Kindlers Literaturlexikon* (München, 1974), VI, 2285f.; Salingar, *Shakespeare and the Traditions of Comedy*, p.172.

[65] F. della Corte, *Da Sarsina a Roma* (Genova, ²1967), p.171ff.

of a Plautine comedy was comparable to our musical comedies. To me it seems not at all unlikely that Shakespeare knew of the importance of this musical component, because many Renaissance editions of Terence contained an introductory chapter on metre, written by Erasmus, in which the use of music in ancient comedy was explicitly mentioned.

The range of emotions aroused in these soliloquies as well as in the plays as a whole is surprisingly wide: there is the feeling of disappointment and anger of a duped father, the despair of a kidnapped girl, a character's pathetic experience of a sudden change of fortune, as well as the exuberance of young lovers.[66] There is a widespread prejudice against Plautus that he treats the emotion of love in a light, frivolous and cynical manner. This is in fact a vast over-simplification, because it must be said that his plots are 'basically moral'.[67] It is, of course, true that the treatment of love in Plautine comedy is often markedly different from the romantic love of Elizabethan comedy; what interests Plautus is not so much the process of falling in love but rather the confusions which arise once a character has fallen in love.[68] Love scenes are frequently presented in a burlesque and sometimes even coarse manner, and often a lover is made the butt of comedy or irony. Furthermore, it is common for a character in love to talk about his own love or to complain about the unhappiness of his love and to formulate moral maxims.

However, although genuine love scenes are rare, the common view that love scenes in Roman comedy take the form of libidinous sexuality takes no account of the situations where the lover's unfulfilled desires and longings are given dramatic expression. Friedrich Schlegel was right when he contended that 'The tender warmth, the urban grace, the liberal humanity that flowed through the erotic presentations of Attic New Comedy, is still preserved in many plays by Plautus and Terence.'[69] Thus love in Plautus sometimes resembles the presentation of an enamoured lover in Elizabethan romantic comedy.[70] To some extent we can even observe the dramatist's interest in presenting the various psychological conditions of a lover. His (or her) 'reason' may be clouded in such a way that he (or she) becomes a downright fool (*Truculentus*, V, 26). Many inconveniences, troubles and pains await the lover. He feels miserable and melancholy, he becomes pale, sighs and suffers. In *Bacchides*, a young man is asked to discern whether it is 'Cupid, or Love, raging within' ('Cupidon tecum saevust anne Amor?') (Fragm. XIV). Clearly, love is sometimes recognized as a most intense human experience permeating the deep recesses of the human heart or affecting the whole

---

66 Cf. Blänsdorf, op. cit., p.174; on love in Roman Comedy cf. also P. Flury, *Liebe und Liebessprache bei Menander, Plautus und Terenz* (Heidelberg, 1968).
67 Duckworth, op. cit., p.303.
68 Blänsdorf, op. cit., p.164.
69 *Über das Studium der griechischen Poesie* in: *F. Schlegel, Schriften zur Literatur*, ed. W. Rasch (München, 21985), p.164.
70 Cf. Duckworth, op. cit., p.415.

person. Occasionally, a character thinks that suicide may be a way out of his love-sickness (*Cistellaria*, II, 638, *Mercator*, III, 472). One of Plautus's lovers expresses his sufferings with a surprisingly original and suggestive image: Alcesimarchus in *Cistellaria* complains that he is 'whirled on the wheel of love' ('versor / in amoris rota' 206f.). The rhythm of this entire soliloquy is so moving that the reader is reminded of the love lyrics of the *Carmina Burana*, although rhyme in the modern sense is lacking. The speaker then goes on to confess that he is 'done to death', 'torn asunder, disrupted, dismembered':

> iactor agitor stimulor, versor
> in amoris rota, miser exanimor,
> feror differor distrahor diripior,
> ita nubilam mentem animi habeo.
> ubi sum, ibi non sum, ubi non sum, ibist animus,
> ita mi omnia sunt ingenia;
> quod lubet, non lubet iam id continuo,
> ita me Amor lassum animi ludificat,
> fugat, agit, appetit, raptat, retinet . . .   II, 206 – 215

> I'm tossed around, bandied about, goaded, whirled on the wheel of love, done to death, poor wretch that I am! I'm torn, torn asunder, disrupted, dismembered – yes, all my mental faculties are befogged! Where I am, there I am not; where I am not, there my soul is – yes, I am in a thousand moods. The thing that pleases me ceases to please a moment later; yes, Love mocks me in my weariness of soul, – it drives me off, hounds me, seeks me, lays hands on me, holds me back . . .

In the *Curculio* we have a young couple whose feelings might almost be called 'romantic'. This mood finds beautiful expression in a nocturnal serenade, a feature which also occurs in *The Two Gentlemen of Verona*. The play *Trinummus* deserves to be examined more closely in our context. It is a play in which the lovers' feelings are taken seriously in an unexpected way. First of all, it contains the famous *oxymoron*, used as a *topos* in Renaissance literature, that love is 'bitter-sweet' (*Trinummus*, V,259). Plautus is the first in Latin literature to express this idea by way of a pun on 'amor' and 'amarus', which is so characteristic of his comic language. As Erasmus in his *Adagia* traces this conceit back to Plautus, we are entitled to say that Plautus must indeed have had a considerable share in the development of this idea.[71]

In *Trinummus*, the character Lesbonicus squanders his material goods and even sells the house of his absent father in order to indulge in his erotic adventures. His friend Lysiteles wants to do him a good turn and relieve him of his poverty. He tells him 'I know your mistakes weren't made wilfully, but you let love cloud your reason; and I myself well understand Love's method' ('scio te sponte non tuapte errasse, sed amorem tibi / pectus opscurasse; atque

---

[71] Cf. E. Wind, *Pagan Mysteries in the Renaissance* (London, 1958), p.136 – 137.

ipse Amoris teneo omnis vias.') (666f.). He then proposes to marry Lesbonicus's sister without a dowry. Lesbonicus, however, cannot agree to this because he fears it would completely destroy his social standing — he would rather sell his farm, which is his last financial resource, than allow his sister to be married without a dowry. Then Callicles, who has been left in charge of the money belonging to Lesbonicus's father, contrives a 'scheme'. He engages a man who is to pretend that he is handing over the money from Lesbonicus's father so that the girl can be given a dowry. The scheme, however, 'explodes' on the unexpected return of the father, who, in a very comic scene, faces the swindler pretending to come from the absent father. Thereupon the marriage between Lysiteles and Lesbonicus's sister is about to take place, and Lesbonicus, too, as a kind of penitence, agrees to marry. He also promises to lead a less libidinous life and to 'keep myself in hand' ('posthac temperabo' 1187). His father is ready to pardon him in response to Lysiteles's plea on his behalf: 'If your son did act a bit foolishly, do overlook it all.' ('si quid stulte fecit, ut ea missa facias omnia' (1168). Although the scheme, which forms the central part of the action, is a farcical element, the play nevertheless articulates human and social problems and discusses the necessity of maintaining Roman values. The 'arts of Love' ('Amoris artis' 236), which have nothing to do with marriage, are verbalized in an astonishingly exhaustive way. With the final moral improvement of Lesbonicus the play achieves an element of 'correction' which, as we shall see, was an essential part of New Comedy right from its beginnings in Menander.

This also accounts for the fact that Plautine comedy can sometimes be satirical as well, a fact too often forgotten by Shakespeare critics, although the satire on the braggart soldier in the *Miles Gloriosus* is a most famous example.[72] In this context a long satirical passage in *Trinummus* should also be mentioned, where the manners ('mores') of the time are satirized (V, 1028 – 1054).

The opening dialogue of the Plautine *Stichus*, a pure Menandrian comedy, in which one of the characters is called Antipho, brings us back once more to Shakespeare's *Errors*. Panegyris and her sister are discussing the fact that their husbands have been absent for three years and that therefore their father wants to dissolve their marriage. Panegyris is unable to account for her husband's disregard of his duty towards her, while she is faithfully doing hers. Her sister then advises her that 'right . . . thinking people should all have regard for what's their own . . . duty and do it.' ('omnis sapientis / suom officium aequom est colere et facere.' V, 39 – 40), and she specially warns her 'to keep your own duty in mind' ('moneo, ut tuom memineris officium' 42). There is a remarkable parallel between the two sisters' views about marital duty and the scene between Adriana and Luciana in *Errors* (II, i), where the duties of husband and wife are discussed in a similar manner.

---

[72] A notable exception is C. Hoy in his excellent study *The Hyacinth Room* (London, 1964).

As we see, Plautus is indeed concerned in his comedies with moral themes; some of these recur frequently, and occasionally they are exploited for philosophical moralizing. In particular, many comments on Roman virtues can be found. If these are sometimes dealt with in a comic manner, this does not mean that Plautus is slighting them in a cynical way, as we have seen. On the contrary, their temporary reversal is a saturnalian topsyturvydom that in the end only serves to confirm the established system of values. Since, however, the saturnalian element plays a far smaller role in Terence than in Plautus, Erasmus and some other continental humanists gave preference to Terence, who, no doubt, preserved the marked humanism of Menandrian New Comedy in an unadulterated way. This humanist stance is admirably reflected in Chremes's comment in the Terentian *Heautontimoroumenos*: 'I am a man, I hold that what affects another man affects me.' ('Homo sum: humani nil a me alienum puto.' I, 77). Nevertheless, as we have seen, many humanists also recognized the educational qualities of the plays of Plautus, and they read and recommended them for their didactic value. Erasmus included in his pedagogical programme a selection of those Plautine comedies which were devoid of 'obscenitas'.[73]

We observe in Plautus a remarkably critical stance towards the gods,[74] and this reminds us somewhat of the way the gods appear in Euripidean tragedy, from which New Comedy is ultimately derived. In some plays by Plautus, a character complains of being exposed to the fitfulness of the gods. Thus, in *Mercator*, Demipho expresses the belief that 'The Gods do make sport of us mortals in amazing ways!' ('Miris modis di ludos faciunt hominibus' 225), and the Prologue to the *Captivi* complains that they 'use us mortals as footballs' ('enim vero di nos quasi pilas homines habent.' 22). Do we not find a similar view of the gods in Shakespeare, too? Does this not remind us of Gloucester's famous cry of despair in *King Lear*: 'As flies to wanton boys are we to th' gods, / They kill us for their sport'? (IV, i, 36f.) By contrast, as in Euripides and Plautus, Shakespeare in his late plays stresses the idea that the nature of the gods is benign.

On the other hand, the notion that human life is subject to the whims of Fortune forms part of the basic structure from the very beginning of New Comedy in Menander. Omnipotent Tyche is seen to be behind human

---

[73] *De Ratione Studii* in: *Opera Omnia Desiderii Erasmi Roterodami*, ed. J.-C. Margolin (Amsterdam, 1971), I, 2, 116.

[74] Cf. E. Lefèvre, 'Theatrum Mundi: Götter, Gott und Spielleiter im antiken Drama' in: *Theatrum Mundi: Götter, Gott und Spielleiter im Drama von der Antike bis zur Gegenwart*, ed. F. Link und G. Niggl (Berlin, 1981), p.74. He points out that Plautus felt free to present the gods as he wished because the gods in comedy were already distinguished from those in contemporary religion. However, according to Duckworth, 'in general Plautus' comedies do not display an attitude of irreverence.' (op. cit., p.298).

actions, and the gods are no more than her agents.[75] In the Menandrian play *Aspis*, she even appears in person on stage.[76] By their emphasis on adventurous happenings, through which family bonds are dissolved and then retied, the plots of New Comedy adopt a quality of romance. The virtue or *virtus* by which man may oppose the malevolent aspects of Tyche/Fortuna is patience (*patientia*). It is clear that this didactic quality of the plays of New Comedy especially appealed to the humanists, and this is why they had a marked preference for the specifically 'romantic' comedies of Plautus, such as the *Rudens* or the *Captivi*. The *Captivi* has neither a love story nor any coarse comic character, because the plot, based on the caprices of Fortune, develops and unfolds through human virtues such as the faithfulness of a servant to his master or the natural longing of a father for his son. The misfortunes which the characters of New Comedy experience are partly caused by their inability to distinguish between appearance and reality, but also to some extent by their lack of self-knowledge and their ignorance of their own faults which are in need of correction.

3. *New Comedy and romance*

The importance of these romance elements has not been sufficiently recognized by most Shakespeare critics. Madeleine Doran's conjecture that New Comedy was 'one of the lines that entered into the composition of romantic comedy'[77] can now be taken as an established fact. It is certainly true that the romantic or romanesque plots of the Elizabethans 'were less unclassical than we think them'.[78] The Renaissance dramatists felt that, in putting on stage their own plays, they were performing 'simply the extension of an old authoritative' comedy[79] that had been established by Menander and other Greek New Comedy dramatists, and which was further developed by Plautus and Terence. It follows from this that, when Shakespeare added the romance subplot to the suggestions he took from the *Menaechmi* for his *Errors*, we *cannot* maintain that he 'medievalized the story', as Nevill Coghill[80] put it in his well-known article. Nor was Shakespeare's impulse to include suggestions from the *Apollonius* romance of late antiquity in *Errors* 'rather odd',[81] as Adelman has claimed. Instead, Shakespeare was 'only' enlarging

[75] Lefèvre, 'Theatrum Mundi', p.71.
[76] *Aspis* in: *Menander*, ed. W.G. Arnott, The Loeb Classical Library (Cambridge, Mass./London, 1979), I, 24.
[77] *Endeavors of Art*, p.172.
[78] Ibid., and Duckworth, p.415.
[79] Ibid., p.174.
[80] 'The Basis of Shakespearean Comedy', *E&S*, n.s. (1950), 1 – 28.
[81] J. Adelman, 'Male Bonding in Shakespeare's Comedies' in: *Shakespeare's Rough Magic*, ed. Erickson and Kahn (Newark/London/Toronto, 1985), p.93.

and elaborating a romantic plot pattern already familiar in some plays of Plautus (as well as in the New Comedy tradition itself), although it was not prominent in the *Menaechmi*. Yet in the Prologue to this play the romance motif of the separation of family members is directly referred to, and Antipholus's narration of his long sea voyage at the beginning of Act II further suggested the romance-like extension of the plot.

Coghill's distinction between the 'medieval' or 'romantic' and the 'satirical' types of comedy is based on a thorough misunderstanding: none of these three adjectives is appropriately used here. We shall see that Shakespeare's comedies cannot simply be called 'romantic', that, like the humanists, he had a considerable satirical interest and that this aspect of his comedies is too often played down. Of course, 'he does not make it a habit to denounce bad men',[82] as is pointed out by Tillyard, who also has a critical objection to Coghill's view; yet there are many degrees of satire: it is not always vitriolic, it can both range from the coarse to the subtle, Shakespeare's satire being of the greatest subtlety.

Recent research has shown that the traditional view, according to which in the Middle Ages the term 'comedy' meant a 'story starting in trouble, ending in joy, and centred in love',[83] is one-sided, if not downright wrong. The Middle Ages had a more precise idea of the nature of comedy, and there was even a basic 'theory' of comedy.[84] Its major points continued to be accepted in the Renaissance so that we are no longer entitled to speak of 'medieval comedy' as though it were a special kind of comedy that paved the way for Shakespeare's comic vision. Suchomski, who has done away with the confusion about the nature of comedy in the Middle Ages, has pointed out that epic comedy came into existence as an *additional* variety of comedy only by way of a misunderstanding: it was thought that the plays of Terence were never performed but only read,[85] recited and accompanied by mime and gesture. Thus, the notion developed that the dialogic interplay was not indispensable for comedies and that therefore they could also be *narrated*. Up to the 13th century the Terentian and Plautine tradition was the only standard for the concept of comedy.[86]

With John of Garland in the 13th century, however, we come across an extension of the idea of comedy: he makes a division into 'comoedia' and 'comoedia perfecta', that is, he distinguishes between the *genuine* Terentian comedy and the epic, narrative comedy composed in the *Terentian tradition*.[87] This observation made by Suchomski is most interesting because it

---

[82] E.M.W. Tillyard, *The Nature of Comedy and Shakespeare*. The English Association, Presidential Address 1958 (Oxford, 1958), p.7.
[83] Coghill, op. cit., p.14.
[84] Cf. J. Suchomski, op. cit., p.143.
[85] Suchomski, op. cit., p.90.
[86] Suchomski, op. cit., p.146.
[87] Suchomski, op. cit., p.97.

3 From the Duc de Berry's *Terence* about 1400, B.N. MS Lat. 7907, f.2v

undermines the nebulous concept of a special 'medieval [romantic] comedy'; instead, even epic comedy is now seen to have been developed by adopting Terentian structural models. Thus, epic comedy in the Middle Ages was a new comedy only in the restricted sense of a narrative *substitute* for *classical* comedy.

What the medieval and the Renaissance definitions of Comedy have in common is the idea that a comedy has to present a fictive world, but still a true one, which may function as a *speculum* providing *utilitas*, didactic usefulness, for the reader or audience. Whereas 'movere' was considered as the primary function of tragedy, 'delectare' was a special quality expected from comedy.[88] The Renaissance editions of Terence and Plautus, which Shakespeare must have used, did not contain a new theory of comedy; instead, the humanists in their introductions and dedicatory epistles preferred to quote traditional authorities or else, like Melanchthon, they enlarged on traditional views.[89] It is the *selection* of thoughts, however, which they make, that is interesting. They saw in comedies a picture of human life, of its problems and dangers, and they considered them as providing illustrations of how these may be overcome or avoided. I have already mentioned that even a play like *Menaechmi* was regarded as useful because Messenio warns his young master against light women and because the play contains other proverbs and *sententiae*. This sporadic proverbial lore was seen to provide the Aristotelian dramatic category of 'thought'. In the context of his definition of comedy, Sir Thomas Elyot refers to the Plautine *Amphitruo*, which, as we shall soon see, has much to offer, and he quotes Alcumena's beautiful words about 'virtue' (I, 64 – 51)[90] as proof of the play's moral content. Many of the maxims, proverbs and tags which Erasmus collected in his famous *Adagia* were adopted from Roman comedy, and it is interesting that the number taken from Plautus is far greater than those derived from Terence. Kenneth Muir is thus perfectly right in claiming that the chief Elizabethan comic playwrights (including Shakespeare) 'were all influenced by the theory that comedy should be didactic.'[91]

On the whole, the humanists thus considered tragedy *and* comedy to be similarly useful and they even hesitated to make any clear-cut distinction between these two dramatic kinds. Did not Plato in his *Symposion* make Socrates emphasize the interrelation between the tragic and the comic?[92] In

---

[88] Suchomski, op. cit., p.95, 146f. Castelvetro is exceptional in claiming that comedy should provide nothing but delight (H.B. Charlton, *Castelvetro's Theory of Poetry* [Manchester, 1913], p.66.).

[89] Cf., for example, the edition: *Terentii Afri Comoediae Sex*, ed. Philip Melanchthon and Desiderius Erasmus (Nürnberg, 1558).

[90] *The Book Named the Governor*, p.48.

[91] *Shakespeare's Comic Sequence* (Liverpool, 1979), p.8.

[92] *Symposion*, 223d; cf. also G. Williams, ' "The Comedy of Errors" Rescued from Tragedy', *REL*, 5 (1964), 63.

the tradition of Aristotle, Evanthius and Diomedes, comedy was defined and described in terms *analogous* to those of tragedy. This can be clearly studied in the *Tractatus Coislinianus*, which, according to the latest research, may have preserved Aristotle's own thoughts on comedy.[93] It points out that the function of comedy is to purge through the effects of the laughter which it evokes. Guarini believes the cathartic effects of comedy to be much greater: he claims that it achieves the purgation of the affections of sadness and melancholy.[94] When the earlier humanists defined comedy as representing the *ethos* or manners of the dramatic characters, then they also implied that their emotions were put on stage in order to purge the audience from these emotions – emotions which, compared to those evoked by tragedy, are 'mitiores',[95] that is, they do not reach the intensity and height of tragedy.

Such is the background against which we have to consider the origins of *Errors*. This picture is essentially different from Coghill's suggestion that the 'simple formula' of 'a tale of trouble that turned to joy [. . .]' is the true basis of Shakespearean Comedy'[96] and that Plautus is replete with 'coarseness and selfishness'.[97] We shall see on many occasions how Shakespeare's reception of Plautus resembles that of the humanists. Although, unlike most of them, Shakespeare usually was not overtly didactic, his plays are nevertheless concerned with central human as well as humanist issues and with the correction of human weaknesses. Most often, Shakespearean comedy dramatizes the problem of human identity with both its comic and its tragic implications. The fact that precisely this problem could be studied in classical Comedy as well, becomes abundantly clear if Shakespeare's second source for *Errors*, the *Amphitruo*, is at last given the attention it deserves.

---

[93] Cf. R. Janko, *Aristotle on Comedy. Towards a Reconstruction of Poetics II* (Berkeley/Los Angeles, 1984), p.83.

[94] Guarini's *Compendium of Tragicomic Poetry* in: A.H. Gilbert, *Literary Criticism. Plato to Dryden* (Detroit, 1962), p.524.

[95] Erasmus in: *De Ratione Studii*, ed. J.C. Margolin in *Opera Omnia Desiderii Erasmi Roterodami*, I, 2 (Amsterdam, 1971); English translation: *On the Method of Study* in: *Collected Works of Erasmus. Literary and Educational Writings*, 2, ed. C.R. Thompson (Toronto/Buffalo/London, 1978), p.687: 'In comedy decorum and the portrayal of our common life must be observed, and the emotions are more subdued: that is, engaging, rather than passionate.' Personally, Erasmus disliked tragic παϑος, and in his own poetry avoided every kind of violent affection (Huizinga, *Erasmus and the Age of Reformation* [Princeton, 1984], p.94); Quintilian defines the emotions of ηϑος as 'calm and gentle' – 'mites atque compositos' (*The Institutio Oratoria of Quintilian*, ed. and transl. H.E. Butler [London/Cambridge, Mass., 1922], II, 423 (VI, ii, 9)).

[96] Coghill, op. cit., p.4.

[97] Coghill, op. cit., p.10.

4. *The relevance of* Amphitruo *as a source for* The Comedy of Errors

With *Amphitruo*, Plautus has no doubt exerted his greatest influence on European comedy. The play was known even in the Middle Ages[98], and, more than any other of his works, has inspired a large number of new versions and still continues to do so.[99] Recently critics have become increasingly interested in the play, whose impact on Shakespeare was far greater than simply to suggest the ideas of having Antipholus locked out of his own house and of doubling the twins. That there was an English translation, dating from 1562 – 3[100] escaped Baldwin's notice and that of later scholarship.[101]

Before embarking upon our comparison, we would do well to recall that the myth of Jupiter's visit to Alcumena was originally dramatized in Greek *tragedies* which are now lost; it is certain that Aeschylus, Sophocles and Euripides were also authors of *Amphitryon* tragedies.[102] Euripides may have concentrated on the fact that Alcumena is about to give birth to twins (Heracles and Iphicles), although her husband had not touched her before he went to battle. His plot may have been along the following lines: Amphitruo believes Alcumena to be guilty of adultery, and since she protests that he has indeed enjoyed her (she is unaware of Jupiter's disguise), his suspicion of her supposed adultery increases. Her 'guilt' cries out for his punishment; she seeks sanctuary at the altar, which Amphitruo intends to be the very place of her execution. At the last minute, Jupiter may have appeared as *deus ex machina* and prevented Alcumena from being sacrificed. In the Sophoclean *Amphitryon* the protagonist may have been similar to other Sophoclean characters; for example, like Oedipus, he may have relentlessly tried to clear up the mysterious past, to find a truth which he is unable to bear: here, too, the inevitable consequence would be his decision to punish his wife for her supposed transgression. (The parallels to *Othello* which are opened up here are remarkable.)[103]

Thus, a far greater 'seriousness' is implied in the plot material of the Plautine *Amphitruo* than in that of *Menaechmi*. The very first scene of Plautus's *Amphitruo* establishes this serious tone. The physical aggression, which in

---

[98] Cf. Suchomski, op. cit., p.120.

[99] Cf. C.D.N. Costa, 'The Amphitruo Theme' in: T.A. Dorey and D.R. Dudley, eds., *Roman Drama* (London, 1965), p.87 – 122.

[100] Cf. C.H. Conley, *The First English Translations of the Classics* (New Haven, 1927), p.143 and Duckworth, op. cit., p.412.

[101] As the real and very close connections between *Errors* and *Amphitruo* have gone unnoticed, the passages from this source that Bullough reprints are far from giving an adequate picture, *Narrative and Dramatic Sources of Shakespeare*, I,, 40 – 49.

[102] Cf. P. Szondi, 'Fünfmal Amphitryon: Plautus, Molière, Kleist, Giraudoux, Kaiser', in: *Schriften*, (Frankfurt/M., 1978), II, 170 – 204.

[103] On these reconstructions cf. F. Stoessl, 'Amphitryon, Wachstum und Wandlung eines poetischen Stoffes', *Trivium*, 2 (1944), 96ff. and E. Lefèvre, *Maccus Vortit Barbare* (Mainz, 1982).

Menaechmi does not go beyond threatening language, becomes real when Sosia is about to be beaten by Mercury. The audience, who have been informed by the Prologue about the identity of the characters, see two Sosias facing each other and acting together, Mercury disguised as Sosia, beating the real one for claiming to be Sosia. (In Italian, the name Sosia still has the sense 'Doppelgänger'.) Sosia's experience with his *alter ego* leads him into serious trouble. Whereas in *Menaechmi* the problem of human identity, so important in *Errors*, is scarcely touched upon, it assumes central significance in *Amphitruo*. Mercury takes great pains to persuade Sosia that he is a different person. Perceiving that he is confronted with an impostor-Sosia, he feels compelled to look for a new name: 'I've got to find me a new name' ('aliud nomen quaerendum est mihi.' 423). He then complains that he has also been deprived of his own form by another person: 'he had stolen my looks along with my name.' ('tum formam una abstulit cum nomine.' 600). Mercury even succeeds in awakening in him doubts concerning his own self:

> Mercury.   Quid nunc? Vincon argumentis, te non esse Sosiam?
> Sosia.   Tu negas med esse?   433 – 434

> Mercury.   Well, have I convinced you that you are not Sosia?
> Sosia.   You deny it, do you?

While here Sosia still insists that he is himself, a little later his doubts increase: 'For mercy's sake who am I, if I'm not Sosia?' ('Quis ego sum saltem, si non sum Sosia?' 438). And then he asks in dismay: 'For heaven's sake, where did I lose myself? Where was I transformed? Where did I drop my shape?' ('di immortales, obsecro vostram fidem, / ubi ego perii? ubi immutatus sum? ubi ego formam perdidi?' 455 – 456). Sosia goes so far as to believe that, rather than having been beaten by Mercury, it is his *alter ego* who has beaten him (607). Thus, not only has Mercury deprived Sosia of his name, he has also deprived him of his identity. The slave Sosia is the first to realize that his identity has become problematic. And Barnes has rightly called him 'the truly tragicomic figure' of the play, because he 'is in conflict with himself' and because he 'ultimately' even becomes 'a stranger to himself'.[104] In this play we are made to realize 'that the self [. . .] remains a mystery'.[105] Furthermore, it has, I think, been correctly maintained that 'even if Plautus had been incapable of seeing more than the comic possibilities, the play would have had a serious undertone in spite of him'.[106]

A comparison between Sosia and Shakespeare's Dromios is most revealing. Dromio S is the first to notice that his identity and that of his master have come under serious attack; there is even a verbal echo of *Amphitruo* when Dromio assumes that they have been 'transformed':

[104] H.E. Barnes, 'The Case of Sosia Versus Sosia', *CJ*, 53/54 (1957/8), 19.
[105] Ibid., p.21.
[106] Ibid.

Syr. Dro.   I am transformed, master am I not?
Syr. Ant.   I think thou art in mind, and so am I.
Syr. Dro.   Nay, master, both in mind and in my shape.
Syr. Ant.   Thou hast thine own form.
Syr. Dro.   No, I am an ape.
Luciana.   If thou art chang'd to aught, 'tis to an ass.
Syr. Dro.   'Tis true, she rides me, and I long for grass.

II, ii, 195 – 200

Before the same Dromio tells his master about his experience with the kitchen wench in III,ii, he, in the ensuing short dialogue, jestingly asks Antipholus whether he is really his master's old Dromio:

Syr. Dro.   Do you know me sir? Am I Dromio? Am I your man?
            Am I myself?
Syr. Ant.   Thou art Dromio, thou art my man, thou art thyself.
Syr. Dro.   I am an ass, I am a woman's man, and besides myself.

72 – 76

The Dromio of the denizen Antipholus is less occupied with questions of his own identity, yet when his master tells him, 'I think thou art an ass', he unhesitatingly agrees with Luciana: 'Marry, so it does appear / By the wrongs I suffer and the blows I bear' (III, i, 15 – 16). We have, then, a most interesting parallel between *Errors* and *Amphitruo* when in III, i the two Dromios are simultaneously present on stage, while the audience are aware of the real identity of the two. The difference between *Errors* and *Amphitruo* is, however, that Dromio E cannot *see* but only hear his double; yet, like Sosia, Dromio considers the other to be an impostor. The recognition of the parallel situation in *Amphitruo* helps us to understand more clearly the following exchange between the two Dromios:

Eph. Ant.   What art thou that keep'st me out from the house I owe?
Syr. Dro.   The porter for this time, sir, and my name is Dromio.
Eph. Dro.   O villain, thou hast stol'n both mine office and my
            name;
            The one ne'er got me credit, the other mickle blame;
            If thou hadst been Dromio to-day in my place,
            Thou would'st have chang'd thy face for a name, or thy
            name for an ass.   43 – 47[107]

Like the real Sosia, the doorkeeper of Amphitruo, Dromio E, the real 'porter', has been manoeuvred into a position where he has to look for a new name; yet whereas Sosia also feels the necessity of looking for a new shape ('formam una abstulit cum nomine'), Dromio E thinks he has to look for a new office: 'O villain, thou hast stolen both mine office and my name.'

---

[107]   Here we follow the Folio reading rather than the emendations by Foakes and the New Cambridge Shakespeare.

Amphitruo, too, experiences an identity crisis of his own, although this is more difficult to analyse because the text of this comedy has come down to us in a fragmentary state. Amphitruo is puzzled so much by what he hears from Alcumena and his Sosia that he begins to question whether he is still the same person. Sosia then reassures him that he has not changed, but he nevertheless warns his master: 'be careful that you do not *lose* yourself' ('cave sis ne tu te usu perduis' italics and translation mine 845). Shakespeare is so interested in this problem that he articulates it directly in *Errors*: Antipholus S is aware of the danger of 'losing' himself (I, ii, 40); finally, however, he finds himself through the discovery of his brother and mother.

From the moment of his first appearance in Ephesus, the life of Antipholus S is threatened because he is a Syracusian, and therefore the First Merchant advises him to 'give out' (I, ii, 1) that he has come from Epidamnum. He increasingly feels the loss of his self until he acquires self-knowledge. In his dialogue with Adriana and Luciana he believes himself to have been 'transformed' (II, ii, 195 – 196) and to be 'disguis'd' (214) from himself. In Act V, as Adriana and her company approach to bind him, it seems to him that the initial threat to his life has become real.

Whereas the plot of *Amphitruo* is on the one hand a comic amorous adventure of the Supreme God, on the other hand the suspicion of adultery which arises from the confusions develops both comic and tragic complications. Amphitruo has good reason to suspect his wife of having spent a night with another man. In *Errors*, too, adultery is a major concern and cause of trouble; yet, in contrast to *Amphitruo*, it presents itself exactly in reverse: here it is the wife who suspects the husband, and without real cause. Adriana suffers so much from the thought of her husband's having a paramour that she thinks her very own identity to be threatened (II, ii, 119 – 146), and even wishes to die: 'Since that my beauty cannot please his eye, / I'll weep what's left away, and weeping die' (II, i, 114 – 115). However, she rebukes the wrong husband and, as a consequence, Antipholus S in turn begins to have serious doubts about whether he is still the same person. In the scene following the dialogue between Adriana and Antipholus S, the adultery motif is further reinforced and made more similar to *Amphitruo*: when Antipholus E is locked out of his house, and a second Antipholus is performing his 'office' at home, the situation is at least sexually ambiguous, as Michel Grivelet and Ralph Berry have remarked.[108] For if Adriana, believing that her husband has returned, did allow Antipholus S to make love to her, she would actually have been committing adultery with a stranger. We shall see in a later context that the sexual punning during this situation emphasizes its ambiguity.

---

[108] M. Grivelet, 'Shakespeare, Molière, and the Comedy of Ambiguity', *ShS*, 22 (1969), 15 – 26, esp. p.15f.; R. Berry, *Shakespeare and the Awareness of the Audience* (London, 1985), p.40.

There are further parallels between Antipholus E and Amphitruo. Both are passive victims of what happens to them. After Antipholus's wife has complained to the other twin, she begins to pity her real husband again on false grounds, this time for his supposed madness. The confusion about the *golden chain* greatly increases her suspicion that Antipholus has gone mad. Wanting to help and rescue her 'poor distracted husband' (V, i, 39), she is on the verge of destroying his identity. Adriana and the Courtesan, who received a ring from him, consider him possessed of the devil and therefore make preparations for his exorcism. Amphitruo's doubts about his identity begin when after his return from the battlefield his wife Alcumena behaves in a way that must appear shocking to him because she is entirely unaware of the fact that it is Jupiter, and not her husband, who visited her the previous night. When she claims to have been given a *golden cup*, his bewilderment increases even more, because the object is real and cannot be talked away. Thereupon Amphitruo considers her possessed by evil spirits (776, fr.8), and Sosia confirms him in this view by asking whether he intends to make a purifying sacrifice for the benefit of his wife: 'Quaeso, quin tu istanc iubes / pro cerrita circumferri?' (776 – 7); this means: 'Please, why don't you have her exorcised?' (my translation). (And even in *Menaechmi* Menaechmus' supposed madness is suspected to be the work of evil spirits, 890.) It follows from this that the introduction of Dr Pinch the exorcist is not an entirely new and Christian element, by which Shakespeare radically changed the atmosphere of New Comedy, but a motif already *suggested* in the Plautine *Amphitruo*; Shakespeare extended it and turned it into a most effective scene, unparalleled in Plautus.

Amphitruo's perplexity at the thought of what has happened to him increases to the point where he no longer knows who he is: 'Upon my soul, I have been so bewitched I don't know who I am!' ('Delenitus sum profecto ita, ut me qui sim nesciam.' 843). The same happens, as we have seen, to Antipholus S. When at the close of scene IV, iii, Jupiter enters *Amphitruo's* house, he is about to despair and feels himself to be on the verge of madness: 'Oh, of all miserable men in Thebes! What shall I do now? Disowned and humbugged by every mortal soul to suit their humour!' ('qui me Thebis alter vivit miserior? quid nunc agam? / quem omnes mortales ignorant et ludificant ut lubet.' 1046 – 1047). Now he no longer asks who he is because he thinks he has been made the dupe of a juggler or conjurer, and yet he complains that the image which society has of him has been destroyed. Later on, he, like Adriana, wishes he were dead ('mortuom satiust' 1018). In order to define Amphitruo's problem precisely, it is advisable to adopt Jauss's distinction between 'personal' and 'role' identity.[109] Amphitruo fears having been

---

[109] H.R. Jauss, 'Poetik und Problematik von Identität und Rolle in der Geschichte des Amphitryon' in: *Identität*, ed. D. Marquard and K. Stierle, *Poetik und Hermeneutik*, VIII (München, 1979), p.220 – 221. On this point cf. also M.D. Boesel, *Identitäts- und Rollenproblematik in den englischen Komödien der Amphitryon- und Menaechmi-Tradition* (Diss. Stuttgart, 1976), p.73.

deprived of his social identity because, as he says, he is 'humbugged by every mortal soul to suit their humour' ('quem omnes mortales [. . .] ludificant ut lubet.' 1047), and this is the cause of his loss of self-confidence. Somewhat later he even feels that he is about to be killed. We see him lying as though dead in front of his house and calling himself a broken man ('Interii.' 1076). Like Amphitruo, yet in contrast to his twin brother, Antipholus E does not really question his personal identity; however, he becomes furious when he is forced to assume that his own wife has annihilated his social identity.

Alcumena is indeed much more passive than Adriana. However, as has been observed by Percy Simpson, both women are characterized by a 'rich poetic colouring'.[110] Plautus gives her a moving soliloquy in II,ii, in which she acquires the stature of a tragic character and comes to the conclusion that in life sorrow is a constant companion to pleasure (635). Somewhat later, the Supreme God himself assures her that she is right in thinking that human lives vacillate between extremes: 'Human beings lay hold on pleasures and then again on pains.' ('capiunt voluptates, capiunt rursum miserias' 939). Yet what troubles her most is her husband's suspecting her of adultery, which has deeply wounded her: 'I know one thing — that joke of yours cut me to the heart, sir' ('Ego illud scio quam doluerit cordi meo.' 922). Conversely, Adriana, as we have seen, feels wounded to death because she thinks her husband has committed adultery. She articulates her sorrow and despair in moving monologues by which she develops into an individual character. At the end of both comedies the question remains whether the couples have really managed to overcome the problems that have arisen in their marriages.

In his Prologue to the Plautine *Amphitruo*, Mercury alludes to the fact that the Amphitruo myth was originally dramatized as a tragedy. After a while he makes the surprise announcement that a 'tragicomoedia' (59) is to be presented. The immediate cause for this creation of a new, mixed genre is, as Mercury himself points out, the intermingling of high and low characters in the same play. Yet this does not seem to be the sole justification for calling the play a 'tragicomoedia'. Jauss has convincingly argued that, by calling this play, in which no less than a temporary loss of identity is shown, a tragicomedy, Plautus subtly indicates the possibility of a double reception of the work.[111] As Mercury suggests, it depends entirely on the perspective of the audience whether the play is seen as a comedy or as a tragedy. From the omniscient point of view of the gods, the play is a comedy, in the eyes of the human beings who suffer because of Jupiter's erotic adventure, the plot takes on an almost tragic note. The audience, who from the beginning are given the superior vantage point of the gods, can laugh both *with* the gods and even *at* the gods. Furthermore, they may enjoy the comedy of the confusions and *also* at times sympathize with the tragic predicament of the human characters, that

---

[110] P. Simpson, *Studies in Elizabethan Drama* (Oxford, 1955), p.83.
[111] Jauss, op. cit., p.217.

is, they may experience both comic and tragic emotions. The fact that the audience, because of their superior awareness, know that there is no real cause for Alcumena's and Amphitruo's despair, does not prevent them from feeling sympathy for their affliction. The happy ending is achieved only by Jupiter's sudden appearance as *deus ex machina*, a device borrowed from tragedy (and lacking in Terence[112]). When Amphitruo learns that it was the Supreme God who, in his absence, visited his wife and enjoyed her love, he shudders at the thought of this ineffable experience and, as a consequence, becomes aware of his own smallness (1117ff.). It seems, then, very fitting that Plautus should have called this play a tragicomedy. Whenever the history of Renaissance tragicomedy is discussed, the shaping influence of the Plautine *Amphitruo* has to be taken into consideration. It should be added here that the Plautine *Rudens* and *Captivi*, too, are tragicomedies in that they likewise invoke both tragic *and* comic emotions.

Turning again to *Errors*, we are, of course, aware that this play begins in an entirely different way, as it has no Prologue. Yet, although Shakespeare has dispensed with this dramatic device, he not only mixes high and low characters in a social pyramid governed by a Duke, he also, like Plautus, tries to evoke opposing reactions in the audience. The title 'The Comedy of Errors' and the unhappy beginning of the play, as well as some comic pointers in the first scene,[113] suggest to the spectator that he is about to witness a play with a happy ending, and yet the action on several occasions verges on the tragic in a way reminiscent of *Amphitruo*. Because of their superior awareness, the audience can anticipate that all will be well in the end, yet in a good performance, in which the threatening elements are not suppressed, they also sympathize with the extreme bewilderment, the existential fear, of the major characters. In order to bring about the final resolution, here too a *deus ex machina*, 'borrowed' from tragedy, is required.

If it is a special characteristic of this early Shakespearean play that the comic action is fused with the possibility of tragedy, then *Errors* can be seen as an anticipation of Shakespeare's later interest in tragicomedy. He took the 'comoedia motoria' of *Menaechmi* as a basis and added to it some important suggestions from *Amphitruo*, where Plautus dealt with the problem of losing and finding one's identity in a much more profound way; the effect of his *tragicomoedia* is much more than playful and tentative.[114] Shakespeare thus adopted an aspect of tragicomedy that some years later (in 1599) was formulated as part of a theory of tragicomedy by Guarini, who, interestingly

---

[112] This was first observed by Baldwin, *Shakspere's Five-Act Structure*, p.61.

[113] Cf. on this point K. Tetzeli v. Rosador, 'Plotting the Early Comedies: "The Comedy of Errors", "Love's Labour's Lost", "The Two Gentlemen of Verona" ', *ShS*, 37 (1984), 14 – 15.

[114] Cf. also W. Habicht, 'Tragicomedy, Mediaeval Drama, and Shakespeare' in: *L'Europe de la Renaissance. Mélanges offerts à Marie-Thérèse Jones-Davies* (Paris, 1989), p.447-461.

enough, also referred to the Plautine *Amphitruo*.[115] The point I am aiming at is that Guarini gives a detailed description of a view only touched upon by earlier humanists, and put into practice in Shakespeare's *Errors*, namely that tragicomedy, too, offers a special purgation of the affections. It purges 'the sadness of the hearers' 'with pleasure'.[116] It achieves this because 'the end of tragicomedy [. . .] is to imitate with the resources of the stage an action that is feigned and in which are mingled all the tragic and comic parts that can coexist in verisimilitude and decorum, properly arranged in a simple dramatic form'.[117] And Guarini goes on to state that the *Amphitruo* of Plautus has more of the comic, the *Cyclops* of Euripides more of the tragic.[118] *Errors*, one would like to add, achieves a remarkable balance between the two dramatic modes.

From a thematic point of view, *Errors* is, then, much more indebted to *Amphitruo* than to *Menaechmi*. It is one of the strange facts of Shakespeare scholarship that these intertextual links have not been sufficiently recognized. Yet, because of these links we cannot confine ourselves to a comparison with the *Menaechmi*, but we shall also have to consider in detail structural and dramaturgic aspects of the Plautine masterpiece *Amphitruo*.

---

[115] In Gilbert, op. cit., p.523.
[116] Gilbert, op. cit., p.524.
[117] Ibid.
[118] Ibid; Cinthio, too, had taken *Amphitruo* as an example when explaining the use of rhyme in comedy (Gilbert, op. cit., p.255 and 260).

II

Characterization in Plautus and in The Comedy of Errors

As New Comedy developed from Greek tragedy, plot is a most important structural element, although the genre of comedy in general tends more towards a dramatization of the characters' social behaviour and manners, their ηϑος, as opposed to their παϑος in tragedy. That Menander shows an equal interest in both character and plot has been well described, for example, by Sandbach; he points out that plot in New Comedy is important not so much because of the events, but primarily because of 'the means by which those events of the plot are brought about; they include the psychology of the persons in the play, since the way in which they choose to act determines its course. Hence the imaginative creation of characters is part of the playwright's business.'[1] In this chapter we are interested in the ways in which Shakespeare in his *Errors* extended and transformed techniques of characterization common in the New Comedy tradition. Although in his later plays he developed far more subtle means of depicting a dramatic character, it is nevertheless interesting to observe his early experiments with a well-established tradition.

The usual assumption that New Comedy used only stock figures is not entirely true because Menander, like other authors after him, knows how to surprise us by rounding off some of the characters with remarkably individual traits. He takes delight in making a 'character react and clash startlingly against the type', by his technique of 'effective highlighting [. . .] of vivid, realistic and significant detail'.[2] Each detail, even if it is not given direct verbal expression, is significant and most telling. Arnott reminds us of the fact that Menander 'defines' character as 'the sum of a person's idiosyncrasies' with regard to 'behaviour' and 'speech'.[3]

To some extent this individualizing of types can also be found in Plautus, especially in his adaptations of Menandrian plays. Yet in many cases the

---

[1] F.H. Sandbach, *The Comic Theatre of Greece and Rome* (London, 1977), p.77.
[2] Cf., for example, W.G. Arnott in the preface to his edition of *Menander*, The Loeb Classical Library (Cambridge, Mass./London, 1979), I,xxxi – xxxii.
[3] Arnott, ibid., p.xxxii.

Plautine characters are primarily functions of the plot.[4] Among the techniques which Plautus took over from New Comedy, direct characterization takes pride of place.[5] A character either defines himself or else is reflected, as it were, in a description by another character. There are a number of situations of direct characterization in *Menaechmi* and in *Amphitruo*. For example, in his first soliloquy, Peniculus, the Parasite, presents a detailed description, both of the type and of his own habits:

> quem tu adservare recte, ne aufugiat, voles,
> esca atque potione vinciri decet.
> apud mensam plenam homini rostrum deliges;
> dum tu illi quod edit et quod potet praebeas,
> suo arbitratu adfatim cottidie,
> numquam edepol fugiet, tam etsi capital fecerit;
> facile adservabis, dum eo vinclo vincies.
> ita istaec nimis lenta vincla sunt escaria:
> quam magis extendas, tanto adstringunt artius.
> nam ego ad Menaechmum hunc eo . . .   II, 87 – 96

> The man you really want to keep from running off ought to be bound with [. . .] food and drink. A loaded table [. . .] tie his snout to that. Just you deal him out meat and drink to suit his pleasure and his appetite each day, and he'll never run – Lord, no! – no matter if he's done a deed for hanging. You'll keep him easily so long as you bind him with these bonds. They're such extraordinarily tenacious bonds, these belly-bands: the more you stretch 'em, the closer they cling. Here's my case – I'm going to Menaechmus here . . .

Shakespeare significantly refines this technique in *Errors*: nowhere in this play do we find a direct self-explanation in this extended manner. Antipholus S, it is true, on his first appearance in I, ii, characterizes himself in a self-referential way, reminiscent of the New Comedy tradition; yet he does it with the greatest dramatic economy and, as we shall see in a later context, he organizes his self-characterization around a central image which is admirably suited to concretize his feelings at that moment:

> He that commends me to mine own content
> Commends me to the thing I cannot get.
> I to the world am like a drop of water
> That in the ocean seeks another drop . . .   I, ii, 33ff

In *Errors* we also find interesting examples of one character characterizing

---

[4] Cf., for example, J. Blänsdorf, 'Plautus' in: *Das römische Drama*, ed. E. Lefèvre (Darmstadt, 1978), p.177.

[5] On direct characterization in Plautus cf. O.L. Wilner, 'The Technical Device of Direct Description of Character in Roman Comedy', *CP*, 33 (1938), 20 – 36; cf. also W.H. Juniper, 'Character Portrayal in Plautus', *CJ*, 31 (1936), 276 – 88.

another – we need only think of the description of Nell, of Antipholus E taken prisoner, of the punishing of Dr Pinch.

A further device of New Comedy, by which character portrayal, *ethopoeia* in the broad sense,[6] is achieved, is the contrasting and paralleling of characters. Modern scholarship has recognized that Plautus, following Menander, knows how to contrast his characters effectively.[7] This technique has been observed in fourteen of twenty plays by Plautus. The '*Bacchides* abounds in contrasts',[8] especially as far as the two fathers are concerned; in *Casina* we find several contrasted pairs, and in *Epidicus, Mercator, Trinummus* and *Stichus*, fathers, old or young men, or wives and husbands are set in dramatic contrast. The contrast may be expressed either directly by way of description or indirectly by contrasting reactions.[9] There are particularly dramatic parallels and contrasts in *Amphitruo*, 'where first Sosia is the victim of a situation that deprives him of his identity (*Amphitruo*, 248 – 462, I; 551 – 632), then his master is treated likewise (ibid. 676 – 854)',[10] and the 'strong and unyielding'[11] Amphitruo is juxtaposed to the coward Sosia.

The technique of contrasting characters is skilfully adopted and developed in Shakespeare's 'classical' play, particularly in the dramatization of the two sisters, Adriana and Luciana. It will therefore no longer do to explain Shakespeare's addition of Luciana by merely referring to the symmetry of Lyly's plays or to Italian adaptations of Roman comedy. It seems rather that Shakespeare is also following one of the structural principles of New Comedy itself. As we shall see, at the same time he is already beginning to experiment with combining contrasting as well as parallel effects arising from one and the same pair of characters.[12]

One of the most important aspects of dramatic characterization is the specific kind of linguistic register which a particular *dramatis persona* employs. Menander's characters already speak an appropriate language, in accordance with the requirements of πρεπον or *decorum;*[13] they have their distinctive

---

[6] On *ethopoeia* cf., e.g. M. Doran, *Endeavors of Art*, p.240.

[7] On this aspect cf. O.L. Wilner, 'Contrast and Repetition as Devices in the Technique of Character Portrayal in Roman Comedy', *CP*, 25 (1930), 56 – 71; cf. also Arnott in the introduction to his edition of Menander.

[8] Wilner, 'Contrast and Repetition', p.57; cf. also Duckworth, op. cit., p.269.

[9] Cf. J. Blänsdorf, op. cit., p.181.

[10] Wilner, 'Contrast and Repetition', p.63.

[11] Wilner, ibid.

[12] On this dramaturgic technique in Shakespeare cf. especially R. Fricker, *Kontrast und Polarität in den Dramen Shakespeares* (Bern, 1951).

[13] Cf. Arnott, op. cit., p.xxxv. Arnott has also examined Menandrian patterns of linguistic characterization in Plautus and Terence: 'Targets, Techniques, and Tradition in Plautus' Stichus', *Bull. Inst. of Class. Studies*, 19 (1972), 54ff; and 'Phormio Parasitus: A Study in Dramatic Methods of Characterization', *Greece and Rome*, 17 (1970), 32ff.

4 From *Liber Chronicarum* by the humanist
Hartmann Schedel

modes or habits of speech,[14] a fact which was discussed by Quintilian.[15] Donatus was probably the first to discover that in Terentian comedies, the language of which on the whole produces a fairly unified impression, characters are sometimes differentiated by their linguistic peculiarities;[16] low comedy characters in particular may speak in a grammatically incorrect way, use rustic images, metaphors or even vulgarisms.[17]

Plautus, whose linguistic variety is far greater than that of Terence, has a number of ways of individualizing characters through the manner in which they speak, though we do not find any thoroughgoing consistency. A good deal of research remains to be done here, but some interesting results have already been achieved. It has been shown, for instance, how in *Aulularia*

[14] The *Tractatus Coislinianus* mentions the fact that the characters in comedy speak in their own proper idiom (Janko, *Aristotle on Comedy*, p.39).
[15] The *Institutio Oratoria of Quintilian*, ed. and transl. by H.E. Butler (Cambridge, Mass./London, 1968), IV, 41, 173ff.
[16] Donatus, op. cit., I, 125, 331, 348.
[17] Cf., for example, W. Stockert, 'Zur sprachlichen Charakterisierung der Personen in Plautus' "Aulularia" ', *Gymnasium*, 89 (1982), 4 – 14. The aspect of characterization through language is also pointed out in Renaissance editions, e.g. by G. Fabricius in the Terence edition (Strasbourg, 1548), f.V.

Euclio's language has a marked terseness and is enriched by metaphors taken from his rustic environment; Staphyla, who functions as a foil to Euclio, is notable for her loquaciousness; and Megadorus uses a noble language contrasting with Euclio's rusticity.[18] The *Miles Gloriosus*, too, provides good examples of the art of characterizing through language. No other character is, however, so clearly distinguished by the individuality of his language as the slave.[19]

Although the slaves in Plautus cannot be said to be fully individual characters, they often develop into more than just types by the sheer brilliance of their dramatic language. They sometimes even become intellectually superior to their masters by the subtle wit and ingenuity with which they plot intrigues for them. In *Menaechmi*, the slave Messenio, though he does not devise an intrigue, outdoes his master through his verbal wit, which he displays in a soliloquy concerned with the burden of being a slave (II, 966ff.). Being cunning, however, he knows how to make the best of his social position. Yet in two significant situations Messenio is outwitted by his master: whereas Messenio at first believes that the other Menaechmus is dead and will therefore never be found, the quest of Menaechmus S proves in the end that Messenio was wrong. Secondly, he is mistaken when he tries to prevent his master from entering the house of Erotium because, contrary to Messenio's expectations that Menaechmus would be duped by Erotium, he in fact succeeds in enjoying her gratuitous love. It is only in the very last scene that Messenio comes fully into his own as the *servus callidus*. He is the first to realize that the two Menaechmi, who are facing each other, must be twins, and, having full command of the situation, he directs them towards the realization of the truth.

The slave Sosia in *Amphitruo* comes much closer to the Shakespearean Dromios, and yet Shakespeare critics have not examined his role in detail. Although he is, at heart, the cunning slave capable of advising his master (702 – 705), he becomes an unforgettable dramatic character by his individual and spontaneous reactions. It has been rightly said that he, like the other major characters in *Amphitruo*, documents the maturity of Plautus's art.

He introduces himself as a character who does not lack self-confidence: 'Who's a bolder man, a more audacious man than I am [. . .]' ('Qui me alter est audacior homo aut qui confidentior' 153). This first dramatic situation is rich in comic potential because Sosia presents himself as an expert in deceitful cunning: he is rehearsing the report of a battle he did not attend, and his report reflects his rhetorical versatility. When the disguised Mercury appears and overhears him, a basic and very comic irony arises because Sosia's deceitful cunning is seen to resemble Mercury's major 'quality': he has come to use his own cunning in order to assist Jupiter in his new erotic adventure.

---

[18] Stockert, op. cit., p.14.
[19] Cf. Duckworth, op. cit., p.270.

Sosia's self-confidence is then put to the test by Mercury, who, by his own individual method, which includes beating, persuades him into believing that there are two Sosias instead of one. Sosia, who is at first frightened, finally adapts himself to the new situation and begins to act on these new premises. He thinks that he has had a miraculous experience and advises his master Amphitruo accordingly, and this gives him superiority over his master. The way in which Amphitruo reacts to Sosia's report of what has happened to him reminds us of the anger of the Antipholi. He feels mocked and flouted (565, 571 cf. *Errors* I, ii, 91); he suspects the slave of being drunk (574, cf. *Errors* IV, i, 97); he calls him downright mad (604, cf. *Errors* IV, i, 94; iii, 40); he threatens to beat him, but he never carries out his threat. Sosia is usually in better command of the situation than Amphitruo and he continues to advise him; on one occasion he increases the comedy of the situation by an ingenious pun (812 – 814) which we shall have to discuss in a later context. Although he comes near the truth about the confusion of identities when he suspects that there may be another Amphitruo (785), even he is, of course, deceived about the reality behind it. He is unable fully to understand Alcumena's consternation, and therefore he suggests to Amphitruo that her madness should be exorcised.

The self-confidence and intellectual brilliance of Shakespeare's Dromios is far greater than that of even Sosia. This enables them to maintain their witty play even under a real and dangerous threat and during a heavy flogging. Like Sosia (and Messenio), they too are liable to confusion about the characters' real identity; and like Sosia, Dromio S, on one occasion, comes near the truth when he refuses to attribute the confusions to the influence of witches and considers the Ephesians as basically 'gentle' (IV, iv, 151). The dialogue between Antipholus S and his Dromio in II, ii is especially significant. At first, Antipholus treats Dromio as the subordinate slave who has to obey his master, yet Dromio, knowing that he has given his master no cause for dissatisfaction, refuses to be treated in this way. When, however, Dromio adds that in his being beaten there is 'neither rhyme nor reason' (II, ii, 48), he reveals that he, too, is in full command of the situation, because his explanation for the blows he has received, is the confusion of identities. But then we have an abrupt change of gear, and Dromio, with his witty reasoning, takes the lead in the dialogue. The clever scheming is replaced by the servant's superiority in clownesque mock-reasoning. He has more to say than his master on the highly philosophical subject of the nature of time, which is taken up again in IV, ii. It has been observed how skilfully the Dromios know how to adapt themselves to the individual register of their respective partner and how Dromio S in particular has a thorough knowledge of rhetorical tropes and schemes.[20]

A further aspect of the individuality of the Dromios which points forward to Shakespeare's later clowns and fools is the fact that they have a particularly

[20] Cf. Foakes, op. cit., esp. p.69, n.31 – 47.

keen eye for the concrete, realistic detail.[21] In this respect scenes IV, ii and IV, iii are very important: master and servant are taken by surprise by the appearance of the courtesan demanding a chain from Antipholus. To Dromio's question: 'Master, is this Mistress Satan?', Antipholus answers quite distinctly: 'It is the devil.' (IV, iii, 47 – 48), but a few moments later Dromio rightly identifies her as a 'light wench' (50). While Antipholus is seriously affected by the apparition of the 'sorceress' (64), Dromio immediately recovers his composure so that he is able to make a witty comment about her invitation to dinner. The situation ends with the slave's typical warning of imminent danger: 'Master, be wise . . . ' (72). Dromio appears in a similar role at the end of Act IV: by his superior intelligence and insight he is the first to recognize that they are not confronted with a dangerous menace. By suggesting that they should stay in Ephesus, Dromio is really preparing for the comic catastrophe.

Although twins, the Dromios are not just two identical characters. The Ephesian Dromio, who has a greater preference for doggerel verse, on the whole has less opportunity than his brother to display his intelligence and flexibility. Indeed, he is never portrayed as intellectually superior to his master. This becomes especially obvious in III, i: he himself has no idea of how to overcome the difficulty of the locked door to his own house. The proposal to use an iron crow bar is his master's, while Dromio merely carries out this suggestion. The same observation can be made in IV, i, where Dromio is ordered to buy a rope. He has no opportunity to give his master any kind of advice as to how he might avenge himself on his wife. He knows that the situation makes him look a complete fool. It becomes apparent, especially when both Dromios are simultaneously present on stage, that Dromio S has greater dramatic energy and wit. In the dinner scene in III, i, Dromio S dominates the dialogue. When in the last Act Antipholus S and his Dromio appear from the Priory, thereby completing the two pairs of twins, the same thing can be seen: immediately after he has recognized his double on stage, Dromio S claims to be the real Dromio: 'I, sir, am Dromio, command him away.' (335). However, in the very last situation of the comedy, Shakespeare skilfully redresses this slight 'imbalance' by having Dromio S once more mistake his master's identity. Thus, at the very end of the play, the audience are given the feeling that the two Dromios are equally important in the play as a whole. The Dromios' witty use of language will be considered in another context.

A word must now be said about the assumption that the Dromios owe a considerable part of their vitality to the *commedia dell'arte*. This attempt to establish a close link between the Dromios and the zanies (abundantly reflected in the recent BBC production directed by J. Cellan Jones) is

---

[21] Cf. on this point M. Pfister, *Studien zum Wandel der Perspektivenstruktur in elisabethanischen und jakobäischen Komödien* (München, 1974), p.67.

unconvincing for several reasons. First, it is based on K.M. Lea's comprehensive study on the *commedia dell'arte* and its possible influence on the English stage. However, the evidence which she is able to put forward is disappointingly sparse, and the connections with *Errors* are particularly slight. As far as Shakespeare is concerned, there are, of course, some references to the *commedia dell'arte* in *The Taming of the Shrew* and *Love's Labour's Lost*; yet there is no cogent reason to claim that the zany was in any way a model for the Shakespearean Dromios, as Lea would have it. Lea herself is conscious of the difficulty of assessing this particular influence: 'the issue is confused by the partial coincidence of the roles of the clown and the servant'. In *Errors*, correspondences between the Dromios and the zany, even the knocking scenes, can be traced back to the slave in Plautine comedy, the common 'basis' of both *Errors* and the *commedia dell'arte*, as Lea herself admits.[22] On no occasion could we say that the Dromios perform the special *lazzi* of the zany because these are part of the *extempore* character of the *commedia dell'arte*; they function as a digression and halt the action so that the actor has a few moments to think about what he is going to say next. A good example of these *lazzi* is, for instance, a scene where a zany is bothered by a fly: he will indulge in a great deal of gestural or even acrobatic activity, none of it remotely *connected* with the action of the play, and all happening on the spur of the dramatic moment.

A further reason why we should hesitate to associate the Dromios with the zanies is the fact that these serve an *old* master, whereas the Dromios are not supposed to be any younger than the Antipholi.[23] Unlike the zany, the Dromios in *Errors* serve their master for the sake of serving and not in order to promote their own ends. Even the fact that a zany is often involved in a relationship with a maid is not enough to establish a connection with Dromio S' brilliant narration of how he was pursued by the kitchen-maid Nell. It is wrong, therefore, to isolate single elements and account for them by referring to a different tradition and then to conclude that 'in behaviour and misfortunes they [the Dromios] are the servants of the Commedia dell'arte'.[24] The resemblances which exist have come about, as it were, incidentally, by Shakespeare's transformation of the classical plot. When Shakespeare worked with the *Menaechmi* and *Amphitruo*, he had no need to integrate further *commedia dell'arte* details, as he saw no reason to give this play a touch of popular Italian comedy.

---

[22] K.M. Lea, *Italian Popular Comedy: A Study in the Commedia dell'arte, 1560 – 1620, with Special Reference to the English Stage* (Oxford, 1934) II, 398 – 399; for a more recent claim of the dependence of the Dromios on the zany cf. Foakes, op. cit., p.xxxiii.

[23] Cf. D. Esrig, *Commedia dell'arte* (Nördlingen, 1985); cf. also A. Nicoll, *The World of Harlequin* (Cambridge, 1963), V. Pandolfi, *La Commedia dell'arte, Storia e testo* (Firenze, 1957ff.), 6 vols, and G. Oreglia, *The Commedia dell'Arte* (London, 1968).

[24] Lea, op. cit., II, 438.

A particularly interesting example in *Menaechmi* of the Plautine technique of linguistic characterization is the Senex, the typical Old Man of classical comedy, although his role here is brief and he, like the Matrona and Erotium, is excluded from the final *anagnorisis*. He is, as both he himself and Menaechmus acknowledge, a caricature of physical decrepitude, and this is reflected in the way he speaks. His soliloquy is an instance of his senile macrology. The opening verses deserve our special attention:

> Vt aetas mea est atque ut hoc usus facto est
> gradum proferam, progrediri properabo.   II, 753 – 754

> Yes, I'll step out, I'll step along as fast as my age permits and
> the occasion demands.

The verses suggest a rather slow speaking speed, the alliteration as well as the repetition of the same verbal prefix ('pro-pro-pro') seem almost to echo the sound of his stick beating on the ground.[25]

Plautus is even capable of using stylistic nuances to indicate differences of mood, as in the short verbal exchange between father and daughter at the moment of meeting. To her 'salve multum, mi pater' (775) the father replies laconically and rather sharply: 'salva sis', that is, he reduces the formula of greeting to its absolute minimum. This no doubt suggests that he already bears a grudge against her. When somewhat later he commands her: 'paucis, non longos logos' (779), there is an ironic contrast to the long-windedness in which he himself has just indulged. However, the comic decay of the Senex is merely physical; he is still a genuine representative of patriarchal Roman society. The original audience would surely have considered his behaviour towards his daughter and son-in-law as perfectly sound. In their view, he would be arguing very reasonably in claiming that his daughter must recognize her husband's superiority and turn a blind eye to his sexual licence.

Shakespeare's Egeon is, of course, a character entirely different from the Plautine Senex; when he describes his physical weakness ('Though now this grained face of mine be hid / In sap-consuming winter's drizzled snow, / And all the conduits of my blood froze up' V, i, 311 – 313), he reveals how different he is from the Senex. Whereas the Senex produces a merely comic effect, Egeon distinguishes himself by his emotional depth, and the audience respond to his feelings. He is in no way a comic figure, but rather a man who has learnt patience by long suffering. In the first scene, Egeon expresses his readiness to die in order to end his 'tragic' (!) life (I, i, 64). The verse he speaks has a poetic quality designed to evoke the affective response of 'pity', which is indeed expressly referred to by the Duke (I, i, 97). In his narration of the blows of Fortune he has suffered, the image of the sea becomes the familiar symbol of the vicissitudes of human life. And so, in feeling pity for Egeon, the

---

[25] The fact that he at the same time tries to emulate the *servus currens* adds to the comic effect which he produces.

audience are also reminded of the dangers involved in human life, to which no one is immune. When in the last Act Egeon is confronted with his long-lost son, his emotional depth, the very quality of which distinguishes him from the Plautine Senex, is as strong as ever, and thus, unlike the other characters in the play, he 'cannot err' (317), but rightly recognizes his son.

The Senex is in some scenes accompanied by another hilariously comic figure, the Doctor, who is totally incompetent and whose nonsensical diagnosis is meant as a caricature of contemporary physicians. Shakespeare, by his creative power, transformed him into Dr Pinch, the schoolmaster and exorcist. To some extent, he too is a caricature; both are utterly deceived into thinking that their patient suffers from madness. Yet in a manner characteristic of *Errors*, Pinch combines within himself both comic and threatening aspects, because the power he exerts is dangerous. Anyone who has seen a good performance of *Errors* or has directed the play will know how important the character of Dr Pinch is, although Shakespeare has given him only 12 lines. Much depends, of course, on his mask and costume, and particularly on his gestures and movement, that is, on non-verbal by-play. Directors often make the mistake of interpreting him as outrageously funny. Funny he is, but if this aspect is overemphasized, the whole climax of Act IV, which is the threat to Antipholus's identity, will be lost. Pinch's exorcism is not merely hilarious, but reminds us of the terrible reality of the *Malleus Maleficarum*,[26] the notorious continental handbook for witch hunters by two Dominicans, Sprenger and Institoris. If this aspect is lost in a performance, the audience will miss the important point that Antipholus E seems to be heading towards a tragic fate. We might even add that in this respect *Errors* has a special relevance to our own days: it produces an absurd, almost kafkaesque situation to which a modern audience are particularly sensitive: it is not inconceivable that someone might be taken for another and, perhaps, be subjected to treatment in a clinic according to a wrong diagnosis, and, when he tries to rectify the error, simply may not be believed.[27]

It is interesting to note that Shakespeare introduces a Duke into his comedy and thus completes the social pyramid. He thus *extends* and transforms the character pattern of New Comedy. This is important to realize, because it implies that, if in his later plays we are confronted with a wide social range of the acting characters including both Dukes and servants, then this by no means disproves the structural influence of New Comedy, as Mincoff has argued.[28] More remarkable is the fact that, despite his superior position, the Duke fails sadly; he is unable to discover the truth because he is utterly at a

---

[26] *Malleus Maleficarum*: J. Sprenger and H. Institoris, *Der Hexenhammer* (München, 1982).

[27] This point has also been made by S. Wells in the introduction to his edition, p.31.

[28] M. Mincoff, 'Shakespeare's Comedies and the Five-Act Structure', *Bulletin de la Faculté des Lettres de Strasbourg*, 63 (1965), 131 – 146.

loss in the face of the 'intricate impeach' (270) of the last Act, and his helplessness has a particularly comic effect on the audience. Interestingly enough, the authority which the audience would have expected him to command is, as it were, transferred to a woman, Aemilia, something inconceivable in Plautus. She proves to be the only character who is able to resolve the complex situation.

The women characters in Plautine comedy differ in social rank. They are either freeborn or freedwomen or slaves, those in the first category forming the great majority. In line with contemporary Roman social reality, women in these comedies do not enjoy the same rights as men; in household matters they are dependent on the decision of the *pater familias*.[29] Plautus does seem to take a critical stance towards certain aspects of the established family structure. In some plays, for instance, he advocates marriage based on the love and faithfulness of the wife towards her husband, and he strongly emphasizes the virtue of *pudicia* (marital fidelity) on the part of the wives. The prostitutes, such as Erotium in *Menaechmi*, who are dramatically very effective, reflect the double moral standard of Roman society. However, as *Menaechmi* is a turbulent comedy, social criticism of this kind is not brought into focus. The Matrona is somewhat privileged because she is an *uxor dotata*, that is, she has been given a dowry of which her father, not her husband, is in charge. She can therefore afford to behave self-assertively towards her husband and this is reflected in her way of speaking. She threatens to divorce him and return to her father because she has discovered not only that her husband has a paramour, but that this paramour even receives gifts from her possessions. Plautus derives comic effects from her shrewish behaviour towards her husband. Her shrewishness, so typical of an *uxor dotata*, does not increase matrimonial concord, of course, and the consequence is that Menaechmus seeks satisfaction with Erotium. The nameless Matrona is, however, merely a functional character, and when she is no longer needed, she is disposed of and excluded from the final *anagnorisis*. On her first appearance she is overshadowed by the Parasite, who takes the lead in the revenge plot against her husband. When the Parasite realizes that she has forgotten her 'part', he soon takes over (619). However, towards the end of the brilliant second scene of Act IV, she comes into her own, as it were, and acts with great resolution. The only other occasion where she appears is at the beginning of Act V. The comedy concludes with Messenio's playful announcement that not only Menaechmus's household but also his wife are to be sold at auction; in real life he would not have been entitled to sell his wife, and therefore this must not be taken seriously.

When Shakespeare studied the *Menaechmi*, he will not, of course, have recognized all the social implications of the Matrona. To him she may have appeared as the typical shrew who revolts against her social position. Thus,

[29] Cf. E. Schuhmann, 'Zur sozialen Stellung der Frau in den Komödien des Plautus', *Altertum*, 24 (1978), 97 – 105.

her shrewishness seems to have been the starting point from which Adriana's character grew. Yet to consider Adriana as simply shrewish, as those critics do who see the play as merely farcical, is to neglect Shakespeare's significant departure here from *Menaechmi*: his concern was to present the psychological factors that lead Adriana to behave like a shrew. The first thing that strikes us from a comparison of the two wives is the fact that Adriana appears to be far more 'emancipated' than her Plautine model. She is not the anonymous Matrona but an individual character of considerable depth. In no respect is she inferior to any of the play's characters; on the contrary, she leaves a strong impact on the spectator or reader. She rebels against the traditional assignment of roles to the sexes and complains that she has fewer rights and less chance of self-realization than her husband; with regard to the rights of men she asks: 'Why should their liberty than ours be more?' (II, i, 10). She contends that both men and women should have equal liberties, and that a partnership in marriage should lead to perfect union. This tone in one of Shakespeare's first women characters is remarkable, and its significance should not be underestimated. However, Adriana adjusts her conduct to that of the male members of society, she knows how to act like a man. We observe how she treats a person who is socially inferior to her: she uses exactly the same authoritarian manner as her husband when she scolds Dromio and threatens him with a severe beating.

Especially in scene II, ii with Antipholus S, she proves to possess not only considerable intellectual power but also emotional intensity and passion. However, the problem in her marriage has to do with the fact that her unwarranted jealousy is a threat to the 'liberty' which she herself has described as essential. Because of her jealousy she is also incapable of recognizing her husband's real nature. She wrongly feels that she has been betrayed by him, whereas the Plautine Matrona discovers that her husband has really committed adultery. There is a moment when Adriana succumbs to self-pity, but this soon gives way to more healthy feelings. In the 'Pinch scene', her suspicion that her husband has gone mad is for the first time confirmed, as it seems. Although she considers him guilty of having made love to her sister and of having a paramour besides, she feels compassion for him because of his supposed madness and calls him a 'poor distressed soul' (IV, iv, 57). This new capacity for compassion helps her to overcome her former self-pity and reinforces the active side of her character. It is through her care for her 'poor distracted husband' (V, i, 39) that she comes into conflict with the authority of the Abbess. The Abbess helps her to renounce her excessive claims upon him: 'I will attend my husband, be his nurse, / Diet his sickness, for it is my office' (V, i, 98 – 99). Nonetheless, we cannot be quite certain whether the Abbess has finally succeeded in correcting Adriana's views. What gives us some reason for doubt is the fact that Adriana has a strong feeling that she has been wronged by Aemilia. After she has been dismissed by the Abbess, her only desire is to obtain justice from the Duke. Yet she has to realize that if she claims justice, then her husband, too, will do the same. When at the moment of recognition she says that she sees two husbands, this is true in a higher, symbolic sense. She has constantly been deceived by her eyes: she has always lived with two husbands, with an imaginary one, as he appeared in her mind, as well as with the true one, whom she did not fully recognize.

In a sense, it could be said that Adriana has closer connections with the Alcumena of the *Amphitruo* play than with the Matrona of *Menaechmi*. It is not easy to understand why this comparison has hardly ever been made,[30] although both women believe that they have been wronged by their husbands and that this has provoked the crisis in their marriages. Unlike the Matrona, Alcumena is not a farcical character but a woman with emotional depth, and therefore we may say that she comes closest to the characters in Shakespeare's *Errors*.[31] At first she tries to understand the fact that her husband left her so soon, yet she comforts herself with the thought that human 'voluptas' is short-lived and that it must often be sacrificed to deeds of 'virtue' (633ff.). The way in which Alcumena describes sexual purity in marriage (*pudicia*) comes very close to Adriana's ideas on marital fidelity. However, when the 'real' Amphitruo returns and believes she has gone mad and that she has committed adultery, she determines to leave him unless he revokes it (882ff.). It is through the intensity of her language that Alcumena characterizes herself and the depth of her feelings.

Adriana, too, becomes an individual character above all through the individual kind of language she employs. She appears on stage as a woman of considerable intellectual power and capable of meaningful 'discourses' (II, i, 91) and of creating some brilliant metaphors. In her dialogue with the Abbess, she indirectly characterizes herself by way of *ethopoeia* when she narrates the way in which she reprehended her husband in the following manner:

> It was the copy of our conference;
> In bed he slept not for my urging it,
> At board he fed not for my urging it;
> Alone, it was the subject of my theme;
> In company I often glanced at it;
> Still did I tell him it was vile and bad.   V, i, 62 – 67

Adriana does not need to speak at length about her marriage problems, because this short comment, by its very rhetorical organization, is far more revealing than a long speech could be. Her speeches in particular bear witness to the fact that in his *Errors* Shakespeare has already achieved great rhetorical skill, something which will need to be discussed later (cf. chapter V).

---

[30] Cf. chapter I, p.41.
[31] Cf. P. Simpson's chapter 'Shakespeare's Use of Latin Authors', *Studies in Elizabethan Drama* (Oxford, 1955).

Although Luciana's part is much shorter than that of Adriana, she provides an important foil to her sister, as is most evident on her first appearance, when she seems to speak in defence of the 'degree' structure of the Elizabethan cosmos. Here she articulates the same conservative humanist teaching as is expressed in Kate's final speech in *The Taming of the Shrew* and in Ulysses's 'degree' speech in *Troilus and Cressida*. Luciana suspects her sister of being dissatisfied with this view of the world and of revolting against it. Yet the way in which Luciana puts forward her arguments has an almost tongue-in-cheek quality that has not been recognized: when at the end of her teaching she announces that she will marry some time 'but to try' (II, i, 42), this may not strike us as unusual, yet the Elizabethans must surely have found Luciana's intention to marry in order to 'see what it is like' as rather frivolous and flippant. In fact, it appears that Luciana is herself not free from the spirit of revolt which she detects and condemns in her sister. When the occasion arises in III, ii, she does not hesitate to disregard the moral norms in order to satisfy her personal desires. It seems to me that one grave mistake in scholarly criticism of *Errors* is the constant misunderstanding of Luciana's character. When describing her advice to Antipholus in III,ii as moderate, reasonable or commonsensical, critics must either have failed or have refused to recognize that she is boldly opposed to the established moral standards of the time. Although she, of course, believes she is being wooed by her own brother-in-law, she does not try to deflect him from his supposedly adulterous, indeed *doubly* illicit, intentions — for not only is he, as she thinks, a married man, but also her brother-in-law; on the contrary, she even gives him a lesson on how he might secretly achieve his goal. There is no doubt that this makes her an excitingly ambiguous character, whose true significance for the entire play will have to be discussed later.

Apart from the two merchants, Antipholus's paramour is the only character without a proper name. In the stage directions of the Folio she is called 'curtizan'. In some Renaissance plays such as *Cambises*, written at Gray's Inn, and *La Calandria* by Cardinal Bibbiena or Aretino's *Il Filosofo*, we find the generic term 'meretrix' (or 'meretrice') of Roman Comedy; in other plays, for instance in the comedy *Chrysis* by Enea Silvio Piccolomini, courtesans are given individual names. In the *Menaechmi* the meretrix Erotium is a woman capable of enticing a man and promising him refined sensual pleasures, and this, precisely, is indicated by her name. The language she uses characterizes her as a woman providing 'voluptas', and her first appearance on stage is described by Menaechmus as an impressive dramatic moment: 'oh, solem vides / satin ut occaecatust prae huius corporis candoribus?' (180 – 181) ('Ah, you see the sun — is it not positively bedimmed in comparison with the brilliance of her body?'). When she feels cheated by him, she immediately shuts the door against him without, however, considering avenging herself on him. Whereas it is true that the Plautine courtesans sometimes display a certain quality of wit, this does not become prominent in Erotium.

It is therefore interesting that Shakespeare turns the prostitute into a woman who is both physically and intellectually attractive; on the one hand she is described as 'a light wench' (IV, iii, 50) who is 'pretty' and 'wild', but on the other hand she is also credited with 'excellent discourse' (III, i, 109 – 110), and this implies more than the quality of wit. And finally Antipholus praises her for being 'gentle' (III, i, 110), which seems to imply a cultivated quality. Thus Shakespeare, by turning his courtesan into a woman of physical *as well as* intellectual charms, involuntarily 'revived' the tradition of the cultivated *hetairai* of Menandrian comedy.[32]

The two twins in *Menaechmi* are in the main functional characters; the sole purpose of their entrances and exits is the development of the turbulent action. Nevertheless, they are impressive representatives of the *adolescens* in New Comedy, and in the first half of the play they exhibit an unalloyed *joie de vivre*. Both have a sense of game-playing; both know perfectly how to employ ruse in order to deceive others. Both are also interested in material gain. Menaechmus S is overjoyed at receiving the mantle (*palla*) and bracelet (*spinter*) from Erotium, and his brother, on hearing that Messenio wants to offer him a purse, hastens to tell him that he should lose no time in fetching it. These are facets which Shakespeare has eliminated from his portraits of the Antipholi. In *Menaechmi* Plautus prefers to shift the point of view alternately to each Menaechmus by giving both of them important soliloquies. This alternating of the perspective of the audience is actually a characteristic feature of *Menaechmi*. Yet critics have not adequately explained this technique: while Harry Levin maintains that 'we tend to visualize what goes on in the Latin play from the denizen's standpoint', Leach takes exactly the opposite view.[33] It is clear, however, that Acts I and IV are seen from the point of view of Menaechmus E and Acts II and III from that of his brother, while in the fifth Act the dramatic interest is first focused on Menaechmus S and then on his brother.

Does Plautus provide the two twins with any characteristic traits by which they are distinguished from each other? The denizen Menaechmus is caught up in the everyday world of business and duty from which he finds only a momentary release. Plautus suggests this confining force of duty by a series of military images.[34] In the second part of the play Menaechmus is involved in several situations in which he is compelled to react in a violent manner. Menaechmus E is much concerned with justifying his previous conduct and

---

[32] It is worth noting that the Italian cortigiana gave pleasure not only by fulfilling sexual desire, but also by her cultural refinement, and in particular by her witty conversation (cf. G. Masson, *Courtesans of the Italian Renaissance* [London, 1975], e.g. p.64).

[33] H. Levin, 'Two Comedies of Errors', *Stratford Papers on Shakespeare* (1963), p.52; E.W. Leach, '*Meam Quom Formam Noscito*: Language and Characterization in the *Menaechmi*', *Arethusa*, 2 (1969), 30 – 45, esp. p.33.

[34] Cf. E.W. Leach, op. cit., p.34.

with finding a way out of the scrape into which he has unwittingly manoeuvred himself. Scene V,v appears to form an exception. As he is now considered to be mad, he feels bound to avenge himself on the Senex by charging him with a series of libels.

Menaechmus S represents the holiday spirit of comedy, and yet he himself tells his slave that he is choleric and easily provoked to wrath ('ego autem *homo iracundus*, animi perditi' 269, italics mine). Indeed, a short while later, during his unexpected encounter with the Cook, we are given an example of how easily he can lose his temper. When in III, ii he is maligned by Peniculus, he threatens him with violence: 'Vae capiti tuo' 512 ('Curse you!'). There is verbal aggression in the way he addresses the Matrona in V,i, and this reaches its climax in his pretended madness in V, ii, where he uses the most intense verbal violence: '[. . .] ut ego huius membra atque ossa atque artua / comminuam illo scipione quem ipse habet.', 855 – 56 ('[. . .] that I crush his limbs and bones and joints with that same staff which he doth carry!'). The last time he becomes very angry is in V, viii, when he believes that he is being deceived by his own slave; he answers Messenio's request for manumission with vehemence: 'Quin certissimumst, / mepte potius fieri servom, quam te umquam emittam manu.', 1058 – 1059 ('Well, the most certain thing in the world is this – I had rather become a slave myself than ever free you.'). This reminds the audience of his earlier warning to the slave to beware of his irascible temper unless he wants to risk being beaten (II, 270f.). Shakespeare adopts this element of aggression for his Antipholus S and even intensifies it. However, whereas Antipholus S shows his quick temper when he beats his Dromio, Menaechmus S never actually beats Messenio. As a result of our comparison, we find that, contrary to the common view, Menaechmus S is in fact a more complex and dramatically effective character than Menaechmus E, and our reading is fully borne out in performance.

The manner in which Shakespeare transforms the two Menaechmi into his Antipholi is most interesting and has not been considered clearly enough by the critics. The sharp contrast which most commentators have found between the two brothers does not in fact hold true and certainly does not correspond to the experience one has during a stage performance, because it is Shakespeare's intention to make the twins *resemble* each other. The critics see in Antipholus S an introverted melancholy character and regard his brother as a choleric. This is a strange misunderstanding because, as we shall see, Antipholus E is less choleric and Antipholus S is more inclined to aggression than is generally believed. His own Dromio uses the word 'choleric' to define the nature of his master (II, ii, 61). Although Antipholus S differs from Menaechmus S because he does not exhibit the same holiday spirit as his Latin model, his self-characterization as 'melancholy' (I, ii, 20) is not entirely reliable. In the late sixteenth century, as is well known, many Englishmen suffered from bouts of the 'Elizabethan malady'. It is most important to recognize that Shakespeare did not intend his Antipholi to differ *radically* because, as this play is a comedy about a young man in search of his identity, Antipholus S achieves this goal by finding a brother, who is *both like and unlike* him, so that he can become aware of the nature of his own individual self. He defines his business, which has brought him to Ephesus, as a 'quest' (40), a word with distinct romance implications. Just as the hero of many medieval romances is in search of his identity, so is Antipholus S: his task is a 'spiritual' one, despite the fact that he takes a fuller part in the turbulent action than his brother and even occasionally joins in his Dromio's verbal jokes. Since he is the quester, consciously trying to find his identity, he 'appears, archetypally, to be the "younger" brother'.[35]

Just as on his first entrance his brother was in high spirits, so is Antipholus E in good humour when we first see him. He has invited guests to dinner, and he is enjoying entertaining them. He addresses his guests with these words:

> Ant. E.   . . . pray God our cheer
>   May answer my good will, and your good welcome here.
>   III, i, 19 – 20

This reflects a relaxed behaviour comparable to that of his brother in I, ii, 19ff. We see that the first impression we have of Antipholus E does not in fact corroborate the usual view that he is choleric, aggressive and irascible. His ensuing dialogue with Dromio is not to be taken as a scolding but rather as a kind of coarse jesting. When, a few minutes later, he realizes that he has been locked out from his own dinner, his language remains remarkably composed. Note how easily he is persuaded by Balthasar to give up his attempts to break into the house and how soon he is prepared to be 'merry' (III, i, 108). This is hardly in line with a choleric character. On the contrary, his deliberate intention to be merry is somewhat reminiscent of the merriment which Menaechmus E relishes at the beginning of the Plautine comedy. It is true that Antipholus E takes brutal revenge on Dr Pinch, yet, after what has happened, the force of his aggression is understandable and, more importantly, it has no great effect on the audience's image of him because it happens *offstage* and is merely reported. From now on, the similarities between the denizen Menaechmus and the denizen Antipholus become even more pertinent because both are constantly forced to *react* aggressively to the complications of the action; therefore this can hardly be taken as their normal behaviour. Antipholus E cannot be blamed for believing that he has been deceived all the time. Yet again it should be noted that even after his decision to purchase 'a rope' in order to castigate his wife and her confederates, he remains relatively calm. This may be inferred from the fact that his dialogue with Angelo and the Second Merchant can be interpreted by Angelo as a 'merry humour' (IV, i,

[35] Leach, op. cit., p.35.

27). Furthermore, it is remarkable that he shuns a direct confrontation with Angelo and prefers instead to be taken into custody until the money to bail him out has arrived: 'I do obey thee, till I give thee bail' (IV, i, 81).

Our picture of Antipholus E is further corroborated by the fact that he is again very calm and composed at the beginning of IV, iv: 'Fear me not, man, I will not break away' (1). Could we expect him to react more reasonably, given the extremity of his situation? It is true that his Dromio complains that he has to endure blows from his master (IV, iv, 30), yet in the play it is Antipholus S who is the first to beat his Dromio. He does this twice, whereas Antipholus E is driven to beating his servant only in IV,iv. Antipholus E's aggression is perfectly understandable because he is now finally beginning to lose his long-kept patience after realizing the fundamental threat to his identity. Adriana and her confederates, however, − and many critics too − mistake this behaviour for 'incivility' (IV, iv, 44) and choler.

When, a few moments later, Antipholus E is confronted by Dr Pinch, he cannot but feel even more threatened. Are not his acts of aggression the natural reaction of a man who finds himself in a situation which presents a danger to his very life? 'What, will you murder me?' (IV, iv, 107) he exclaims in despair. His address to his wife: 'Dissembling harlot, thou art false in all' (IV, iv, 99) reveals the depth of his consternation.

Antipholus E's behaviour in the last Act provides even less justification for the judgement critics have passed on him. In spite of the injustice he has experienced, his plea for justice before the Duke is remarkably free from any specifically aggressive tone. On the contrary, the way he presents his case is surprisingly composed, and he remains in full command of his language. Throughout the scene he retains his self-control, although he is, of course, very upset. This impression is even confirmed by the Duke himself when he says: 'If he were mad, he would not plead so coldly.' (V, i, 273). With these words the Duke confirms that Antipholus has kept the promise with which he began his long narration:

> My liege, I am advised what I say,
> Neither disturb'd with the effect of wine,
> Nor heady-rash, provok'd with raging ire,
> Albeit my wrongs might make one wiser mad.   V, i, 214 − 217

It thus appears that the two twins are more similar to each other than is usually assumed; the only real distinguishing mark by which Antipholus S is set off as an individual from his twin brother is his introverted imagination. Our close comparison of the characters in *Errors* and the Plautine plays has shown how thoroughly Shakespeare studied the dramaturgy of characterization in the New Comedy tradition and how varied the different suggestions are which he has taken up; yet far more important are the numerous transformations by which Shakespeare has achieved a fascinating dramatic intensification that already points forward to his later plays.

We shall now have to turn our special attention to a major New Comedy convention of dramatic characterization, namely the use of soliloquy.[36] The view is commonly held that the convention of the soliloquy was established in the classical tradition on the basis of the audience accepting a technical, non-realistic device of the dramatist.[37] However, this definition is not fully appropriate because this so-called classical convention was already used by dramatists like Menander, Plautus and Terence in a number of ways and to considerable artistic effects. Therefore Slater's definition of the term 'convention' seems more to the point: for him, a convention is simply a 'highly structured means of dramatic communication', and he rightly adds that the 'success of such conventions [. . .] is [. . .] to be measured by their [. . .] effectiveness as communication'.[38] Indeed, many soliloquies in the New Comedy tradition testify to this effectiveness. In the classical tradition we have both an anti-illusionist tendency *and* the attempt at a temporary establishing of 'illusion', though not of realism; on similar lines the convention of the soliloquy, too, can be made subservient to one intention or the other. It is a mistake, therefore, albeit a common one, to assume that the more artistic forms of the soliloquy which disclose the inner life of a character do not yet occur in New Comedy.

This point has recently been made by Karen Newman. She has reminded us that, beginning with Menander, the convention of the soliloquy was also used to reveal the characters' thoughts and feelings without destroying the dramatic illusion, sometimes even without the characters' directly addressing the audience. Unfortunately, the usefulness of her book is somewhat impaired by a too narrow concept of the structure of soliloquy in New Comedy and in Shakespeare. She argues that a self-revealing soliloquy is a self-representation, a dialogue of the speaker with his own self conducted according to a 'rhetoric of inner life'.[39] However, in interpreting all kinds of dialogic elements, even, for instance, an apostrophe to the gods, as a dialogue with the *self*, she carries her approach too far and lays too much stress on 'rhetoric', instead of emphasizing the great variety of dialogic elements that may occur in a soliloquy in New Comedy.

[36] On the soliloquy in classical drama cf. F. Leo, *Der Monolog im Drama* (Berlin, 1908); W. Schadewaldt, *Monolog und Selbstgespräch* (Berlin, 1926); J.D. Bickford, *The Soliloquy in Ancient Comedy* (PhD Diss. Princeton, 1922); J. Blundell, *Menander and the Monologue* (Göttingen, 1980); L. Braun, *Die Cantica des Plautus* (Göttingen, 1970); B. Denzler, *Der Monolog bei Terenz* (Diss. Zürich, 1968); M.H. Shackford, 'Stichomythia, Chorus, Soliloquy as Dramatic Forces', in: *Shakespeare, Sophocles: Dramatic Themes and Models* (New York, 1960).

[37] D. Bain, *Actors and Audience* (Oxford, 1977), p.1 – 12.

[38] N.W. Slater, *Plautus in Performance*, p.11.

[39] K. Newman, *Shakespeare's Rhetoric of Comic Character* (New York/London, 1985), p.5.

We should first consider the soliloquizing technique in Menander, where we shall see that the soliloquy has already become a *dramatic process.*[40] The fourth scene of Act III of *Samia*, for example, consists of Demeas's soliloquy, which throughout reveals his thoughts and feelings.[41] He finds himself in a very precarious and painful situation; he is trying to find excuses for his son, who has seduced the girl Chrysis, to whom he is himself attached. The way in which he justifies his son's behaviour and his readiness to send Chrysis away, produces an almost desperate impression, so that the soliloquy reflects a psychological struggle with his own feelings. He opens and concludes his speech by addressing himself as his own partner in his quasi-dialogue; however, as the soliloquy continues, he addresses the audience in a direct way. He concludes with an appeal to himself to pull himself together and to show moral strength:

> O citadel of Cecrops' land, O vault of heaven on high, O – why the noisy imprecation, Demeas? Why all the shouting, you fool? Control yourself, stiffen the upper lip. It's not *Moschion* who's done you wrong [. . .] For if he'd done this from malice aforethought, or in the grip of the passion of love, or from dislike of me, he'd still be brazening it out and marshalling his forces against me. As it is, he's cleared himself completely, in my judgement, by his enthusiastic agreement to this marriage, when it was proposed to him. It wasn't love, as I thought then, that prompted his enthusiasm, but a desire to get away somehow from the house, and from that Helen of mine. *She's* the one to blame for what's happened. She caught him, I imagine, when he'd had a spot too much to drink, when he wasn't quite in control of himself. Yes, that's obviously what happened. Strong wine and young blood can work a lot of mischief, when a man finds at his side someone who has used these things to set a trap for him. I *cannot* believe that a boy who's always been well-behaved and considerate to others could treat me like this: not if he's ten times adopted and not my natural son. It's not his origins I care about, it's his character. But that – creature – she's a trollop. She's poison. She'll have to go.   325ff [42]

It would be wrong to define this speech merely as a self-dialogue. Scene IV,ii opens with another of Demeas's soliloquies, a relatively short one and perhaps the most interesting of all. At first, he speaks facing the house at the back, and

---

[40] W. Schadewaldt says of the Menandrian soliloquy that it is a most effective instrument of dramatic characterization by showing a character to be alone 'with himself' in the act of thinking aloud. (*Menander. Das Schiedsgericht, Der Menschenfeind* [Frankfurt, 1963], p.144).

[41] The soliloquies in *Samia* have been perceptively analysed by H.D. Blume, *Menanders Samia. Eine Interpretation* (Darmstadt, 1974), and also S.M. Goldberg, *The Making of Menander's Comedy* (London, 1980), p.98 – 99.

[42] *Menander. Plays and Fragments*, ed. and transl. N. Miller (London, 1987), p.64.

he addresses those standing in front of it. Then he changes his position and goes up to the stone column of Apollo in midstage, where he begins to pray to the god:

> If I get my hands on a stick, I'll knock tears out of you all right. Stop this nonsense! Get on and help the cook [. . .] There's really something to cry about, I must say; our house has lost a really valuable treasure. Her behaviour makes that quite clear. [*He bows to the altar*] Grant us, Lord, successfully to effect this marriage we are about to celebrate. For [*turning to audience*] celebrate it I shall, Ladies and Gentlemen, and swallow my rage. [*Turns back to altar*] Guard me, O Lord, from self-betrayal, and constrain me to sing the marriage-hymn . . .   439ff

There can be no doubt that this soliloquy is dialogic throughout, but with the change of addressee the nature of the dialogue alters entirely. The soliloquy is very effective not least because it is *acted* on stage and accompanied by dramatic movement. Thus, a single Menandrian soliloquy may consist of different elements, all of which contribute to the overall dramatic effect.

Of course, Shakespeare cannot have been directly familiar with Menander's art of the soliloquy. Yet, indirectly, this tradition was strongly present among the Elizabethans because four of Terence's plays and three Plautine comedies, the *Bacchides*, *Cistellaria* and *Stichus*, are adaptations of Menandrian plays. Let us therefore first turn our attention to one of these 'Menandrian' plays in Roman comedy.

The second Act of the Plautine *Stichus*, a comedy read at some Elizabethan Grammar Schools,[43] opens with a long and exuberant soliloquy by the boy Pinacium who has to inform his mistress that her husband will soon arrive, and he is seen to be in high spirits: 'onustum pectus porto laetitia lubentiaque' V; 276 ('this breast of mine is brimming with delight and delectation!'). He then tells himself to hurry up: 'curre ut lubet' 284 ('run as thou likest!'). The audience know from the comment of the eavesdropper Gelasimus that Pinacium is approaching in a state of excitement, carrying all his fishing tackle. Pinacium's high spirits are thus expressed not only by verbal utterance but also by physical action. Then, suddenly, he halts because a *thought* crosses his mind: 'Sed tandem, opinor, aequiust eram mihi esse supplicem / atque oratores mittere ad me donaque ex auro et quadrigas, / qui vehar [. . .]' (290 – 292) ('[. . .] And yet, methinks, 'twere more fitting for mistress to petition me and send me envoys and gifts of gold and a four-horse chariot for transportation [. . .]'). He therefore *returns* to where he started running: 'ergo iam revortar.' 292 ('So back I go forthwith.'). Then, on second thoughts, it occurs to him that he cannot expect his mistress to approach him because she cannot know the important message he has to deliver to her, and he realizes

---

[43] Cf. Baldwin, *Shakspere's Small Latine and Lesse Greeke*, II, 436.

that he 'must return, speak out, unfold it all, and sweep away her sorrow' ('non enim possum quin revortar, quin loquar, quin edissertem / eramque ex maerore eximam' 302 – 393). Thereupon he decides to be the best of messengers and to outdo even the Herald of Agamemnon, and, by way of association, he adds: 'cursuram meditabor ad ludos Olympios' 306 ('I'll try my stride for the Olympic games.'). Again he starts running, yet he finds that this is 'a rotten place to run! This track's too short.' ('sed spatium hoc occidit: brevest curriculo' 307). Having arrived at the house of his mistress, he notices that the door is shut. He then starts, as it were, a game of knocking at the door and shouting into the house until the Parasite Gelasimus accosts him. We see how this soliloquy, far from being a direct audience address, is throughout accompanied by comic action and stage business.

In the 'Menandrian' play *Bacchides,* Mnesilochus enters from Bacchis's house and speaks a soliloquy, whose sole function is to express *credibly* the disconsolate state of his mind; he perceives that he has acted like a complete fool; he is a lover without money because he has given all his gold to his father:

> Petulans, protervo iracundo animo, indomito incogitato,
> sine modo et modestia sum, sine bono iure atque honore,
> incredibilis imposque animi, inamabilis inlepidus vivo,
> malevolente ingenio natus. postremo id mi est quod volo
> ego esse aliis. *credibile hoc est*? [. . .]
> qui patri reddidi omne aurum amans, mihi
> quod fuit prae manu. sumne ego homo miser? . . .
>
> I, 612 – 623 (italics mine)

> A hasty fool, a reckless, passionate, uncontrollable, unthinking fool without method and moderation, that's what I am − a creature without any sense of right and honour, distrustful, hotheaded, loveless, graceless, crabbed and born crabbed! Yes, yes, I'm everything that I wish some one else was! Is this credible? [. . .] I to give all that gold to my father, and I in love − gold I had in hand! If I'm not a poor, poor fool!

The eavesdropper Pistoclerus then decides to 'console' him.

In the play *Trinummus*, adapted from the New Comedy author Philemon, Lysiteles opens Act II with a long soliloquy in which he complains that his *mind* is full of things that need thinking about. He then becomes more specific: 'amorin med an rei opsequi potius par sit . . . ' V; 230 ('Should I go in for love affairs or attend to business?'). He mulls over the question without finding an answer. Then an idea comes to his mind: 'nisi hoc sic faciam, opinor, / ut utramque rem simul exputem, iudex sim reusque ad eam rem. / ita faciam, ita placet; omnium primum / Amoris artis eloquar quem ad modum expediant.' 232 – 235 ('The only thing to do, it seems, is examine 'em both together and serve as judge and advocate in the case. That's what I'll do, that's a good idea. I'll begin by exposing the arts of Love and their procedure.'). He then tries to explore the nature of love and of the individual lover, he imagines the lover's words and quotes his exchanges with his beloved. This leads him to reject love: 'mille modis, Amor, ignorandu's' 263 ('No, Love, you must be shunned by every means'). And then he decides: 'certumst ad frugem adplicare animum, / quamquam ibi labos grandis capitur.' 271 – 272 ('I devote myself to things worth while, even if it does involve a lot of effort.'). This soliloquy, anything but a mere address to the audience, is conceived as a meditating *process*. The dramatic effect is due mainly to the alternation between various dialogic elements and to the fact that the speech lends itself to being *acted*.

If, as Duckworth rightly observes, 'A true soliloquy is one in which a character, believing himself to be alone, talks alone under the stress of strong emotion',[44] then Plautus also knows how to write true and really dramatic soliloquies; he often succeeds in transforming the convention into something new and original. There are many instances where 'the characters express perplexity, indignation, anger, remorse, anxiety'.[45] Donatus, in his criticism of the Plautine soliloquy, was merely thinking of the relatively frequent soliloquies in which the audience are directly addressed; he failed to consider the fact that the soliloquies in Plautus are not always a form of 'extra comoediam loqui', nor are the Terentian monologues always purely spontaneous expressions of thoughts and feelings ('non quaesitum [. . .] sed [. . .] sua sponte').[46]

The soliloquies in *Menaechmi* and *Amphitruo* are skilfully organized, and many of them have an interesting characteristic in common: they share subdivisions into different parts which are marked by a change not only of theme, but also of *metre* [47]. Many Renaissance editions faithfully print the lines of these *cantica* as verse, and they differ considerably in length. In *Menaechmi*, the soliloquies are given an important function: they influence the focal position of the two twins. Although we cannot expect the soliloquies in this light comedy to provide us with any deep psychological motivation, it is nevertheless worthwhile examining them in greater detail. Menaechmus S concludes the third Act with a soliloquy in which he takes leave of Erotium's maid by assuring her that he will take care of her *palla* and *spinter*: 'Say I'll take care of these things' (II; 548), and when, looking back, he is sure that she is gone, he, like the medieval Vice, converts the meaning of his sentence into its very opposite and comes forward to the audience:

---

[44] Duckworth, op. cit., p.103. On the typically Plautine soliloquy cf. also E. Fraenkel, *Elementi Plautini in Plauto* (Firenze, 1961), p.105ff.

[45] Ibid., p.104.

[46] Donatus, op. cit., I, 330.

[47] This had been pointed out by Braun, *Die Cantica des Plautus* (Göttingen, 1970), p.34 – 42; 111 – 119.

> Haec me curaturum dicito –
> ut quantum possint quique liceant veneant.   II, 548 – 549

> Say I'll take care of these things [. . .] take care they're sold as
> soon as possible for what they'll bring.

Then he expresses the boundless joy he feels because of the great love the gods have shown him, and he tells himself to hurry up: 'propera, Menaechme, fer pedem, confer gradum.' (554). He even accompanies his words by some stage business: in order to deceive the others, he takes the wreath from his head and throws it to the left, while he exits in the opposite direction. This dramatic soliloquy is an effective means of revealing the speaker's mood in his particular situation, and the effect is further intensified by the brevity of the speech.

Menaechmus E, having returned from the Forum, addresses the audience in IV,ii in a long monologue in order to explain the reason for his long absence. Yet the second part of this soliloquy is more than a mere set speech; with its abrupt exclamations and spontaneous questions, it reflects the speaker's excited state of mind:

> Vt hoc utimur maxime more moro
> molestoque multum [. . .]
> apud aediles pro eius factis plurumisque pessumisque
> dixi causam, condiciones tetuli tortas, confragosas;
> aut plus aut minus quam opus fuerat dicto dixeram
> controversiam, ut
> sponsio fieret. quid ille? qui praedem dedit [. . .]
>> di illum omnes perdant, ita mihi
>> hunc hodie corrupit diem,
>> meque adeo, qui hodie forum
>> umquam oculis inspexi meis . . .   II, 571 – 597

> What slaves we are to this consummately crazy, confoundedly
> chafing custom! [. . .] Before the aediles I spoke in defence of his
> countless atrocities, and proposed provisos that were intricate and
> difficult; I had put the case more or less as was necessary to have a
> settlement made. But what did he do? [. . .] What? Named a
> surety! [. . .] Heaven curse the man, with the way he spoiled this
> day for me; yes, and curse me, too, for ever taking a look at the
> forum to-day! . . .

The growing excitement of the speaker is here also reflected in the change of metre, which is, as we said, faithfully preserved in the Renaissance editions. We may see from this example that one and the same soliloquy in Plautus may combine both anti-illusionist and 'realistic' elements, that it may be both an address to the audience and a self-referential reflection.

The soliloquy which Menaechmus speaks on his first entry is even more interesting. What we find here is not a dialogic self-reference; the monologue is dialogic throughout, though not in Newman's sense, because Menaechmus speaks with his back to the audience and facing the house where his wife has remained:

> Ni mala, ni stulta sies, ni indomita imposque animi,
> quod viro esse odio videas, tute tibi odio habeas [. . .]
> nam quotiens foras ire volo, me retines, revocas, rogitas,
> quo ego eam, quam rem agam, quid negoti geram,
> quid petam, quid feram, quid foris egerim . . .   II, 110 – 116

> If you weren't mean, if you weren't stupid, if you weren't a violent virago, what you see displeases your husband would be displeasing to you, too [. . .] Why, whenever I want to go out, you catch hold of me, call me back, cross-question me as to where I'm going, what I'm doing, what business I have in hand, what I'm after, what I've got, what I did when I was out.

His disgust at his family situation is admirably 'mirrored' in the staccato rhythm of the verse. Turning to the audience, in a sudden comic volta, he abandons his quarrelsome tone and begins to express his joy about his triumph over his wife:

> Euax, iurgio hercle tandem uxorem abegi ab ianua.
> ubi sunt amatores mariti? dona quid cessant mihi
> conferre omnes congratulantes, quia pugnavi fortiter?
>
> II, 127 – 129

> Hurrah! By Jove, at last my lecture has driven her away from the door! Where are your married gallants? Why don't they all hurry up with gifts and congratulations for my valiant fight?

After the Matrona and Peniculus have convicted him of stealing her *palla* in IV, ii, she shuts the door against him. He comments on this, addresses his absent wife, then moves to the door of Erotium's house, where he expects to find admittance. There is irony involved here because the audience know that Erotium, too, has a bone to pick with him, since the other Menaechmus has not returned the *palla* and *spinter*. When he appears in V, v, the Senex and the Doctor are waiting for him in order to set about curing his madness. He delivers an emotional soliloquy, in which his lamenting over his wretched state is taken to confirm that he is mad. When they have gone to fetch slaves to carry him away to the clinic, he again reflects on his miserable condition:

> Abiit socerus, abiit medicus. solus sum. pro Iuppiter,
> quid illuc est quod med hisce homines insanire praedicant?
> nam equidem, postquam gnatus sum, numquam aegrotavi unum diem,
> neque ego insanio neque pugnas neque ego litis coepio.

salvus salvos alios video, novi homines, adloquor.
an illi perperam insanire me aiunt, ipsi insaniunt?
quid ego nunc faciam?   II, 957 – 963

Father-in-law's gone. Doctor's gone. All alone! Lord save us!
What is it makes those men declare I'm insane? Why, as a matter
of fact, I've never had a sick day since I was born. I'm neither
insane, nor looking for fights, nor starting disputes, not I. I'm
perfectly sound and regard others as sound; I recognize people,
talk to them. Can it be they're insane themselves with their absurd
statements that I'm insane? [. . .] What shall I do now?

This soliloquy, which expresses the speaker's psychological condition, is
remarkable throughout. Menaechmus asks himself what reason people can
have to consider him mad; he has not been aggressive in any way, nor does he
recognize any change for the worse in himself. This leads him to the daring
idea that perhaps it is the others who have gone mad. He considers what he
should do next and decides to move over to his own house and to wait outside
to be let in. Menaechmus talks to himself here in a spontaneous and 'realistic'
way, and we, the audience, witness his thinking as a dramatic process that
ends up in a concrete decision. It is true that the rhetorical questions which
Newman emphasizes do recur, but they are not sufficient to characterize this
soliloquy as merely dialogic. What strikes us most in these soliloquies is their
conciseness and the way in which they arise naturally out of a specific dramatic
and 'affective' situation.

This does not apply to all of Plautus's soliloquies, because they tend at times
to become exceedingly long, and thus they hold up the dramatic flow of the
action, especially when one soliloquy immediately follows another. But in
Menaechmi, as can easily be seen in stage performances, the soliloquies are
distributed with considerable dramatic skill; they almost always form an
effective contrast with turbulent and agitated scenes and situations. By this
very fact the soliloquies are an essential means of establishing the dramatic
rhythm of the play. Sometimes a soliloquy in Plautus helps to build up the
pyramidal structure of a scene, as, for example, in IV, ii of *Menaechmi*; the
scene starts quietly with Menaechmus's soliloquy, then gradually develops
into a climax with the attacks of the Matrona and Peniculus, until the scene
again returns to a more normal pace with Menaechmus' soliloquizing
reflection on his precarious situation. Plautus, too, knows how to employ 'the
lesser units of structure' which Brooks examined in Shakespeare's *Errors*: he
achieves rhythmical variety and contrast by the regrouping of the characters
on stage, by a new entrance or an exit in the course of a scene, so that the
scene is divided into a number of 'sub-scènes'.[48]

---

[48] H.F. Brooks, 'Themes and Structure in "The Comedy of Errors"', *Early Shakespeare*, p.55.

The wide range of the Plautine technique of soliloquy is amply documented in *Amphitruo*. First of all, the gods direct long addresses to the audience and explain the action to them, thus making them partners in the play. Jupiter admits having come on stage with the sole purpose of helping the comedy to advance: 'nunc huc honoris vostri venio gratia, / ne hanc incohatam transigam comoediam' (I; 867 – 868) ('I now appear out of regard for you, so as not to terminate this inchoate comedy.').

Mercury has a very interesting soliloquy in III, iv; he not merely addresses the audience but even delivers his address while *running* onto the stage. He takes his course through the middle of the audience, whom he first commands to make way for him: 'Concedite atque abscedite omnes, de via decedite, / ne quisquam tam audax fuat homo, qui obviam obsistat mihi.' (984 – 985). This lively and dramatic soliloquy recalls the fact that it is meant to be *acted* instead of being merely delivered. Furthermore it closely resembles the famous entrance soliloquies of Vice characters such as, for example, Ambidexter in *Cambises* or Merry Report in John Heywood's *The Play of the Weather*, where, be it noted, Jupiter, too, dominates the play. The soliloquies of the human characters in the *Amphitruo* play are also spoken with a view to the audience, yet in some of them we notice a personal self-revelation and even a direct verbalisation of personal emotions and feelings. Thus scene II, ii begins with Alcumena appearing in front of the Palace Gate. She starts with some maxims concerning the general lot of mankind: 'Satin parva res est voluptatum in vita atque in aetate agunda / praequam quod molestum est? ita cuique comparatum est in aetate hominum; / ita divis est placitum, voluptatem ut maeror comes consequatur . . .' I; (663 – 665) ('Oh, are not the pleasures in life, in this daily round, trifling compared with the pains! It is our common human lot, it is heaven's will, for sorrow to come following after joy . . .'). But then she reflects on what has just happened to her and, while doing so, in very moving lines she concentrates on her own individual experience. When, in III, ii, she appears from the Palace, after she has been accused of adultery, her words become even more personal because she has been deeply hurt. Her soliloquy, therefore, is an immediate verbal expression of her feelings rather than an explanatory address to the audience:[49]

> Durare nequeo in aedibus. ita me probri,
> stupri, dedecoris a viro argutam meo!
> ea quae sunt facta infecta ut reddat clamitat,
> quae neque sunt facta neque ego in me admisi arguit;
> atque id me susque deque esse habituram putat.
> non edepol faciam, neque me perpetiar probri
> falso insimulatam, quin ego illum aut deseram
> aut satis faciat mi ille atque adiuret insuper,
> nolle esse dicta quae in me insontem protulit.   I, 882 – 890

---

[49] Cf. P. Simpson, *Studies in Elizabethan Drama* (Oxford, 1955), p.15.

I can't stand staying in the house! To be branded so with shame, disloyalty, disgrace, by my own husband! How he clamours to make facts no facts! And what never happened, things I never, never did, he accuses me of, and thinks I'll consider it quite immaterial. Good gracious, but I won't! I won't endure such an awful, unjustified accusation: I will leave him, or he must apologize, one or the other, yes, and swear he is sorry, too, for the things he has said to an innocent woman.

To conclude this survey, we can say that the tradition of New Comedy and Roman comedy in particular provided a technique of the soliloquy which lent itself to various functions. In many cases the soliloquy is far from being a static address to the audience; instead, even in Greek comedy, playwrights were already aware of the dramatic potentialities contained in this convention. A major function of the soliloquy has always been the verbal reflection of the psychological condition of the speaker. No doubt, this tradition of dramatically complex soliloquizing contributed to the development of Shakespeare's art of soliloquy, which surprises us by its dramatic and poetic variety and intensity. As Shakespeare's soliloquies have been most perceptively analysed by Wolfgang Clemen, it will suffice here simply to concentrate on a few salient points.[50]

Although *Errors* is an early Shakespearean comedy and although it would be wrong to expect in it examples of Shakespeare's famous comic soliloquies, he nevertheless employs the convention here with considerable skill and economy, while at the same time he develops various dramaturgic elements from the soliloquy tradition of New Comedy. All the dramatic qualities of the Plautine monologue are found here. Even more than in *Menaechmi*, the soliloquies in *Errors* help to create the play's dramatic rhythm. As the action is more turbulent than in *Menaechmi*, soliloquies provide an even more effective contrast, as they are usually set against agitated situations. They are decidedly short and they do not suspend the dramatic illusion but are always a verbal reflection of the thoughts or feelings of the speaker. Apart from the soliloquy

[50] W. Clemen, *Shakespeare's Soliloquies*, The Presidential Address of the Modern Humanities Research Association (Cambridge, 1964); repr. in: Clemen, *Shakespeare's Dramatic Art. Collected Essays* (London, 1972, repr. 1980). *Shakespeares Monologe. Ein Zugang zu seiner dramatischen Kunst* (München and Zürich, 1985); English version: *Shakespeare's Soliloquies* transl. by C. Scott Stokes (London/New York, 1987). Earlier studies on Shakespeare's soliloquies include M.C. Arnold, *The Soliloquies of Shakespeare. A Study in Technic* (New York, 1911); N. Coghill, *Shakespeare's Professional Skills* (Cambridge, 1964) and K. Muir, *Shakespeare the Dramatist and other Papers* (London, 1961). On the impact of the soliloquy tradition on English Renaissance drama cf. W. Clemen, *English Tragedy Before Shakespeare. The Development of Dramatic Speech* (London, 1961, repr. 1980), M.C. Gingrich, *Soliloquies, Asides, and Audience in English Renaissance Drama* (PhD thesis Rutgers Univ. New Brunswick, 1978) and L.A. Skiffington, *The History of English Soliloquy. Aeschylus to Shakespeare* (London/New York, 1985).

given to the Courtesan in IV, iii, they are assigned exclusively to the traveller Antipholus, who is thus given greater profile than his brother. Each soliloquy is triggered off by the dramatic situation to which the speaker is trying to react. Antipholus's very first monologue admirably expresses his state of mind:

> He that commends me to mine own content
> Commends me to the thing I cannot get.
> I to the world am like a drop of water
> That in the ocean seeks another drop,
> Who, falling there to find his fellow forth,
> (Unseen, inquisitive) confounds himself.
> So I, to find a mother and a brother,
> In quest of them, unhappy, lose myself.   I, ii, 33 – 40

That this text is supposed to be 'generated' in and through the act of speaking, is clear from the syntax, which becomes increasingly complicated and thus reflects the speaker's unresolved situation. The particular skill of Shakespeare's later soliloquies, in which images and metaphors are used to objectify a specific emotion,[51] is here to a certain extent anticipated by Antipholus's famous water-drop image, which Shakespeare extended and developed from an image Plautus had used in the recognition scene in *Menaechmi*, where Messenio comments on the likeness of the twins with the words: 'neque aqua aquae nec lacte est lactis, crede mi, usquam similius, / quam hic tui est, tuque huius autem' II; 1089 – 1090 ('No drop of water, no drop of milk, is more like another, believe me, than he's like you, yes, and you like him, sir.').[52] Shakespeare's use of this image is nevertheless highly original; by its refinement it is admirably suited to express Antipholus's vital concern, which has brought him to come to Ephesus: his attempt to discover his true identity. He unwittingly anticipates what will happen to him on his quest: he will indeed come near to 'confounding' and 'losing' himself.

His next soliloquy, at the end of the scene, reveals the specific quality by which he distinguishes himself from his brother: his imagination, which leads him astray as much as it helps him to preserve his integrity. On the one hand, he clings to a prejudiced view of Ephesus, which suggests that the town is full of evil spirits, and hence he 'transforms' the city and the inhabitants he meets according to his biased view. He himself is afraid that his mind is being 'transformed' by sorcerers, something which does indeed happen to his brother, and he fears 'soul-killing witches', whom a little later he believes he has recognized in the form of Adriana, Luciana and the Courtesan. The other, positive, aspect of his imagination is, however, that he does not lose

---

[51] On this aspect in Shakespeare cf. W. Clemen, *The Development of Shakespeare's Imagery* (London, 1977).

[52] Shakespeare's brilliant extension and transposition of the Plautine image has, for example, been observed by Baldwin, *On the Compositional Genetics of The Comedy of Errors* (Urbana, 1965), p.159f.

sight of his prime objective. He knows that, in order to find his true self, he has to preserve his mind and soul intact and free from the 'liberties of sin'.

After Adriana has expressed her wish to cling to Antipholus as a 'vine' clasps itself around an 'elm', he reacts with words which he speaks half to himself and half as an aside:

> To me she speaks, she moves me for her theme;
> What, was I married to her in my dream?
> Or sleep I now, and think I hear all this?
> What error drives our eyes and ears amiss?
> Until I know this sure uncertainty,
> I'll entertain the offer'd fallacy.   II, ii, 181 – 186

The rhetorical questions, which we have already found in Plautine soliloquy, are not so much an instance of self-address but rather the expression of his utter helplessness; the effect is comic because the audience *know* the reason for his confusion.[53]

The longer Antipholus stays in Ephesus, the greater is the menace to which he believes he is exposed. In III, ii, after his encounter with Luciana, he speaks another soliloquy, in which he forms the idea that he may have met another witch, and now he can hardly forgive himself for having succumbed to her charms. As he thinks that 'none but witches do inhabit here' (III, ii, 155), he is bound to interpret the appearance of Angelo with the chain as a further temptation. In IV, iii he has just been asking himself why people are doing him so many favours and offering him money; when his own Dromio brings him gold, his 'quest' is for a moment submerged beneath the desire for material gain, and he is brought almost to breaking-point: 'The fellow is distract, and so am I, / And here we wander in illusions . . .' (IV, iii, 40 – 41). As his Dromio tries to explain that 'Here are the angels that you sent for to deliver you.' (39), he thinks the remark has a spiritual meaning and hopes that real angels ('some blessed power' 42) will deliver him from this devilish situation. Thus we see that his soliloquies, short as they are, all mark decisive moments in his quest for identity. They are dramatic expressions of his fear of losing himself, which is the necessary prerequisite for his self-discovery.

The remarkable fact that a soliloquy in this tradition is a text to be *acted* on stage is, of course, powerfully continued in the soliloquies in Shakespeare's tragedies.[54] Yet, in Iago's soliloquies, for instance, an underlying comic structure is clearly discernible. Let us consider his first soliloquy in I,iii, in which he begins to develop his intrigue against Othello:

---

[53] Newman is wrong when she argues that in his question: 'What error drives our eyes and ears amiss?' (184) the audience are included in Antipholus's errors, because we by this stage have no doubt whatsoever about the characters' identity. (Newman, op. cit., p.80).

[54] Cf. Clemen, *Shakespeare's Soliloquies*, p.90 – 177.

> I hate the Moor,
> And it is thought abroad that 'twixt my sheets
> [H'as] done my office. I know not if't be true,
> But I, for mere suspicion in that kind,
> Will do as if for surety. He holds me well,
> The better shall my purpose work on him.
> Cassio's a proper man. Let me see now:
> To get his place and to plume up my will
> In double knavery — How? how? — Let's see —
> After some time, to abuse Othello's [ear]
> That he is too familiar with his wife. [. . .]
> I have't. It is engend'red.   I, iii, 386 – 403

In this soliloquy, we as the audience are made witnesses of Iago's attempts to devise an effective intrigue; we watch him develop his plot. This implies, of course, that the actor does not merely deliver the soliloquy as a speech to the audience but accompanies it with nonverbal gestural and physical, 'kinesic' by-play. That this was already the case in Plautine comedy, that obviously there was no essential difference in the gestures on the Plautine and the Elizabethan stage, can be inferred from the theatrically very interesting scene II, ii in *Miles Gloriosus*. Here we are given the opportunity to watch the slave Palaestrio hatching a plot; however, he does so completely without words, merely using mime and gestures, as is reflected in the comments of Periplectomenus:

>   illuc sis vide,
> quem ad modum adstitit, severo fronte curans cogitans.
> pectus digitis pultat, cor credo evocaturust foras;
> ecce avortit: nixus laevo in femine habet laevam manum,
> dextera digitis rationem computat, ferit femur dexterum.
> ita vehementer icit: quod agat aegre suppetit.
> concrepuit digitis: laborat; crebro commutat status . . .
>   III, 200 – 206

> Just look at him, how he stands there with bent brow, considering
> and cogitating. He's tapping his chest with his fingers. Intends to
> summon forth his intelligence, I suppose. Aha! Turns away! Rests
> his left hand on his left thigh, and reckons on the fingers of his
> right hand. Gives his right thigh a smack! A lusty whack — his
> plan of action is having a hard birth. Snaps his fingers! He's in
> distress. Constantly changes his position! . . .

Here, too, the dramatic situation of the engendering of a plot is credibly presented on stage.[55] Furthermore, it is interesting that one of the soliloquies of Terence, although they are less theatrical than those of Plautus, resembles

---

[55] On this aspect cf. my article 'Shakespeares monologische Redeformen dramaturgisch betrachtet', *ShJW* (1985), 28 – 44.

in its form Iago's soliloquies: when in the *Heautontimoroumenos* the slave Syrus finds himself in a scrape, he realizes the necessity of devising a new ploy:

> *quid agam?* aut quid comminiscar? ratio de integro ineundast mihi.
> nil tam difficilest quin quaerendo investigari possiet.
> *quid si* hoc nunc sic incipiam? nil est. *quid, sic?* tantundem
> egero.
> at sic opinor: non potest. immo optume. euge habeo optumam.
> I, 674 – 677

> *What plan now?* what device? I must clean all the old figures off the slate. Nothing is too hard for a detective's industry. *Let me see let me see* [. . .] Start that way? That's no go. Or that? No go either. Or that perhaps? No, can't be done. Can't it, though? It can, excellently. Hurrah! I've got an excellent scheme. (italics mine)

Great soliloquies occur in Shakespeare's comedies too;[56] let us take as an example Viola's famous and important monologue with which she concludes scene two of Act II in *Twelfth Night*. She has just been informed by Malvolio that Olivia, who has fallen in love with Viola disguised as a man, refuses to accept a ring from the Duke Orsino:

> She loves me sure, the cunning of her passion
> Invites me in this churlish messenger.
> None of my lord's ring? Why, he sent her none.
> I am the man! If it be so, as 'tis,
> Poor lady, she were better love a dream.
> Disguise, I see thou art a wickedness
> Wherein the pregnant enemy does much.
> How easy is it for the proper-false
> In women's waxen hearts to set their forms!
> Alas, [our] frailty is the cause, not we,
> For such as we are made [of,] such we be.
> How will this fadge? My master loves her dearly,
> And I, (poor monster), fond as much on him;
> And she, (mistaken) seems to dote on me. [. . .]
> O time, thou must untangle this, not I,
> It is too hard a knot for me t'untie.   22 – 41

Viola tries to grasp a situation that puzzles her completely: she begins with a reflection and becomes aware of Olivia's altered way of speaking, which she correctly interprets as a sign of her infatuation. Viola even repeats Olivia's words: 'None of my lord's ring . . .' and adds that she is 'the man of Olivia's choice'. Yet this soliloquy, which masterfully reflects the development of the speaker's thoughts by way of association, does not continue in the same way;

---

[56] Cf. Clemen, *Shakespeare's Soliloquies*, p.46 – 87.

we observe a change of tone, which to the actor suggests a change of position on stage or some kind of movement. Viola now addresses personified Disguise and formulates a gnomic maxim: 'Disguise, I see thou art a wickedness . . .' She continues her new generalizing tone, in the course of which she speaks for all women. This means that Viola, momentarily giving up her concern with her own private problems, is now establishing contact with the audience, because she has become aware of the paradigmatic nature of her own experience: 'Alas, our frailty is the cause, not we . . .' From this point, she alternates between reflecting on her own situation and addressing the audience, a technique familiar to us from the soliloquy in New Comedy. Just as the second part of the soliloquy was introduced by an apostrophe to a personification, so the whole monologue ends with an address to personified Time. Thus, the soliloquy not only fulfils an important function for the action of the play; it is also an impressive example of concentrated and poetic language and, beyond that, it is a highly dramatic *playtext* because, through the specific sequence of its thoughts and through the characteristic alternation between private and general considerations, the soliloquy acquires the quality of dramatic movement. Although these elements evoke some reminiscences of the soliloquizing technique of New Comedy, Viola's soliloquy has all the marks of a Shakespearean masterpiece.

III

The Structure of Plautine Comedy and its Impact on Shakespeare

1. Some basic elements of scenic dramaturgy

In turning to questions of plot and the dramaturgic organization of the action, we shall not be concerned with a detailed structural comparison between *Errors* and *Menaechmi*, since several critics have already examined the process by which Shakespeare transforms the plot of Plautine comedy. Nor shall we consider the question of the Elizabethan attitude towards the classical unities which has also been previously discussed.[1] We shall, instead, choose to concentrate on a number of essential structural aspects of New Comedy, and shall investigate the ways in which Shakespeare makes use of them. The first area we shall look at is that of scenic dramaturgy.

It is well known that in New Comedy there are no changes of locality, whereas in tragedy as well as in Old Comedy such changes are common. The acting area in New Comedy is always a street or the space in front of a house. Indoor scenes, when they become necessary, are also sometimes played in front of the house, and the dramatist is unconcerned about dramatic verisimilitude. This kind of scenic dramaturgy has important implications. As the action unfolds in one place, there is no need for the characters on stage to clear it so as to create the illusion that the next scene will take place in a different setting. In New Comedy, therefore, one scene is distinguished from the next by a change in character grouping, brought about either by the arrival of a further character or (much less frequently) by a character's exit.

In his *Errors*, Shakespeare has not only preserved the unity of time, for the most part he has also remained remarkably faithful to the dramaturgy of space in New Comedy. For example, Menander's *Dyskolos* is opened by the Prologue spoken by Pan who invites the audience to 'Imagine that the scene's

---

[1] For a structural comparison cf. especially the profound analysis by H.F. Brooks, 'Themes and Structure in "The Comedy of Errors"', *Early Shakespeare*, Stratford-upon-Avon Studies, 3 (1961), p.54–71 and the article by E.M. Gill (cf. Introduction, note 10). On Shakespeare's use of the classical unities cf. Salingar, *Shakespeare and the Traditions of Comedy*, p.77ff.

in Attica' ('της Αττικης νομιζετ' ειναι τον τοπον'),[2] and the Prologue to *Menaechmi* concludes with the remark that today the stage 'is' Epidamnus and tomorrow it may 'be' any other place, depending upon the plot of the next play (72 – 76). Shakespeare's attitude towards the creation of dramatic space through the imagination of the audience is very similar; we need only think of the Prologue to *Troilus and Cressida*, which begins by informing us: 'In Troy there lies the scene . . .', then the bare stage is given a particular individuality in a manner corresponding to the transformation of the Menandrian or Plautine stage. The similarities between the Plautine and the Elizabethan dramaturgy of space are very close indeed. And there is surely no *decisive* qualitative difference between the so-called Terentian screen stage, for which *Errors* was most probably written, and the Elizabethan popular stage. The neutral space where the action develops becomes an individual place only through the action. That this dramaturgy in *Errors* is not simply concerned about 'realism', can be seen, for example, in the interesting situation in IV, i. When Antipholus E is hard pressed by Angelo and the Second Merchant, who want his money, he orders Dromio to fetch it. Dromio, however, does not do what would be the most obvious thing from a realistic point of view, namely cross the stage and enter the house of Antipholus E; instead, he exits hurriedly and returns only after some time, sweating. The audience are not disturbed by this anti-illusionist dramaturgy, since they have no time to become aware of it, for Shakespeare uses Dromio's absence as an opportunity for Adriana's and Luciana's reappearance, so that Dromio's hasty and exhausted return and his encounter with the two ladies produce another very effective confusion.

In a discussion of the dramaturgy of space, the use of offstage localities cannot be ignored. Plautus is one of the very first dramatists to make offstage scenery into an important part of the total dramatic design. There is an effective contrast between the everyday business world of the Forum and the offstage holiday area of the harbour, with the pleasures of Erotium lying in wait.[3] Menaechmus E oscillates between the two worlds, whereas Menaechmus S belongs entirely to the latter. He is a born traveller and uses the search for his brother almost as a pretext for travelling. For a few moments, his narration of his long journeys creates an imaginary world which forms a contrast to the action of the play itself. Again, in the brilliant scene V, ii, he succeeds in imaginatively extending the actual space when he plays the madman and suggests that he is performing a chariot race on the orders of Apollo.

In *Errors*, offstage locality becomes even more important; it can be seen as an extension and transformation of the Plautine dramaturgy of space.

---

[2] *Dyskolos* quoted from W.G. Arnott, ed., *Menander*, p.184 – 85; on the point of locality in Old and New Comedy and in Plautus cf. J. Blänsdorf, 'Plautus' in: *Das römische Drama*, ed. E. Lefèvre (Darmstadt, 1978), p.188.

[3] This contrast has been pointed out by Segal, *Roman Laughter* (Cambridge, Mass., 1968), p.42 – 70.

Whereas Menaechmus E is saved from being carried off to the clinic, Antipholus E is actually sent to prison, which Dromio metaphorically associates with Hell, and is then thrown into a 'dark and dankish vault' (V, i, 248). This dark vault, which marks the nadir of Antipholus's fortunes, is the exact counterpart of the Priory in which his brother is detained. In the one place, identity is about to be destroyed, while by the other its final attainment is made possible.

Scene III, i of *Errors* deserves our special attention. Here, the acting space is again extended beyond the visible part of the stage. It is often claimed that, for the scene to make its proper impact, both pairs of twins should be clearly visible to the audience. I am rather inclined to believe that the overall effect of this magnificent scene is greater if the acting space is divided into a visible and an invisible half. Staged in this way, the scene is extremely funny. In my own production, both Dromios were visible to the audience only for the short moment when Dromio E succeeded in pulling open the door, whereupon Dromio S at once pulled it to again.

In our discussion of the characters in *Menaechmi* we have seen that two contrasting backstage locations – the Forum and the harbour – are essential for a proper understanding of the play's movements because the one represents the everyday world of business and constraint, whereas the other symbolizes the spirit of holiday and sexual liberty, and the comedy moves between these two worlds. It is, I think, very likely that there are direct links between this kind of spatial opposition and the contrasting of localities in some of Shakespeare's comedies. Again Shakespeare may have taken up a suggestion which he developed into a dramaturgic device of great originality. In fact, as early as the 'classical' *Errors*, we find that Shakespeare employs two contrasting *kinds* of space. In the very first scene, which is exceptional in that it takes place within the Duke's palace, Shakespeare widens the narrow confines of the play by evoking an *imaginary* space in the minds of the audience. Egeon mentions his misfortunes on the boundless ocean, and from then on, as R. Berry has remarked, 'always at the back of the action is the sea'.[4] This boundlessness of the imaginary space is reinforced by Luciana in II, i, when she describes the cosmic order and refers to the creatures 'in earth, in sea, in sky', 'The beasts, the fishes, and the winged fowls', and then goes on to call Man 'Lord of the wide world and wild wat'ry seas' (18ff.). Thus Shakespeare achieves an effective contrast with the real acting space, the city of Ephesus, which gives the impression of a continually narrowing acting area: whereas, as the play progresses, the major characters increasingly experience a feeling of claustrophobia, the references to the sea provide the audience with a momentary relief by offering a view outside the narrowing confines of the play world. Shakespeare further elaborates this same technique in his later plays, for example in *A Midsummer Night's Dream*, where we find a comparable

---

[4] R. Berry, *Shakespeare and the Awareness of the Audience* (London, 1985), p.34.

narrowing of space in the woods of Athens, while the poetical and mythological descriptions, such as the picture of Oberon sitting on a 'promontory', hearing 'a mermaid on a dolphin's back' (II, i, 148ff.), briefly open up a liberating vista into the world outside the woods, as Young has shown.[5]

The city of Ephesus is a common locality in New Comedy. However, Shakespeare is not content merely to distance the action of his play by transferring it to a far-off place; he is concerned to evoke in the audience the opposing reactions of 'engagement and detachment'.[6] Not only in the second scene but on some later occasions, too, there are references to familiar English locations, particularly when Dromio S gives his description of Nell, the buxom kitchen wench. Berry was the first to conclude that these associations give the audience the 'reassurance that all will be well'.[7]

In this context a further interesting aspect of the dramaturgic affinity between Shakespeare and Plautus becomes evident. As is well known, Plautus takes over the Greek settings of his sources; on the other hand, however, he occasionally includes in his plays some references to Roman place names as well as official and legal terms.[8] One effect of the combination of Greek and Roman elements is certainly to create an imaginary world of play set at some removes from everyday experience; at the same time these Roman references reassure the audience of the eventual resolution in a way quite comparable to Shakespeare's homely allusions in *Errors*. This is particularly striking since, in contrast to Plautus, we do not find any references to contemporary Rome in the plays of Terence.

We must now pay special attention to the way in which in Plautine Comedy and in Elizabethan drama space is used for the meeting and parting of the *dramatis personae*. As both classical and many Elizabethan comedies are 'plays of meeting', to use a term coined by Clifford Leech,[9] we find a great many variations on the act of meeting. In both traditions we have frequent scenes in

---

[5] D.P. Young, *Something of Great Constancy. The Art of 'A Midsummer Night's Dream'* (New Haven/London, 1966), p.76 – 81.

[6] Cf. M. Mack, 'Engagement and Detachment in Shakespeare's Plays', *Essays on Shakespeare and Elizabethan Drama in Honor of H. Craig*, ed. R. Hosley (Columbia, 1962), 275 – 96.

[7] Berry, op. cit., p.42.

[8] Cf. Duckworth, op. cit., p.272, and especially K. Gaiser, 'Zur Eigenart der römischen Komödie: Plautus und Terenz gegenüber ihren griechischen Vorbildern' in: *Aufstieg und Niedergang der römischen Welt*, ed. H. Temporieri (Berlin/New York, 1972), I,2,1027 – 1113, esp. p.1079; cf. also M. Fuhrmann, 'Plautus' in: *Der Kleine Pauly. Lexikon der Antike*, ed. K. Ziegler and W. Sontheimer (München, 1979), IV, 914.

[9] C. Leech, 'The Function of Locality in the Plays of Shakespeare and his Contemporaries', in: D. Galloway, ed., *The Elizabethan Theatre* (Oshawa, 1969), p.103ff.

which the action develops simultaneously on different parts of the stage, as envisaged by Bain:

> That X can be on stage concurrently with Y and unaware of Y's presence or that they can be mutually unaware of each other's presence is an established convention of the Greek stage. When an actor enters an already occupied stage, he is in comedy usually represented as at first unaware of the presence of the other people on stage. On some occasions they are represented as unaware of him and the two actors or groups of actors proceed in mutual unawareness for some time.[10]

Bain rightly points out that this dramaturgic convention, which is related to the multiple setting familiar to us from the medieval tradition, does not put great strain on the audience's belief because 'the [. . .] characters are [. . .] too occupied in their own thoughts to notice each other.'[11] The very length of the Plautine stage too adds credibility to this convention. It is nevertheless clear that these scenic situations, with the exception of the 'classical' eavesdropping convention,[12] are far less dramatic than situations beginning with a dialogue. In Plautus and in New Comedy proper, we find many examples of these scenic types. Yet Plautus also knows how to make good dramatic use of an 'open' dialogue, where characters appear to be continuing on stage a discussion which they had already begun beforehand.

In Shakespeare's plays, we admire the 'infinite variety' of the ways in which his characters meet. In our present context, it is particularly interesting to note that he shows an increasing reserve in the use of less 'dramatic' scene openings involving soliloquies or the soliloquy of a new character which is overheard and commented on by another; when this latter situation is necessary, Shakespeare, as a rule, sees to it that after a short while a dialogue between the characters is established. On the other hand, his art of beginning a scene in the middle of a dialogue can already be studied in *Errors*, where this technique adds a strong touch of 'realism' to the play's overall impact. The beginning of the so-called wooing scene, III, ii, is especially noteworthy because, as we shall see in a later context, the pattern of an ordinary wooing is, as it were, undercut by the fact that we meet Luciana and Antipholus *after* they have already exchanged a dialogue behind the stage, and the new scene opens with Luciana taking the initiative and giving Antipholus some strikingly odd advice for what she interprets as an amorous adventure.

In New Comedy, there are frequent scenes in which a newcomer on stage does not notice that his arrival has been observed by a character or a group of characters hiding behind a suitable object; these eavesdropping scenes always

---

[10] D. Bain, *Actors and Audience* (Oxford, 1977), p.162.
[11] Bain, ibid.
[12] On overhearing in classical comedy cf. V.E. Hieatt, *Eavesdropping in Roman Comedy* (Diss. Chicago, 1946).

provide opportunities for effective stage comedy. The great variety of eavesdropping scenes in the comedies of Plautus served Shakespeare as a kind of skeletal basis around which he built his own brilliant scenes of overhearing. Two of the best scenes of this kind appear in plays well known during the Renaissance, namely in *Miles Gloriosus* (IV, iv) and *Amphitruo* (I, i). In *Amphitruo*, the way in which Mercury and Sosia observe each other and comment on one another from a distance is masterfully contrived. *Menaechmi* also contains an interesting example: at first, Peniculus thinks his Patron, who has just returned from the Forum, has come from the dinner and cheated him, whereupon he plans his revengeful intrigue in his cynical asides. Plautus adds complexity to the situation through the fact that, just as Menaechmus is unaware of Peniculus's thoughts of revenge, so Peniculus fails to realize that he is being deceived about Menaechmus's real identity. In *Errors* Shakespeare disposed of the eavesdropping convention because, unlike his Latin sources, he had no real need for it. Since *deliberate* deception is the prerequisite of an intrigue, it would be wrong to call *Errors* a comedy of intrigue.[13] The Courtesan, it is true, plans to avenge herself on Antipholus, but she is prevented from putting her plans into practice; nothing else in the play can properly be called an intrigue. Nevertheless, we have, of course, in *Errors* a great deal of *passive* self-deception. It would exceed the limits of this book to examine Shakespeare's reception of the dramaturgic elements of intrigue and disguise, particularly Roman elements occurring in Plautus, not least in the splendid *Amphitruo*; instead we must refer the reader to existing studies on these points.[14]

Shakespeare's transformation of the eavesdropping convention in his later comedies is stunning, especially in *Troilus and Cressida* and in the famous gulling of Benedick and Beatrice in *Much Ado About Nothing*. Benedick begins scene II, iii with a soliloquy and then, as so often happens in New Comedy, the soliloquizer notices other people coming on stage and decides to overhear them. At this point, the pattern of the scene becomes more and more complicated because, when Benedick starts reflecting about Claudio's having become a 'fool of love', he does not realize that at this very moment that is precisely what he himself is about to become too. The complexity of the situation is then further increased by a doubling of eavesdropping: just as Benedick reacts in asides to what he has heard, so the intriguers secretly comment on the progress of their scheme. Benedick's aside: 'I should think this a gull, but that the white-bearded fellow speaks it. Knavery cannot sure hide himself in such reverence.' (II, iii, 118 – 120) is overheard by them and interpreted as signalling their success: 'He hath ta'en th'infection' (121). In

---

[13] For example, J.R. Brown calls *Errors* 'in the main, an intrigue comedy' (*Shakespeare and his Comedies* [London, [2]1962], p.54).

[14] Cf. S. Brotherton, *The Vocabulary of Intrigue in Roman Comedy* (Diss. Menasha, 1926); V.O. Freeburg, *Disguise Plots in Elizabethan Drama* (New York, 1915).

the gulling of Beatrice, the situation is then paralleled, most skilfully varied and even contrasted, because, although the intrigue takes on a parallel form, the method which Hero, Margaret and Ursula employ is different: whereas the men had cajoled Benedick into believing that Beatrice was deeply in love with him, the women point out to the eavesdropping Beatrice her own proud and disdainful attitude towards Benedick.

The great length of the Plautine stage and the vast size of the Elizabethan platform were certainly favourable to the frequent employment not only of eavesdropping, but also of the aside, which occurs above all in the superb overhearing scenes in both Plautus and Shakespeare and which has an interesting and even contrasting variety of forms in Roman comedy.[15] Plautus often has a character secretly address the audience and is not concerned about illusion, when a character produces a whole chain of asides, yet he also knows how to add credibility to this convention when he wants to. We find this especially in his eavesdropping scenes, where a character's aside is often a *spontaneous* but brief emotional reaction; and spontaneous asides, not simply directed at the audience, occur in ordinary dialogue as well. The speaker may even secretly address his partner, so that the aside retains a dialogic element. Although Plautus ultimately 'derived' this convention from Greek New Comedy, it has been shown that he sometimes transforms it into something new and original[16] and even *increases* the dramatic plausibility of the aside by additional devices. This happens when an aside is noticed or 'discovered' by the dialogue partner(s); either the character's silence is commented on, or the aside has been heard indistinctly, and therefore the speaker of the aside is asked to repeat his comment; formulae such as the following are used: 'Quid tu solus *tecum* loquere?' (*Aulularia* 190); 'quid tute *tecum*?' (*Mostellaria* 551).[17] The aside may be noticed as an inarticulate murmur (*Aulularia*),[18] or one character may make a secret remark while another is engaged with an occupation of some kind, so that he does not notice that an aside is being made.

Plautus developed a further type, namely the aside accompanied by the actor's turning or even moving away from his partner. Thus, in *Truculentus*, for example, a character addresses the following question to another *dramatis persona*: 'Quo te avortisti?' (357); this implies no less than a '*post eventum* stage direction for the delivery of the aside',[19] because here the speaker, besides talking secretly, has also changed his position. This device too is clearly meant to add verisimilitude to the convention, and the size of the platform stage

---

[15] Cf. also Duckworth, op. cit., p.82f.
[16] A. Barbieri, *Das Beiseitesprechen im antiken Drama* (Diss. Innsbruck, 1966), p.312; D. Bain, *Actors and Audience*; Donatus, in his commentary on Terence, was the first to discuss this quality of the aside, op. cit., I, 278.
[17] Bain, op. cit., p.156f.
[18] Barbieri, op. cit., p.224.
[19] Bain, op. cit., p.157.

provides the opportunity for this kind of delivery. According to Bain, the aside which is observed but not understood by the partner can even be traced back to Euripidean tragedy.[20]

In the plays of Shakespeare, the aside holds a very important dramaturgic position,[21] and there are some interesting connections between Plautus and Shakespeare in the use of this technique. If Plautus employs both the anti-illusionist secret address to the audience and the more 'realistic' forms of the aside, so does Shakespeare. It would be wrong to claim that Shakespeare gradually replaced the direct address to the audience by types fully compatible with the dramatic illusion. Yet we may say that there is a gradual increase of the latter types until the final plays, where a new 'Plautine' unconcern about more primitive dramaturgic elements makes itself felt. We find a similar 'Plautine' disregard of realism in the aside in the very early trilogy *Henry VI* and the early *Richard III*. Like Plautus, Shakespeare here inserts whole 'chains' of asides which awkwardly interrupt the regular flow of the dialogue. In the first part of *Henry VI*, Suffolk ponders in frequent asides whether he should woo Margaret (V, iii, 60 – 99), and in *Richard III*, Margaret, having entered the stage from a back door, showers Gloucester with curses in a series of asides (I, iii, 109 – 156).

On the other hand, *Richard III* also contains Gloucester's famous and 'realistic' aside-comment on a remark made by young Prince Edward. Since the young Prince has indistinctly heard, but not understood, Gloucester's aside: 'So wise so young, they say do never live long', Gloucester turns the original meaning of his comment into its very opposite and then, in a second aside, he compares his own verbal ingenuity, by which he manages to produce deceptive ambiguity, with that of the Vice of the Moralities:[22]

> I say, without characters fame lives long.
> [Aside] Thus, like the formal Vice, Iniquity,
> I moralize two meanings in one word.   III, i, 79 – 83

Like a Vice character, Gloucester deceives his victim with a double meaning so that young Edward is bound to mistake his words. Not only does Gloucester deceive Edward, but in two asides he even makes the audience aware of his deceptive verbal ambiguity. The fact that his first aside has been half perceived by his victim, and has to be re-formulated in order to provide it with an opposite meaning, reminds us of an aside-type in Plautus. The very

---

[20] Bain, ibid.

[21] On the aside in Shakespeare cf. my doctoral dissertation *Das Beiseitesprechen bei Shakespeare* (München, 1964), and more recently M.C. Gingrich, *Soliloquies, Asides, and Audience in English Renaissance Drama* (PhD thesis New Brunswick, 1978), and R. Weimann, *Shakespeare and the Popular Tradition in the Theatre* (Baltimore/London, 1978).

[22] Cf. W. Clemen, *A Commentary on Shakespeare's Richard III*, transl. by J. Bonheim (London, 1963), p.125.

content of Gloucester's first remark, too, is connected with the New Comedy tradition because it closely resembles the famous tag: 'Whom the gods love die young', found in Menander.[23] Furthermore, it is no mere coincidence that Shakespeare's *Errors*, too, contains this Plautine technique of a person 'discovering', but not fully understanding, an aside. In the first encounter of Antipholus S and Dromio with Adriana and Luciana, Dromio, imitating his master, tries in an aside to account for the incredible situation he finds himself in: 'O for my beads; I cross me for a sinner. / This is the fairy land . . .' (187 – 192). Again, this aside, spoken in an 'incredible' situation, is given dramatic verisimilitude by the fact that Luciana has noticed Dromio talking aside: 'Why prat'st thou to thyself and answer'st not?'. With regard to its form, this aside corresponds to the Plautine type of 'Quid tute tecum?'. Elsewhere in Shakespeare, we find a variety of responses from characters who observe another character talking aside. For example, in *Cymbeline*, Belarius notices that Arviragus, who has just spoken aside, 'wrings at some distress' (III, vi, 78), and in *The Tempest*, Ferdinand remarks to Miranda that her father, speaking aside, must be 'in some passion' (V, i, 143). There are, then, a number of dramatic situations in Shakespeare in which the content of an aside remains hidden from both the audience and certain of the characters on stage because the aside is merely whispered.

The turning or even moving away of the character who speaks the aside was taken over in Elizabethan and Shakespearean drama as an effective means of adding plausibility to the convention. In the anonymous play *A Pleasant Comedie of Faire Em The Miller's Daughter*, a stage direction suggests that the character Blanche is to make her aside-comment 'secretly at one end of the stage'.[24] Another stage direction in *The Famous Victories of Henry V* shows that Lady Katheren, who wants to make an aside, thinks it best to withdraw for a while from the dialogue situation and to conceal her words by moving away: 'She goes aside, and speakes as followeth'.[25] In Tourneur's *Revenger's Tragedy*, Lussurioso asks his partner, who has spoken an aside, 'Why dost walk aside?'.[26] Likewise, the 'turning away' of a character in order to make an aside is found in Elizabethan drama, as in *The Taming of a Shrew*.[27] All these examples clearly continue the Plautine tradition. Shakespeare does not find the need to insert stage directions suggesting the moving away of a character speaking aside; instead, he prefers to use situations for an aside in which a character is already standing outside the ordinary dramatic situation or in

---

[23] Menander Fragm. 111.

[24] In *The Shakespeare Apocrypha*, ed. C.F. Tucker Brooke (Oxford, 1908), p.290.

[25] In: *Chief Pre-Shakespearean Dramas*, ed. J.Q. Adams (Cambridge, Mass., 1924), p.668.

[26] C. Tourneur, *The Revenger's Tragedy*, ed. R.A. Foakes (London, 1966), I,iii,127, p.24.

[27] In: *Narrative and Dramatic Sources of Shakespeare*, ed. G. Bullough (London, 1957), I, 77.

which two separate groups have been formed. These types of the aside are, however, surpassed in effectiveness by those which, in form and content, are spontaneous reactions of a speaker to a certain dramatic situation. Effective instances of these can already be found in *Errors*.[28] The way in which Adriana in II, ii addresses Antipholus as her husband evokes an emotional response from him which is released in his talking to himself, as we have already seen:

> To me she speaks, she move s me for her theme;
> What, was I married to her in my dream?
> Or sleep I now, and think I hear all this?
> What error drives our eyes and ears amiss?   181 – 184

His secret attempt to cope with the confused situation culminates in his resolution: 'Until I know this sure uncertainty, / I'll entertain the offer'd fallacy.' Some moments later, he again tries to explain to himself the unexplainable: 'Am I in earth, in heaven, or in hell?', and again he makes up his mind to act according to what the people of Ephesus expect of him: 'I'll say as they say, and persever so, / And in this mist at all adventures go' (212 – 216). It would be quite wrong to assume that these asides were designed to be directly addressed to the audience in order to inform them beforehand of Antipholus's intentions; on the contrary, judged from the point of view of providing information, they are superfluous because the plot will soon develop in quite a different direction from that which Antipholus has anticipated, and therefore he fails to carry out his intention of *deliberately playing* the madman; all he can do is to *react* to situations which become increasingly threatening. A comparison with *Menaechmi* makes the point abundantly clear. In V, ii Menaechmus S notices that Senex and Matrona are beginning to take him for a madman. Then the idea occurs to him on the spur of the moment that *playing* the madman may be the only way to escape from them. In an aside directly addressed to the audience Menaechmus informs them of his intentions. Here the aside is necessary because the audience have to know in advance that his ensuing mad behaviour is to be taken as deliberate role-playing.

In *Errors*, soliloquies as well as asides are used very economically; they are always brief and do not get in the way of the dramatic opening of a scene, as they often do in the comedies of Plautus. Shakespeare seems already to have become aware of the dangers inherent in this convention. It would be beyond the scope of this book to give a survey of the variety of the asides in Shakespeare; suffice it to say that Shakespeare enormously extended the ways in which a speaker may express his emotional condition and articulate his innermost thoughts and feelings. It is, therefore, not surprising that the greatest examples occur in Shakespeare's tragedies, rather than in his comedies. In no other play is the convention of the aside transformed with

---

[28] That these already occur in Roman comedy was observed by Donatus, for example, op. cit., I, 278.

such originality and perfection as in *Macbeth*. Here the dramatic situation created by the Weird Sisters with their prophecies releases in Macbeth an inner process during which he becomes conscious of his secret desires and expresses them in a series of asides. He thus becomes increasingly isolated from his companions (I, iii, 116ff.). They notice his change of behaviour and observe how he is 'rapt'. At the end of this process Macbeth is absorbed in his evil thoughts to the point of forgetting that he is not alone, and so his asides give way to mere soliloquizing, whereupon he leaves the stage in order to put his evil plans into practice.[29]

The structure of a play is essentially determined by the interaction of the characters' entrances and exits. It is therefore worth asking the question how and with what kind of motivation the playwright causes his characters to meet and to separate; yet, strangely enough, this aspect is too often neglected in scholarly research. Menander's dramaturgy of entrances and exits produces a natural effect.[30] Plautus is sometimes not concerned with motivating the appearance of his characters; thus he has them enter 'on cue', just as they are expected or mentioned by the persons present on stage. This *lupus in fabula* effect may seem clumsy or artificial, and indeed, on one occasion Plautus makes fun of himself, as it were, when a character comments on the sudden arrival of another as an appearance similar to the 'lupum in sermone' (*Stichus*, V, 577). But in the theatre, rules other than 'realistic' ones are valid. Nor, indeed, is this convention so completely unrealistic; we all know from everyday experience that the 'speak of the devil' effect occurs in real life as well. Like Plautus, Shakespeare makes quite frequent use of this technique. Yet he very often adds credibility to the convention. We find a very good example in *Richard III*, where much is made of the contrast between reality and dramatic illusion. Richard, who is an excellent actor as well as a director, suggests that the action on stage is 'real' by the very fact that he occasionally compares it with a stage play; and Buckingham likens Richard's appearance in III, iv at the right moment to the entrance of an actor on his cue (26).[31]

How, then, do *Errors* and its Plautine sources compare in their motivation of the characters' entrances and exits? It has recently been suggested that Plautus motivates both entrances and exits carefully,[32] but this is not entirely borne out by *Menaechmi* and *Amphitruo*. Exits are sometimes not provided with credible motivation and are not always conducive to the further development of the plot. For example, after she has convicted her husband of his theft, the Matrona exits in IV, ii with the remark: 'never shall you enter the house

---

29 Cf. my discussion of the aside in *Macbeth*, *Das Beiseitesprechen bei Shakespeare*, p.71 – 74.
30 Cf. F.H. Sandbach, *The Comic Theatre of Greece and Rome* (London, 1977), p.77.
31 Clemen, *A Commentary on Shakespeare's Richard III*, p.138.
32 Blänsdorf, 'Plautus', p.190.

unless you bring the mantle with you.' ('nam domum numquam introibis, nisi feres pallam simul.' 662). She does not suggest that she intends to take any further action against him; it appears that she is waiting at home for his return. In V, i she re-enters unexpectedly because she wants to see why her husband has been away for so long: 'I'll go out and see if my husband won't soon be back home.' ('Provisam quam mox vir meus redeat domum.' 704). This re-entry, which lacks any connection with her earlier exit, is necessary at this point because Menaechmus S must have a chance to meet her. Peniculus and Erotium leave the stage for good while the action is still in full flow, and the Matrona, having fled in panic from her 'mad husband', does not return either. As these loose ends show, we have in *Menaechmi* some comparatively slack links between scenes.

There are a good many examples where the entrance of a character lacks motivation. When Menaechmus S enters from Erotium's house, he appears with no particular intention – he is still relishing in his mind the pleasures he has just experienced. The other Menaechmus, too, enters on several occasions without having a real motive. For example, in IV, iii he leaves the stage with the intention of asking his friends what he should do next after Erotium has turned her back on him. This is a somewhat clumsy trick the author is forced to use in order to keep him off-stage for some time. When he returns in V, i, he still does not know what to do, and is complaining even more bitterly: 'Well! By Jove, I certainly do lead a miserable life!' ('eu edepol! ne ego homo vivo miser.' 908). His reappearance is, however, necessary from a dramaturgic point of view because the Senex and the Medicus have to mistake him for his 'mad' twin brother.

In *Amphitruo*, most entrances and exits are much better motivated, but even here some of them serve merely to provide opportunities for new mistakings of identity. Thus Alcumena on one occasion enters from her house for the sole purpose of delivering a reflective soliloquy, whereupon she meets her real husband (II, ii, 633 – 653). Later on, the real Amphitruo leaves the stage with the intention of fetching Naucrates from the boat; again, it is necessary for Amphitruo to be temporarily absent so as to provide an opportunity for another mistaking of identity. Yet, he returns without Naucrates, because the introduction of a new character at this point would have been superfluous. However, this should not be condemned as lack of motivation, for, as Marti has shown, there is a dramatic purpose behind Amphitruo's failure to fetch Naucrates: it is a further disappointment for him, and thus his isolation increases dangerously.[33] Moreover, inconsistencies of motivation are not noticed during a performance; indeed, they are perfectly in tune with the 'logic' of theatrical game-playing.

---

[33] H. Marti, *Untersuchungen zur dramatischen Technik bei Plautus und Terenz* (Winterthur, 1959), p.44.

Our comparison with Plautus helps us to realize that Shakespeare, by contrast, pays much closer attention to both the entrances and the exits of his characters. There is practically no exit in *Errors* which is not clearly motivated in the sense that it is the immediate cause of the character's re-entry. Thus, in contrast to the convention of New Comedy, the scenes in Shakespeare are on the one hand frequently distinguished from one another by the 'clear stage' convention, while on the other hand they are closely linked together by the interdependence of exits and entrances. Shakespeare's principal device here is the series of orders which the Dromios are given and which they attempt to carry out. Whereas in *Menaechmi* there is only one occasion on which the slave Messenio exits with a particular order, in *Errors* most of the confusions occur precisely because one of the Dromios is carrying out the order of his own Antipholus, when he happens to meet the other one.[34] The knot of the action is thus bound much more tightly than in Plautus. This produces a certain 'cogency' completely lacking in *Menaechmi*.

2. *The problem of Act division*

It is impossible to examine Shakespeare's reception of the comedies of Plautus without discussing the vexed question of Act division. The view shared by most Shakespeare critics has been discussed at length by H.C. Snuggs,[35] who tries to show that Shakespeare did not care much about the convention of the five-Act structure, but rather composed his plays in terms of scenes. There is, however, far too much evidence which speaks against this conclusion. The soundest view appears to be that of Emrys Jones and G.K. Hunter, who take a middle position: Shakespeare did not abandon the five-Act convention altogether, but neither did he adhere to it strictly and consistently. Nevertheless, 'many of Shakespeare's plays observe the five-Act arrangement'.[36]

This whole question is far from being of secondary importance because it would be interesting to know whether Shakespeare wrote in terms of five

---

[34] Cf. also M. Pfister, who finds that in *Errors* two independent chains of events are formed, which continually interfere with each other (M. Pfister, *Studien zum Wandel der Perspektivenstruktur in elisabethanischen und jakobäischen Komödien* [München, 1974], p.64).

[35] H.L. Snuggs, *Shakespeare and Five Acts* (New York/Washington/Hollywood, 1960); cf. also W.T. Jewkes, *Act Division in Elizabethan and Jacobean Plays 1583 – 1616* (Hamden, 1958) and G. Heuser, *Die aktlose Dramaturgie William Shakespeares* (Diss. Marburg, 1956).

[36] E. Jones, *Scenic Form in Shakespeare* (Oxford, 1971), p.67; G.K. Hunter, 'Were there Act-Pauses on Shakespeare's Stage?' in: *English Renaissance Drama. Essays in Honor of Madeleine Doran & Mark Eccles*, ed S. Henning, R. Kimbrough, R. Knowles (Carbondale, 1976), p.15 – 35; Leech, too, argues in favour of five distinct stages ('The Use of a Five-Act Structure', *Neuere Sprachen*, 1 [1957], 249 – 263).

rhythmically alternating movements; if he did, then they must in some way or other have been conveyed to the audience during a performance. In his fine article G.K. Hunter also argued in favour of short Act pauses because 'it often seems that a pause, of the appropriate length, can cause tension to increase rather than elapse'.[37] And these pauses must have been filled by brief music performed by the musicians of the public theatres. In any case, Hunter has collected enough evidence for the existence of the five Act convention even on the popular stages. Our own considerations will confirm Hunter's findings from a different perspective.

The confusions that arise in this matter can mainly be traced back to T.W. Baldwin's lengthy study, which, like his book on the compositional genetics of *Errors*, distorts the facts. Baldwin calls his book *Shakspere's Five-Act Structure*, but in fact only about a quarter of the work is concerned with Shakespeare. He starts with the assumption that 'Terence was at the basis of the grammar-school system. Along with him, Plautus was frequently used as a supplement'.[38] Because of his strong bias against Plautus his argument falters and even becomes contradictory, and it is most strange that practically all critics have nevertheless accepted his 'conclusions'. He tries to persuade us into believing that Lambinus's edition of Plautus of 1576 was the 'standard annotated edition'[39] — he has to base his argument on an edition like this one which does not always use Act divisions. However, even Baldwin has to concede two facts which completely undermine his argument: a) Lambinus was 'exceptional in that he regarded these act-divisions as unwarranted innovations'.[40] b) As the overwhelming majority of Plautus editions had these divisions, Shakespeare 'may [. . .] also still have had his old grammar school edition of Plautus in addition to that of Lambinus. This old edition might have proved handy on act-divisions.'[41] There is, then, no reason to doubt that Shakespeare worked with a text of Plautine comedies containing these divisions, and indeed, as we shall see, the evidence for this is overwhelming. Many English dramatists looked to Plautus rather than Terence for their classical model for comic drama. The plain facts are that no Terentian play served Shakespeare as a source for any of his comedies, whereas he made extensive use of the Plautine *Menaechmi* and *Amphitruo*. I shall argue, therefore, that Shakespeare quite 'naturally' became familiar with the convention of Act division through the plays of Plautus and that it is absurd to assume with

---

[37] Hunter, op. cit., p.31.

[38] *Shakspere's Five-Act Structure*, p.3.

[39] *Five-Act Structure*, p.667 – 81, 668 – 94. Baldwin is unable to present any hard facts in support of his view that Shakespeare worked with the Lambinus edition. The scholia to which he refers are not exceptional, but are made in analogy to Donatus's comment on Terence.

[40] Ibid., p.668.

[41] Ibid. The Lambinus edition of 1588 has Act divisions in eight plays, among them being *Amphitruo*.

Baldwin that he 'reconstructs [*Menaechmi* and *Amphitruo*] into the *Andria* formula of Terentian structure'.[42] Yet first of all it is necessary to consider briefly the use of the Act convention in the tradition of New Comedy.

In the comedies of Menander and those of his contemporaries whose names have been preserved, the action was divided into Acts by the appearance from time to time of a Chorus.[43] Plautus and Terence disposed of this Chorus completely and this, together with the fact that the Plautine and Terentian manuscripts do not contain Act divisions, has led scholars to assume that Acts lost their importance in Roman comedy, despite the fact that both Horace and Varro define a play as being divided into five Acts.[44] Along with other classicists, Duckworth argues that, since the plays of New Comedy have an *actio continua*, a 'continuous action', the question of whether there were acts becomes immaterial.[45] However, it seems to me that such a view does not do full justice to the practical concerns of the theatre. It is helpful to the audience if they are made to realize that the action is unfolding in several units and movements, and these may be pointed out by the rhythmic recurrence of brief pauses, filled, perhaps, by a few 'flourishes' of music or other pointers which do not really interrupt the continuous flow of the action, but which help to make the structural organization more lucid. The written text of Plautine and Terentian comedy as we have it does not, of course, indicate these non-verbal elements of the original performance; yet we can be fairly certain that such devices were used, and may indeed have contributed considerably to the overall effect, because there is an interesting exception: in the Plautine *Pseudolus* a character leaves the stage telling the audience: 'I'll soon be back, though, and won't keep you waiting. Meantime you'll be entertained by the fluteplayer here.' ('sed mox exibo, non ero vobis morae; tibicen vos interibi hic delectaverit', 573a), and then Act II starts afresh.

The Act divisions of modern editions of Plautus go back to manuscripts of the 15th century, and in the 16th century the humanist J.B. Pio inserted them into all editions.[46] The same had first been done with the comedies of Terence. The humanists took it for granted that comedies had to be divided into Acts, not least because Donatus discussed the plays of Terence in terms of Acts. How, then, did Pio decide where an Act division had to be? He followed the *scaena vacua* or 'clear stage' criterion that somehow seems to reflect the Act division of the Greek models of the Roman comedies. However, since the Roman transformations are often considerable, and since in a play there are sometimes more and sometimes fewer than the four required *scaena vacua*

---

[42] Ibid., p.666.

[43] Cf., for example, Duckworth, op. cit., p.99.

[44] Horace, *Ars Poetica* 189 – 90: 'neve minor neu sit quinto productior actu fabula quae posci et spectanda reponi'; Varro is referred to by Donatus, cf. Duckworth, op. cit., p.98.

[45] Duckworth, op. cit., p.101.

[46] Cf., Duckworth, op. cit., p.98.

Plautus Comicus

5 From *Liber Chronicarum* by the humanist
Hartmann Schedel

situations, his decision must necessarily have been difficult or even haphazard. Nevertheless, many of his divisions make very good sense, and those Renaissance humanist editions of Terence which have Act divisions generally accepted his decisions.

Since Baldwin has a marked and even 'irrational' preference for Terence and a much lower opinion of Plautus, he presents the factual evidence uncritically: For instance, while he has a chapter on 'Terence Texts in England', he fails to give us a corresponding account of the spread of Plautine texts in England. What makes his whole line of argument so wrong is that he does not see that Shakespeare's own dramatic temperament is far more akin to Plautus than to Terence. Since most Plautus editions, too, were divided into Acts, we have the best of reasons for assuming that the edition Shakespeare used will also have contained these divisions. Yet the really important question has still to be asked: in what way are Act divisions that were inserted by the humanists structurally motivated and plausible? If there is a positive answer to this question, we are fully justified in examining the effect they had on Shakespeare.

Before beginning our closer inspection, two misunderstandings must be cleared up which have so far hindered critics from taking an unbiased view of the problem. Just as classicists have argued that the *actio continua* in New Comedy makes the question of Act division irrelevant, so Shakespeare critics have adduced the 'continuous action' of Shakespeare's plays as proof that he composed his plays without paying any attention to dividing them into Acts. Thus W.W. Greg pointed out that, shortly after the beginning of Act V, Antipholus and his Dromio reappear, although they left the stage only a short while before, at the end of the preceding Act. From this Greg concluded that Act division in the Folio was inserted by the editors in the process of printing.[47] Given the correspondence of the *actio continua* and the 'continuous action', Greg's argument appears to be really without force. He failed to realize, for example, that at the end of Act IV in the *Amphitruo* comedy Amphitruo falls to the ground and continues to lie there until the beginning of Act V. Similar occasions can be found in French classical drama,[48] and in the division between Acts III and IV of *A Midsummer Night's Dream* the Folio has the famous stage direction that the lovers should 'sleepe all the Act'. We must therefore conclude that continuous action and Act division need not be mutually exclusive, as long as the interval between the Acts remains short.

The second misunderstanding is the notion that the exposition of a drama is complete only after *all* the characters have been introduced to the audience. Snuggs, who takes this view, thinks that in *Menaechmi* the exposition ends *after* the first appearance of the traveller twin in II, i, so that he considers the Act division before the end of the first scene of Act II unjustified.[49] Snuggs and others do not seem to have read carefully enough the Evanthian definition of *protasis*, according to which, as we shall see, part of the action is withheld from the audience in order to create suspense.[50] Besides, the very Prologue to a play like *Menaechmi* mentions the arrival of the traveller Menaechmus so that there is no need to regard the exposition as extending to II, 1.

As far as *Menaechmi* and *Amphitruo* are concerned, the Act divisions do on the whole make good sense in that they coincide with the various stages of the plot development and agree with the Evanthian and Donatian definitions of the structure of comedy, which we shall discuss below. The first Act of both *Menaechmi* and *Amphitruo* contains the exposition, although not all the characters have been introduced yet. The action of *Menaechmi*, which consists mainly of confusions of identity, starts with the beginning of Act II, when the other twin arrives only to be taken for Menaechmus E by the Cook and Erotium. The third Act forms a unit of its own, since the Parasite, having returned from the Forum in disappointment, mistakes the identity of Menaechmus S and therefore begins to plan his revenge on his Patron. It is very interesting that the beginning of each new Act appears to be emphasized by the entry of a *new* character. If Acts II and III started with an emphatic

---

[47] Greg, *The Shakespeare First Folio* (Oxford, 1955), p.201.
[48] E.g. in Racine's *Britannicus*.
[49] Snuggs, op. cit., p.66.
[50] 'pars reticetur ad populi exspectationem tenendam', *Aeli Donati Commentum Terenti*, I, 27.

beginning in the first appearance of Menaechmus S and the return of the Parasite, the fourth Act is again set off as a separate entity by the very first entry of the Matrona, who immediately joins in the revenge of the Parasite. This revenge, carried out as an intrigue, then forms the dramatic focus of Act IV. Act V of *Menaechmi* is exceptional in so far as here the confusions continue right into the *anagnorisis*. In any case, this final Act presents a new phase of the play's dramatic development, especially in the appearance of the Senex as an entirely new character. In *Menaechmi*, the dramatist succeeds in maintaining dramatic suspense right until the end, not least by means of the appearance of a new character in each Act (even if in Act III the new character is only the maid of the Courtesan).

In a perceptive article W. Steidle has shown that scene III, i should be regarded as the pivotal centre of the whole play.[51] This scene consists of Peniculus's soliloquy, which he delivers returning from the Forum in disappointment about his missed lunch. Here it can be seen that Plautus is a master of symmetrical structure. The soliloquy is symmetrically flanked on each side by two scenes of mistaken identity − the two scenes preceding III, i, (in II, ii Menaechmus S is mistaken by the Cook and in II, iii by Erotium) and the two scenes following it (in these he is taken for his brother by Peniculus and Erotium's maid). Steidle also points out that the two scenes next to the pivot, namely II, iii and III, ii, are the more important ones.[52]

The Act structure of *Amphitruo* presents a surprisingly comparable picture. The exposition in Act I is followed by the beginning of the complications in Act II with the return of the real Amphitruo, and the Act then focuses on Alcumena's despair. Scene III, i is again the pivot of the play: Jupiter enters as the 'stage director' of his own play and informs the audience of what he intends to do in order to make sure that the play ends like a proper comedy. This soliloquy is then flanked by two scenes resembling each other, since they are both dominated by Alcumena. All these Acts are marked by an emphatic beginning with the appearance of an important character: Act IV, for example, begins with the return of the real Amphitruo, who finds himself locked out of his own house. Jupiter, who has come from the house in order to face Amphitruo, at the end of the same Act exits into the house with thunder and lightning, whereupon Amphitruo falls to the ground. After Jupiter's theophany, Act V starts by bringing the truth gradually to light. The answer to the question of what the individual Acts contribute to the development of the action is simply: dramatic intensification.

Some interesting connections between Plautus's technique of paralleling and contrasting and Shakespeare's use of the same devices have been pointed

[51] W. Steidle, 'Zur Komposition von Plautus' "Menaechmi" ', *RhM*, 114 (1971), p.247 − 61.

[52] Steidle, op. cit., p.251.

out above all by H.F. Brooks,[53] and it is unnecessary to repeat his findings. Instead, we shall concentrate here on the fact that Shakespeare's use of symmetry and Act division should be seen in close relation to the Plautine *Menaechmi* and *Amphitruo*. Just as Plautus makes scene III, i the centre of his comedies, so does Shakespeare. In III, i of *Errors*, the real husband Antipholus E is locked out of his own house, and this produces a splendid major climax in the long series of confusions beginning as early as Act I. Whereas in *Menaechmi* Peniculus in a soliloquy complains about having been tricked out of a meal he had been promised, in Shakespeare the real husband returns home to have his meal, only to be locked out by his own wife. The soliloquy is replaced by a brilliant dramatic scene, which ironically anticipates the final 'gossips' feast'.[54] Yet the symmetrical structure bears an astonishing resemblance to that of *Menaechmi*. Just as the central scene in the latter play is flanked by scenes which have important features in common, so in *Errors* the scenes next to the pivotal centre III, i are related to each other by a thematic similarity, although at first sight this is perhaps less clearly noticeable than in *Menaechmi*. If in III, ii Antipholus S voices feelings of possessive love towards Luciana, then this was in a way 'triggered off' in II, ii by Adriana, when she articulated her possessive desire for him as her supposed husband. Furthermore, at the end of Act III Antipholus S comes very close to meeting his twin brother; he, as it were, just fails to find him by the 14 lines which are exchanged between Angelo, the Second Merchant and the Officer. Interestingly enough, at the end of Act III of *Menaechmi*, too, the twins likewise miss each other by a few moments – the 12 lines by which Menaechmus E comes too late.

Although surprisingly close links between the structural symmetry in Plautus and Shakespeare have emerged, we have to bear in mind Brooks's sound warning which he expressed when he discussed the balanced groupings of characters, namely 'that one and the same feature commonly has antecedents in more than one tradition',[55] and especially in the Moralities and Interludes. This is quite true, although the authors of these plays were 'humanists' themselves and may owe to classical drama more than is usually recognized. We remember that we have seen how, for example, the comic subplot of *Cambises* reflects quite clearly the atmosphere of Plautine comedy.

There can be no doubt that the structural correspondences between *Errors* and *Menaechmi* are anything but accidental. Over and above these, however, there is the dramaturgic similarity of Act division. Shakespeare employs the same technique of marking the beginning of a new Act by the appearance of a new character. After the exposition has been presented in Act I, a new tone is set by the first appearance of the two sisters Adriana and Luciana. At the

[53] H.F. Brooks, op. cit., p.58ff.
[54] This has, for example, been observed by Foakes, op. cit., p.40.
[55] Brooks, op. cit., p.64.

beginning of III, i the denizen Antipholus makes his first, delayed entrance. At the opening of Act IV, we encounter the second merchant as a new character, and the Act reaches its climax in the only situation in which Dr Pinch is seen on stage. Act V opens with characters we already know, but before long a final new character, Aemilia, makes her entrance as the important *dea ex machina*.

Shakespeare not only emphasizes the beginning of most Acts in *Errors* by a new character, he also concludes Acts II to IV by means of deliberately parallel situations, a fact which was remarked by Baldwin. He shows that at the end of each of these Acts Antipholus soliloquizes about the effects of witchcraft, to which he attributes his predicament, and declares that he wishes to leave the city as soon as possible.[56] The effect of this concluding situation is reinforced by a final couplet. (Only the two concluding lines of Antipholus S in Act IV are exceptional in that they do not form a rhyming couplet.) These parallel endings make a strong impact of their own in a performance; with them, Shakespeare achieves a rhythm which makes the audience aware of the great movements of the plot, each of which marks an intensification of the confusions of the major characters.

It is now clear that in *Errors* Shakespeare adopted the structural convention of Act division, and evidence from elsewhere in his dramatic work points in the same direction.[57] Apart from the four appearances of the Chorus in *Henry V* and *Pericles*, this evidence is very strong in *The Tempest*, where the Act divisions are generally believed to derive from Shakespeare's own hand.[58] Here he begins Act V with the same characters who have just left the stage. There can, then, be no serious doubt that, when Shakespeare studied the Plautine *Menaechmi* and *Amphitruo*, he became directly acquainted with the five-Act convention. Since most editions of Plautus, too, had Act divisions, there is no need whatsoever to follow Baldwin's curious view that, in order to study this convention, Shakespeare had to turn to Terence. We shall see that in a good number of his later plays he employed the convention and that he adopted it in some of his tragedies as well. G.K. Hunter is, I think, right in claiming that in this respect New Comedy was more influential than Senecan tragedy. However, Hunter concludes that the ultimate authority behind Elizabethan Act division was Terence because he, rather than Seneca, was the major author studied in the Grammar Schools.[59] Although this is true, it must be objected that what really counts is not what the immature schoolboy studied at school but what the adult dramatist took as his model; in England, as we have seen, the dramatists in most cases preferred to follow Plautus in the art of

[56] *On the Compositional Genetics of 'The Comedy of Errors'* (Urbana, 1965), p.73ff.

[57] Snuggs's claim that there is an 'artificiality of the act-divisions' in *Errors* is unfounded (p.59).

[58] Cf. W.W. Greg, *The Shakespeare First Folio*, p.418, n.l.

[59] 'Seneca and the Elizabethans: a case-study in ''influence'' ' in: *Dramatic Identities and the Cultural Tradition. Critical Essays by G.K. Hunter* (Liverpool, 1978), p.166 – 7.

play-writing. However, Hunter's attempt to argue in favour of Act pauses on the Elizabethan stage is convincing and confirms our own results. In any case, the view that the 'theory of the five-act structure is largely a red herring'[60] should at last be discarded.

3. *Towards a definition of the action in New Comedy*

We do not really know how Aristotle, in the lost second part of his *Poetics*, defined the nature of comedy. Yet a tentative reconstruction seems possible, although opinions are divided on this matter. It is probable that he defined the structure of comedy as he found it in New Comedy, although this has recently been questioned.[61] However, it is certain that 'only in New Comedy are comedy's principles in terms of plot construction closely assimilated to those of tragedy.'[62] This is supported by a well-known anecdote which tells how Menander on one occasion said he had almost finished a new play, having just invented its plot; the only minor thing still left to do, he said, was to write the verse. For our purpose it may suffice to recall that, from the beginning of the European reception of classical comedy, the notion of the close interrelation of tragedy and comedy was prevalent – and New Comedy itself developed from Euripidean tragedy. As we have seen, this interrelation was something which particularly interested the humanists. In the Evanthian Essay *De Fabula*, included in many Renaissance editions of Terence and in some of Plautus, and undoubtedly familiar to Shakespeare, certain comic plot elements reveal their 'origins' in tragedy; yet at the same time a new attempt is made to define the overall comic structure. According to Evanthius and Donatus, a comedy consists of four parts: *prologue*, *protasis*, *epitasis* and *catastrophe*.[63] This structural organization is again based on the assumption of Act division. When Shakespeare critics use the terms *protasis* and *epitasis*, they generally follow Baldwin's interpretation, which here again, however, is not altogether reliable.

---

[60] M. Mincoff, 'Shakespeare's Comedies and the Five-Act Structure', *Bulletin de la Faculté des Lettres de Strasbourg*, 63 (1965), 131 – 146, esp. 145. This does not contradict the argument put forward by E. Jones (*Scenic Form in Shakespeare*, p.69f.), that many Shakespearean plays are marked by a notable two-part structure and that during an Elizabethan performance there was obviously an interval after the end of Act III. On the contrary, it is, I think, remarkable that this notable two-part structure has been anticipated by a play such as the *Menaechmi*. The action of this comedy makes a fresh start after Act III with the first appearance of the revengeful Matrona and with Menaechmus E returning from the Forum after his long absence.

[61] Cf. R. Janko, *Aristotle on Comedy*, p.67.

[62] Ibid.

[63] Evanthius, *De Fabula* in: *Aeli Donati Commentum Terenti*, I, 22.

Baldwin is responsible for the common false belief that the *protasis*, the exposition of a play, comprises Acts I and II;[64] he misrepresents and partly misunderstands the definitions of Evanthius and Donatus and their reception by the humanists. The Evanthian definition which we find, as a rule, in the humanist editions, reads as follows: 'protasis primus actus initiumque est dramatis';[65] and Donatus adds that in the protasis 'pars argumenti explicatur, pars reticetur ad populi expectationem tenendam.'[66] That is to say, as we have already argued, that the *protasis* does not give a complete introduction to the 'argument', it reveals only part of it and remains silent on the rest so as to keep the audience in suspense. This does not mean to say that the *protasis* could never extend well into the second Act. In *Miles Gloriosus*, for example, Plautus inserts the Prologue in Act II, but this is an exceptional case within the still valid Evanthian definition. Although Baldwin does not disregard this clear-cut definition of the *protasis*, he unduly concentrates his attention on a few exceptional humanist definitions, which, however, were by no means as influential as he would have us believe. One of these, and, for Baldwin, the most important one, comes from the humanist Willichius, who found it necessary to modify the Evanthian theory and to maintain that the *protasis* comprises Act I *and* Act II.[67] However, this theory ran counter to the received opinion in humanist circles. If Baldwin rightly admits that not even Scaliger was a universally recognized authority (although Scaliger, be it noted, confined the *protasis* to Act I with the exception of the *Miles Gloriosus*[68]), then he would have had still more cause for reservation in the case of Willichius.

The *epitasis*, the proper development of the action, which begins with Act II, is described by Evanthius as '*incrementum processusque turbarum* ac totius [. . .] nodus erroris', and Donatus further defines it as the 'involutio argumenti, cuius elegantia connectitur'.[69] It ends with Act IV and is then followed by the catastrophe of the final Act. Again Baldwin has recourse to less common theories and tries to persuade his readers that the *epitasis* is situated mainly in Act III (or in Acts III and IV).[70] The picture which he presents is again quite incorrect, since he misinterprets some of the evidence. There can be no denying the fact that the received opinion on matters of dramatic construction was that, while the *protasis* takes place in Act I, the *epitasis* happens in Act II to

---

[64] Baldwin, *Shakspere's Five-Act Structure*, p.312 – 332 and esp. p.703; cf. also M.T. Herrick, *Comic Theory in the Sixteenth Century* (Urbana, 1950), p.109.

[65] Evanthius, op. cit., p.32.

[66] Donatus, *Excerpta de Comoedia in Aeli Donati Commentum*, I, 27.

[67] Baldwin, *Shakspere's Five-Act Structure*, p.575.

[68] Julius Caesar Scaliger, *Poetices Libri Septem*, ed. A. Buck (Stuttgart/Bad Cannstatt, 1964), p.14.

[69] Evanthius, op. cit., p.22; Donatus, p.27 – 28.

[70] *Five-Act Structure*, passim. Leech, too, thinks that the *epitasis* takes place mainly in Act III with an added movement in Act IV ('The Structure of the Last Plays', *ShS*, 11 [1958], 19 – 30).

IV, and the play concludes with the catastrophe of Act V. If sometimes the term *epitasis* seems to be applied to Act III, then the term is used in the restricted sense of the *intensified* stages of the tying of the knot; yet the 'involutio argumenti' undoubtedly begins with Act II.

Baldwin very frequently speaks of the tripartite structure which was, of course, not *created* by Terence, who adapted Menander's plays. Yet Baldwin wrongly claims that this tripartite structure which, he thinks, can best be seen in *Andria*, was *perfected* by Willichius, and that this marked the end of Renaissance theory of comic structure. Willichius, who, according to Baldwin, had a practical sense of theatre, tried to assign a certain function to each Act: the *protasis*, which for him comprises Acts I and II is followed by the *epitasis*, located in the third Act, while Act IV contains the preparation for the final catastrophe in Act V. Baldwin finds that this structural division underlies the play *Studentes* by the humanist Stymmelius. He appears to admire the fact that the plot of this play unfolds with a 'machine-like precision'.[71] In his later discussion of *Menaechmi* and *Amphitruo* he likewise praises the alleged 'machinery' of the plot. While we may well doubt the usefulness of such a concept of dramatic structure for our understanding of Shakespeare's dramatic art, critics have followed Baldwin's estimation of Willichius. He even suggests that, when Shakespeare worked on *Errors*, he also used a copy of the Willichius Terence which 'would have furnished the *Andria* five-act formula which Shakespeare used.'[72]

How superfluous all these assumptions are, becomes clear when we realize that Shakespeare came to know the received Donatian and Evanthian definition of *protasis* and *epitasis* through his close study of the Plautine *Menaechmi* and *Amphitruo*. To assume with Baldwin and others that Shakespeare looked for a complicated definition of comic structure of the kind offered by Willichius is to imply that Shakespeare had the temperament of an academic scholar, which he certainly hadn't. Surely, Shakespeare was a practical dramatist who was not excessively concerned with the intricacies of dramatic rules, and, as his plays show, Evanthius and Donatus, reprinted in the Renaissance editions, were sufficient for him. His dramatic temperament was obviously similar to that of his Spanish contemporary Lope de Vega, who likewise wrote his plays for the popular stage. In his famous essay *Arte nuevo de hacer comedias* (*The New Art of Making Comedies*) of 1609, Lope claims with some pride that he accepts only the basic rules for writing comedies, such as Act division, but that when he starts writing a play, he locks up the more intricate rules with six keys, that is, he considers it most important to give free rein to his dramatic imagination.[73] And Shakespeare would also probably have agreed with Uranie's view in Molière's *Critique de l'Ecole des Femmes*, that those

---

[71] *Five-Act Structure*, p.246.
[72] Ibid., p.714.
[73] In A.H. Gilbert, ed., *Literary Criticism. Plato to Dryden* (Detroit, 1962), p.542.

who talk most about the *epitasis* and the rules of dramatic construction and pretend to know them better than everyone else, write plays which nobody likes.[74] Shakespeare too refused to allow his dramatic imagination to be constrained by any minute theoretical considerations. Indeed, we can only be grateful for the fact that Donatus did *not* define the *epitasis* in greater detail and that he did *not* identify its various stages with the Acts, thus leaving enough scope for the playwright to develop the structure of each individual play.

In *Menaechmi* the *protasis* coincides with Act I, where Menaechmus E unfolds his plan to deceive his wife, the starting point for all the subsequent confusions. The *epitasis* starts with II, i, when Menaechmus S and Messenio appear for the first time. Similarly, in *Amphitruo* the *epitasis* begins with II, i, when the real Amphitruo enters, and this has the same effect of increasing the complications of the plot. In this comedy the end of the *epitasis* is marked by the conclusion of Act IV, whereas in *Menaechmi* it extends well into Act V. To be more precise, what we often find in Menandrian New Comedy as well as in Roman Comedy, and frequently in Shakespeare, is an intensification of the *epitasis* in the third Act which then appears like a nodal point; but even so, further complications are often added in Act IV so that the movement leading to the catastrophe does not begin before Act V.

Turning to *Errors*, we can now see clearly that here, too, the *protasis* ends when Act II begins, because the first appearance of the new characters Adriana and Luciana increases the confusions of identity. The *epitasis*, beginning with Act II, reaches a first climax in Act III. In Act IV, however, the 'involutio' of the action is further intensified by the appearance of the conjurer, and it is finally resolved in the comic catastrophe of Act V. Yet, Shakespeare also masterfully 'undercuts' the concepts of *protasis* and *epitasis* by making Dromio E, who first appears towards the end of Act I, the cause of the first confusion so that the 'incrementum processusque turbarum' already starts within the *protasis* itself. Shakespeare's expository technique in *Errors* prompted an admiring remark from Friedrich Schiller in a letter to Goethe of April 25, 1797, when he called the opening of *Errors* exceptional in that 'the exposition is already part of the development'.[75]

According to Evanthius, the comic catastrophe is the 'conversio rerum' and leads to 'iucundos exitus',[76] 'happy endings', in Act V with the final recognition of the errors and of the influence of a benign Fortune. But can the 'conversio' of the action in any way be located in the play's structure? Neither Evanthius nor Donatus is inclined to define precisely where the beginning of the resolution must come. A more categorical statement on this was made by

---

[74] *Critique de l'Ecole des Femmes* in: *Oeuvres Complètes de Molière*, ed. M. Rat (Paris, 1951), p.541–2.

[75] *Der Briefwechsel zwischen Schiller und Goethe* (Leipzig, 1955), I, 326; in *Amphitruo* Plautus had anticipated a similar technique.

[76] Evanthius, op. cit., p.22.

J.C. Scaliger in his over-elaborate and oversystematic *Poetics*. He calls this final complication the *catastasis* and defines it as 'that phase of the plot or situation where it is thrown into confusion by the tempest to which fortune has led it.'[77]

Baldwin, who seems to have had a foible for exceptional definitions, has no doubt that this concept reinforced the structural system of Willichius.[78] In a recent article D.C. Boughner makes a fresh attempt to demonstrate that the concept of *catastasis* must have been familiar to Shakespeare[79] and that he adopted it from Ben Jonson. Boughner maintains that, particularly in his *Tempest*, Shakespeare 'manipulates the four-part structure invented by Terence and described by Donatus, revived by Machiavelli and given a final critical explanation by Scaliger, and naturalized on the English stage by Ben Jonson'.[80] However, this line of argument, working with wrong assumptions, does not really carry conviction: Ben Jonson, who, as Boughner correctly states, did not consider Terence, but rather Plautus, as his model, merely discussed the *catastasis* as a term, yet he did not develop any theory of comedy which Shakespeare might have adopted in his *Tempest*.[81] It is impossible to see in the *catastasis* an important new element that is not already included in the definition of *epitasis*, which in the words of Evanthius implies not only the 'incrementum processusque turbarum' but also '*totius* nodus *erroris*', that is, the entire *complexity* of the entanglements. Introducing the *catastasis* involves a playwright in unnecessary complications, and it seems almost certain that it would have appeared too schematic and therefore unattractive to Shakespeare.

In order to understand more fully the nature of the action of New Comedy and how it was seen in the Renaissance, it is necessary to consider briefly the precise meaning of the definition of the development of the action as 'totius nodus *erroris*'. This definition provides important proof of the fact that the classical theory of comedy was closely modelled on that of tragedy. 'Error' is here supposed to be the major *agens* of the comic plot. It is interesting to observe that the Renaissance humanists did not always take this definition of comic action literally, because they did not strictly consider the stages of the comic action to be interrelated by causal logic. The admirers of Plautus in particular knew only too well that he often prefers a looser conjunction of the different parts. And the followers of Terence blamed Plautus for being too careless about a plausible coherence of the action in his comedies.[82] Moreover,

---

[77] Scaliger, op. cit., p.5; I have used D.C. Boughner's translation, 'Jonsonian Structure in *The Tempest*', *SQ*, 21 (1970), 3 – 10.

[78] *Five-Act Structure*, p.235.

[79] D.C. Boughner, op. cit., p.3 – 10.

[80] Ibid., p.10.

[81] This has been claimed by Boughner, op. cit., p.6.

[82] Cf., for example, the edition *Publii Terentii Afri Comoediae Sex* (Frankfurt, 1562): 'Hiant non nunquam, neque satis cohaerent Plauti Comoediae', f.II.

the action in New Comedy in general can often be defined as an interplay of accident and deliberate planning. The plots of New Comedy are generated, as it were, by the interaction of Tyche with skilfully devised intrigues. Yet there is also the notion that man's fortune is the result of his character. Plautus does not simply replace Tyche by the concept of Fortune and her wheel[83] – the term Fortune is in fact surprisingly rare in Plautus,[84] so that we do not so much have the impression that the action is *guided* by Fortuna; rather, the characters avail themselves of propitious moments and either thank the *gods* for their benignity or complain about their cruelty. In *Menaechmi*, the first mistakings of identity caused by the appearance of the twin Menaechmus are merely accidental; yet he himself deliberately brings about a series of further confusions by his role-playing. Peniculus and the Matrona further complicate the action by their intrigue. After Menaechmus S has succeeded in escaping by feigning madness, Plautus has some difficulty in providing an opportunity for a further mistaking of identity; he is therefore compelled to create an 'artificial' situation by having the other Menaechmus make an unmotivated appearance, merely to allow him to be mistaken for his twin brother. It is perhaps because of this kind of looseness of the *nodus* that some humanist editions replace the term 'nodus' in the Evanthian definition by such totally different words as 'motus' or 'modus'.[85]

How, then, is 'error', as the basic agent in New Comedy, to be described? In his valuable book on the traditions of comedy, Salingar offers too limited a view of the problem. He maintains that comedies in which a character commits errors by misinterpreting a situation are much less frequent than those in which a victim is caught in a net of errors by the intrigue of a trickster figure. Thus, even the Plautine *Rudens* with its fine 'humanist' tone is interpreted as a play in which 'trickery' brings about 'the restoration of [. . .] social relationships .'[86] Duckworth provides a more balanced description of the nature of 'error' in New Comedy. He thinks that 'deception is the chief interest in spite of the fact that few comedies lack some type of trickery',[87] and he adds that at the basis of these plays is 'mental error, or misapprehension'.[88] In his *Poetica*, Trissino defines the comic error as deception of expectation and self-deception, and this he considers as 'the mode most appropriate to the ridiculous'.[89] Castelvetro prefers to include the deformities of character in the

---

[83] This claim had been made by Salingar, op. cit., p.159.

[84] Cf. G. Lodge, *Lexicon Plautinum* (Leipzig, 1933), s.v. 'Fortuna'.

[85] 'motus' for example in *P. Terentii Afri Comoediae* (Cologne, 1534), f.VIII.; 'modus' in a commentary by Pylades Brixianus, quoted in Baldwin, *Five-Act Structure*, p.693.

[86] Salingar, op. cit., p.165 and 157ff.

[87] Duckworth, op. cit., p.141.

[88] Duckworth, ibid., p.140.

[89] Trissino, *Poetica*, in: Gilbert, op. cit., p.231.

concept of error.[90] This idea is in accordance with the *Tractatus Coislinianus* and may perhaps go back to Aristotle.[91]

A more helpful explanation of the meaning of 'error' is given by H.W. Prescott, who claims that the genre of New Comedy was a 'comedy of errors' based on 'agnoia', that is, the characters' ignorance of reality.[92] We are indeed reminded here of tragedy, especially tragedy of the type of the Sophoclean *Oedipus Rex*. When Oedipus kills his father and marries his mother, it is through *agnoia*, his inability to distinguish between appearance and reality. The concept of error thus seems to bear some similarity to the Aristotelian *hamartia*. Whereas a close analogy between the tragic and the comic plot has been claimed, recently the objection has also been raised that such a definition of error would not include Aristophanic Old Comedy.[93] However, what has influenced the European tradition of comedy is the concept of error in New Comedy, both in the sense of being deceived or mistaken and in the sense of *committing* an error by wrongdoing. Although the element of 'guilt' is frequently lacking in comedy, there are plays, even among the canon of Plautus, in which the characters' behaviour necessitates an act of forgiveness.[94] New Comedy as a whole is a comedy not only about the discrepancy between appearance and reality but sometimes also about self-deception, wrong-doing and the conduct of a character which requires correction and pardon. From a structural point of view, the recognition of error is similar in both comedy and tragedy.

Salingar was the first to suggest that with his title 'The Comedy of Errors' Shakespeare may have been alluding to the classical origin of his play.[95] By exploiting all the possibilities which this tradition offered, Shakespeare did indeed write 'The Comedy of Errors'; he drew the maximum effect out of this dramatic tradition. We now realize how absurd Baldwin's claim really was that 'Directly or indirectly [. . .] The Comedy of Errors owes its title to Lambinus'.[96] In this early comedy, he conceives error not only as a mistaking of appearance for reality but also as a deficiency in a character's behaviour which leads him or her to commit further deceptions. Adriana provides an illustration of this, because, as we have seen, she acts according to her erroneous, possessive views about marriage, which are in need of correction. It appears, therefore, that it is wrong to confine corrective comedy to Ben Jonson and to ignore the corrective element in Shakespeare's romantic

[90] Cf. Salingar, op. cit., p.86.
[91] Cf. Janko, *Aristotle on Comedy*, p.84.
[92] H.W. Prescott, 'The Comedy of Errors', *CP*, 24 (1929), 32 – 41; cf. also Duckworth, op. cit., p.141.
[93] Janko, op. cit., p.67 – 68.
[94] For example, in *Rudens* or *Captivi*.
[95] Salingar, op. cit., p.324.
[96] *Five-Act Structure*, p.692.

comedies.[97] They are different from those of Ben Jonson *not* because they lack the quality of correction, inherent in the New Comedy tradition, but because they offer an incomparably rich and complex world in which correction, too, has its place.

Furthermore, in *Errors*, even in the absence of any trickster figure, the 'nodus erroris' is exceedingly tightly knit. Salingar has already rightly pointed out that one part of the lessons Shakespeare learnt from classical art was the fact that a story can be more effectively dramatized if rather than beginning *ab ovo*, it follows the ' "artificial order" beginning at a high point of action'.[98] The action in *Errors*, then, develops with an almost uncanny 'logic', and thus it approaches the structure of tragedy. By doubling the romance motif of the separated twins, Shakespeare seems to have discarded the principle of verisimilitude, which is valid in New Comedy and which had been discussed by Aristotle.[99] Yet, since it is a psychological truth that two improbabilities joined together are more readily accepted than just one, the initial improbability of the action does not in any way impair the forcefulness of its impact on the audience.

In this context it is surprising to note how many dramaturgic aspects of New Comedy were already recognized by Donatus's commentary on Terence, and far too little attention has been given to this work. It may suffice here to mention that Donatus praises Terence's dramatic *oikonomia*.[100] Shakespeare probably did not know this Donatian comment, yet Ben Jonson, in his *Timber, or Discoveries*, was obviously aware of it when he preferred the *Oeconomy* of Plautus to that of Terence.[101] This term should not, of course, primarily be understood in its modern sense: it implies the art of 'disposition' of the plot, especially the art of preparation of coming events, and it articulates the playwright's 'determination' to approach the resolution of the action; however, the modern meaning of 'dramatic economy' is also implied in the term. We may infer from this that there was indeed a most acute Elizabethan awareness of New Comedy as very skilfully contrived drama.

Another aspect of the dramaturgy of New Comedy which Donatus points out quite frequently is dramatic irony. Indeed, New Comedy is inconceivable without an underlying irony. In comedies in which family members are reunited without being aware in advance of the impending reunion, the action itself is basically ironic. The audience are given necessary advance

---

[97] Salingar, op. cit., p.77.

[98] Ibid., p.79.

[99] Janko, *Aristotle on Comedy*, p.96.

[100] Donatus, I, 98, 157, 163, 193, 348 and passim; οικονομια has already been discussed by Herrick, *Comic Theory in the Sixteenth Century* (Urbana, 1950), p.104, and E. Klien, *Aelius Donatus als Kritiker der Komödien des Terenz* (Diss. Innsbruck, 1948), p.58.

[101] Cf. *Ben Jonson*, ed. C.H. Herford, P. and E. Simpson (Oxford, 1954), VIII, 618, and Herrick, op. cit., p.104; Klien, op. cit., p.58.

information and are made aware that this central irony is mainly due to the workings of wilful Fortune. In Plautus, there is a considerably greater variety of ironic effects than in Terence. [102] In *Menaechmi*, the confusions of identity all produce ironic effects and they culminate in the assumption of a character that there may be a second Menaechmus. It testifies to the maturity of Plautus's art that occasionally a character involuntarily makes a comment which is revealed to contain a dramatic irony later on, but which at the time cannot be recognized as ironic even by the audience. The very first words of the traveller Menaechmus, when he arrives with his slave in Epidamnus, are an example of just such an irony: 'Voluptas nullast navitis, Messenio / maior meo animo quam quom ex alto procul / terram conspiciunt.', 226 – 228 ('There is no pleasure sailors have, in my opinion, Messenio, greater than sighting from the deep the distant land.'). When he describes his coming ashore as 'voluptas', neither he nor the audience know that before long he will be enjoying an even greater 'voluptas' in the arms of Erotium. [103] Plautus is here employing a type of irony that even anticipates some of the great ironic moments in Shakespeare. The omniscience of the audience as a prerequisite for dramatic irony is momentarily discarded, and only through the unforeseen development in the play is the irony here gradually revealed.

Furthermore, it seems that Plautus even intentionally included irony in the very structure of *Menaechmi* through having the motif of 'stealing' recur in several forms and situations. The Prologue itself introduces Menaechmus E as the twin who was kidnapped ('surreptus') and abducted to Epidamnus. Structural irony is achieved when this same Menaechmus, who had himself been 'surreptus' – 'stolen' has the idea of *stealing* his wife's *palla*, which then becomes the major 'agent' of the development of the turbulent action. Yet the same motif is also turned *against* Menaechmus when Peniculus, on realizing that he has lost his patron at the Forum, is forced to assume that Menaechmus has secretly 'stolen' away ('surrupuisti te mihi dudum de foro!' 491). This discovery generates Peniculus's revenge on Menaechmus. As we can see, and Salingar was the first to realize it, [104] there is every reason to believe that Plautus used the idea of 'stealing' as a kind of *leitmotif* in ironic transformations, and for structural purposes.

The ironies in *Menaechmi* are, however, far less subtle than those by which Plautus has enhanced the complexity of his *Amphitruo*; yet the ironic texture of this play has only recently been recognized in critical circles, although it is obvious to anyone embarking on a close study of the play. Through the development of the action, Alcumena has arrived at a paradoxical situation that is familiar to us from the *tragedy* of *Oedipus Rex*: she is both innocent and

---

[102] Duckworth, op. cit., p.232; on ειρωνεια in Terence cf. Donatus, I, 93, 151, 299, 365, 438, 456, 496.
[103] This has already been observed by E. Segal, op. cit., p.48.
[104] Salingar, op. cit., p.161.

guilty; innocent in her belief that she has spent the night with her husband and at the same time actually guilty of having committed adultery with Jupiter.[105] In this comedy a statement may be both true and untrue. Most ironies of the plot result, of course, from the fact that two gods play a major part in it and that especially 'the obvious incongruity between what the gods really are and the human roles they play provides the setting for much comic irony'.[106] Plautus also succeeds in an ironic contrasting of scenes, for example 'Mercury's treatment of Sosia and the harassment of Amphitruo by Mercury and Jupiter'[107] are set in ironic contrast.

And then there are numerous effects of verbal irony. The fact that the name of *Iuppiter*, who is an actor in the play, occurs no less than forty times, suggests that it is used for ironic purposes; oaths are sworn by Jupiter and thus 'almost at every turn in the play's language'[108] irony is produced – and most effectively when the gods swear by themselves.[109] It has been rightly said that the most striking example of verbal irony is given by Alcumena when she confesses to Amphitruo with an oath that she has remained faithful to him:

> per supremi regis regnum iuro et matrem familias
> Iunonem, quam me vereri et metuere est par maxume,
> ut mi extra unum te mortalis nemo corpus corpore
> contigit, quo me impudicam faceret.   831 – 4

> I swear by the kingdom of the king on high and by Juno, the matron goddess I most should reverence and fear – so may she bless me as no mortal man, save you only, has taken me to him as a wife.

She swears by Jupiter and is unaware of the fact that it is he who has caused her troubles. And, as she will soon give birth to two twins, it is fitting that she should include the name of Juno too, the goddess of childbirth, yet as she has served Jupiter as a paramour, she has offended the very Juno she is just invoking, a goddess who can be very revengeful to Jupiter's sweethearts.[110]

Subtle though the irony is in these Plautine comedies, it is far surpassed by Shakespeare's multifarious use of irony in *Errors*. Both the plot and the dialogue are replete with ironic effects, and it is possible here to discuss only a few examples. In this play, where reality is constantly transformed, ironic metaphors are particularly frequent, as when, for example, Dromio S calls the fat Nell who pursued him a 'kitchen-vestal' (IV, iv, 73). That Shakespeare in his 'classical' play should allude to the Roman vestal, the personification of virginity, is most fitting; but Dromio, by replacing the Temple of the Vestal

[105] W.E. Forehand, 'Irony in Plautus' *Amphitruo*', *AJP*, 92 (1971), 640.
[106] Forehand, op. cit., p.643.
[107] Forehand, op. cit., p.647.
[108] Forehand, op. cit., p.638.
[109] Forehand, op. cit., p.636.
[110] Forehand, op. cit., p.639.

by the kitchen, yokes together the most heterogeneous images and produces an ironic effect. In the opening scene of the play we find some instances of *dramatic* irony in utterances that come true in a sense different from the speaker's intention (10; 27; 104; 139). Even stylistic features such as verse or prose are used for specifically ironic purposes; for instance, when Dromio S rebukes his master for beating him, although 'there is neither rhyme nor reason' for it, he changes over at this point from prose to a rhyming couplet (II, ii, 48).[111]

If there was irony in the very structure of *Menaechmi*, we also find irony as a structural principle in Shakespeare's *Errors*. As we know, the action very much centres on the gold chain which Antipholus E has ordered and which is erroneously delivered to his brother. We may say that the chain, itself the cause of so many confusions, becomes a visual symbol of the kind of action we find in this comedy: the way in which the events follow one another is strongly reminiscent of a chain because the two 'strands', that is, the two actions of the Antipholi, continually interfere with each other in such a way as to form an 'imaginary' chain.

The plot itself is made to produce multiple ironic effects that by far exceed those in the Plautine plays. All the mistakings of identity which are perceived by the audience are highly ironic. Furthermore, it is ironic that, in the very first scene, Egeon should first have to receive a death sentence before he can be given a new life with his family. The fact that Shakespeare introduces here a basic paradox reminds us somewhat of Alcumena's paradoxical situation. The second scene of *Errors* is especially interesting from the point of view of irony: in it we have the contrasting of the 'thousand marks' as the ransom needed by Egeon and the sum which Antipholus S has brought with him. The audience, who notice the identity of the sums, may draw their own inferences and may in some way anticipate a happy ending,[112] yet nevertheless they are deceived: it is not through the thousand marks that Egeon is given back his life again, but through the quality of forgiveness and pardon. Antipholus's announcement in this scene that he is going to 'lose' himself in the 'quest' for his brother begins, ironically, to come true the very next moment when the 'wrong' Dromio addresses him as the other Antipholus. Shakespeare achieves many ironical effects of this kind by his characteristic dramaturgy of juxtaposition, a refinement that he developed from a specific dramaturgic device of New Comedy. It has, for example, been pointed out that Menander parallels situations and scenes for comic and ironic purposes, for example, when 'two different groups of characters experience or appear to experience parallel fates.'[113] In *Menaechmi* we have a situation of ironic humour when Menaechmus E, who had just been excluded from his own house by his wife,

---

[111] Cf. Foakes, op. cit., p.29, n.48.

[112] Tetzeli v. Rosador, 'Plotting the Early Comedies . . .', *ShS*, 37 (1934), 13ff.

[113] W.G. Arnott, ed., *Menander* (Cambridge, Mass./London, 1979), I, xxxix.

goes to the Courtesan in the belief that she will receive him kindly, yet he finds that she excludes him just as firmly. The situations of ironic paralleling in *Errors* are far more subtle. There is a further highly ironic situation in II, ii, when Adriana rebukes her husband with the words: 'O, how comes it, / That thou art then estranged from thyself?' (119 – 20); in a way quite unbeknown to herself, her 'strange' behaviour contributes to Antipholus's estrangement from himself. For this reason it is so fitting that Adriana should in this context repeat his own image of a water-drop: 'For know, my love, as easy mayst thou fall / A drop of water in the breaking gulf, / And take unmingled thence that drop again / Without addition or diminishing, / As take from me thyself, and not me too.' (125 – 29).

Most of the ironies we have discussed are fully noticed by the audience who, by their superior awareness, are capable not only of merely *watching* the play but also of critically examining and *judging* the events as well.[114] They are thus in a position to connect events taking place on different levels and in different dramatic contexts. While Plautus only occasionally experiments with this technique, it is fully developed in *Errors*. For example, when Luciana quotes the proverbial tag that 'a man is master of his liberty' (II, i, 7), we are called upon to ask how far this is confirmed by the action in the comedy; in other words, are men *really* shown to be in command of their fate? Antipholus E, for one, is far from enjoying absolute freedom (and it was he that Luciana was thinking of), and, indeed, we sympathize with the ways in which he loses it. Nor does his brother feel free in the world of Ephesus; he desires nothing so much as to escape from Ephesus as soon as possible. That he is here caught up in a web of deceptions is fully recognized by the audience who, on the one hand, sympathize with his fears, while at the same time knowing, by the very title of the play, that Antipholus E and Dromio are but part of the game of comedy. This discussion of ironic developments of the plot could be continued; suffice it to point to a major irony in the pivotal scene III, i: it concludes with a brilliantly ironic situation when Balthasar takes great pains in persuading Antipholus E to leave off trying to break open his door. If he had done so, he would have been prevented from all the ensuing confusions by discovering his brother. These examples, to which others could be added, are, I think, sufficient proof to show how, in his dramatic use of irony, Shakespeare developed a great variety of forms, yet he did so by extending and transforming the ironic dramaturgy of the New Comedy tradition.

An important means of providing advance information, necessary for the perception of dramatic irony, is the convention of the Prologue, which, according to the Evanthian definition, is a major part of the comic structure. This device was taken over from Greek tragedy, where it was necessary to introduce the myth of the play to the spectators. The Prologues were spoken

---

[114] On the discrepancy of awareness in Shakespeare's comedies cf. especially B. Evans, *Shakespeare's Comedies* (Oxford, 1960).

by the gods, or by a character from the play. As Walter Jens has shown in a study of Euripides' tragedies,[115] in some of his plays the audience know beforehand, from the Prologue's narration of the entire action, that the complications will be resolved, and so attention is concentrated on discovering *how* this resolution will be brought about. Jens sees here a very early instance of the Brechtian dramaturgy of *Verfremdung*. Menander preferred a god for the Prologue because only a god could be credited with the required omniscience. By including the necessary expository information in the Prologue, the dramatists of New Comedy were able to concentrate entirely on the *final* stages of the action. Plautus composed highly individual Prologues, yet he used them in only eleven out of his twenty extant plays.[116] He was fully aware of the advantages and also of the artistic requirements of this device. This can, for example, be seen in his *Mercator*, where he has a character poke fun at the bad motivation of some Prologue-monologues which remain outside the play proper. As Duckworth has pointed out, Plautus does not dispose of dramatic suspense or effects of surprise; he rather 'foreshadows' only 'part of the plot but refrains from revealing the main action'[117] in order 'to quicken the interest of the audience in what is to come',[118] and the Prologues to both *Menaechmi* and *Amphitruo* are excellent examples of this. Plautus thus creates in the audience a kind of twofold suspense, namely suspense of anticipation and suspense of uncertainty[119] as to the complete development of the plot. Surprise thus plays an important role in Plautine drama, because only fragmentary advance information is given to the audience.

As is well known, Shakespeare makes relatively scarce use of the Prologue, namely in *Romeo and Juliet*, the introduction to *Henry IV* Part II, in the Chorus before each Act of *Henry V* and of *Pericles*. The Chorus of Time, occurring in *The Winter's Tale* after Act III, continues the same tradition.[120] The very first scene of *Errors*, with Egeon's narration of past events, replaces the conventional Prologue and strikes a tragic note which is counterbalanced, as it were, by the title, which clearly denotes that the play will be a '*Comedy* of Errors'. It is of particular interest in our context that Shakespeare's technique of preparation in this play reminds us for a moment of Terence, who has no *expository* prologues, but at the same time it reveals some striking affinities with the technique of Plautus, although Shakespeare has disposed of the convention of the Prologue. Through Egeon's narration, Shakespeare, too, enables the audience to anticipate *part* of the plot; he does it in order to arouse interest in

---

[115] W. Jens, *Zur Antike* (München, 1978), p.51.

[116] F. Stoessl, 'Prologos', in: *Realencyklopädie der classischen Altertumswissenschaft*, 23 (1959), 2384ff.

[117] Duckworth, op. cit., p.215.

[118] Ibid., p.227.

[119] Ibid., p.223 – 235.

[120] Cf. also C.C. Coulter, 'The Plautine Tradition in Shakespeare', *JEGP*, 19 (1920), 72.

what is to come, so that his audience, too, experience a two-fold suspense, namely suspense of anticipation as well as of uncertainty. Although *Errors* surprises us by the many transformations of the Plautine models, we recognize at the same time a most deliberate continuation of the basic New Comedy tradition.

IV

Game-Playing in the Theatre of Plautus and the Early Shakespeare

It is with regard to the theatrical and metadramatic element that there is a particular affinity between the two playwrights. Both dramatists often make the audience aware of the play *as* a play being *acted* on stage; and in recent research on both Plautus and Shakespeare this aspect has received the attention it deserves. In *Bacchides*, for example, as Slater has shown, the characters' consciousness of their 'social role' leads to their conscious 'adoption of comic roles'.[1] One character even begins to act as a playwright within the play by writing a 'role' for another character. The direct contact with the audience, which is frequently established, sometimes becomes so close that a character asks them to take an active part in the action, and we are reminded of a *Punch and Judy* show. Thus Menaechmus E asks all married men who have a paramour to participate in his triumph over his wife (128f.), and the other Menaechmus, trying to escape from Epidamnus, appeals to the audience not to tell the Senex which way he has gone (879 – 81). (However, as we can infer from a play like *Cistellaria* (II, 678ff.), the original audience did not directly respond to this kind of address.) Shakespeare never goes so far as to make the audience *part* of the action itself. It is true that in *The Taming of the Shrew* Petruchio wants to know from the audience whether anyone has a more effective method than his own for taming a shrew (IV, i, 210 – 211), and Launce in *The Two Gentlemen of Verona* asks the audience to judge for themselves the behaviour of his dog; yet Launce certainly does not wait for a possible response (IV, iv, 16), and none of these examples goes so far as to make the audience co-actors in the drama.

The very Prologue to *Menaechmi* begins a play with the audience, and the comedy as a whole is presented as a 'game'. The events prior to the beginning are narrated so that the audience are capable of enjoying the game-character of the ensuing action. Even a playful comment on the 'style' of the comedy is included: *Menaechmi* is not presented in the usual Attic manner, but in a Sicilian style (12). The speaker of the Prologue then goes on to say that, as he is himself on his way to Epidamnus, he is prepared to deliver mail from the

---

[1] Slater, *Plautus in Performance*, p.97.

audience to that city. The Prologue to *Amphitruo* reveals a remarkable complexity. Mercury, the speaker, relishes the chance to play a role, disguised as, or rather transformed into Sosia; he is also the messenger god, the son of Jupiter, the Roman god of commerce, and the god of cunning and deception as well as of rhetoric. He introduces the action as a splendid game for the gods as well as for the audience. The spectators are fully capable of enjoying this game because they are given privileged advance information which enables them to share the point of view of the gods. They are told that Jupiter will approach Alcumena, whose love he desires, in the shape of her husband so that he may spend a long night with her. When Mercury tells them that they are going to witness a tragedy, he notices that they react by frowning (I; 52), and so he promises that he will change the text into a comedy (55). His question whether they accept this transformation is answered by himself in the affirmative: 'utrum sit an non voltis? sed ego stultior, / quasi nesciam vos velle . . .' (56 – 57) ('Do you wish me to do it, or not? But there! how stupid of me! As if I didn't know that you do wish it').

Throughout the play, Jupiter, too, is 'playing', he is performing the role of Amphitruo – with the exception of his final monologue in which he as the supreme god explains to Amphitruo the reason for his errors. He has been the director of the comedy and so he sees to it that the human couple will not end up in a tragic catastrophe. Nevertheless, the essence of this play is the constant interference of game and seriousness: what is a game for the gods has serious and near-tragic effects for Alcumena, Amphitruo and even Sosia, and we have seen how this brilliant structure provides the play with an exceptional richness. The audience share the gods' pleasure, but they are also on the side of the human beings, as when, for example, Jupiter/Amphitruo tries to explain to Alcumena the reproaches of the real Amphitruo as mere jokes: 'If something is said in joke, it's not fair to take it in earnest', and Alcumena replies: 'I know one thing – that joke of yours cut me to the heart, sir.' ('Si quid dictum est per iocum / non aequom est id te serio praevortier.' 'Ego illud scio quam doluerit cordi meo.' 920ff.).

Slaves and parasites, characters who reflect the dramatic vitality of the popular mime, are great experts at game-playing. Although his part in the play is not a large one, the slave Messenio in *Menaechmi* is a skilful player. His entire role reflects the holiday spirit of comedy. Even the brawling scene, for all the violence with which Menaechmus is carried off by four slaves, has a playful aspect: for Messenio it is no hardship to fight with the slaves in order to rescue his supposed master. However, his principal piece of play-acting occurs in the final recognition scene. As soon as he begins to anticipate the revelation that the two Menaechmi are twins, he takes the initiative and, like a stage director, manipulates and directs the two brothers until they recognize each other. Messenio then provides the comedy with a coda, a situation of rollicking game-playing. He asks Menaechmus E for permission to announce the auction of his goods, including his wife. This auction should not, of course, be misunderstood as suggesting Plautus's cynicism;[2] what we have here is a merely temporary saturnalian reversal of order. When the play-world of the comedy ends, Menaechmus is supposed to *return* to his wife. The many intrigues of Plautine comedy, usually performed by the slave, are basically games, and are referred to as such in the phrase 'ludos facere'.[3] In *Menaechmi*, the role of setting off the intrigue is transferred to the parasite Peniculus,[4] who is himself a totally saturnalian character.

Menaechmus S, as soon as he is certain about who it is that Erotium takes him for, ignores his slave's warning and decides to pretend to be his brother in order to enjoy the pleasures of the courtesan's company. He even goes so far as to apologize for having dared to contradict Erotium (418). The reason he gives for his former 'misbehaviour' is that he feared Messenio had informed his wife of the mantle (*palla*) and the lunch (*prandium*) (419 – 420). In the great scene V, ii, Menaechmus S, who is hard-pressed by the Senex and the Matrona, suddenly has the idea that it may be possible for him to escape from the serious scrape he is in by pretending to be the madman for whom the Matrona and the Senex take him. By his superb acting he indeed succeeds in making his 'insanity' credible. The strong saturnalian element in his acting becomes particularly manifest if Menaechmus in fact jumps onto the altar, present on the Roman stage, and there imitates a chariot driver who receives his commands from Apollo and who then allows himself to fall down in order to terrify the trembling Senex. There is an additional saturnalian quality in this situation, because it is a comic inversion of the famous madness scenes of Greek tragedy.

The game-playing of Menaechmus E, too, is of special interest. Since in the first Act he has already won a game over his wife by outwitting her, he finds himself in high spirits. For instance, we see him act out a little pantomime for the benefit of Peniculus, who is a spectator on stage. Wearing his wife's *palla* across his breast, he by his gestures brings to mind two famous mythological motifs, namely Ganymede being raped by Jupiter's eagle and Adonis being abducted by Venus. While he expects Peniculus to testify to his being true to the mythological types, the parasite discerns only the comedy in this acting, since Menaechmus has not the slightest justification for comparing himself with either Ganymede or Adonis (143 – 146).

When he returns from the Forum, the spirit of comedy has disappeared, but in the splendid scene IV, ii Menaechmus E is forced to play a role again, this time in self-defence. He has to pretend not to be guilty of stealing the *palla*, although he knows only too well that his role-playing is totally unconvincing.

---

[2] This charge against Plautus has been made, for example, by Wells in the introduction to his edition of *The Comedy of Errors*, p.26; and Salingar thinks that Menaechmus's marriage is 'breaking up', *Traditions*, p.124.

[3] Cf. Blänsdorf, op. cit., p.167, and Salingar, *Traditions*, p.115.

[4] On the saturnalian element in Plautus cf. especially E. Segal, *Roman Laughter* (Cambridge, Mass., 1969), passim.

He pretends not to know the reason for his wife's sadness and asks her whether her servants or her maids have insulted her. A little later, he rightly claims not to have enjoyed the *prandium* at Erotium's house. While the audience know this to be true, his accusers take it to be merely another lie. Playing the innocent, he even goes so far as to ask who it was that stole the *palla*. His wife then sarcastically remarks that it was 'a certain Menaechmus'. Interestingly enough, he now asks her to specify which Menaechmus it was (651), as if he knew that there were two of them. As he is entirely concerned here with defending himself, we must cease to speak of his consciously playing a role. Nevertheless, from the point of view of the audience, this splendid situation is a superb saturnalian game, in which the mistaking of identity functions as the *qui pro quo* of carnival. And there are further similar highlights, such as the encounter between the Cook and the traveller Menaechmus or the helplessness and fright of the quack doctor and the Senex, caused by the supposed madness of Menaechmus, which have a strong and powerful saturnalian effect.

Shakespeare thus worked with two comedies in which game-playing is an essential part of the dramatic experience. It is therefore interesting to ask in what way this element recurs in *Errors*. By disposing of the Prologue and by opening the play with Egeon's 'tragic' narration, Shakespeare introduces an element of seriousness which sets all the later situations of a play within the play in sharp relief. This serious and 'illusionistic' opening already suggests to the audience that more is at stake than just the playing of a game. The dramatic illusion is suspended only occasionally, and when this does happen, it serves a distinct dramatic purpose. In fact, there are only a few moments when the audience are directly made aware of the play as a play. At the end of II, ii, Adriana, who is about to leave the stage for dinner, commands the 'wrong' Dromio to 'play the porter well' (211). She does not, of course, invite Dromio to start a comic game, but she expects a function and role which is alien to the twin Dromio. The audience are, however, called upon to view the following scene as a magnificent theatrical game, and Dromio indeed performs his role to perfection. Thomas van Laan has pointed out that identity in this play is defined in terms of 'the various functions a character acquires through participating in a number of social relationships'.[5] 'In this world there is no real difference between being something and playing something.'[6] Some lines earlier in II, ii, Adriana blamed Antipholus S for his puzzling behaviour: 'How ill agrees it with your gravity / To counterfeit thus grossly with your slave' (168 – 169). Here Antipholus's consternation about the fact that his identity is being mistaken is in turn interpreted by Adriana as play-acting.

Errors contains a number of situations where a character believes that his or her partner is just playing a game. At first sight, this parallels the Cook's or

---

[5] T. van Laan, *Role-Playing in Shakespeare* (Toronto/Buffalo/London, 1978), p.25.
[6] Ibid., p.23. A similar point has been made by M.D. Boesel, *Identitäts- und Rollenproblematik*, esp. p.143.

Erotium's assumption that Menaechmus is playing one of his usual tricks. The Shakespearean Courtesan also believes that Antipholus is jesting, and Angelo, who offers him a chain, has the same impression (III, ii, 165ff.). Unable to account for Angelo's behaviour when he urges him to pay money for a chain he never received, Antipholus reproaches him for indulging in a most offensive 'dalliance' (IV, i, 48).[7] The more, however, we examine the various situations where identities are confused, the more we observe how interesting and how different in character they really are. Some of them are apt to evoke rather complex reactions in the audience. In the first of these scenes (I, ii, 43ff.), Dromio E reveals so many details about his and his master's domestic circumstances in Ephesus that the traveller twin could be expected to anticipate that his brother might live here; yet Antipholus does not react in this realistic way. Since Dromio is playing the double role of the 'serious' messenger and the punning and jesting servant (in the tradition of the *servus callidus*), Antipholus does not hit upon the idea that this might be a different Dromio. Conversely, Antipholus's concern about his money is misinterpreted by Dromio as the role play of a buoyant and jesting master. This dialogue, in which each thinks the other is speaking in jest, is enjoyed by the audience as a saturnalian *qui pro quo*, because the mistaking of identity does not yet carry any deeper implications.

Deliberate game-playing is in *Errors* confined almost exclusively to the two Dromios. Of course, if one merely reads the play, these situations may easily be overlooked; they have to be performed on stage and they require good comic actors, capable of comic by-play. Adriana and Luciana watch the first of these games when Dromio E narrates his supposed master's refusal to come home to dinner. Instead of merely reporting his encounter with the 'wrong' Antipholus, he re-enacts the whole scene in a one-man show:

> When I desir'd him to come home to dinner,
> He ask'd me for a thousand marks in gold;
> ''Tis dinner-time', quoth I; 'my gold,' quoth he;
> 'Your meat will burn', quoth I; 'my gold', quoth he,
> 'Will you come?', quoth I; 'my gold', quoth he,
> 'Where is the thousand marks I gave thee, villain?'
> 'The pig', quoth I, 'is burn'd'; 'my gold', quoth he;
> 'My mistress, sir . . .', quoth I; 'hang up thy mistress;
> I know not thy mistress, out on thy mistress . . .'   II, i, 60 – 68

The way in which Dromio plays both himself and his master is very funny. The sequence of questions and the monotonous answer 'my gold', the abrupt changing from one role to the other and the final climactic exclamation 'hang up thy mistress' (which, by the way, is an invention of Dromio's for the sake of heightened effect) make the passage into a comic scene *en miniature*.

---

[7] Cf. Foakes, op. cit., p.64, n.59.

In scene II,ii the encounter between Antipholus and the other Dromio develops in the reverse manner: not only does Antipholus mistake Dromio's comments for jesting, but he also feels himself taunted by him, and this so exasperates him that he immediately beats Dromio. It is remarkable that, on the one hand, Dromio comments on his being beaten, but on the other hand he does not stop quibbling and playing his comic role. Even when he characterizes this situation as 'earnest', he uses it as an occasion for a pun.[8] Thus, in this whole encounter between Antipholus and Dromio, the saturnalian spirit is allowed to prevail. It is, of course, strongly present in the great dinner scene with the comic play of the Dromios and not least in the numerous sexual innuendos in that scene. The playful competition between the two Dromios at times becomes the major focus of interest, so that the serious purpose of the scene, Antipholus's desire to enter his house, is temporarily forgotten. The game-playing of the Dromios is once more the dramatic centre in III,ii, when Dromio informs his master how he was pursued by the kitchen wench Nell. The point is again that he is not supposed to merely *narrate* his encounter with the kitchen wench, but to re-enact on stage his meeting with her behind the scene.[9] However, the game-playing abruptly changes over into fear, because master and servant suddenly think to have encountered witches. On other occasions a playful dialogue ends in violence, and this increases greatly as the play proceeds. We have seen that masters beating their servants violently was a fact of Elizabethan everyday life. This is not expressly criticized here — Dromio is not prepared to accept the beating but runs away — yet violence is introduced, as it were, as a counterweight to the saturnalian lightness. In a comparison between Plautus and Shakespeare it should not go unobserved that in Shakespearean comedy there is much more violence than in the comedies of Plautus, where violent punishments are, as a rule, merely announced but not performed.

Furthermore, what from the superior point of view of the audience appears as a comic, playful confusion of identity between the two Antipholi is experienced by them as a radical and very dangerous transformation of 'reality'. Here we have an interference of the comic and serious perspective that so strongly reminds us of Plautus's double strategy in *Amphitruo*. Antipholus S begins to fear that his very identity is becoming involved in this process. In these scenes, something quite different from a saturnalian topsy-turvydom is implied, and therefore they also begin to evoke complex emotions in the audience which go far deeper than the pleasures of carnival. We may observe this even more clearly in what happens to the other Antipholus. In the confusions about his own identity, reality begins to transform itself because,

---

[8] Cf. Foakes, op. cit., p.28, n.29.

[9] Since he begins his description of her by calling her 'spherical, like a globe' (112), we may suppose that he picks up a round object such as a casket as a 'substitute' for Nell before beginning to play the episode with the 'kitchen wench' (93).

although he has not been guilty of misbehaviour, his social reputation appears to be seriously affected if not even destroyed as he is taken to prison. We should note how Dromio S in Act IV takes this as an opportunity for comic punning and quibbling, yet the holiday spirit of comedy is no longer given the free rein it had on earlier occasions, and the element of threat that we witnessed in the very first scene of the play is once more emphasized. Antipholus E, who does not understand why reality is beginning to change, is inclined to think that he has been the victim of a practical joke: 'But sirrah, you shall buy this sport as dear / As all the metal in your shop will answer.' (IV, i, 82 – 83). And when Adriana appears with Dr Pinch, who, as we have seen, is not merely a farcical character, he cannot believe that his own wife is playing a wicked game of 'dissembling' (IV, iv, 99) and indulging in 'shameful sport' (103). Yet a few moments later he fully realizes the most serious nature of this 'sport' and feels an immediate threat to his own life. The contrasting elements of game-playing and violence, of carnival and brutal 'real' aggression, are brought very closely together in this play.[10] They provide *Errors* with an incomparably greater dramatic intensity than *Menaechmi*, and they surpass even the excellent *Amphitruo*.

Errors concludes with a dialogue between the two Dromios, who have remained on stage. Contrary to the usual practice, this should not be omitted in a modern performance, because it provides a brilliant *coda* to the comedy and offers the final instance of a subtle improvisational game.[11] As the Dromios are overjoyed at having finally found each other, their playing is now more relaxed than before, while the 'theme' of their game remains the same: they now playfully act out the discovery of their own identities and find that they are each other's 'glass' (V, i, 417). That Dromio S suggests the game of drawing 'cuts' (422) in order to decide who has the prior claim, is a small but most fitting detail: it once again reminds us of the workings of Fortune, so important from the very first scene in the process of their finding each other. Moreover, the drawing of lots is a dramatic motif which occurs also in Plautus.[12] Shakespeare uses the last minutes of his comedy to bring to mind once more the fact that he draws the most comic as well as the most serious effects in his *Errors* from the basic problems concerning human identity.

Yet on the other hand we should be careful not to interpret the difference in the use of play elements as greater than it actually is. In her excellent book on the play element in Shakespeare, Anne Righter argues that the concept of the stage play as presenting a dramatic reality was developed by the Elizabethans.[13] According to Righter, Diccon's claim in his song in II, ii of *Gammer*

---

[10] Ralph Berry rightly says that 'In this most binary of plays, there are always two sides to events: what it looks like and what it feels like.' (*Shakespeare and the Awareness of the Audience*, p.44).

[11] Cf. also S. Wells in his edition of *The Comedy of Errors*, p.38.

[12] For example in *Casina*, 298.

[13] Anne Righter (Barton), *Shakespeare and the Idea of the Play* (Harmondsworth, 1962).

Gurton's Needle that the factual story of the lost needle is such that 'A man might make a play out of it' (II, ii, 10) reflects a specifically Elizabethan attitude.[14] Righter acknowledges that in classical antiquity Terence occasionally refers to details of the theatrical performance in order to provide the action of his play with a quality of 'reality'. She quotes a character in the Terentian *Hecyra* saying: 'There's no need to breathe a syllable of it. I have no wish for it to be as in the comedies where everybody gets to know everything.' ('non placet fieri hoc item ut in comoediis, / omnia omnes ubi resciscunt.' 866 – 867). She claims that in Terence, much more 'than in the more artificial, audience-conscious comedy of Menander and Plautus', this comparison between the theatre and real life 'serves [. . .] to define the depth and realism of the play world itself. It provides a vivid demonstration of the fact that characters – and by implication the audience – can accept the imaginary environment of the play as reality.'[15]

Here Righter's comment on classical comedy is, however, not quite appropriate. She fails to see the close connection between Terence and Menander, who was the first to establish a play world through the creation of a dramatic illusion which is seldom suspended.[16] Furthermore, it is not without significance that Diccon's comment occurs in a comedy strongly influenced by *Plautus*. Falling victim to the old prejudice against Plautus as an 'artificial' playwright, Righter is unaware of the fact that Plautus, although he delights in dissolving the dramatic illusion, is in many situations and scenes also intent on producing effects of dramatic illusion and 'verisimilitude'.[17] In fact, the example Righter quotes from Terence has a far more impressive counterpart in the Plautine *Bacchides* (an adaptation of a Menandrian play) where Chrysalus rebukes Pistoclerus for his behaviour, which appears to him to be merely 'confounding acting' ('actor mihi cor odio sauciat.' I; 213).[18] More than that, Pistoclerus then refers to Plautus's own play *Epidicus* and confesses that even this pleasant comedy displeases him if the bad actor Pellio plays a role in it (214f.). This metadramatic reference has the effect that Chrysalus and Pistoclerus become, for the moment, very real by setting themselves off from fictional comedy. Similarly, in *Miles Gloriosus*, as we have seen, Periplectomenus, in a typically Plautine situation, concludes from Palaestrio's gestures and mimic expression that he is hatching an intrigue. The fact that one of these gestures reminds Periplectomenus of the slaves in comedies

[14] Righter, ibid., p.61.
[15] Ibid.
[16] Cf. for example, W. Schadewaldt, ed., *Menander. Der Menschenfeind. Das Schiedsgericht* (Frankfurt, 1963), p.144 and W. Görler, 'Über die Illusion in der antiken Komödie', *Antike und Abendland*, 18 (1973), 41 – 57.
[17] This is a major point in Slater's book, *Plautus in Performance*.
[18] Cf. also C. Knapp, 'References in Plautus and Terence to Plays, Players, and Playwrights', *CP*, 14 (1919), 35 – 55.

('euscheme hercle astitit et dulice et comoedice' III, 213) provides the present situation with a temporary 'reality'.

Mostellaria contains an especially interesting illustration of the relationship between the elements of play and reality. The slave Tranio is famous for his play on two levels. Not only does he play a role, but he also causes others to play roles in turn. In doing so, he creates a theatrical world which, even after it has been discovered to be false, is still maintained in the fifth Act.[19] In order to ensnare Tranio, the old man, his opponent, has to perform an intrigue in the manner of a slave by pretending to believe the lie that the haunted house has been bought. It has been said that, by pretending to accept Tranio's deception as true, the old man is operating on a *second* fictional level in order to get the better of Tranio.[20] Conversely, Tranio pretends to take the old man's 'game' for real, although he has already noticed that the latter has only been playing with him. This famous example shows that Plautus was indeed sometimes intent on providing dramatic situations with an effect of reality, and we must conclude that, whereas the plot of *Gammer Gurton's Needle* is specifically English, its elements of dramaturgy are certainly more 'Plautine' than Righter and others are willing to acknowledge.

As far as *Amphitruo* is concerned, may we not say that it contains a paradox comparable to the one we have just seen in *Mostellaria*? Does not the very fact that, within the fictional world of comedy, Jupiter performs his own play of trickery and deception make the private and shocking experience of Alcumena and Amphitruo all the more 'real' by contrast? Turning again to *Errors*, we observe that, for Antipholus, the city of Ephesus becomes increasingly un-real because he believes that he has arrived in an 'illusionary' setting, created by witchcraft, whereas he, who defines the world around him as 'imaginary', himself paradoxically becomes more 'real' as a fictional character in an unreal theatre world; yet, while he becomes more 'real', he also approaches madness. Foucault has pointed out that 'Madness is the purest, most total form of *Qui pro quo*; it takes the false for the true, death for life, man for woman . . .';[21] Antipholus does indeed take the false for the true, but only because society has already confused his identity by a *qui pro quo*. Thus, in a sense, society goes 'mad' first.

The element of game-playing, so prominent in New Comedy, sometimes even extends to a play with the two genres of comedy and tragedy in the sense that the frontiers of comedy are crossed and a tragic perspective is opened up. Even Aristophanic Old Comedy is sometimes concerned with aspects of Greek tragedy, which it likes to parody, as, for instance, in *The Acharnians*.[22] In

---

[19] This point has been made by J. Blänsdorf, 'Plautus' in: *Das römische Drama*, ed. E. Lefèvre (Darmstadt, 1978), p. 168.

[20] Blänsdorf, ibid.

[21] M. Foucault, *Madness and Civilization. A History of Insanity in the Age of Reason*, transl. by R. Howard (London, 1967), p. 33 – 34.

[22] *The Acharnians of Aristophanes*, ed. W.J.M. Starkie (Amsterdam, 1968), p.228.

Menander's *Epitrepontes* (*The Arbitration*) we find a character quoting part of a soliloquy from a Euripidean tragedy, and tragic pathos is transformed into comic burlesque.[23] By this parodying of elements of the older tragic genre, New Comedy indirectly suggests that it originated and developed from tragedy. In Plautus, too, tragedy is parodied; we have already seen how Mercury playfully first announces a tragedy and then promises a comedy instead and how *Menaechmi* contains a witty parody of tragic madness scenes such as we find in the Euripidean *Hecabe* or *The Trojan Women*. In her very interesting book Joan Hartwig has perceptively analysed the dramaturgy of parody in Shakespeare. She does not, however, consider the fact that there is a dramatic tradition behind it.[24] It may suffice here to refer to *A Midsummer Night's Dream*, a play which has certain connections with New Comedy, and which draws great parodic effects from the performance of the 'play' of Pyramus and Thisbe. The brilliant and highly original Pyramus and Thisbe scenes on the one hand parody the early pathos of Elizabethan tragedy and make fun of the artisans' hopelessly inappropriate understanding of dramatic illusion as well as of their way of acting; on the other hand, although he was not aware of the structure of the Menandrian plays, Shakespeare nevertheless developed with these scenes a dramaturgic device of parody present in New Comedy from the beginning and brought it to its absolute climax.

[23] *Epitrepontes*, in *Menander*, ed. W.B. Arnott, The Loeb Classical Library (Cambridge, Mass./London, 1979), I, 519. On the mixing of the comic and the tragic in Menander cf. especially S.M. Goldberg, *The Making of Menander's Comedy* (Berkeley, 1980), p.29ff.

[24] J. Hartwig, *Shakespeare's Analogical Scene. Parody as Structural Syntax* (Lincoln, Nebr./ London, 1983).

V

Dramatic Language in Plautus and in
The Comedy of Errors

1. *The ideal of* copia *in Plautus and Shakespeare*

Critics have too often lost sight of the fact that the principal element in comedy is language. In his fine book on the language games in *Love's Labour's Lost*, Keir Elam has argued that one reason for this state of affairs lies in Aristotle's subordination of dramatic language to dramatic action, in the fact that Aristotle obviously did not realize that language can itself *be* action.[1] It must be added that in comedy the *meaning* of language is less important than its *gaming* character, and our view on this has been sharpened by the insights of Derrida and others. In the famous *Tractatus Coislinianus*, in which comedy is defined in terms analogous to tragedy, language, in particular popular and conversational language, is assigned an important function for the achievement of the comic catastrophe.[2]

Plautus's comedies excel by the author's almost inexhaustible linguistic imagination, by his brilliant use of sound effects, metaphors and puns. We are unable to judge precisely the original effect of these comedies on the Roman stage. Yet we know that they were accompanied by music, that the soliloquies were sung as *cantica*, thus reminding us of operatic arias, as E. Fraenkel has pointed out.[3] He draws a parallel to modern works, such as Beaumarchais's *Mariage de Figaro* and Lorenzo da Ponte's libretti for Mozart's Italian comic operas; a performance of a Plautine comedy must have resembled a modern musical comedy. It has to be emphasized here that the Elizabethan dramatists will have been familiar with the role of music in Plautus; this was mentioned and even explained in the introductions to the major Renaissance editions of Roman comedy.[4] The dialogue of Plautine comedy is stylized, as the lines are often symmetrically balanced, so that we are sometimes reminded of an exchange of 'musical' phrases. The overall effect of Plautine theatre language

---

[1] K. Elam, *Shakespeare's Universe of Discourse. Language-Games in the Comedies* (Cambridge, 1984), p.6.
[2] R. Janko, *Aristotle on Comedy* (Berkeley/Los Angeles, 1984), p.221 – 225; 167 – 186.
[3] *Elementi Plautini in Plauto* (Firenze, 1961), p.151.
[4] Cf., for example, *Publii Terentii Afri Comoediae Sex* (Frankfurt/M., 1562), p.44f.

is one of patterned artificiality,[5] and this is surely how it was received by the Elizabethans.

The Renaissance humanists appreciated the Roman comedies as model texts in which the art of writing good Latin could be studied. In some important Renaissance editions, Plautus is highly recommended for the 'elegantia' as well as the 'copia', the stylistic copiousness, of his language.[6] How much this ideal meant in humanist education during the Renaissance has been shown by Marion Trousdale in her book on rhetoric in Shakespeare. She concentrates on Erasmus, and especially on his treatise *De Copia*, in which he instructs a writer how to acquire the rhetorical quality of 'richness'.[7] Trousdale goes on to demonstrate how this is reflected in the scenic art of Shakespeare. Although her analysis is very helpful (even if not all the examples she offers are fully convincing), one important link is missing in her argumentation. She remains silent on the fact, essential in our context, that Shakespeare and other Elizabethan dramatists did not only study the art of copiousness in Erasmus's prose treatise *De Copia*,[8] which, besides, offers only a selection of rhetorical conventions, but were primarily interested in the way in which a playwright made *dramatic* use of the elements of *copia* in a specific situation; that is, they studied *dramatic* models of copiousness, models that *exemplified* the use of *copia* in dialogue or in a scene, and these models were the Roman comedies, those of Plautus even more than those of Terence. So far only the dramatic rhetoric of Terence has been examined in detail by students of Elizabethan drama,[9] whereas Plautus's great rhetorical skill has been totally neglected by Shakespeare critics.

Indeed, it must be said that all the elements mentioned by Trousdale as contributing to the effect of *copia* are to be found in Plautus. Erasmus not only expressly advised the schoolmaster that, when teaching Roman comedies, he should point out the rhetorical figures and schemes,[10] but he also illustrated many of the elements of *copia* with examples taken from Terence and, more frequently, Plautus.[11] To begin with, Plautus has a special penchant for 'semantic repetition', a stylistic device that was known as 'amplificatio': a concept is expressed in different ways in a succession of phrases. The following example is taken at random: Sosia comments, by way of 'amplificatio', on the

[5] Fraenkel, op. cit., e.g. p.217f.
[6] Cf. for example, the edition *Plautus Poeta Comicus* (Strasbourg, 1508), f.IIff.
[7] M. Trousdale, *Shakespeare and the Rhetoricians* (London, 1982).
[8] Erasmus, *De Copia*, English translation in: *Collected Works of Erasmus*, vol.24, Literary and Educational Writings, 2 ed. C.R. Thompson (Toronto/Buffalo/London, 1978).
[9] E.g. M.T. Herrick, *Comic Theory in the Sixteenth Century* (Urbana, 1950), p.12ff.
[10] In *On the Method of Study* (*De Ratione Studii*), *Collected Works of Erasmus*, vol.24, p.683.
[11] Cf., for example, the notes in the English translation of *De Copia*, *Collected Works of Erasmus*, 24, passim.

fact that Jupiter has prolonged the night so that he may have a longer enjoyment of Alcumena's love:

> Certe edepol, si quicquamst aliud *quod credam* aut *certo sciam*,
> *credo* ego hac noctu Nocturnum obdormivisse ebrium.
> nam *neque* se Septentriones quoquam in caelo commovent,
> *neque* se Luna quoquam mutat atque uti exorta est semel,
> nec Iugulae *neque* Vesperugo *neque* Vergiliae occidunt.
> ita statim stant signa, *neque* nox quoquam concedit die.
>
> I, 271 – 276 (italics mine)

> My goodness, if there's anything I can believe or know for sure, I surely do believe old Nocturnus went to bed this night in liquor. Why, the Great Bear hasn't moved a step anywhere in the sky, and the moon's just as it was when it first rose, and Orion's Belt, and the Evening Star, and the Pleiades aren't setting, either. Yes, the constellations are standing stock still, and no sign of day anywhere.

Plautus here employs the device of 'artful redundancy', which Trousdale discusses in detail.[12] In our next example, already familiar to us, the repetitive variations used by Sosia appropriately reflect his anxiety about his identity being denied by Mercury:

> ubi ego perii? ubi immutatus sum? ubi ego formam perdidi?
> an egomet me illic reliqui, si forte oblitus fui?
> nam hic quidem omnem imaginem meam, quae antehac fuerat, possidet.
> vivo fit quod numquam quisquam mortuo faciet mihi possidet.
>
> 456-459

> For heaven's sake, where did I lose myself? Where was I transformed? Where did I drop my shape? I didn't leave myself behind at the harbour, did I, if I did happen to forget it? For, my word, this fellow has got hold of my complete image, mine that was. Here I am alive and folks carry my image – more than anyone will ever do when I'm dead.

'Artful redundancy' is further achieved by language 'varied by the use of synonyms [. . .], by *antonomasia* [. . .] paraphrase [. . .] metaphor, metonymy, synecdoche, hyperbole [. . .] *interrogatio*, irony [. . .]'[13], as well as the use of *incrementum* leading to a climax. Instead of discussing all these rhetorical schemes, so frequent in Plautus, we concentrate on just a few of them. Plautus has a special fondness for the asyndetic piling up of synonymous expressions, which adds intensity to a dramatic situation, as when Menaechmus S articulates his great joy over his good fortune in a series of exclamations:

---

[12] Trousdale, op. cit., p.52.
[13] Trousdale, ibid.

di me quidem omnes *adiuvant, augent, amant* [. . .]
propera, Menaechme, fer pedem, confer gradum.

II, 551-552 (italics mine)

Well, well, all the gods do aid, augment, and love me! [. . .]
Quick, Menaechmus! forward, march!

Metaphors are employed to great effect with reference to 'trickery and love'.[14] We also find in Plautus remarkable instances of 'comparatio', arising immediately and naturally from a dramatic situation: when Peniculus, for example, is faced with his Patron, who is wearing the stolen *palla* across his breast, Menaechmus, as we have seen, draws a comparison with two famous mythological motifs: Jupiter carrying away Ganymede, and Venus in the company of Adonis. Furthermore, the principle of 'climax' frequently shapes the whole structure of a dialogic situation.

The exchange of dialogue is itself given added intensity by a variety of means which were to become stock elements in European comedy. One of these is rapid repartee, a feature which has been commented on by classicists[15] and which occurs, for example, in IV, ii of *Menaechmi* (602ff.). An effective way of linking dialogue exchanges is the 'catchword' technique: a speaker picks up the last word or one of the last words of the preceding speaker and comments on it, sometimes turning the meaning into its exact opposite.[16] This is very common in Plautus; there is a good example in the concluding situation of scene V, vii of *Menaechmi*, where Messenio has just freed Menaechmus from the four slaves, and asks his master in return for his manumission:

MES.   Ergo, edepol, si recte facias, ere, med emittas manu.
MEN.   Liberem ego te?
MES.   Verum, quandoquidem, ere, te servavi.
MEN.   Quid est?
        adulescens, *erras*.
MES.   *Quid, erro?*
MEN.   Per Iovem adiuro patrem,
        med erum tuom non esse.
MES.   Non taces?
MEN.   Non mentior;
        nec meus servos umquam tale fecit quale tu mihi.
MES.   Sic sine igitur, si tuom negas me esse, abire liberum.

---

[14] Cf. Duckworth, op. cit., p.337; on 'variatio' cf. Erasmus, *De Copia*, op. cit., esp. p.307ff.

[15] J.N. Hough, 'Rapid Repartee in Roman Comedy', *CJ*, 65 (1969/70), 163 – 167; cf. also G. Thamm, 'Beobachtungen zur Form des plautinischen Dialogs', *Hermes*, 100 (1972), 558 – 567.

[16] For this technique cf. B. Seidensticker, *Die Gesprächsverdichtung in den Tragödien Senecas* (Heidelberg, 1969), p.26 and J.L. Hancock, *Studies in Stichomythia* (Chicago, 1917), p.36.

MEN. Mea quidem hercle causa liber esto atque ito quo voles.
MES. Nempe *iubes?*
MEN.   *Iubeo* hercle, si quid imperi est in te mihi.

                                        1023-1030 (italics mine)

MES. Then, by Jove, master, if you did the right thing you'd set me
      free.
MEN. I set you free?
MES. Yes indeed, seeing I saved your life, master.
MEN. What's this? You're making a mistake, young man.
MES. Eh? A mistake?
MEN. Why, I swear by Father Jupiter I'm not your master.
MES. [. . .] Oh, none of that, sir!
MEN. I'm not lying; no slave of mine ever did such a thing as you
      did for me.
MES. Very well then, sir, if you say I'm not yours, let me go free.
MEN. Lord, man, be free so far as I am concerned, and go where
      you like.
MES. [. . .] Those are your orders, really?
MEN. Lord, yes, if I have any authority over you.

This passage also contains an instance of *interrogatio* as a further means of
achieving *copia*. In *Amphitruo* we have an especially fine example of catchword
exchanges; Mercury, playing the part of Sosia, intimidates the real slave
Sosia; he rebukes him for lying and threatens to beat him:

MERC. At mentiris etiam: certo pedibus, non tunicis venis.
SOS.   Ita *profecto.*
MERC.   Nunc *profecto* vapula ob mendacium.
SOS.   Non edepol volo *profecto.*
MERC.   At pol *profecto* ingratiis.
       hoc quidem *profecto* certum est, non est arbitrarium.

                                        369-372 (italics mine)

MERC. Ha, lying again! Thou dost clearly come with thy feet, not
       thy tunic.
SOS.   [. . .] Naturally.
MERC. And naturally now get thrashed for fibbing [. . .]
SOS.   Oh dear, I object, naturally.
MERC. Oh well, naturally that is immaterial. My 'Naturally', at
       least, is a cold hard fact, no matter of opinion.

This is also a good example of the figure of *ploce*, the repetition of a word after
another one has been inserted, a figure very common in Plautus.[17] Sometimes
the more emphatic form of *epizeuxis*, the immediate repetition of the same
word, is used, as when Menaechmus, on discovering Erotium entering the

---

[17] For a further discussion of rhetorical figures in Plautus cf. Duckworth, op. cit.,
     p.331ff.

stage, tries to keep Peniculus back: 'Mane, mane obsecro hercle: eapse eccam exit.' (179) ('Wait, wait, for heaven's sake, wait! Look! she's coming out herself!'). As Plautus is an author fond of *playing* with language, he especially favours *polyptoton*. We find a most skilful example of *polyptoton* combined with *antimetabole* in the first scene of *Amphitruo*, where Sosia anxiously comments on the words and actions of Mercury; Mercury's threat 'Haud malum huic est *pondus pugno*' (312; 'There's some weight in that fist') is followed by Sosia's 'Perii, *pugnos ponderat*' ('I'm finished! He's a-weighing his fists!'). If *anaphora* is very common in Plautus, *epistrophe*, the obverse of this figure, is sometimes also used for dramatic effects. Again the encounter between Mercury and Sosia provides good examples, as Sosia anxiously echoes Mercury's threats:

> MERCURY.   Hinc enim mihi dextra vox auris, ut videtur, *verberat*.
> SOSIA.   Metuo, vocis ne vicem hodie hic vapulem, quae hunc
>   *verberat*.
>
> MERCURY.   Yes, a voice from the right here, as it seems, doth strike
>   my ear.
> SOSIA.   I'm afraid he'll soon pummel me instead of my voice for
>   its striking him.   333-334

In the great quarrel scene IV, ii of *Menaechmi* the Matrona adds intensity to the dramaturgic situations by five times completing lines spoken by Menaechmus with the 'choric' comment: 'nugas agis' (621-625) ('Nonsense'). Forms of *epanalepsis* are also to be found in the comedies of Plautus, as when Mercury threatens Sosia: '*familiaris* accipiere faxo haud *familiariter*' (355) ('I warrant ye I'll welcome servants of the family with strange familiarity.'). Other tropes and figures will be considered in our discussion of the Plautine art of punning. Here it is necessary to point out that the Plautine dialogues, despite their rhetorical and metrical stylization, often produce a colloquial or conversational tone.[18] The best examples are perhaps the opening dialogue in *Amphitruo* between Mercury and Sosia and the brilliant situation in scene IV, ii of *Menaechmi* where the Matrona and Peniculus try to prove Menaechmus E guilty of the theft of the *palla*:

> MEN.   Quid negotist? MA. Pallam- MEN. Pallam?
>   MA.Quidam pallam- PEN. Quid paves?
> MEN.   nil equidem paveo [. . .]   608-609
>
> MEN.   What does this mean? MA. A mantle- MEN. [. . .] A
>   mantle?

---

[18] According to the *Tractatus Coislinianus*, 'Comic diction is common and popular. The comic poet must endue his characters with their own native idiom, and (use) the local (idiom) himself.' (Janko, op. cit., p.39); cf. also Duckworth, op. cit., p.332.

MA.   A mantle someone-   PEN. [. . .] What are you frightened at?
MEN.   [. . .] Frightened? I? Not in the least.

Here the Matrona is unable to finish her accusation against her husband, because he is so agitated that he interrupts her. Then the subject matter changes, and further incriminations are voiced by the Matrona and by Peniculus. Some moments later, Menaechmus E asks his wife what it is that the parasite has told her. As she does not answer at once, he is forced to repeat his question, and only then does she break her silence and tell him that he himself knows the answer well enough:

MEN.   Quid hoc est, uxor? quidnam hic narravit tibi
          quid id est? quid taces? quin dicis quid sit?
                                        MA.   Quasi tu nescias.
          me rogas?   638-40

MEN.   What's all this my dear? What sort of a tale has he been
          relating to you? What is it? What? are you silent? Why don't
          you tell me what it is?
MA.   As if you didn't know! Asking me!

Menaechmus then replies that he would not have asked if he had known the answer, which is, of course, a lie. It is only then that the Matrona is able to complete the accusation which she had begun a considerable while before: 'palla mi est domo surrupta.' (645) ('A mantle has been stolen from me at home.'). When Menaechmus E hears this sentence, he is so shocked that he mechanically repeats it without even changing the personal pronoun: 'Palla surruptast *mihi*?' (italics mine). This kind of an uncontrolled and perplexed reaction of a character is well known in modern productions of farces.

The dialogue likewise approaches 'realism' when one character commands another to be silent. For example, Messenio warns his master of the fraudulent Erotium, but Menaechmus is unwilling to listen to him because he accepts full responsibility for the consequences of his visit to the courtesan: 'Tace, inquam / mihi dolebit, non tibi, si quid ego stulte fecero.' (438-439) ('Hold your tongue, I tell you. It will hurt me, not you, if I play the fool.'). However, the tables are turned in the final scene when Messenio is in command of the situation and assumes an authority which is fully accepted by both Menaechmi. When, in his uncontrolled outbursts of joy, Menaechmus S interrupts him, Messenio strictly forbids him to interfere with his investigation into whether the two young men are twins (II, 1114).

Shakespeare's *Errors* reflects the stylistic ideal of *copia* par excellence, because the play as a whole can be understood as an 'incrementum' or 'amplificatio' of the Plautine model: the doubling of the twins motif, the intensification of the confusions, the addition of the Egeon subplot and the introduction of Luciana as well as the extension of the role of the denizen's wife, all reflect the Elizabethan delight in amplified copiousness that goes far beyond the stylistic ideal of *copia* in language.[19] As far as this linguistic *copia* is concerned, it is not surprising that rhetorical elements, schemes and tropes which are common in Shakespearean drama are already to be found in *Errors*, and it is interesting that many of them not only occur in the rhetorical handbooks of the Renaissance but also in Shakespeare's Plautine sources.

Errors, although characterized by compactness and great dramatic intensity, contains forms of stylistic *amplificatio*, too. Dramatic economy and *copia* are not mutually exclusive. We need only think of the extensive dialogue between Antipholus S and his Dromio about the nature of time, where the frequently punning redefinitions of time may be taken as instances of *amplificatio* (II, ii). These are most skilfully inserted into the development of the action in order to provide the audience with a few moments of relaxation. There are other occasions, too, where *amplificatio* occurs, as when, for example, Adriana uses it to reveal her despair about the supposed cooling of her husband's love: 'Hath homely age th' alluring beauty took / From my poor cheek? [. . .] Are my discourses dull? barren my wit? [. . .] Do their gay vestments his affection bait? [. . .] What ruins are in me that can be found / By him not ruined?' (89-97). One of the great dramatic situations is Adriana's encounter with the 'wrong' husband in scene II, ii; Adriana's monologue addressed to him is an excellent example of Shakespeare's brilliant command of rhetoric in this play, of his ability to combine a whole series of figures and tropes in order to achieve a heightened overall effect:[20] Adriana uses a rhetorically charged language because she knows that her marriage is at stake:

> Ay, ay, Antipholus, look strange and frown,
> Some other mistress hath thy sweet aspects;
> I am not Adriana, nor thy wife.
> The time was once when thou unurg'd wouldst vow
> That never words were music to thine ear,
> That never object pleasing in thine eye,
> That never touch well welcome to thy hand,
> That never meat sweet-savour'd in thy taste,
> Unless I spake, or look'd, or touch'd, or carv'd to thee.
> How comes it now, my husband, O, how comes it,
> That thou art then estranged from thyself? —
> Thyself I call it, being strange to me,
> That undividable, incorporate,
> Am better than thy dear self's better part.

---

[19] Cf. H.F. Brooks, 'Themes and Structure in "The Comedy of Errors" ', *Early Shakespeare*, p.63.

[20] On Shakespeare's rhetoric cf. especially Sr. M. Joseph, *Shakespeare's Use of the Arts of Language* (New York, 1947) and B. Vickers, 'Shakespeare's Use of Rhetoric', in K. Muir and S. Schoenbaum, eds., *A New Companion to Shakespeare Studies* (Cambridge, 1971), p.83 – 98.

[. . .]
I am possess'd with an adulterate *blot*,
My *blood* is mingled with the crime of lust [. . .]
Keep then fair league and *truce* with thy *true* bed,
I live unstain'd, thou undishonoured.   110-146 (italics mine)

The first lines, which begin with a small instance of *epizeuxis*, have the form of *amplificatio*, they are also an excellent example of irony, because Adriana is addressing her memories of her husband's former behaviour to a stranger. The rhetorical patterning of the lines by *anaphora*:

> *That never* words were music to thine ear,
> *That never* object pleasing in thine eye,
> *That never* touch well welcome to thy hand,
> *That never* meat sweet-savour'd in thy taste . . .

adds further emphasis and may be compared to the end of *Menaechmi*, where Messenio announces in anaphoric lines the auction of all his master's possessions, including his wife:

> *venibunt* servi, supellex, fundi, aedes, omnia
> *venibunt* quiqui licebunt, praesenti pecunia.
> *venibit* uxor quoque etiam, si quis emptor venerit.
>
> 1158-1160 (italics mine)

> For sale . . . slaves, household, goods, land, houses . . .
> everything! . . . For sale . . . your own price . . . cash down!
> . . . For sale . . . even a wife, too . . . if any buyer appears!

However, whereas Messenio uses the figure for a merely playful purpose, Adriana achieves through it an intensification of her entreaties. Adriana's anaphoric lines are at the same time organized according to the figure of *isocolon*. As each line exceeds the former in intensity, we have a kind of climax which results in her dramatically effective question: 'How comes it now, my husband, O, how comes it, / That thou art then estranged from thyself? – / Thyself I call it, being strange to me . . .' This effect is enhanced by the use of *ploce* (comes . . . comes), *anadiplosis* (thyself / Thyself), and *polyptoton* (estranged-strange). Although the tension decreases for a while, rhetoric is still present when Adriana continues: 'Thyself I call it [. . .] That undividable, incorporate, / Am better than thy dear self's better part'. By the use of 'better' in a double sense, she employs the figure of *antanaclasis*. The juxtaposition of the words 'blot' / 'blood' and 'truce' / 'true', in the last lines of the above quotation produces the additional figure of *paronomasia*. This example provides abundant proof of Shakespeare's rhetorical skill in this early comedy; it shows how he aims at an effect of intensification by *fusing* a great number of rhetorical elements. In the last scene, in her encounter with the Abbess, Adriana directly refers to *copia* as a stylistic ideal. Justifying herself, she claims that she constantly reprehended her husband, so that his behaviour was the topic, 'the *copy* of our conference' (62).[21] Interestingly enough, the lines in this monologue, as in all the other verse parts of the comedy, are structured with a far greater regularity than the verse of a Plautine comedy, where, for example, we do not find many instances of *isocolon*. And yet the overall effect of Shakespeare's lines is far more dramatic than anything we find in the Plautine comedies.

In the above quotation there is a further very characteristic rhetorical device, namely the technique of *incrementum*, the heaping up of synonyms by way of *asyndeton*. This deserves special mention because it is particularly prominent in *Errors* and because it has striking analogues in Plautus's dramatic language. Towards the climax in the first part of her monologue quoted above, Adriana reminds Antipholus of the fact that 'The time was once when thou unurg'd wouldst vow [. . .] That never meat sweet-savour'd in thy taste, / Unless I *spake*, or *look'd*, or *touch'd*, or *carv'd* to thee'. The same scene contains further interesting examples, as when Luciana playfully scolds Dromio S using a number of animal metaphors: 'Dromio, thou *drone*, thou *snail*, thou *slug*, thou *sot*' (194), or when Adriana builds up another climax in her exchange with Antipholus (168 – 180). Indeed, the accumulation of synonyms for dramatic purposes occurs very frequently in *Errors*; note how in this way Shakespeare achieves a mimetic or 'subtextual' suggestion of Adriana's frustration concerning her husband in IV, ii:

> I cannot, nor I will not hold me still.
> My tongue, though not my heart, shall have his will.
> He is *deformed*, *crooked*, *old* and *sere*,
> *Ill-fac'd*, *worse bodied*, *shapeless everywhere*;
> *Vicious*, *ungentle*, *foolish*, *blunt*, *unkind*,
> *Stigmatical* in making, *worse* in mind.   17 – 22 (italics mine)

Here a comparison suggests itself with the way in which Plautus dramatizes Menaechmus's impatience with his wife – he, too, uses the accumulation of synonyms in a specially dramatic situation:

> Ni *mala*, ni *stulta* sies, ni *indomita imposque animi*,
> quod viro esse odio videas, tute tibi odio habeas [. . .]
> nam quotiens foras ire volo,
> me *retines*, *revocas*, *rogitas*,
>   quo ego *eam*, *quam rem agam*, *quid negoti geram*,
>   *quid petam*, *quid feram*, *quid foris egerim* . . .
>   110 – 116 (italics mine)

If you weren't mean, if you weren't stupid, if you weren't a violent virago, what you see displeases your husband would be displeasing

---

[21] The rhetorical meaning of the term *copy* has been explained by Foakes, op. cit., p.91, n.62.

to you, too [. . .] Why, whenever I want to go out, you catch hold
of me, call me back, cross-question me as to where I'm going,
what I'm doing, what business I have in hand, what I'm after,
what I've got, what I did when I was out . . .

While it is true that Shakespeare is much more successful in the art of
building up a climax in the dialogue or in a whole scene, some of the means he
employs to achieve this intensification are familiar to us from our study of
Plautus. We find rapid repartee on various occasions, such as in the witty
dialogic exchange between Antipholus and his Dromio in II, ii. (40ff.).[22]
Furthermore, the catchword technique, also familiar to us from Plautus, has
an important function in *Errors* and is especially favoured by the Dromios,
who like to take up the last word of their master in order to turn the meaning
on its head. This technique is introduced in the very first scene of mistaken
identity, when the puzzled Antipholus S asks Dromio E: 'How chance thou art
return'd so soon?' and Dromio, no less bewildered, retorts: 'Return'd so
soon? rather approach'd too late . . .' (I, ii, 43). In this way they produce
another rhetorical scheme, *asteismus*, which was to become one of the
prominent devices of Shakespearean dialogue.[23] This scheme comes quite
naturally in a comedy about the confusion of identity, and we find a number
of effective and comic examples in both *Menaechmi* and *Amphitruo*. (e.g.
Menaechmi 685, 724; *Amphitruo* 309, 317, 333ff; 367, 434, 530, 537, 697, 719.)
   Elements such as these produce verisimilitude that is in sharp contrast to the
overall stylizing tendency. In both Plautus and Shakespeare the juxtaposition
of poetic stylization and colloquial 'realism' is most deliberate. The notion is
common among classicists that in his comedies Plautus merely uses the
everyday Latin language of his own time. However, recent criticism has
shown convincingly that this impression of a 'conversational' language is
deceptive, because Plautus knows very well how to use *poetic* language for
dramatic purposes.[24] His language is that of a poet, and this is already suggested
by the metrical structure of his verse. And that the Elizabethans were well
aware of Plautus's *poetic* qualities is documented by both Ben Jonson and by
Francis Meres, who, as we remember, considered Plautus such a great master
of language that, if the Muses spoke Latin, then it was surely in the manner of
Plautus that they would speak. Indeed, there is poetry in Plautus, yet what
Meres did not realize is that in the plays of both Plautus and the whole New
Comedy tradition as well as in Shakespeare's play there is a deliberate contrast
between poetic stylization and conversational 'realism'. In *Errors*, the stylizing
is a necessary formal equivalent to the artificiality and improbability of the

---

22 This has also been recognized by Foakes, op. cit., p.xlix.
23 Cf. Vickers, in Muir and Schoenbaum, op. cit., p.89.
24 Cf. I. Fischer, 'Encore Sur Le Caractère de la Langue de Plaute', *Studii Clasice*, 13
    (1971), 59 – 78.

plot. It would, therefore, be dangerous to take stylization in *Errors* as proof of the hypothesis that it is a *very* early work. It is equally wrong to qualify Shakespeare's use of rhetoric in the comparatively early *Errors* as 'stiff',[25] because rhetoric is here deliberately used as a development of the classical tradition.

The conversational tone within the stylized framework is a major reason for the brilliant actability of Plautine and Shakespearean comedy. Along with this tendency we frequently find nonverbal, mimic and gestural elements. The Renaissance humanists had at least some knowledge of the performative quality of comedy, and they referred to Donatus, who claimed that sometimes 'gesture is more powerful than speech'.[26] Lucian, who was highly esteemed by them, wrote a perceptive and most interesting essay on the communicative qualities of the nonverbal element in theatre.[27] Yet above all they quoted Evanthius's definition that 'comoedia autem, quia poema sub imitatione vitae atque morum similitudine compositum est, *in gestu et pronuntiatione consistit*'.[28] Because of their performative character, the Plautine play-texts contain a great many implied or indirect stage directions which the actor has to add to the spoken word.[29] The great scene IV, ii of *Menaechmi* presents a good example of this technique in Plautus. Here the actor can infer from the reactions of his partner what gestures he has to use in this situation: the Matrona commands her husband to stop his caresses ('Aufer hinc palpationes.' 607) and to take his hands off her ('Aufer manum.' 627). Peniculus notices that Menaechmus turns pale with fear. In the dramatic dialogue between Alcumena and Jupiter in III, ii of *Amphitruo*, Alcumena has been accused by her husband of adultery, and now she shows her indignation to Jupiter, who, in the shape of Amphitruo, is standing in front of her. He asks her: 'quo te avortisti?' ('Turned away? Where to?'), and a little later she rebukes him for his caresses: 'Potin ut abstineas manum?' (899 – 903) ('Can't you keep your hands off?'). The Roman comedies are particularly rich in deictic gestures, and it is certain that these were used to add emphasis to personal pronouns. The use of implied gestures in Elizabethan drama is very similar to the Roman practices,[30] and *Errors*, too, continues the tradition. In

---

[25] Sr. M. Joseph, op. cit., p.80 and Vickers, op. cit., p.94.

[26] Cf. E. Klien, *Aelius Donatus als Kritiker der Komödien des Terenz* (Diss. Innsbruck, 1948), p.197.

[27] *On Dance* in Lucian, ed. and transl. by A.M. Harmon, The Loeb Classical Library (London/Cambridge, Mass., 1915), V, 219 – 289.

[28] Evanthius, *De Fabula* in: *Aeli Donati Commentum Terenti*, ed. P. Wessner (Stuttgart, 1962), I, 23. Quoted from Klien, op. cit., p.12.

[29] Cf. E.G. Loitold, *Untersuchungen zur Spieltechnik der plautinischen Komödie* (Diss. Wien, 1975). A further useful study is B.A. Taladoire's *Commentaires sur la Mimique et l'Expression Corporelle du Comédien Romain* (Montpellier, 1951), esp. p.13 – 58.

[30] This has been clearly demonstrated by G. Rudolf, *The Theatrical Notation of Roman and Pre-Shakespearean Comedy*, The Cooper Monographs, 29 (Bern, 1981); for this aspect in Shakespeare cf. J. Hasler, *Shakespeare's Theatrical Notation* (Bern, 1974).

Errors the use of deictic language is nowhere more clearly visible than in the final recognition scene, where the Duke is trying to work out who is who:

> *These* two Antipholus', *these* two so like,
> And *these* two Dromios, one in semblance,
> Besides her urging of her wrack at sea.
> *These* are the parents to *these* children . . .
>
> 347 – 350 (italics mine)

The first indirect suggestion of gestures is to be found in the opening scene, when the Duke speaks of his own 'threat'ning looks' (10). Adriana, who in II, i was described by her sister with the comment: 'Fie, how impatience loureth in your face' (II, i, 86), reproachfully addresses her 'husband' in the next scene: 'Ay, ay, Antipholus, look strange and frown' (110). She later entreats him: ''do not tear away thyself from me' (124) and adds: 'I will fasten on this sleeve of thine' (173). There is an echo of this later when she advises Antipholus S in III, ii: 'Though others have the arm, show us the sleeve' (23).

The dialogue of the 'Pinch scene', one of the play's most dramatic situations, contains the largest number of implied gestures. Luciana and the Courtesan comment on the outward appearance of Antipholus E: 'Alas, how fiery, and how sharp he looks. / Mark how he trembles in his ecstasy' (48 – 49). Dr Pinch's first words: 'Give me your hand, and let me feel your pulse' (50) are answered by Antipholus's aggressive retort: 'There is my hand, and let it feel your ear'. Furthermore, the grotesque appearance of Dr Pinch is graphically described by Antipholus E, who calls him the 'companion with the saffron face' (59). Later, in the last scene, Antipholus draws a very detailed picture of the dreadful appearance of the conjurer (V, i, 237 – 246). The gestures in this scene culminate in Antipholus's outraged: 'with these nails I'll pluck out these false eyes' (102). This reminds us of the aggressiveness of Menaechmus S in his 'madness' scene (V, ii), where we also have a series of important implied gestures.[31]

So far we have not considered the most effective use of a gesture contained in the text of *Errors*: it occurs at the climax of Antipholus's 'wooing' in III, ii, when he concludes his address to Luciana with the words: 'Give me thy hand.' (69). This moment, when Antipholus takes Luciana's hand, is very powerful on stage. The comedy of the situation, which is fully enjoyed by the audience, culminates in Luciana's concluding words: 'O, soft, sir, hold you still; / I'll fetch my sister to get her good will.' But beneath the comic veneer we are touched by the human fallibility and instability which Luciana exhibits here. This situation already reminds us somewhat of the great effects Shakespeare draws from gestures in his later plays: Antipholus's asking for Luciana's hand can be seen as an early comic anticipation of the famous gesture of Coriolanus, who takes his mother's hand in silence (V, iii, 182): he has been persuaded to

---

[31] These gestures are meant to parody the madness scenes of Greek tragedy.

give up his plan of sacking Rome. But whereas Coriolanus's holding Volumnia's hand signals his final tragedy, the gesture in *Errors* is a great comic moment.

2. *Special dialogic strategies: questions and persuasions*

In her analysis of *copia* in Shakespeare, Trousdale refers to the opening scene of *Hamlet* and argues that the frequent questions can be understood as an elaborate use of the rhetorical figure of *interrogatio*.[32] Yet what she sees as a characteristic of this particular play may, on closer inspection, be seen to be a basic element of Shakespearean dramaturgy. Moreover, it is used with considerable skill in *Menaechmi* and especially in *Amphitruo*, and in the early *Errors* we find a fully developed pattern of question and answer. Frequently in this play, questions are caused by the bewildering confusions of the action, and their regular recurrence effectively contributes to the play's overall rhythm. The opening scene modifies the pattern in a subtle way. There, the extensive narration of Egeon's adventures is the answer to the Duke's question: 'say in brief the cause / Why thou departedst from thy native home' (28 – 29). The pattern first emerges fully in I, ii after an introductory dialogue and a short soliloquy from Antipholus S: on seeing Dromio 'reappearing', he addresses his servant as 'the almanac of my true date' (I, ii, 41). Then he asks him why he is about to mar this image which he has of him by returning too soon (42). As we have seen, this causes the 'wrong' Dromio to ask a question in return; and he adds that he is afraid he has arrived too late to bring his master home in time for dinner. The dialogue then continues with further questions and seemingly nonsensical answers until Dromio receives the first slap in the face. This is the moment when the dialogic situation is exactly reversed, because now it is the servant who is unable to understand his master's behaviour: 'What mean you, sir? for God's sake hold your hands.' (93).

In the next scene, the first of the second Act, Shakespeare skilfully varies the pattern with the entrance of Adriana and Luciana. Adriana's worries about her husband predispose her to ask questions. Not only does she ask why her husband and servant have not returned, but she goes so far as to question the traditional definition of male liberty; and she wants to know whether her sister is of the same opinion – she expects, of course, a positive answer. When Dromio E at last returns, the two ladies shower him with questions, while he unwittingly provokes them by talking in an enigmatic and quibbling manner. Towards the end of the same situation, the pattern of question and answer is again reversed because it is now Dromio who asks: 'Go back again, and be new beaten home?' (76). What makes this scene even more effective is the fact

[32] Trousdale, op. cit., p.52.

that it contains another 'inset scene': Dromio skilfully acts out the confrontation between his 'master' and himself, using the same question and answer pattern (II, i, 60 – 70). When, still in II, i, Adriana begins a monologue in which she reflects on the mysterious behaviour of her husband, she repeatedly formulates her thoughts as questions, a technique which is so typical of *Errors*. She addresses questions to herself in self-pity, but she does not know how to answer them. This monologue ends therefore with the speaker's total isolation: '. . . I'll weep what's left away, and weeping die.' (115).

The dialogic pattern first introduced in I, ii is extensively repeated in II, ii when Dromio S reappears and when for the first time we have a long dialogue between Antipholus S and his own servant. Dromio S, too, is bombarded with questions which he does not understand, just as in I, ii, the servant receives a beating from his master, whereupon he starts asking questions as to the reason for his master's exasperation. It is interesting that Dromio's questions differ markedly from those of his master, because he is not only concerned with discovering the reason for his master's behaviour, but aims rather to find a deeper level of meaning in his master's comments. So to a large extent the ensuing dialogue develops as a language game of questions and answers. In III, i this pattern dominates the entire dialogic exchange. Occasionally this is skilfully stylized in that question plus answer together form a couplet:

> Adriana. Who is that at the door that keeps all this noise?
> Syr. Dro. By my troth, your town is troubled with unruly boys.
>
> 61 – 62

The same pattern is maintained in Acts IV and V, especially in the dialogues between Adriana and Luciana in IV,ii and Antipholus and Dromio in IV, iii. It then achieves most dramatic effects in the Pinch scene (IV, iv). For instance, the stichomythic exchanges of question and answer between master and servant (66 – 76) remind us, as Foakes has observed, of an 'interrogation of a witness'.[33] At the culmination of the fifth Act, even the Duke can do nothing but ask the question: 'Why, what an intricate impeach is this?' (270). Interestingly enough, the next person he addresses with a question in the hope of getting help is a character of the lowest social rank, namely a Dromio: 'Sirrah, what say you?' (275).

There is an even more interesting pattern which contributes to the shaping of the dialogic structure of *Errors*, and this is its abundance of persuasion scenes; the play contains no fewer than eight of these. Rhetoric as a means of persuasion is thus used in a sense propagated by the Renaissance humanists.[34]

---

[33] Foakes, op. cit., p.82, n.66.
[34] Cf., for example, Sr M. Joseph, *Shakespeare's Use of the Arts of Language*, esp. p.242ff. and Trousdale, op. cit., p.55ff.

Commenting on the Elizabethan dramatists, R.Y. Turner observed that 'The dialogue of persuasion would have a ready appeal to playwrights trained in rhetoric because they could transpose to the stage with very few adjustments a traditional deliberate oration.'[35] As far as the early Shakespeare is concerned, Turner discovered that in the early histories persuasion scenes are used frequently and occupy a central position,[36] although in these plays most persuasions end unsuccessfully. In *Errors* too we find that some persuasions do not lead to the desired end. These persuasions and other aspects of style in this comedy are, of course, incompatible with the notion sometimes found among critics that the 'sermo humilis' is appropriate to the genre of comedy.[37] Yet already in Quintilian is the middle style assigned to comedies. The reason he gives is that, since the emotions in comedy ($\eta\vartheta o\varsigma$) are milder than those in tragedy ($\pi\alpha\vartheta o\varsigma$), they require an intermediate style. Shakespeare's comic style is always intensely varied and differentiated. On a considerable number of occasions he adds elements of the grand style, and one of these is, of course, persuasion. The persuader, trying to influence his dialogue partner and change his mind and affections, employs figures of rhetoric, such as we found in Adriana's address to Antipholus S, and in this way, particularly in the tragic opening scene, the style may even approach $\pi\alpha\vartheta o\varsigma$.

When *Errors* opens, we are meant to assume that Egeon has already delivered his plea for mercy. Both at the beginning and at the end of this scene, Egeon shows that he cherishes little hope of being pardoned, and he starts his narration only at the Duke's request. Yet while narrating his misfortunes, he does begin to feel some hope and this causes him to intensify the $\pi\alpha\vartheta o\varsigma$ of his narration by the use of figures of rhetoric, especially of moving metaphors so that his language acquires the quality of 'energeia', and the entire situation assumes the nature of persuasion. In telling his misfortunes, Egeon first characterizes himself by way of *ethopoeia*. When the Duke asks Egeon 'to dilate at full / What have befall'n of them and thee till now' (122 – 1230, the verb 'to dilate' alludes to the *dilatatio* recommended by writers of textbooks of rhetoric in instructions about composing a *narratio*;[38] with this metapoetic reference, the Duke draws the attention of the audience to the scene's rhetoric. To heighten this effect, Egeon skilfully includes in his narration the small scene of 'piteous plainings of the pretty babes' (72). It is especially interesting that the way in which Egeon narrates the sea-storm closely follows Quintilian's suggestion regarding the presentation of a storm: he says that the description should be so vivid that the storm can be clearly

---

[35] R.Y. Turner, *Shakespeare's Apprenticeship* (Chicago/London, 1974), p.67.
[36] Ibid., p.68ff.
[37] Cf., for example, Herrick, *Comic Theory in the Sixteenth Century*; yet Herrick admits that 'Terence's style is not always exclusively humble', p.215.
[38] Cf. Foakes, op. cit., p.9, n.122.

seen before the mind's eye, and this vividness, which Quintilian calls 'enargeia',[39] is splendidly achieved by Egeon. The most important means by which he succeeds in this style is the frequent use of adjectives and verbs charged with emotion. As a result, the Duke, Egeon's judge, is moved to pity, and he pardons him on condition that he procure the ransom of 1000 marks.

A second persuasion scene comes at the beginning of Act II, when Luciana discusses with her sister the rights and duties of husband and wife, and tries to convince her of the necessity of patience. Yet how different is the tone of this scene from that of the earlier persuasion. Luciana attempts to persuade her sister by means of an intellectual argument, yet Adriana's disdain at the 'fool-begg'd patience' (II, i, 41) shows that Luciana has not succeeded in changing her sister's mind.

When Adriana meets the wrong husband in II, ii, a masterfully devised persuasion scene is built up. It is also splendidly comic on account of her efforts to arouse his emotions by frequent use of figures of rhetoric. Ignorant as Adriana is about the real identity of her partner, she nevertheless brings about a change in him. Her monologue, beginning with the words: 'Ay, ay, Antipholus, look strange and frown . . .' has a strong impact on Antipholus, although the effect is different from the one she intended. This effect increases when she asks him why he is estranged from himself (120), and also when she applies to him the same simile of the water-drop which, a short while before, he *himself* had used. It must appear to Antipholus that she is familiar even with his thoughts. From this it is only a short step to his assumption that she may be one of the Ephesian witches.

But the influence she exerts on him by her persuasion goes still further, and the more we proceed with this scene the more 'ambiguous' it becomes. When Antipholus hears a woman who is entirely unknown to him confess that she is 'incorporate' with him and that she is better than his 'dear self's better part' (122 – 123), then this most unusual and powerful experience continues to work within him and, as it were, triggers off his use of the same kind of language with her sister in the next scene but one. He seems to have come unwittingly under Adriana's spell. This accounts for the similarity between his love language and Adriana's.[40] The final part of her speech, which, as we have seen, is very rich in rhetorical devices, again shows Adriana's great capacity for intellectual 'discourses' (II, i, 91). If we do not take offence at the fact that Antipholus never assumes that he has been mistaken for Adriana's husband, then this is certainly due to Adriana's rhetorical mastery and the comic potential of the situation.

---

[39] *The Institutio Oratoria of Quintilian*, ed. H.E. Butler (London/Cambridge, 1922), VIII,iii,60ff.; cf. also Doran, *Endeavors of Art*, p.242 and H.F. Plett, *Rhetorik der Affekte*, Tübingen, 1975, esp. p.39ff.; on 'ενεργεια' cf. Quintilian, VIII,iii,89.

[40] J.R. Brown, *Shakespeare and his Comedies* (London, 1962), p.45 – 55, has pointed out that Luciana, too, adopts possessive language.

Though not very long, Balthasar's persuasion speech in III,i is dramatically effective and, as a result, Antipholus E decides to go to a courtesan instead of breaking open his own house. Again, rhetoric is made use of, yet the main argument which Balthasar puts forward concerns social 'reputation' (86). Antipholus, Balthasar suggests, will lose his good reputation if he acts in an antisocial way by forcefully opening his locked door, not knowing the reason why it was barred.

When scene III, ii opens, we see Luciana and Antipholus in the midst of a dialogue (a scenic opening, we remember, not unknown to Plautus), where Luciana has taken the lead because she is giving her supposed brother-in-law a strange piece of advice. Luciana quite unabashedly suggests to Antipholus that he conceal his real intentions and employ the language of dissimulation for his purpose. In a metapoetic pointer she implies that in order to attain his purpose he should make effective use of rhetoric: 'Be not thy tongue thy own shame's *orator*; / Look sweet, speak fair, become disloyalty.' (10 – 11). Note how well Luciana herself knows how to apply figures of rhetoric such as *erotema*, *paronomasia* and *chiasmus* in her attempt to persuade Antipholus.

The immediate consequence of her address to Antipholus is a long speech of his, aimed at persuading her to become his lover; the persuading situation is thus redoubled. He immediately avails himself of the advice she has just given him, and his style, too, is rhetorically embellished. He has felt deeply moved by her words, and thus it is no accident that he calls her 'mermaid' and 'siren'. In addition, her words also remind him of a sibyl because he discovers some hidden meaning in them, and what is most remarkable, he associates this hidden quality with deceit: 'the folded meaning of your words' deceit' (36). The more he proceeds, the more intensely he uses rhetorical figures and schemes. Note, for instance, how he takes an image from her earlier advice that he should not 'play truant' with his '*bed*' (17) and uses it to form the climax of his own persuading strategy: 'and as a *bed* I'll take thee . . .' (49), and how he adds the favourite Elizabethan paradox: 'He gains by death that hath such means to die'. The exchange of arguments which then follows further increases the intensity of the situation by its pointed form of *stichomythia*, the last words of Antipholus forming the emotional apex. In a later context we shall have to return to this ambiguous scene which is so important for a deeper understanding of the play.

The last Act assembles a number of situations of persuasion. The first of these is the confrontation between Adriana and the Abbess. Aemilia, it is true, is not trying to persuade Adriana to do anything or to perform any action; yet the rhetorical situation is similar to a persuasion scene. From her superior vantage point she makes Adriana see her misbehaviour towards her husband and change her mind. The tone in which she puts forward her arguments is firm. Adriana's reaction 'She did betray me to mine own reproof' (90) suggests that she senses the truth in the reproaches of the Abbess; but she is nevertheless unwilling to accept her authority, and as, with increasing intensity, she pleads for the release of her husband, we again have a double persuasion scene, and a unique one in that it culminates in the clash of two strong wills. The situation ends in a stalemate because neither woman succeeds in changing the other's mind, and thus dramatic suspense is achieved, to be finally resolved by the Duke's appearance. Adriana's pleading to the Duke ends with a powerful climax and, like the other speeches of persuasion, is most effective theatrical language. It has been observed that Adriana does not merely repeat the reproaches concerning her husband which she expressed earlier to the Abbess, but that here her tone is more restrained. She succeeds in persuading the Duke to call for the Abbess. It is a stroke of genius on Shakespeare's part that the entry of the Abbess is delayed by other unexpected events, the first being the excited entry of the Messenger (168 – 184). His entrance gives rise to what may be called a persuasion scene *en miniature* because he seeks Adriana's help to prevent her husband from doing great harm and Antipholus from killing Dr Pinch. The dramatic impetus of this appeal is, however, thwarted by the surprising entrance of Antipholus E. He immediately begins another persuasion scene – the last one in the play – by urging the Duke to grant him justice. Once more the persuader is unsuccessful: the Duke is unable to comply with Antipholus's plea because he is caught up in the 'intricate impeach' (270) of the situation in the same way as the other characters.

The dramatic strategy of persuasion in particular reveals the wide range of Shakespeare's transformation of the plays of the New Comedy tradition which served as his sources. Neither in *Menaechmi* nor in *Amphitruo* is there a fully worked out persuasion scene. As we have seen, rhetorical elements certainly do have considerable importance in these comedies, but they are used in a play with language in order to heighten the *ad hoc* effects of a dramatic situation; they are not employed to form great scenic persuasions. In *Menaechmi* there are only two occasions which would perhaps lend themselves to a brief comparison; in both of them Messenio is the 'persuader': in II, iii he gives advice to his master which at times comes close to being a persuasion, but Menaechmus refuses to listen to him. Although Messenio tried to prevent him from entering Erotium's house, Menaechmus nevertheless visited her, and so Messenio in a soliloquy bewails his own powerlessness over his master. In V,vii there is another brief dramatic moment of persuasion when Messenio, who thinks that it is his master that he has rescued, tries to persuade Menaechmus S to set him at liberty. Although he is unable to make head or tail of the situation, Menaechmus E assents to Messenio's request, and they both anticipate the manumission in a game:

MEN.   Mea quidem hercle causa liber esto atque ito quo voles.
MES.   Nempe iubes?
MEN.   Iubeo hercle, si quid imperi est in te mihi.
MES.   Salve, mi patrone, cum tu liber es, Messenio,

        gaudeo. credo hercle vobis. sed, patrone, te obsecro,
        ne minus imperes mihi quam cum tuos servos fui . . .

MEN.   Lord, man, be free so far as I am concerned, and go where
        you like.

MES.   [. . .] Those are your orders, really?

MEN.   Lord, yes, if I have any authority over you.

MES.   [. . .] Hail, patron mine! 'Messenio, I congratulate you on
        your freedom!' By gad, I take your word for it! But, patron, I
        beseech you, don't order me about any less than when I was
        your slave.   1029ff

This spirit of game reveals where the great difference between these situations and the persuasion scenes in *Errors* really lies. The widespread use of persuasion in *Errors* is one of the major elements that make for the specifically 'Elizabethan' quality of Shakespeare's 'classical' comedy.

3. *The verbal game of puns and quibbles*

A number of explanations are generally advanced for the prevalence of punning and quibbling and other kinds of verbal play in Elizabethan drama and especially in Shakespeare's comedies.[41] One concerns the development of the English language, particularly the changes that occurred with the Great Vowel Shift in the fifteenth century. Frequent punning was made possible by the many homophones which arose in the formative stages of Early Modern English. These new possibilities in the language were welcomed by English authors who had a fine sensitivity to semantic ambiguities and the effects of homophony. In addition, the use of punning in drama had a native popular tradition of its own, especially in the character of the Vice in the Moralities and Interludes. Punning has also been considered in connection with the fact, examined by Foucault, that in the Renaissance there emerged 'a new experience of language and things'[42] – the experience of the separation of things and signs and the discovery that similar or identical signs can signify different things. The prevalence of punning in Shakespeare's plays, particularly in his comedies, has frequently been commented on. We have,

[41] Cf. also the perceptive article by N. Kohl, 'Die Shakespeare-Kritik zum Wortspiel. Ein Beitrag zur historischen Wertung eines Sprachphänomens', *Deutsche Vierteljahrsschrift für Literaturwissenschaft und Geistesgeschichte*, 44 (1970), 528ff. On Shakespearean word play cf. especially L. Wurth, *Das Wortspiel bei Shakespeare*, Wiener Beiträge zur Englischen Philologie, 1 (Wien, 1895), and M.M. Mahood, *Shakespeare's Word Play* (London, 1957).

[42] M. Foucault, *The Order of Things. An Archaeology of the Human Sciences* (New York, 1973), p.49.

however, also to remember the warning by Sister Mirjam Joseph that what looks like a pun may be one of the traditional figures of rhetoric and that, according to the OED, the term 'pun' is not attested before 1660.[43] Nevertheless, it is clear that many of the quibbles are also to be understood as manifestations of a *play* with language, something which, before Shakespeare, is particularly discernible in Plautus.

I do not claim that this influence on Elizabethan comedy was always a direct one, but on the other hand it is important to realize that Roman, especially Plautine comedy appealed to the Elizabethan taste for puns and quibbles. In Plautus, the Elizabethans found an author who had succeeded in drawing brilliant effects from witty verbal gaming. The Romans themselves recognized that this was Plautus's particular strength. He is so successful with his verbal play because he draws heavily on the popular tradition of the Roman Atellana and the Mimus, which also had a playful attitude towards language.[44] We can thus appreciate that in the Elizabethan reception of Plautine comedy the classical and English popular traditions *merged* to an extent that has so far not been sufficiently recognized.

According to Cicero, the most important form of word-play is *paronomasia* (*adnominatio*), which he defines as the similarity, indeed the almost identical forms of two or more words;[45] they need not, however, be etymologically related. In Plautus, this is the most common form of punning.[46] For example, the extravagant voracity of the Parasite is suggested in the following pun which he utters towards the end of his self-characterizing soliloquy: 'neque *edo* neque *emo* nisi quod est carissumum.' (106) ('For not a thing do I eat or buy that isn't, oh, so dear!'). Menaechmus E ironically confesses by way of a pun that he has stolen the *palla* from his wife at no small risk to himself: 'meo *malo* a *mala* apstuli hoc' (133) ('I've done the wretch out of this . . . and done myself, too!'). There is a most comic example in *Amphitruo*: Mercury, who impersonates Sosia and effectively intimidates the true Sosia with his beating, asks Sosia his name. The slave admits being 'Amphitruonis Sosia', whereupon Mercury beats him again. He asks again whether he claims to be Sosia. The slave, afraid of another beating, says that he made a mistake and that instead of 'Amphitruonis *Sosia*' he meant to say 'Amphitruonis *socium*'. He looks for a word which sounds similar to his name in order to make the retraction plausible (383f.). Among the especially remarkable sound effects in Plautus we find Bromia's description of Jupiter's theophany in *Amphitruo*: she admirably describes the *miraculous* supernatural experience of Jupiter's thundering theophany by a most unusual sequence of two pairs of words

---

43 Sr M. Joseph, *Shakespeare's Use of the Arts of Language*, p.340.
44 Cf., for example, Duckworth, op. cit., p.10 – 17.
45 Duckworth, op. cit., p.350ff.
46 Cf. W. Schmidt, *Die sprachlichen Mittel des Komischen bei Plautus* (Diss. Tübingen, 1960).

related to each other by their almost mannerist play with sound effect: 'strepitus, crepitus, sonitus, tonitrus' (1062).

Furthermore, Plautus knows how to play with semantic ambiguity (*syllepsis*), although this play with two meanings of one word is decidedly less common than the formal element of *paronomasia*. We find a good example of this in Peniculus's first soliloquy, because there he puns very nicely on the two meanings of 'carus' = 'dear' (expensive) and 'carus' = 'dear' (beloved). He says that for a long time he has stayed at home with his dear ones ('domi domitus sum usque cum caris meis.'); yet dearer still to him than his loved ones are his meals which, as we saw above, have become so expensive for him: 'nam neque edo neque emo nisi quod est carissumum. / id quoque iam, cari qui instruontur deserunt.' (105 – 107). The pun is thus used as a means of self-characterization.

Jocular repetitions of a word or the asyndetic enumeration of synonyms are additional aspects of Plautine verbal gaming. The juxtaposing of words with the same stem but different prefixes is another form of Plautine verbal play. When, for instance, Erotium discovers that Menaechmus has brought the *palla* which he is wearing as a present for her, he gives the following explanation: '*Induviae* tuae atque uxoris *exuviae*, rosa.' (191; italics mine) ('You're arrayed and my wife's raided, rosey.').[47] And when in Act IV he denies having received the *palla* from Erotium, she shuts her house door against him in anger; he then describes his desperate situation with a pun which is effective because of its conciseness by which the new dramatic situation is described: 'abiit intro, *occlusit* aedis. nunc ego sum *exclusissimus*' (698; italics mine) ('She's gone inside! She's closed the door! Well, if I'm not getting the most exclusive reception!'). Sometimes Plautus even creates a new word, as when Mercury threatens to break Sosia's ribs: 'hodie *lumbifragium* hinc auferes.' (454; italics mine), ('today you will "catch" a fracture of your loins'; my translation).[48] By coining a new and pompous word, Mercury succeeds in intensifying the threatening effect.

Furthermore, Plautus has a penchant for playing with names. In *Menaechmi*, the city name Epidamnus is used in a pun: Messenio warns his master of the dangers of this town by drawing a lively picture of the corruption of its inhabitants and by interpreting the stem of the name Epidamnus as the word 'damnus' = 'damage'. Thus, the very name of the town suggests the dangers that lurk there: 'propterea huic urbi nomen Epidamno inditumst, / quia nemo ferme huc sine damno devortitur.' (263 – 264) ('This city got its name of Epidamnus for just this reason – because almost everyone that stops here gets damaged'). Duckworth gives a whole list of comic 'tell-tale' names or names used for the purpose of a jest. A most elaborate one occurs in *Captivi*, where

---

[47] Cf. Schmidt, op. cit., p.187.
[48] Schmidt, op. cit., p.389. This aspect has also been pointed out by Duckworth, p.334ff.

Philocrates mentions the name of his father as 'Thesaurochrysonicochrysides' (I, 286) (= 'the son of gold surpassing treasures of gold'; Nixon translates this as 'Ducatsdoubloonsandpiecesofeightson'). Here the tell-tale effect is ironic, because Hegio's assumption that the name was given to him on account of his money, is refuted by Philocrates; he says that the father received his name 'on account of his being so greedy and grasping'.[49]

In the play *Bacchides* the enraptured Pistoclerus reveals his fascination for Bacchis by calling her a goddess and then firing off a list of the qualities he finds personified in her; these are: 'Amor, Voluptas, Venus, Venustas, Gaudium, / Iocus, Ludus, Sermo, Suavisaviatio' (I, 115f.) ('Love, Delight, Venus, Grace, Joy, Jest, Jollity, Chitchat, Kissykissysweetkins'). The joke is continued by Lydus's enquiry: 'An deus est ullus Suavisaviatio?' ('You mean to say there is a god Kissykissysweetkins?'). This documents Plautus's singular delight in personifying abstract ideas; it is also an impressive instance of his playful creation of a new word which, by its grotesque form, admirably reflects Pistoclerus's excessive infatuation and elicits the laughter of the audience.[50] In addition, this element serves the function of comedy as a release of sexual energy. It is, however, remarkable that verbal punning in Plautus has this function far less frequently than we might have expected. In *Menaechmi*, we even find an example where the Courtesan is shocked at what she considers an obscene pun by Menaechmus. (She takes his word 'navis' ['ship'] in its second, obscene meaning, 'cunnus').[51] As Donatus's commentary on Terence suggests, Plautus may in these cases be influenced by the stylistic ideal of the 'πρεπον' or *aptum* which prohibited the use of bawdy language;[52] he may also have been motivated in his restraint by his consideration of the women in his audience.

Plautus's play with language exhibits an astonishing variety which cannot be discussed in detail here. Apart from his delight in inventing fantasy names or names with comic effects, he knows how to produce other effects of verbal chiming, such as forming new words or distorting existing words, and in this respect he is totally different from Terence. Furthermore, his texts are interspersed with alliteration, assonance or rhyme, even at the end of a verse. Let us, however, concentrate on Plautine punning. In his comedies, the use of puns differs according to the character type who makes the quibble. The major *dramatis personae* do not favour puns particularly; nor are women (including the courtesans) much given to verbal gaming, because, as we have said, *decorum* would prevent it. The bulk of the verbal games are to be found on the lips of

---

[49] Duckworth, p.349.
[50] E. Segal in his *Roman Laughter* has drawn a parallel between this situation and the revelling scene II,iii of *Twelfth Night*, p.71 – 74.
[51] Cf. Schmidt, op. cit., p.143.
[52] *Aeli Donati Commentum Terenti*, I, 125.

Plautus's slaves and parasites, a fact which once more reflects the strong influence of the popular mime.

For example, Messenio, in his soliloquy on the role of the slave (966ff.),[53] characterizes himself by way of puns in order to describe the cunning and astuteness which enable him to live with his master: 'nam magis multo patior facilius *verba*; *verbera* ego odi' (978) ('I can stand chiding a great deal more easily — but a hiding I can't abide, myself'). 'verba' and 'verbera', lacking any semantic connection, are very similar in sound. When Messenio first enters the stage, he already likes to play the cunning slave who seems better able to assess the advantage of a situation than his master, and he displays his intelligence by punning on his master's quest for his twin ('geminum'); by employing for his comment the verb *gemere*, which looks as if it had the same word-stem as *geminus*, he tries to suggest that sorrows and sighing will necessarily accrue from his master's senseless search: '*geminum* dum quaeres, *gemes.*' (257) ('while you're hunting for your twin, you'll certainly have a twinge.').[54] In the opening scene of *Amphitruo*, which is superb because of its long aggressive dialogue between Mercury and Sosia, the slave on several occasions interprets one of Mercury's words in a sense different from the intended one; he plays either with the homophonic identity of two different words or else with the different meanings of a single word. Mercury shouts 'verbero' at him, meaning that he is about to beat him, whereas Sosia takes the word as a swearword meaning 'Thou whipped slave' (343). A few lines later, Mercury threatens him again: 'Ego tibi istam hodie, sceleste, comprimam linguam.' (348) ('I'll soon make thee hold thy tongue [press thy tongue], miscreant'). The expression 'comprimere linguam' has the double meaning of 'to cause someone to hold his tongue' and 'to rape'; Sosia's answer indicates that he had understood it in the latter sense: 'Haud potes: / bene pudiceque adservatur.' ('No chance: she's chaperoned in nice modest fashion.').[55]

Finally, we should note that the first soliloquy by Peniculus introduces for the first time the theme of 'binding' and 'bond', with which Plautus seems to be playing throughout the *Menaechmi*. As in the course of the action different kinds of 'bond' are set off against each other, the frequent occurrence of the motif acquires a structural function.[56] Peniculus agrees to be 'bound' to his Patron, Menaechmus E suffers from the bonds of his married life and surrenders his will to Erotium; and Messenio, in his own self-characterizing soliloquy, expresses his desire to be freed from the 'bonds' of slavery.

---

[53] Cf. Duckworth, op. cit., p.345.
[54] Schmidt, op. cit., p.69.
[55] Schmidt, op. cit., p.211.
[56] Cf. E.W. Leach, '*Meam Quom Formam Noscito*: Language and Characterization in the *Menaechmi*', *Arethusa*, 2 (1969), 30 – 45.

The range of verbal gaming in Plautus is indeed very remarkable and testifies to his 'language consciousness' and linguistic artistry. As we might expect, though, it is still greatly surpassed by Shakespeare. If Plautus even gives puns a structural function, so does Shakespeare, and he has recourse to the same idea of 'bond' and 'binding'; yet how different is the use he makes of it and how much greater are the dramatic effects he draws from it. As this aspect has, however, already been examined by Leach[57] and by Petronella, a brief mention must suffice here. It has been shown that, by concentrating on the idea of the bonds of family relationship, Shakespeare makes this a part of the play's basic 'structural pattern of separation and union'.[58] The theme is even made concrete in the two symbolic objects, the chain and rope; these, although they 'are instruments for binding, [. . .] do more to cause separation between characters.'[59]

As in Plautus, the quibbles in *Errors* are rarely found on the lips of the female characters. Neither Luciana nor the Courtesan are particularly given to puns, and Adriana has markedly fewer quibbles than other characters (except for her own husband). In any case, she does not join in Dromio's jokes − on the contrary, she is offended by what she takes to be distasteful jesting behaviour from Antipholus and his Dromio. (II, ii, 205). Yet we note that in her reply to Luciana in II, i she employs a linguistic register far above the conversational level, and here she abandons her reservations against punning and includes a play on the double meaning of words. She develops an effective image which she uses as a means of intensifying her persuasive strategy in these lines: 'But, too unruly deer, he breaks the pale / And feeds from home; poor I am but his stale.' (100 − 101).

Her husband is less inclined to verbal play than his brother. However, at the beginning of III, i, he shows his ability to entertain his guests with courteous word-play, and at the end of this scene he informs us of his intention to go and see 'a wench of excellent discourse, / Pretty and witty' (109), which indirectly suggests that he too has a sense of wit. In IV, i he expresses his anger at Angelo's supposed delay in bringing the chain, by using the word 'chain' in a metaphorical sense: 'Belike you thought our love would last too long / If it were *chain'd* together, and therefore came not.' (25 − 26). This pun has the additional function of leading Angelo to believe that Antipholus is merely joking: 'Saving your *merry humour*, here's the note . . .' (27; italics mine).

Antipholus S, on a few occasions at least, joins in the verbal games of his Dromio. When he is 'wooing' Luciana, puns form an important part of his

[57] Leach, op. cit., p.36f.
[58] Petronella, V.F., 'Structure and Theme Through Separation and Union in Shakespeare's ''The Comedy of Errors'' ', *MLR*, 69 (1974), 481.
[59] Ibid., p.483; cf. also R. Henze, 'The Comedy of Errors: A Freely Binding Chain', *SQ,* 22 (1971), 35 − 41.

rhetorical language. For example, when Luciana questions his sanity, he replies with a quibble, playing on the double meaning of 'mated', as 'overcome' and 'partnered', and says that he is 'Not mad, but mated' (54).

Sexual innuendos, very common with figures of the Mime tradition, are a vital element of comedy, and, although critics usually remain silent on this point, *Errors* is no exception. If on the one hand Shakespeare reduces the sexual role of the Courtesan, on the other he reintroduces sexual motifs in the form of puns and quibbles, many of which are made by the Dromios. The first situation of obscene punning occurs in the dialogue between Antipholus S and his Dromio in II, ii; it culminates in the following exchange:

> Syr. Ant.   Why, thou didst conclude hairy men plain dealers
> without wit.
> Syr. Dro.   The plainer dealer, the sooner lost; yet he loseth
> it in a kind of jollity. (= sexual intercourse)
> Syr. Ant.   For what reason?
> Syr. Dro.   For two, and sound ones too.
> Syr. Ant.   Nay, not sound, I pray you.
> Syr. Dro.   Sure ones, then.
> Syr. Ant.   Nay, not sure in a thing falsing.   85 – 93

It has not so far been observed that the sequence of sexual allusions in III, i begins with a verbal game reminiscent of Plautus, because it is triggered off by a name. The only reason why Luce joins in the dialogue in this scene is that she is involved in a typically Elizabethan verbal game which bears a close resemblance to those in Roman comedy. While it is well known that in the next scene her name is changed to 'Nell' for the sake of a pun, it has gone largely unnoticed (and has remained uncommented on in all editions) that her original name 'Luce' is also used for a pun:

> *Enter Luce . . .*
> Luce.   What a coil is there, Dromio? who are those at the gate?
> Eph. Dro.   Let my master in, Luce.
> Luce.   Faith, no, he comes too late,
> And so tell your master.
> Eph. Dro.   O Lord, I must laugh;
> Have at you with a proverb – shall I set in my staff?
> Luce.   Have at you with another, that's – when? can you tell?
> Syr. Dro.   *If thy name be called Luce, Luce thou hast answer'd him well.*
>   48 – 53 (italics mine)

Only H. Kökeritz in his study of Shakespeare's pronunciation has seen that 'Dromio may be punning on the homophones "loose" and "Luce" when he shouts from within . . .'[60] When Dromio addresses the kitchen wench with the words 'If thy name be called Luce, Luce thou hast answer'd him well', the

[60] H. Kökeritz, *Shakespeare's Pronunciation* (New Haven, 1953), p.125.

name 'Luce' is taken by the audience to mean 'loose'. He suggests that she is a loose girl because she has dared to comment in an obscene manner on the situation of the locked door. Whereas Dromio's question: 'Shall I set in my staff?' has been correctly interpreted as having sexual overtones,[61] Luce's reply has not been fully explained. Her 'When? can you tell?' is a proverbial phrase of 'defiance'[62] on one level only. On another level it is also a continuation of Dromio's sexual innuendo. Before she exits, one further double entendre connected with the door motif occurs in the rapid exchanges between herself and Dromio:

> Eph. Dro.   Master, knock the door hard.
> Luce.   Let him knock till it ache.   58

Ralph Berry is right in pointing out that here the punning is extended beyond the purely verbal level, and that the stage symbolism becomes effective: 'the house, perceived from earliest times as the coding for woman, and the knocking at the gates, the male attempts at entry'.[63] This has a certain parallel not only in *Amphitruo* but also in *Menaechmi*, where at the end of Act IV Menaechmus E finds himself placed between the closed doors of both his wife and the Courtesan. Earlier, too, when Erotium goes back to her house and invites Menaechmus to enter, the situation contains obvious sexual symbolism. On the other hand, this comparison also makes it abundantly clear that there is more sexual verbal gaming in Shakespeare than in the Plautine sources.

The next scene, III, ii, is rightly famous for the games of Dromio S when he gives us a most witty and lively report of his experience with the kitchen wench Nell. It is here that the popular Mime, so prominent in Plautine and Shakespearean comedy, is perhaps felt most strongly, because Dromio, as we have said, not only narrates his experience but acts it out with mime and gesture. He develops his quibbles and metaphors, by which he describes her appearance, by way of association, and he succeeds in making her 'present' although she is physically absent from the stage.

Shakespeare's Dromios, by their wide intellectual range and verbal agility, exceed by far the gaming virtuosity of the Plautine parasites and *servi callidi*. They avail themselves of a variety of rhetorical schemes such as *antanaclasis*, *syllepsis*, *asteismus*.[64] We have seen that the most common type of pun in Plautus is the *paronomasia*; if we understand *paronomasia* to be the actual juxtaposition of phonologically or etymologically related words, then in *Errors*

[61] Wells, *Comedy of Errors*, p.149.
[62] Foakes, op. cit., p.44, n.52.
[63] R. Berry, *Shakespeare and the Awareness of the Audience* (London, 1985), p.40.
[64] Cf. B. Vickers, op. cit., p.89; Sr M. Joseph, op. cit., p.340f. and Foakes, op. cit., p.69, n.31; especially in scene IV,iii Dromio S proves to have a masterly command of rhetoric, which he employs for his comic narration of Antipholus's imprisonment, and the overall effect is that of *copia*.

this kind of punning is remarkably 'transformed'. What we often find is a word punning on another one to which it is 'related' by similar sound or near-homophony: however, the second word, rather than being mentioned, has to be supplied by the audience. Thus, when Dromio E tells Antipholus that Adriana will 'scour your fault upon my pate' (I, ii, 65), he also implies the verb 'to score'. The other Dromio, in his narration about fat Nell, 'complains' that 'she would have me as a beast' (III, ii, 84), and he puns on 'abased' as well as on 'baste'. A few lines later, he describes her ugliness as being 'all grease' (93 – 94), while the audience is bound to associate the quality of 'grace' which Antipholus attributes to Luciana.[65]

As we have already noted, the phonological development of the English language multiplied the potential for homophonic puns, and *Errors* contains a few interesting examples of this kind of quibbling. One of these is to be found in Dromio's reaction when he is being beaten by his master in II, ii:

> Hold sir, for God's sake; now your jest is earnest,
> Upon what bargain do you give it me?   24 – 25

Dromio, by associating the homonym 'earnest', meaning 'money paid as a deposit to secure a bargain',[66] tries to explain to himself the situation he is in, and thus produces highly intellectual comedy. Whereas in Elizabethan times the two nouns were often confused with each other, Dromio exchanges them deliberately for the sake of a witty game; ironically, his reference to 'earnest' in the sense of 'earnest money' is perfectly in line with the mercantile atmosphere of Ephesus.

Our second example of this type is used by Dromio in combination with the rhetorical figure of 'asteismus'. This very dramatic punning occurs when a speaker repeats the last word spoken by his partner and changes its meaning: Antipholus S rebukes his Dromio for choosing the wrong occasion for his jokes, and voices the threat that, if he is not careful, then the next time he will 'beat this method' in his 'sconce'. This is immediately followed by Dromio's question: 'Sconce call you it? so you would leave battering, I had rather have it a head' (II, ii, 34 – 36). Dromio is here playing with the homonyms 1. 'sconce' = 'head' and 2. 'sconce' = 'small fort'.[67] Dromio thus playfully transforms reality in a way that goes far beyond anything we find in Plautus.

---

[65] Cf. on these puns Foakes, op. cit., p.16, n.65; p.55, n.94 and Kökeritz, *Shakespeare's Pronunciation*, p.88 and 110.

[66] Foakes, p.28, n.24.

[67] Foakes, p.28, n.34. There is an interesting variant of this purposeful mistaking, namely when a common formula of everyday language, such as a greeting or farewell, is taken in its original sense. In *Asinaria*, for example, Argyrippus takes leave of Philaenium with the formula: 'Salve', which the girl takes literally complaining: 'Salvere me iubes, quoi tu abiens offers morbum?' (I, 593). ('I should fare much better if you'd stay with me.'). This finds a parallel in I,ii of *Errors*: here Antipholus S commands his Dromio: 'Get thee away', because he wants him to deposit his money safely in the Centaur. For a moment Dromio thinks it a good idea

Furthermore, Shakespeare knows how to draw dramatic effects from the polysemic quibble, the punning on several meanings of one and the same word. Antipholus, in his dialogue with Luciana where he tries to persuade her to become his lover, speaks of love as follows: 'Let love, being light, be drowned if she sink.' (III, ii, 52). By playing with the polysemic richness of the word 'light', he skilfully evokes various aspects of the nature of love. The line is therefore a good instance of Shakespeare's linguistic economy. Most examples are, however, to be found with the Dromios. For instance scene IV, ii, in which Dromio S narrates how Antipholus has been taken prisoner, contains a number of these polysemic puns, indeed they are an essential element of his 're-enacting' of the imprisonment. The basis of Dromio's narration is his metaphorical identification of the prison as hell, and it has been pointed out that an actual prison was indeed given this name.[68] He then describes the Officer by means of a number of rhetorical devices, and he puns nicely on the double meaning of the term 'suit'. Following Adriana's question: 'What, is he arrested? tell me at whose suit?', his answer is: 'I know not at whose suit he is arrested well; / But is in a suit of buff which 'rested him, that can I tell' (IV, ii, 43 – 45). When Adriana wants to know whether he was 'arrested on a band', Dromio tells her: 'Not on a band, but on a stronger thing' (50 – 51), thus quibbling on 'bond' and 'band' as 'neckband'.[69] It would be possible to continue the list of examples from this scene; they have a cumulative effect. However, what is most important, and Foakes has already noticed it, is the fact that these rhetorical puns indicate that the free and easy game of the holiday world is here receding, while the element of threat is beginning to assume concrete shape.[70] Dromio's master shares his feeling that Ephesus is under the power of witchcraft. Moreover, Dromio's verbal gaming has the further dramatic function of preparing the audience for the appearance of the Courtesan and above all for Antipholus E's being 'thrust into a real "limbo" by Doctor Pinch'.[71]

Under this 'wicked' influence even the public clock is, as it were, running berserk. Dromio in this scene hears a 'ring' from the 'bell' and remarks "'tis time that I were gone', / It was *two* ere I left him, and now the clock strikes *one*.', and this prompts Adriana to comment: '*The hours come back*; that did I never hear.' (52 – 55; italics mine). The real meaning of this example of the polysemic pun has not been understood. It has been assumed that Dromio still hears the clock striking two, that his intended meaning is therefore: 'the clock strikes *on*', but that he turns 'on' into 'one'. However, this interpretation is extremely improbable. Surely Dromio must have heard one new stroke and

to take Antipholus's order literally: 'Many a man would take you at your word, / And go indeed, having so good a mean.' (17 – 18).
[68] Foakes, p.70, n.40.
[69] Foakes, p.71, n.50, 51.
[70] Foakes, p.69, n.31.
[71] Foakes, ibid.

this makes him wonder because it has already struck 'two'. Only if we assume
Dromio to hear this new stroke does Adriana's comment that the hours 'come
back' make sense. The explanation is quite simple: the clock has just struck *one*
quarter past two. The major Elizabethan clocks did indeed strike the quarter
hours.[72] Thus we have a kind of polysemic pun, because the word 'one' is used
with two meanings.

While the puns of both Plautus and Shakespeare arise from a dramatic
situation, their variety in Shakespeare is, of course, far greater. It is
nevertheless worthwhile pointing out a specific similarity in their dramatic use
of puns: sometimes in Plautus, and very frequently in Shakespeare, puns
develop by way of association on the spur of a dramatic moment. There is a
fine example in *Menaechmi*. During a discussion between Erotium, Peniculus
and Menaechmus E, the Parasite asks why Erotium does not invite him, too,
whereupon she replies: 'Extra numerum es mihi.' ('You don't count.'). The
phrase 'extra numerum esse' alludes to the military sphere. Consequently
Peniculus replies: 'Idem istuc aliis adscriptivis fieri ad *legionem* solet.' ('A
statement that applies in the army, too — it has its supernumeraries.'). And
then Menaechmus, by way of metaphor, refers to the *prandium* in Erotium's
house as a 'proelium', a battle: '[. . .] In eo uterque proelio potabimus; / uter
ibi melior bellator erit inventus cantharo, / tua est legio: adiudicato cum utro
hanc noctem sies.' (182 – 88). ('In this battle we'll both [. . .] drink;
whichever proves himself the better tankard fighter is your army: you be the
judge as to — which you're to spend the night with.').[73] *Errors* offers far more
subtle examples of punning by association; the best ones can be found in the
great scene III, i, 73ff.: Antipholus E is standing in front of the locked door
and wants an instrument to break in: 'Go fetch me something, I'll break ope
the gate.' In the ensuing dialogue the two Dromios play a verbal game of ping
pong as, by way of association, each time the idea of breaking is used with a
different meaning:

Syr. Dro.	Break any breaking here and I'll break your knave's pate.
Eph. Dro.	A man may break a word with you, sir, and words are but *wind*;
Syr. Dro.	Ay, and break it in your face, so he break it not *behind*.
Eph. Dro.	It seems thou want'st breaking; out upon thee, hind.[74]

(italics mine)

---

[72] Cf. C.M. Cipolla, *Clocks and Culture 1300 – 1700* (London, 1967), p.43. Shakespeare himself mentions the 'jack', 'the lifesize figure actuated by the clockwork to
strike the quarter-hours.', A. Hammond, ed., *King Richard III*. The New Arden
Shakespeare (London, 1981), p.270, n.114; cf. also *Richard II*, V,v,60.

[73] Cf. Schmidt, op. cit., p.335.

[74] Dromio E here makes a pun by referring to the bodily functions, and there is a
further parallel in Plautus. In *Curculio*, for example, there is a quibble with 'ventus'
= 'wind' and 'ventum' (= 'ventum esse', the perfect infinitive passive of 'venire',

Antipholus E then repeats his request for a breaking instrument: 'go, borrow me a crow'. When Dromio brings the crow bar, which acquired its name by way of metaphor, the puns which are now produced through association are part of the dramatic situation. For a moment, the crow bar is turned into a 'real' crow, because a moment ago Dromio S answered the other Dromio's request 'I pray thee let me in.' with the words 'Ay, when fowls have no feathers, and fish have no fin . . .'. Now that 'a crow without a feather' is actually present, Dromio playfully concludes that they will be let in: 'For a fish without a fin, there's a fowl without a feather (= a "crow-bar"). However, this is not the end of the verbal game, because the speaker then associates another metaphorical expression derived from 'crow', which he applies directly to the dramatic situation; he uses the crow as a threat to his invisible opponent: 'If a crow [= a "crow-bar"] help us in, sirrah, we'll pluck a crow together' [= "we'll have a bone to pick with you"].[75]

The following answer of Dromio E to Adriana's threat reveals another aspect of Shakespeare's art of punning, the forming of a cluster of puns by way of association:

Adriana.   Back slave, or I will break thy pate *across*.
Eph. Dro.   And he will *bless* that *cross* with other beating;
            Between you I shall have a *holy* head.
                            (italics mine) II, i, 78 – 80

This passage contains a subtle combination of no less than three different puns. Dromio pretends to understand Adriana's words 'I will break thy pate across' in the sense 'that his head will be cut open in such a way as to make the sign of the cross on it'. First, we have a play on the homophones 'across' and 'a cross'; then there is a pun on the homonyms 'to bless' = 'to consecrate' and 'to bless' = 'to wound', and finally there is a second homophonic pun on 'holey' = 'full of holes' and 'holy' = 'marked with a cross'.[76] One could hardly find an example of a comparable *linking* of puns by way of association in a play by any other dramatist. Nor should we overlook the fact that Shakespeare manages to concentrate these puns into so few lines.

In a discussion of the Dromios' art of punning it is interesting to consider for a moment Lyly's *Mother Bombie*, because not only does Shakespeare seem to have taken the name Dromio from this play, but in other respects too *Mother Bombie* is related to *Errors*. Lyly, too, adopted a good many suggestions from

---

to come: 'facite ventum ut gaudeam. / Maxume. / Quid facitis, quaeso? / Ventum . . .' (II, 314 – 316) ('make wind / [approach] to make me happy' [my translation]. 'By all means. What are you two doing, for mercy's sake? Giving you wind . . .').

[75] In his *Love's Labour's Lost* Shakespeare refines this technique when he plays with the homophones 'style' and 'stile', Cf. W.C. Carroll, *The Great Feast of Language in Love's Labour's Lost* (Princeton, 1976), p.26.

[76] Cf. Foakes, op. cit., p.23, n.79 and 80.

Plautus rather than from Terence.[77] His Dromio clearly reveals the type of the Roman *servus*; he is a true descendant of the Latin *servus callidus* in that he uses his intelligence in order to plot an intrigue and, like his Roman models, he is still the slave who hopes to achieve his manumission by the service he renders to his master.[78] So important is the *Latin* basis for Dromio's word play that he sometimes even includes whole Latin sentences; in fact he understands Latin better than his master. Latin quotations, taken directly from Plautine comedy, are sometimes used to describe the characters' movements, as in the following example:

> *Halfpenny.*　We must not tarry. *Abeundum est mihi,*
> 　　　　　　　I must go and cast this matter in a corner.
> *Dromio.*　　*I prae, sequar.* A bowl, and I'll come after with a broom.[79]
> 　　　　　　　　　　　　　　　　　　　　　　　　　　　　II, iv, 21ff

What becomes evident in the examples from *Mother Bombie* is the easy fusion of the 'Plautine' kind of verbal pyrotechnics with his preference for *paronomasia* and the native popular mimic tradition, as in the following example where we have a punning on 'die', 'dice' and '-di' as a Latin inflexion:

> *Mother Bombie.*　Thy father doth live because he doth die, thou hast
> 　　　　　　　　　spent all thy thrift with a die, and so like a beggar
> 　　　　　　　　　thou shalt die.
> *Rixula.*　　　　I would have lik'd well if all the gerunds had been
> 　　　　　　　　　there, *-di*, *-do*, and *-dum*. But all in die, that's too
> 　　　　　　　　　deadly.
> *Dromio.*　　　My father indeed is a dyer, but I have been a dicer.
> 　　　　　　　　　But to die a beggar . . .　　　　　　III, iv, 166 – 172[80]

Whereas Shakespeare in his comedies includes some occasional Latin quotations or allusions to Latin, as for instance in *Love's Labour's Lost*, where he even plays with Ovid's cognomen 'Naso' (IV, ii, 123ff.),[81] he never goes so far as Lyly. In *Errors*, there is one occasion where we have good reason to believe that, in a joke by Dromio E, Shakespeare has included a direct allusion to the Plautine art of punning. When, just before the beginning of the 'Pinch scene', Dromio warns Adriana of her husband's plans to castigate her with a rope, he quotes the end of a Latin tag for the sake of a pun: 'Mistress, *respice*

[77] Foakes is wrong in claiming that *Mother Bombie* is Terentian in character, op. cit., p.18.

[78] Cf. A.H. Andreadis's introduction to her edition of *Mother Bombie*, Salzburg Studies in English Literature, Elizabethan & Renaissance Studies, 35 (Salzburg, 1975), especially p.58.

[79] Quoted from Andreadis, op. cit., p.127.

[80] Op. cit., p.164.

[81] Cf. C.C. Hower, 'The Importance of a Knowledge of Latin for Understanding the Language of Shakespeare', *CJ*, 46 (1951), 221 – 27.

finem, respect your end.' Dromio continues the pun in English, yet in order to understand the word-play fully, the audience has to associate the Latin tag '*respice funem*' ('beware the rope'): 'Mistress, *respice funem*, respect your end, or rather, to prophesy like the parrot, beware the rope's end.' (IV, iv, 39 – 41). The tag '*respice funem*' alludes to the popular Elizabethan habit of teaching parrots to cry 'rope' as a warning against the gibbet.[82] The interesting point here is that in his 'classical' comedy Shakespeare refers to a Latin pun in the manner of the *paronomasia* preferred especially by the Plautine slaves, and then links the Latin pun with the contemporary allusion to the use of the parrot.

Thus, we have seen that both in *Mother Bombie* and in *Errors* there are interesting analogues to the verbal punning of Plautus, especially in the puns of the slaves or servant figures, and that Lyly goes further than Shakespeare in the Latin 'colouring' of the puns. Therefore it is no longer possible to believe in an exclusively native punning influence on the low comedy figures in Elizabethan drama. At the beginning of the present study we remarked that Weimann is wrong in claiming that, in contrast to Shakespearean comedy, the audience in New Comedy always laughs *at* the comic figure, but never *with* him.[83] And we also noticed that Weimann wrongly interprets Speed's comment to Launce, 'your old vice still, mistake the word', as an intentional allusion to the Vice of the Moralities.[84] Whereas the mistaking of words is *extremely* rare in the Vice of the Moralities, it is very common with the slave in the comedies of Plautus, so much so that what Launce is doing might be called very typical of the Roman *servus*, who frequently puns by purposeful misunderstanding. We find many occasions where a character puns, not for the sake of exposing another to laughter, but to make himself a comic character and thus to try to elicit the laughter of the audience. This occurs not only in *Menaechmi* (II, 136; 257), but also especially frequently in *Amphitruo* with the slave Sosia, as in the following example: Amphitruo thinks that his wife has been seduced while he was away; Alcumena, however, believes that he and not Jupiter has enjoyed her:

Alc.	Obsecro ecastor, cur istuc, *mi vir*, ex ted audio?
Amph.	*Vir* ego tuos sim? ne me appella, falsa, falso nomine.

$$812 - 13 \text{ (italics mine)}$$

Alc.	Good heavens! For mercy's sake how can you say such a thing, my dear husband?
Amph.	Am I your husband? Oh, you false wretch, none of your false names for me!

---

[82] T.W. Baldwin, 'Respice Finem: Respice Funem', *J. Quincy Adams Memorial Studies*, ed. J.G. McManaway et al. (Washington, DC, 1948), p.141 – 55.
[83] 'Laughing with the Audience . . .', *ShS*, 22 (1969), p.35.
[84] Cf. Introduction, p.7.

Sosia then 'mistakes' the word 'vir' in its normal meaning 'man' instead of 'husband' and thus produces a witty comment which for this one moment causes the audience to forget the couple's predicament and to laugh *with* Sosia:[85]

> Haeret haec res, si quidem haec iam mulier facta est ex viro.
>
> 812 – 814

> Here's a pretty mess, if he is turned into a *woman* and is not her husband!

Other examples could easily be added.

There can be no doubt that the quibbling of the Dromios is to be viewed in this same tradition, although it is marked by a far greater subtlety. They frequently mistake the sense of their masters' words; sometimes this is because they do not understand their meaning, and in order to make some sense of their masters' comments they interpret them in a different way. Nevertheless, the new precarious situation does not make them inferior to their masters; on the contrary, they retain their intellectual brilliance and even succeed in adding skilful puns of their own.

The correspondences between Shakespeare's and Plautus's delight in playing games with language are far too numerous and subtle to be ignored. The abundant evidence we have put forward in this chapter should prevent us from seeing Shakespearean word play merely in the *native* popular tradition. Shakespeare, as usual blends the English and classical traditions and often surprises us with his most individual transformations. As we have seen, the significance of the classical influence plays more than a merely subsidiary role.

---

[85] Schmidt, op. cit., p.137.

VI

Metre in Plautus
and in Shakespeare's 'Classical' Play

There are two obvious reasons why a comparison between the metrical art of
Plautus and that of Shakespeare in his *Errors* has never been made. First,
critics have considered Shakespeare's early plays as apprentice work. In 1948,
Tucker Brooke, for instance, wrote that Shakespeare imitated Plautus without
any close attention to metre; he maintained that 'it would usually be absurd to
seek any special purpose'[1] in the way blank verse pentameter couplets and
prose were employed. In more recent years advances have been made in
elucidating the specific quality of Shakespeare's early verse. The second
reason why no one has thought it worthwhile to compare these plays from the
point of view of metre is the widespread opinion that during the Renaissance
the Roman comedies were not recognized to be texts written in verse. Baldwin
claimed that only very late in the 16th century did people become 'very
gradually aware that Terence was really verse'.[2] However, such a view can no
longer be maintained.

The major Renaissance editions of Terence contained an introductory essay
on metre (*De Metris*) by Erasmus, which presented detailed information on the
manifold metrical patterns employed in these comedies. Erasmus is critical of
those who are unable to discern metrical structures and who read Terence's
texts as a kind of heightened prose. He starts by pointing out that the Latin
comic poets took great liberties with metre and that no one surpassed Terence
in this regard: 'Comici Latini multam libertatem sibi usurparunt in uersibus,
sed nemo largius Terentio.'[3] He then goes on to explain various metres such
as 'iambicum trimetrum' or 'iambicum tetrametrum'; he adds that occasionally there are to be found the 'tribrachum, spondeum, dactylum,

---

[1] Tucker Brooke, 'The Renaissance (1500 – 1660)', in: *A Literary History of England*,
ed. A.C. Baugh (London, 1948), p.523. F.W., Ness in *The Use of Rhyme in
Shakespeare's Plays*, Yale Studies in English (New Haven, 1941), thinks that rhyme in
the early plays 'seems almost indiscriminate' (p.81).

[2] Baldwin, *Shakspere's Five-Act Structure*, p.545.

[3] In *P. Terentii Afri Comoediae ex D. Erasmi et Jo. Rivii Attendoriensis Castigationibus*
(Cologne, 1534), f.III.

**Publius Terrentius
poeta comicus**

6 From *Liber Chronicarum* by the humanist
Hartmann Schedel

anapaestum'.[4] This gives us an idea of how detailed Erasmus's discussion of
the metrical structure of Roman comedy really is. And in his educational
treatise *De Ratione Studii*, the importance of which we have already noted on
earlier occasions, he advises the schoolmaster that, when teaching Roman
comedy to his pupils, he 'should be careful to point out the type of metre'.[5]

Most Renaissance editions of Terence print the texts as verse; the
humanists paid as much attention to this as to the question of Act division.
The bulk of the editions of Plautus shows the same carefulness. We may
therefore safely conclude that, when Shakespeare studied the Plautine
comedies, he cannot have failed to notice that Plautus employed a great
variety of metrical patterns. It is, I think, quite possible that he may to a
certain extent even have anticipated what recent research has discovered in

---

[4] Ibid. f.IIIf.
[5] *On the Method of Study (De Ratione Studii), Collected Works of Erasmus*, vol.24, p.683.

Plautus, namely that behind a great many of his changes of metre there lies an artistic intention. Madeleine Doran was the first to anticipate that a comparison between Plautus and the early Shakespeare 'might throw light on the *motives* of variation from blank verse to riming couplets or to stanza patterns'.[6]

Classicists tell us that it is difficult to assess the function of metre in Plautus because we do not know how the lines were originally spoken. Nevertheless, while approaching the problem with the necessary caution, it has been possible to achieve at least some concrete results.[7] Plautus gradually learnt the art of adjusting metre to the conditions of the dramatic situation. We find this especially in plays like *Menaechmi* or *Amphitruo*, which are considered to be among his middle if not his later works.[8] It has been shown that he frequently changes his metres according to dramaturgic requirements. Certain metres are given preference for the expression of strong emotion. For example, the exaggerating quality of the 'iambici octonarii' is employed by Plautus when a character experiences fear mixed with anger, as when Menaechmus E is about to be carried away by four strong slaves:[9]

> Occidi,
> quid hoc est negoti? quid illisce homines ad me
> currunt, opsecro?
> quid voltis vos? quid quaeritatis? quid me circumsistitis?
> quo rapitis me? quo fertis me? perii, opsecro vestram
> fidem, Epidamnienses, subvenite, cives. quin me mittitis?
>
> II, 996 – 1000

Murder! What does this mean? What are those fellows rushing at me for, in the name of heaven? What do you want? What are you after? What are you surrounding me for? Where are you pulling me? Where are you carrying me? [. . .] Murder! Help, help, Epidamnians, I beg you! Save me, fellow-citizens! Let me go, I tell you!

It can even be said that Plautus uses metrical differentiation as a means of individualizing characters. Tobias has shown that the dignity and seriousness of a character (*gravitas*) is often emphasized by his or her speaking in bacchiacs (or cretics),[10] as when in *Amphitruo* Alcumena, after she has been accused of committing adultery, speaks her impressive soliloquy.

---

[6] *Endeavors of Art*, p.152.
[7] Cf. the study by A.J. Tobias, *Plautus' Metrical Characterization* (Diss. Stanford, 1970), and Duckworth, op. cit., p.364 – 369.
[8] W.B. Sedgwick, 'The Dating of Plautus' Plays', *CQ*, 24 (1930), 102 – 105; W.B. Sedgwick, 'Plautine Chronology', *AJPh*, 70 (1949), 376 – 383; cf. also F. della Corte, *Da Sarsina a Roma* (Genova, ²1967), p.47 – 69.
[9] Tobias, op. cit., p.60.
[10] Tobias, op. cit., p. 72.

A striking example of metrical characterization can be found with the first appearance of the Senex. Again, bacchiacs are used, but rather than suggesting *gravitas*, they produce a very comic effect because of the incongruity between the elevated tone and the physical deficiency of the speaker:

> Vt aetas mea est atque ut hoc usus facto est
> gradum proferam, progrediri properabo.
> sed id quam mihi facile sit, haud sum falsus.
> nam pernicitas deserit. consitus sum
> senectute . . .   II, 753 – 757

> Yes, I'll step out, I'll step along as . . . fast as my age permits and
> the occasion demands [. . .] But I know well enough how easy it is
> for me. For I've lost my nimbleness . . . the years have taken hold
> of me . . .

In Plautus's use of metres, an element of playfulness is also uppermost when there is a discrepancy between the low social status of the speaker and the dignified metre[11] or when conventional, mainly tragic metres are parodied,[12] or when a metrical pattern like the iambic octonarius is used with 'farcical, ridiculous exaggeration'.[13] In this context the slaves and parasites are again very interesting. In the first scene of *Amphitruo*, Sosia rehearses his 'heroic' report of the battle from which he fled (188ff.); he starts using a metre unfamiliar to him and therefore 'he cannot maintain it. He adopts a formal tone at the end and is ridiculously out of place with it'.[14] He also 'imitates the meter and takes the mood from Mercury'.[15] Conversely, Mercury, the god of the art of language, mocks Sosia's lament, which was uttered in bacchiacs.[16] There are other examples where a slave uses an extravagant metre as a means of pretence.[17] Again, there seems to be good reason to assume that Shakespeare noticed at least some of these skilful metrical variations in Plautus.

Linguistic devices such as word play, internal rhyme and the balance of sentence clauses often enhance the effect of metre. Special mention should be made of the asyndetic accumulation of synonyms, as for instance in Menaechmus S's exclamation: 'di me quidem omnes *adiuvant, augent, amant*' (II; 551, italics mine) ('all the gods do aid, augment, and love me!' 551). It is also worth observing that a change in metre may serve Plautus as a means of skilfully varying the dramatic pace, because these different metres can only be delivered at different speeds. Here it is necessary to remember that the words

---

[11] Tobias, op. cit., p.31.
[12] Tobias, op. cit., p.34ff.
[13] Tobias, op. cit., p.72.
[14] Tobias, op. cit., p.81.
[15] Tobias, op. cit., p.83.
[16] Tobias, op. cit., p.31.
[17] Tobias, op. cit., p.81.

of a Plautine comedy were accompanied by music. Thus, some metrical passages serve to achieve special musical effects so that 'the result is very much like stanzas, music for music's sake'.[18] Since it is very likely that the Elizabethans received Roman comedy as *metrically* organized texts and since in the contemporary editions the soliloquies were correctly defined as *cantica*, songs, we have to assume that the conventional inclusion of songs in Elizabethan comedy may to *some* extent have been suggested by this musical element of Roman comedy. An interesting example is the comic playwright Machiavelli: as he was certainly not an author with a lyrical penchant, the fact that he included songs in his neo-Roman comedies clearly points to a Roman influence.

On the other hand, there was always a mimetic and 'realistic' element in the metrical language of New Comedy, the basis of which in Menander was the iambic trimetre. In Plautus this conversational quality makes itself felt, for instance, when the metre suddenly changes over to iambics (iambic *senarii*), because, since iambics come closest to everyday Latin, they serve to produce a conversational tone in Roman comedy.[19] This special 'conversational', iambic quality of the metres of Plautus was surely noticed by Renaissance students who saw not only in Terence but in Plautus, too, a master of colloquial Latin.[20] It is interesting from this perspective that iambic blank verse became the standard metre of Elizabethan drama, too.

We find a further mimetic feature of Plautine comic dialogue in the frequent device by which several characters share a single line so that it is divided into equal parts. It is advisable to call these parts 'antilabai',[21] using the original classical term instead of 'hemistichomythia', because stichomythia as such is not often found in Plautus. These 'antilabai' serve to furnish the dialogue with a symmetrical and dramaturgically effective structure; they occur above all in scenes of intrigue, persuasion or *anagnorisis*. They are further employed when one character excitedly interrupts another or interjects a witty remark, or even when the effect of a surprise turn is intended;[22] the following passage taken from the first meeting of Menaechmus and his Parasite is a good example:

Pen.　　　　　　　　　　　　　　　Quis istest ornatus tuos?
Men.　　Dic hominem lepidissimum esse me.

---

[18] Tobias, op. cit., p.175; cf. also Duckworth, op. cit., p.370.

[19] Tobias, op. cit., p.158.

[20] Cf., for example, as one of many instances, the interesting edition, made for the purpose of teaching good Latin: *Elegantiarum Puerilium ex M. Tullii Ciceronis Epistolis Libri Tres* (Leipzig, 1554), which contains a second part: *Elegantiarum ex Plauto et Terentio Liber* II: Plautus as well as Terence is used as a textbook of 'elegant' Latin colloquial phrases and sentences.

[21] Cf. B. Seidensticker, *Die Gesprächsverdichtung in den Tragödien Senecas* (Heidelberg, 1969), p.20.

[22] Ibid., p.92.

Pen.   Vbi essuri sumus?
Men.   Dic modo hoc quod ego te iubeo.
Pen.   Dico: homo lepidissime.
Men.   Ecquid audes de tuo istuc addere?
Pen.   Atque hilarissime.
Men.   Perge porro.   II, 146 – 150

Pen.   What sort of a get-up is that?
Men.   Say that I'm a splendid fellow.
Pen.   [. . .] Where are we going to eat?
Men.   Just you say what I command.
Pen.   [. . .] I do – splendid fellow.
Men.   Won't you add something of your own?
Pen.   [. . .] The jolliest sort of fellow, too.
Men.   Go on, go on!

However, Plautus knows that a constant use of the 'antilabai' might have the opposite effect and produce monotony. In V, i, for example, he alternates between 'antilabai' and complete lines, while in the famous madness scene (V, ii) he starts with the soliloquy of the Senex, then allows the lines to break up in the ensuing dialogue between Menaechmus, the Senex and the Matrona, and at the end of the scene he again reverts to complete lines. It appears that the metrical organization of Plautus's comedies is marked by a surprisingly rich variety and a thoroughgoing stylization.

Although Shakespeare, like the Elizabethans in general, contented himself in his plays with blank verse supplemented by the occasional use of rhyme and by lyrical passages with other metres, his work abounds in special metrical effects which far surpass what we found in Plautus. In particular, there are many outstanding examples of the differentiation of metre according to character, mood and situation. As these are well-known, they need not be discussed here. Yet it is surprising that in his *Errors* Shakespeare uses only a *selection* of the metrical elements found in Plautus. It is as though he had composed this play according to the principle of classical restraint and as though he wanted to emphasize the effects of stylization. Particularly striking is the absence of one feature predominant in Plautus, namely the breaking up of a line of verse into small parts assigned to several characters. Even half-lines are very rare in *Errors*, although in the early stage of his career Shakespeare was fully aware of the dramatic effect of this technique, which can be studied, for example, in *Richard III*, where the verse sometimes works 'like a rally at tennis'.[23] The first scene of Act III of *Errors* contains a rare example of such a division of a line. Here, in the passage we have already quoted, the pattern of

---

[23] J. Barton, *Playing Shakespeare* (London, 1984), p.44. The new study *Shakespeare's Metrical Art* by G.T. Wright does not consider *The Comedy of Errors* at length (Berkeley/Los Angeles/London, 1988).

stylized couplets is momentarily disrupted and made 'loose' by the appearance
of Luce, whose character, as we have seen, is that of a 'loose' minion:

Enter LUCE
Luce.	What a coil is there, Dromio? who are those at the gate?
Eph.Dro.	Let my master in, Luce.
Luce.	Faith, no, he comes too late,
	And so tell your master.
Eph.Dro.	O Lord, I must laugh; [. . .]
Luce.	I thought to have ask'd you.
Syr.Dro.	And you said, no.
Eph.Dro.	So come, help, well struck, there was blow for blow.
Eph.Ant.	Thou baggage, let me in.
Luce.	Can you tell for whose sake?
Eph.Dro.	Master, knock the door hard.
Luce.	Let him knock till it ache.

III, i, 48 – 58

The effect of these broken lines is comic rather than dramatic. In the next
scene, however, the breaking up of the lines gives them dramatic intensity: the
increasing emotional excitement of Antipholus S and Luciana is mirrored
appropriately in the way the complete lines of their dialogue are converted into
short, fragmentary eruptions:

Luc.	Why call you me love? Call my sister so.
Syr.Ant.	Thy sister's sister.
Luc.	That's my sister.
Syr.Ant.	No,
	It is thyself, mine own self's better part [. . .]
Syr.Ant.	Thou hast no husband yet, nor I no wife –
	Give me thy hand.
Luc.	O, soft, sir, hold you still;
	I'll fetch my sister to get her good will. III, ii, 59 – 70

On one occasion, in the final recognition scene, Shakespeare adopts the
broken line in order to achieve an effect different from the previous occasion.
When Egeon believes he recognizes his son and Dromio, who do not seem to
know him, he asks them in great bewilderment:

Egeon.	But tell me yet, dost thou not know my voice?
Eph.Ant.	Neither.
Egeon.	Dromio, nor thou?
Eph.Dro.	No, trust me sir, nor I.
Egeon.	I am sure thou dost?
Eph.Dro.	Ay sir, but I am sure I do not . . . V, i, 301 – 305

These lines reflect Egeon's deep feelings at this emotional moment and have to
be spoken rather slowly. They are, of course, different from the *antilabai* found
in classical drama.

To be sure, we do find in *Errors* a few instances of *stichomythia* proper, which is most uncommon in *Menaechmi*. Sophokles and Euripides knew how to produce powerful effects with it,[24] and, as is well known, Seneca too was a master of *stichomythia*. So far it has not been observed that it was a device strictly confined to *tragedy* which Shakespeare introduced into his comedy. On closer inspection of the two stichomythic scenes in *Errors*, we notice that one of these, that in which Dr Pinch the exorcist appears, is particularly suited to the use of *stichomythia* because the way in which Pinch 'attacks' the identity of Antipholus E gives the scene a certain similarity to tragedy. In II, i, the other passage in which *stichomythia* occurs, we notice that the dialogue of Adriana and Luciana is partly an exchange of gnomic sentences and partly an expression of opposite points of view; this pointed articulation of opposite views was often the function of *stichomythia* in Greek and Roman tragedy. Thus, Shakespeare's introduction of *stichomythia* into his classical comedy is a masterly and very deliberate stroke which, interestingly enough, resembles Menander's occasional comic and parodic use of the same device, as in his play *Perikeiromene*.[25]

The parodic use of metre is not lacking in *Errors* either, if we look closely at the verse of the Dromios. It has been said that they are familiar with all the different kinds of language which their partners use at various times. This is, of course, part of their play with language. At the end of IV, i, Dromio S has a short soliloquy in blank verse; here he uses a verse alien to his status because he adopts the function of the final commentator and he playfully concludes the scene with a couplet: 'Thither I must, although against my will; / For servants must their masters' minds fulfil.' In I, ii, the other Dromio appears with the task of urging his master to come home to dinner, yet he fulfils his charge with a brilliant play with iambic verse which is well-balanced and by its very compactness sounds like an accusation spoken in a jesting tone:

> Return'd so soon? rather approach'd too late;
> The capon burns, the pig falls from the spit;
> The clock hath strucken twelve upon the bell;
> My mistress made it one upon my cheek;
> She is so hot because the meat is cold;
> The meat is cold because you come not home . . . I, ii, 43 – 48

This play with metrical language is a major reason why Antipholus S believes Dromio to be jesting. It thus adds verisimilitude to the fact that Antipholus

---

[24] Seidensticker, op. cit., p.27ff.

[25] In: *Menander*, ed. N. Miller (London, 1987), p.114. This has nothing to do with the English comic tradition of 'Dialogue in alternate lines, employed in sharp disputation', which G.K. Hunter has examined. The examples Hunter presents do not reflect any classical influence, whereas *stichomythia* in *Errors* does (G.K. Hunter, 'Seneca and the Elizabethans: a case-study in "influence" ', *ShS*, 20 [1967],1726, esp. p.21 and 25).

does not suspect a confusion of identity. There is a similar situation in IV,i, when Dromio S tells the 'wrong' Antipholus that the ship is ready to set sail, taking pride, as it were, in his own efficiency as a messenger:

> Master, there's a bark of Epidamnum
> That stays but till her owner comes aboard,
> And then she bears away. Our fraughtage, sir,
> I have convey'd aboard, and I have bought
> The oil, the balsamum and aqua-vitae.
> The ship is in her trim, the merry wind
> Blows fair from land; they stay for nought at all
> But for their owner, master, and yourself.   IV, i, 86 – 93

The very brilliance of Dromio's parodic verse play causes the other Antipholus to assume that he is being pestered by a madman.

If in Plautus a change of metre implies a change of pace, then this is even more true of *Errors*; the changes between blank verse, couplets, other rhymed forms and prose passages serve to influence tempo and dramatic rhythm in a decisive way. It is clear, for example, that the prose scenes provide a welcome and necessary opportunity for the audience to relax from the turbulence of the action. Although blank verse as the underlying metre is the basic form of expression of all the major characters, and although Shakespeare, unlike Plautus, does not indicate a change of emotion by a change of metre in this play, it is remarkable how well the blank verse itself alters its form according to the particular speaker and the dramatic situation so that the overall effect is far more dramatic than in Plautus. The dramatic and rhythmic flow of Egeon's narration in I, i and of his soliloquy in Act V is different from the way in which his sons and his wife Aemilia use this metrical pattern, and in each case their blank verse differs from that of Adriana or the Courtesan or from the excited verse of Dromio S in IV, ii. Each character has his or her individual blank verse rhythm. Blank verse in *Errors* has been praised as 'competent', even showing occasional 'brilliance';[26] however, no one has considered it worthwhile examining it in greater detail. It is usually regretted that, unlike the blank verse of the later plays, it is not very rich in suggestive images. The answer to this objection must be that the blank verse offers everything the particular situation requires. The rationale of this play and the nature of its situations do not call for an abundance of metaphor.

However, there are a number of important stylistic elements which give the dramatic verse its characteristic shape, such as the extensive use of figures of rhetoric, in particular of alliteration, internal rhyme, word play, the stylized

---

[26] S. Wells, ed., *The Comedy of Errors*, p.13.

balance of sentence clauses or the asyndetic accumulation of synonyms.[27] A further important feature is the frequent use of epithets, and this fact is all the more striking because in *Menaechmi* as well as in *Amphitruo* (and indeed throughout Plautus) we find surprisingly few adjectives. The reason why Shakespeare here again differs from Plautus is clear from the very first scene. Egeon's narration is interspersed with adjectives which have an affective quality and thus reflect his subjective point of view. Their additional function is to arouse feelings of sympathy in the Duke and above all in the audience.[28] (Plautus has no need of epithets of this kind, because his turbulent comedy is not at all concerned with deep emotion.) Furthermore, many of these adjectives in *Errors* are compounds, which, by their morphological structure, influence the quality of the rhythm.[29] The following, which are all *ad hoc* formations, are a selection: 'well-dealing', 'wind-obeying', 'sinking-ripe', 'dark-working', 'soul-killing', 'fool-begged', 'deep-divorcing', 'secret-false', 'worse-bodied', 'new-apparelled', 'heady-rash', 'sap-consuming'. Vivid adjectives such as these 'need fresh-minting' by the actor on the stage, as John Barton[30] has pointed out.

Very often blank verse producing a lively and vivid rhythm occurs in a scene of persuasion, and it thus fulfils a markedly rhetorical function. Any actor who has played a part in this comedy knows that their very 'natural' rhythm makes these blank verse lines extremely 'speakable'. The common view that blank verse in *Errors* is endstopped and regular is not true, on the contrary, it is in fact rich in skilful variation. Consider for instance the Duke's opening address to Egeon:

> Mérchant of Syracúsa, pléad nò móre.
> I am nót pártial to infrínge our láws;
> The énmity and díscord which of láte
> Sprúng from the ráncorous oútrage of yòur Dúke
> To mérchants, our wéll-deàling cóuntrymèn,
> Whò, wánting guílders to redéem their líves,
> Have séal'd his rígorous státutes with their bloóds,
> Exclúdes áll píty from our thréat'ning lóoks . . .   I, i, 3 – 10

---

[27] On word play cf. chapter IV; internal rhyme III,ii,19; alliteration e.g. II,i,21; balance of clauses, e.g. II,ii,110146, III,i,108; accumulation of synonyms, e.g. IV,ii,1922.

[28] Shakespeare's verse here already exhibits the Elizabethan 'gift of energeia, the quality of style which gives animation to description and to speech' (Doran, *Endeavors of Art*, p.242), cf. chapter V, note 37.

[29] It is interesting that, in his *Rhetoric*, Aristotle claims that composite words and epithets are an important means of stirring the affections of the audience (*The Works of Aristotle, Rhetorica*, transl. W. Rhys Roberts, [Oxford, 1946], XI, 1408b.) That Plautus, too, makes use of composites has been shown by Stein, 'Compound Word Coinage in the Plays of Plautus', *Latomus*, 30 (1971), 598 – 606; cf. also Duckworth, op. cit., p.345.

[30] J. Barton op. cit., p.114.

Many of the devices which a poet has at his disposal in order to avoid rhythmical monotony are assembled here: we have enjambement, 'offbeat'[31] effects, the redoubling of an unstressed syllable, subtle but important variations in the weight and intensity of the stresses, and even variation in the position of the 'obligatory' caesura, usually required after the second foot.[32] If the lines just quoted were more 'irregular', this would destroy the stately tone necessary for the words of a Duke. Examples of this kind can also be found elsewhere in the play. The final situation in the great first scene of Act III deserves our special attention: Balthasar's words with which he persuades Antipholus E to stop trying to break down the door produce a marked rhythmical flow, achieved largely by 'offbeat', which is used in order to influence the emotions of the dialogue partner:

> Have pátience, sír, O, lét it nót bé só;
> Hereín you wár agaínst yòur rèputátion,
> And dráw withín the cómpass of suspéct
> Th'ùnvíolated hónour of your wífe.
> Once thís, – your lóng expérience of her wísdom,
> Her sóber vírtue, yéars and módesty,
> Pleád on hér párt sòme cáuse to you unknówn;
> And doúbt nòt, sír, but she will wéll excúse
> Why at thís tíme the doórs are máde agaínst you.
> Be rúl'd by mé, depárt in pátience,
> And lét us to the Tíger all to dínner . . .   III, i, 85 – 95

In the first sentence of his reply, Antipholus signals his readiness to forget his grudge against his wife and indicates that he is willing to act according to Balthasar's reasoning. Yet the uneasiness of the rhythm in all his lines has the quality of 'subtextual' and, perhaps, 'subliminal' information for the audience; it conveys the effort it costs him to suppress his anger when he thinks that his wife has been maltreating him. Not only do we find that a number of sentences end in the middle of a line, but above all we have a sentence structure marked by syntactical parenthesis, so typical of a conversational register. The more Antipholus develops his new plan, the more we feel the satisfaction he derives from his intended revenge on Adriana:

> You háve preváil'd, I wìll depárt in quíet,
> And in despíte of mírth méan to be mérry.
> I knów a wénch of éxcellent díscourse,
> Prétty and wítty; wíld and yét, tóo, géntle;
> Thére will we díne. Thìs wóman that I méan,
> My wífe (bùt, I protést, withoút desért)
> Hath óftentìmes upbráided me withál;

---

31 We take this useful term from Barton's discussion of Shakespeare's metrical art, op. cit., passim.
32 On this caesura cf. Barton, op. cit., p.36.

To hér will wè to dínner; [*to Angelo*] gét you hóme
And fétch the cháin, by thís I knów 'tis máde;
Bríng it, I práy you, to the Pórpentìne,
For thére's the hóuse — that cháin will I bestów
(Bè it for nóthing but to spíte my wífe)
Upón mine hóstess thère — góod sír, màke háste.
Since mine ówn dóors refúse to èntertáin me,
I'll knóck élsewhère, to sée if théy'll disdáin me.

III, i, 107 – 121

We should also consider the great speech of Antipholus E to the Duke in the
final scene: how well-balanced are his very first lines, which begin and end
with the word 'justice'; they are an impressive instance of affective rhetoric,
reflecting his despair as well as his self-control:

Justice, most gracious Duke, O, grant me justice,
Even for the service that long since I did thee
When I bestrid thee in the wars, and took
Deep scars to save thy life; even for the blood
That then I lost for thee, now grant me justice. V, i, 190 – 194

The underlying blank verse pattern is subtly undercut by two consecutive run-
on-lines. Despite the speaker's excited state of mind, he succeeds completely
in balancing his appeal to the Duke and in rounding it off with the final
repetition of his initial word ('justice'). But when Antipholus comes to report
his 'deep shames and great indignities', his words become intensely dramatic,
although they are still entirely controlled. There is a whole passage in his
speech in which the lines are end-stopped only occasionally. His words have
immediacy and directness as well as a moving quality because they are the
direct linguistic equivalent of the shocking experience he has had:

There did this perjur'd goldsmith swear me down
That I this day of him receiv'd the chain,
Which, God he knows, I saw not. For the which
He did arrest me with an officer;
I did obey, and sent my peasant home
For certain ducats; he with none return'd.
Then fairly I bespoke the officer
To go in person with me to my house.
By th' way we met
My wife, her sister, and a rabble more
Of vile confederates; along with them
They brought one Pinch, a hungry lean-fac'd villain . . .

V, i, 227 – 238

It would be unfair to neglect Adriana's parallel address to the Duke; let us
examine it from a somewhat different angle. Her words are an early example
of Shakespeare's art of creating outstanding 'musical' effects by the

rhythmical structure of the verse lines, something which, as we have seen, occurs in Plautus, too. Perhaps the most essential means by which Shakespeare achieves these effects is his manifold variation of stressed and unstressed syllables. Very often there is a subtle interplay between the beats required by the metrical pattern and the actual accentuation of a line in the delivery on stage. Both the position and the intensity of the stresses are subject to many modifications. Thus, sometimes the beats occur in a position where there should be an unstressed syllable, or the stress required by the metre is spoken in a subdued manner as a 'semi-stress' only, or the stress is not audible at all so that what we get is one or two extra unstressed syllables, as at the beginning of Adriana's speech:

> Mày it pléase your gráce, Antípholus my húsband,
> Who I màde lórd of mé and áll I hád
> At yóur impórtant létters, thís íll dáy
> A móst outrágeous fít of mádness tóok him;
> That désp'rately he húrried through the stréet,
> With hìm his bóndman, áll ás mád as hé,
> Dòing displéasure to the cítizens
> By rúshing in their hóuses; béaring thénce
> Ríngs, jéwels, ány thìng his ráge did líke.
> Once did I gét him bóund, and sént him hóme,
> Whilst to tàke órder for the wróngs I wént,
> That hére and thére his fúry had commítted;
> Anón, I wót not by whàt stróng escápe,
> He bróke from thóse that had the guárd of him,
> And with his mád atténdant and himsélf,
> Éach òne with íreful pássion, with dráwn swórds
> Mét us agaín, and mádly bént on ùs,
> Chás'd us awáy; till ráising of móre aíd,
> We cáme agaín to bínd them. Thén they fléd
> Into thís ábbey, whìther we pursú'd them,
> And hére the ábbess shúts the gátes on us,
> And wíll not súffer us to fétch him óut,
> Nor sénd him fórth that wè may béar him hénce.
> Thérefòre, móst grácious dúke, with thý commánd
> Lèt him be bróught fórth, and bòrne hénce for hélp.
>   V, i, 136 – 160

Note how frequently there are only four, sometimes merely three, actual stresses in a line. This is important, because, as Barton has shown, 'stressed words come into stronger focus'.[33] There is a wonderful vigour in this speech, which admirably reflects the excitement and bewilderment of the speaker and ends in a superb climax.

[33] Barton, op. cit., p.30.

Finally, we must turn our attention to Shakespeare's subtle use of couplets in *Errors*. These couplets have almost always been seen as proof of Shakespeare's metrical immaturity. However, it can be shown that here, as elsewhere in his early plays, his choice of couplets is determined by profound artistic reasons.

That Shakespeare included the couplet passages for artistic purposes can, first of all, be seen from the fact that their metrical organization shows considerable skill. Take, for example, the following passage from the discussion between Adriana and Luciana in II, i:

Adr.	Why should their liberty than ours be more?
Luc.	Because their business still lies out o' door.
Adr.	Look, when I serve him so, he takes it ill.
Luc.	O, know he is the bridle of your will.
Adr.	There's none but asses will be bridled so.
Luc.	Why, headstrong liberty is lash'd with woe.
	There's nothing situate under heaven's eye
	But hath his bound in earth, in sea, in sky.
	The beasts, the fishes, and the winged fowls
	Are their males' subjects, and at their controls;
	Man, more divine, the master of all these,
	Lord of the wide world and wild wat'ry seas,
	Indued with intellectual sense and souls,
	Of more pre-eminence than fish and fowls,
	Are masters to their females, and their lords:
	Then let your will attend on their accords.
Adr.	This servitude makes you to keep unwed.
Luc.	Not this, but troubles of the marriage bed.
Adr.	But were you wedded you would bear some sway
Luc.	Ere I learn love, I'll practise to obey.
Adr.	How if your husband start some other where?
Luc.	Till he come home again I would forbear.
Adr.	Patience unmov'd! no marvel though she pause;
	They can be meek that have no other cause . . . 10 – 33

We notice that the position of the internal pauses is varied very deliberately. In some lines the rhythm is concentrated so that there is no distinct internal pause (10, 11), in others the position of the pauses is varied to great effect (12, 18, 19). On one occasion (18 – 19), the rhythm of a line expands into the next by enjambement. Even more important, however, is the variation of primary stresses, ranging from four to six. When merely reading these lines, one can easily overlook their metrical art. There is practically no line in which the metrical stresses coincide entirely with the speech accents. There are many metrical inversions, and we often have only four primary stresses. By contrast, the line: 'Lord of the wide world and wild wat'ry seas' (21) contains no less than six stresses, which are necessary to convey the impression of cosmic boundlessness evoked in this line. When, in lines 10 – 15 and later in lines 26 – 31 couplets are distributed stichomythically to two speakers, the discrepancy between the speakers' different points of view is ironically brought out by the harmony of rhymes.

When, on the other hand, Luciana addresses Adriana (16 – 25) in couplets, these are a most fitting formal reflection of what she has to say about the harmony of the Elizabethan cosmos. There is irony again when in her later response to her sister's address Adriana adopts Luciana's couplets in an attempt to prove that she is unable to conquer her impatience. The closing part of II, i again consists of a passage in couplets, now spoken by Adriana. The 'natural' sound of these couplets can be best perceived during a theatre performance, where they produce exactly the right effect for the particular situation. For example, when Adriana complains of being neglected by her husband, and indulges in self-pity, the stylized rhymes serve to prevent the audience from identifying with her, so that they are able to perceive the comic side of her behaviour. When Dromio S meets Adriana in order to ask her for her bail money, it is not his master's command that he is fulfilling, and therefore he does not understand the situation; nor does he comprehend why Antipholus has been arrested by the Officer. However, his utter perplexity, rather than being reflected in uncontrolled language, is here, as it were, undercut by his choice of couplets:

> Adr. Where is thy master, Dromio? is he well?
> Syr.Dro. No, he's in Tartar limbo, worse than hell.
> A devil in an everlasting garment hath him,
> One whose hard heart is button'd up with steel;
> A fiend, a fury, pitiless and rough,
> A wolf, nay worse, a fellow all in buff;
> A back-friend, a shoulder-clapper, one that counter-
> mands
> The passages of alleys, creeks and narrow lands;
> A hound that runs counter, and yet draws dry-foot well,
> One that, before the judgment, carries poor souls to hell.
>
> IV, ii, 31 – 40

Note, too, that the lines grow longer and become more verbose as he proceeds. It would seem that here we have a particularly effective stylization because of the interplay between an underlying metrical pattern and the exuberant and creative use of language with which one metaphor is piled up on the other.

The great scene III, i shows still more variation on the stylized use of the couplet. Apart from Antipholus E's light-hearted opening blank verse passage and the concluding dialogue between him and Balthasar, the entire scene is in doggerel verse with between five and seven stresses to the line. First of all, critics have recognized that this doggerel verse serves a specific purpose: it is a conscious imitation of the verse style of earlier English adaptations of Roman comedies.[34] Doggerel on the one hand increases the dramatic effect of this central scene; on the other hand, it is also used as a counterbalance to the chaotic action on the stage. Sometimes a couplet is distributed between two speakers, one standing behind and one in front of the door of the 'Phoenix', so that the second line has the effect of a comically distorted echo. Furthermore, the couplets ironically reflect the fact that for the first time the two couples are present together on stage.

This leads us to recognize a far more important reason why pentameter couplets form an essential part of this comedy. They provide, it would seem, an appropriate verse pattern for a comedy in which two twin 'couples' are the focus of attention. That Shakespeare felt this to be the case can be inferred from the text itself. In the final scene, the two Dromios, meeting for the first time, are bewildered to find themselves each other's counterfeit; each considers the other a rival, and, ironically, the two lines they speak make up a couplet:

> Syr. Dro.   I, sir, am Dromio, command him away.
> Eph. Dro.   I, sir, am Dromio, pray let me stay.   V, i, 335 – 336

As this couplet occurs in a blank verse context (!), its effect is especially strong. Could we not say that the frequent use of *couplets* in the earlier parts of the play indirectly foreshadows the final reunion of the two twin *couples*? Thus it is not by chance that the play in which twins are the main characters both begins and ends with a couplet. The couplets which have so often been looked down upon as reflecting Shakespeare's metrical immaturity are thus in fact quite deliberately employed. It is interesting to note in this context that John Baxter has recently discovered a comparable function of the closed couplets in Shakespeare's *Histories*. He maintains that in the *Histories* they are used to produce a basic irony because 'the heroic couplet, holding out the promise of order in its closed couplet form, becomes an instrument for measuring precisely the violation of that order'.[35] And Baxter rightly concludes that 'It was Shakespeare's genius to discern something of the potential of the couplet for the drama'.[36]

Scene two of Act two is one of the highlights of *Errors*. Adriana addresses her supposed husband with a long blank verse speech which she concludes with the couplet: 'Keep then fair league and truce with thy true bed, / I live unstain'd, thou undishonoured' (145 – 46). She still hopes that her speech will have an atoning, unifying effect, and it is as if her couplets were to remind us of the

---

[34] Cf., e.g. H. Cunningham, ed., *The Comedy of Errors*, The Arden Shakespeare (London, 1907), p.xxf.

[35] J. Baxter, *Shakespeare's Poetic Styles. Verse into Drama* (London/Boston/Henley, 1980), p.155.

[36] Ibid., p.166.

Elizabethan definition of marriage as 'concord',[37] a quality lacking in her relationship with Antipholus. When she does not receive the expected response from her supposed husband, she realizes the necessity of reinforcing her persuasion, and she thus uses couplets as a means of emphasis. She becomes so possessive that she clings to his sleeve and even uses a traditional emblem by identifying him with an 'elm' and herself with an embracing 'vine'. But why should Antipholus S and his Dromio also speak in couplets? The function of their couplets is surely not to mark 'Antipholus's translation from hostility to acceptance of a fantastic situation',[38] because so far he has not been particularly angry; rather, the couplets suggest to us the imaginative impact Adriana has made on Antipholus so that he thinks it best to 'say as they say' (II, ii, 215). Dromio goes even further and adds: 'We talk with goblins, elves and sprites . . .' (190). This has the further consequence that Adriana, who realizes that the two men are imitating her way of speaking, accuses them of laughing her 'woes to scorn' (205).[39]

Scene ii of Act III introduces another facet of Shakespeare's metrical variety. The first 70 lines not only 'recall' the 'debate' between Adriana and Luciana in II, i,[40] but also evoke the lyrical atmosphere of Elizabethan love poetry, not least by the use of quatrains. Luciana's lines are very interesting from the point of view of language and metre. Antipholus S rightly praises her 'enchanting discourse', that is, her elegant and intelligent conversation. When he addresses her: 'Sing, siren, for thyself, and I will dote' (47), he is alluding to the musical effect of her quatrains. Indeed, the whole situation is full of effective 'rhetoric', of figures and schemes such as parallelism and the rhetorical questions which open the dialogue:

> Luciana.   And may it be that you have quite forgot
> A husband's office? shall, Antipholus,
> Even in the spring of love, thy love-springs rot?
>
> III, ii, 1 – 3

These questions give the lines a startling directness of appeal and lead to the climax in the form of a chiasmus: 'spring of love' – 'love springs'. In order to heighten the effect, Luciana uses an internal rhyme: '*Shame* hath a bastard *fame* . . .' (19). By making Luciana speak first, which in a wooing scene is certainly unusual, Shakespeare suggests that Antipholus has come under Luciana's 'spell'. Indeed, Antipholus continues to speak in Luciana's complicated quatrains as he attempts to persuade her to become his love; yet when he claims to be totally united with her, he aptly starts speaking in couplets:

[37] Sir Thomas Elyot, *The Book Named The Governor*, ed. S.E. Lehmberg (London, 1962), p.77.

[38] Foakes, p.36, n.171 – 2.

[39] Other skilful uses of the couplet have already been pointed out by Foakes, p.19; 29, n.48; p.91, n.678.

[40] Foakes, p.49, n.170.

> It is thyself, mine own self's better part,
> Mine eye's clear eye, my dear heart's dearer heart . . .
>
> III, ii, 61 – 62

Our examination of the metrical structure of *Errors* has shown that it is impossible to characterize it as immature, and it seems to be a strong argument against the assumption that *Errors* is Shakespeare's first comedy. On the contrary, the artistic variety, the brilliance of the rhythm of the verse, the exact correspondence between the verse and its content or the dramatic situation, are most striking. For the most part, Shakespeare's metrical art is different from that of Plautus. It seems that his deliberately sparse use of metrical variation serves as an important and *necessary* counterbalance to the turbulence of the action, which is so much greater than in Plautus; and although Shakespeare makes a highly economical use of metrical devices in this play, the overall effect of his classical work is nevertheless much more intense and dramatic than that of his classical sources.

VII

Names and their Meanings

We have seen in the preceding chapters how closely Shakespeare studied his two Plautine sources before composing his own 'classical' comedy; now we shall return to our earlier suggestion that *Errors* should at the same time be viewed as a text documenting Shakespeare's humanist interests. The current underrating of *Errors*, both in the theatre and in criticism, shows only too well that we are still inclined to underestimate the profundity of Shakespeare's education. We have to assume that Shakespeare acquired a fairly solid knowledge of the classics in the Grammar School. In many respects Elizabethan Grammar School teaching seems to have reflected the educational ideas of Erasmus.[1] Although Shakespeare did not study at a university, his intellectual background and thematic interests are in many respects comparable to the 'University Wits', from whom he may have learnt a great deal by way of conversation. It seems to me that Tillyard has given a vivid description of the ways in which Shakespeare may have acquired his intellectual background. He points out that 'a man can be learned in more ways than one and that at least one of those ways fitted Shakespeare'.[2] He maintains that Shakespeare might have drawn an idea directly from a classical author, or he might have learnt it from a contemporary author who himself drew on the classical tradition, or he might have heard the idea discussed. Tillyard then concludes that Shakespeare was indeed learned, albeit not in a strictly academic or systematic way.[3] To a considerable extent this is probably true; yet our examination has shown how intimate his knowledge of Plautine Comedy and of the New Comedy tradition behind it in fact was, and we have seen that, by reading Plautus in the original Latin, he must have acquired important information on Roman comedy and its reception by the humanists from the introductory essays of these editions. An interesting proof of this is the fact that many of these editions contain an explanatory essay on the meaning of the names of the characters appearing in the comedies, and this explanation of the 'ratio nominum' or 'etymologiae' was particularly stressed

---

[1] Cf. Baldwin, *Shakspere's Small Latine and Lesse Greeke* and especially Sr. M. Joseph, *Shakespeare's Use of the Arts of Language* (New York, 1947).
[2] E.M.W. Tillyard, *Shakespeare's History Plays* (Harmondsworth, 1969), p.12.
[3] Tillyard, ibid.

by the humanist editors.[4] In this, they were obviously following a suggestion by Donatus, who laid down that the 'ratio' and the 'etymologia' of the names of the *dramatis personae* must be recognizable.[5] Names and their meanings were also the subject of a detailed debate, which has been examined by J.L. Calderwood, so that there is no need to go into further detail here.[6]

Plautus usually takes over the names of his characters from his Greek sources; he is fully aware of their meanings and sometimes makes effective use of them, as in his *Bacchides*. In this comedy the cunning slave is appropriately called Chrysalus because the golden boy – this is the meaning of the Greek name – has to supply gold for a young master. He knows, however, that his plans may go wrong and that then the young man's father, thinking that he has been cheated by Chrysalus, will change his name from Chrysalus to Crucisalus, because he will in all probability take revenge and have him nailed to a *cross* (*crux*). In *Menaechmi* the seductive nature of the Courtesan is admirably suggested by her name Erotium. The cook Cylindrus, a stock character in New Comedy, derives his name from the 'cylindrus', a rolling pin. The proverbial voracity of the Parasite, who consumes even the leftovers from his Patron's table, is well brought out in the name Peniculus, a name not adopted from Greek but created by Plautus; its meaning is 'table brush', yet the sexual innuendo is, of course, an intentional side-effect.[7]

In his excellent guide to criticism on Shakespeare's reception of the classical tradition, John W. Velz rightly says that 'much yet remains to be said about onomastics in Shakespeare'.[8] The fact that Shakespeare was familiar with the traditional view going back to classical antiquity according to which the name of a person reflects and represents his very nature is most clearly documented by the conclusion of his *Cymbeline*. There Leonatus is made aware of the 'fit and apt construction' of his name: he is 'the Lion's whelp', 'Being *Leo-natus*'. His daughter is truly called a woman, 'mulier', because by her virtue she has become a 'piece of tender air' = '*mollis aer*' (V,v,443 – 49). This explanation of the meaning of the two names is given a special dramatic function: it suggests the final restitution of Posthumus's real nature, and, similarly, Imogen's true self is revealed when her disguise is no longer required. Shakespeare here quite deliberately employs etymologically appropriate, 'telling' names as a way of characterizing the *dramatis personae*.

---

[4] For example, in the edition *P. Terentii Comoediae Sex elegantissimae cum Donati Commentariis* (Basel, 1567); it explains the 'Idiomata Personarum' and 'Ratio Nominum'.

[5] Donatus, *Commentum Terenti*, II, 12.

[6] J.L. Calderwood, 'Elizabethan Naming' in: *Metadrama in Shakespeare's Henriad* (Berkeley, 1979), p.183 – 220.

[7] Cf. *Menaechmi*, ed. H. Rädle (Stuttgart, 1980), p.122.

[8] J.W. Velz, *Shakespeare and the Classical Tradition. A Critical Guide to Commentary, 1660 – 1960* (Minneapolis, 1968), p.36.

The name Solinus directly refers to one of the literary authorities favoured by Renaissance humanists. In the third century A.D., Julius Solinus compiled a compendium of knowledge about the ancient world.[9] It became widely known, and in 1587 was translated into English by Arthur Golding. Foakes wrongly minimizes the importance of this work by calling it a 'description of the Mediterranean countries' written by a 'geographer'.[10] Nor is it correct to claim that there is nothing to suggest Shakespeare's direct use of this book. Not only does Solinus in his book mention Epidaurus (referred to by Egeon in I, i) and give a succinct description of Ephesus,[11] yet, to the Elizabethans, he was more than a 'geographer', as is usually maintained, he was the author of a book of 'res mirabiliae', of the wonders of the world, as its title suggested. We find an interest in the strange, the marvellous and miraculous in Shakespeare too. Thus, the legendary 'anthropophagi', mentioned by Othello in his famous narration of his past adventures, are to be found in Solinus's book.[12] Of course, Shakespeare may have read about them in Mandeville, Raleigh, or Holland's *Pliny*, but the parallels between Shakespeare and Solinus are so numerous that, since the latter's name occurs in *Errors*, we are almost compelled to believe that Solinus served Shakespeare as a mine of information. The name Lysander, one of the male lovers in *A Midsummer Night's Dream*, occurs not only in Plutarch but also in Solinus's *Collectanea*.[13] Shakespeare is said to have taken the name Hermione from Plutarch, Homer or *The Rare Triumphs of Love and Fortune*; however, her life as told in these sources does not bear any resemblance to the Shakespearean character, whereas Solinus mentions that she gives birth to a child, albeit a boy.[14] Considering the interest in the miraculous and strange, which Shakespeare shares with Solinus, we must recognize a subtle irony in the fact that Shakespeare has Solinus open his comedy.

Far more important than these connections is the fact that Solinus is deeply concerned with decidedly humanist values such as *pietas* and *clementia*, and this may account for the special interest Shakespeare took in his work. In the dedication of his book to a certain Adventus, Solinus praises the *clementia* and *benevolentia* of his addressee.[15] And in the book itself, even when describing certain animals, Solinus stresses their capacity for this same *clementia*. He finds it in lions and also in elephants, who are further credited with an almost

---

[9] J. Solinus, *C. Ivlii Solini Collectanea Rerum Memorabilium*, ed. T. Mommsen (Berlin, 1895).

[10] Foakes, op. cit., p.xxx.; Foakes's remark that there is a character called Solinus in Lyly's *Campaspe* is beside the point because he is so insignificant as to speak only two sentences (ibid.).

[11] Op. cit. p.56; p.166.

[12] For example, op. cit., p.82.

[13] Op. cit., p.29.

[14] Op. cit., p.63.

[15] Op. cit., p.1.

7 From *Liber Chronicarum* by the humanist
Hartmann Schedel

human intellect.[16] And so there is an extra irony in Shakespeare's *Errors*: his Solinus, rather than being merciful by nature, has first to learn the superiority of *clementia* over justice. The fact that in his own Solinus Shakespeare dramatizes a ruler's conflict between justice and mercy provides this play, as Tillyard has pointed out, with an additional political dimension: 'The Duke [. . .] is not just the conventional ruler [. . .] he is a human being, in a great office, subjected, as all such people must be, to the conflict between personal feelings and political duty'.[17] Although the general audience do not, of course, notice these subtle interrelations, their existence cannot be denied; they point clearly to the humanist background to this play.

It has been suggested that the name Egeon may have been developed from that of the Aegean Sea, mentioned in Solinus.[18] However, it is probably no mere coincidence that in the Folio the name is spelled 'Egeon'. If the Folio spelling is correct, then the name is not just a reminiscence of the Aegean Sea. Would the fact that Egeon has travelled and suffered on the Aegean Sea be sufficient reason for naming him after the Sea? This seems doubtful, if not

---

[16] Op. cit., p.119, 111.
[17] Tillyard, op. cit., p.143.
[18] The Aegean Sea occurs, for example, on p.58; Solinus also mentions a certain Aegaeon Chalcidiensis who has, however, no connection whatsoever with the Shakespearean character. It is true there is an Aegaeon in Claudian's *De Raptu Proserpinae*, but he is a monstrous giant with a hundred arms (Claudiano, *I Rapimento di Proserpina*, ed. F. Serpa (Milano, 1981), I, 46, p.52.

absurd, especially if we recall the fact that names in the classical comedy tradition often refer to a major quality of the character who bears the name. I prefer to think that Shakespeare here makes use of a further and more subtle linguistic association. The name, which is mentioned on five occasions, may be understood as a derivative of the Latin verb 'egeo' = 'I am poor, in need of, wanting, in search of someone or something'. Only the ending '-on' would then have to be accounted for. If we take it as the common Greek noun ending, as in the name 'Apoll-on', we have in 'Ege-on' a name made up of two hybrid elements, a Latin and a Greek one, which is not unusual. Understood in this way, the name describes admirably Egeon's role in the romance subplot which frames the play: he is the poor one because he wants ransom money and misses his relatives; he goes in search of them and, as a result, runs into extreme danger. It is interesting and most fitting that he is named 'Egeon' for the first time just after he has told us of his unfortunate losses.

The name Antipholus has always been a puzzle to critics. In his New Arden edition Foakes writes that 'Antipholus appears to stem from the Greek "Antiphilos", listed as a proper name for a lover in H. Estienne (Stephanus), *Thesaurus Graecae Linguae* (1572)',[19] and Baldwin refers to the verb 'αντιφιλεω' and the Latin definition as 'Redamo, vicissim amo, amore prosequar';[20] according to Foakes, it is uncertain where Shakespeare found the name.[21] Indeed, the name not only suggests 'a lover', but with the prefix 'anti-' it signifies reciprocity — loving and being loved in return. No doubt Shakespeare was fully aware of the implied meaning of this name. It has been pointed out that there is an Antiphilus in Sidney's *Arcadia* and an Antiphila in the *Heautontimoroumenos* of Terence.[22] In the comedy *Chrysis* by Enea Silvio Piccolomini a Courtesan bears the name Antiphila. We do not know why Shakespeare changed Antiphilos to Antipholus. Perhaps it is a case of partial assimilation, or it was done for reasons of euphony. A possible explanation is the fact that in the Plautine *Stichus* as well as in *Eunuchus* and *Phormio* by Terence there is a character called 'Antipho'. If we add to this the Latin masculine ending '-us', and an intermediate 'l' to make the pronunciation easier, we get the name Antipho-l-us.[23] Thus the name may be explained as a

---

[19] Foakes, op. cit., p.2.
[20] Baldwin, *Shakspere's Five-Act Structure*, p.696.
[21] Foakes, op. cit., p.2.
[22] M.J. Levith, *What's in Shakespeare's Names* (London/Sydney, 1978), p.68. It escaped Baldwin's notice that it was Cicero who, in his famous *De Amicitia*, for the first time translated αντιφιλειν by his newly coined verb 'redamare'. (W.A. Falconer, ed., Cicero. *De Senectute, De Amicitia, De Divinatione*, The Loeb Classical Library [London/Cambridge, Mass., 1964], p.160).
[23] Baldwin already suspected that 'Antipho of Terence's Phormio [. . .] is here really to blame for the *o* interchanged with the final *i* (*Shakspere's Five-Act Structure*, p.696).

contamination of 'Antiphila' and 'Antipho', both frequently found in Roman comedy. Shakespeare's 'Antipholus' is unique, yet its Greek meaning is only slightly blurred. The name suggests that *love* is the motive of his quest for his brother, that *love* rescues the brother from the dangerous situation in which he finds himself, and that *love* brings about their reunion. The name also suggests the idea which Erasmus discusses, and to which we shall have to return, that love is inspired primarily by a partner whose nature is similar to the lover.[24]

In the Folio text of *Errors* we find the speech headings 'Antipholus Sereptus', 'Antipholis [sic] Erotes' and 'A Errotis'. Obviously these additions to the names stem from Shakespeare's own hand. The first has been correctly interpreted as a reminiscence of the Prologue to *Menaechmi*, where the denizen twin is called 'surreptus', and it is assumed that Shakespeare adopted this addition on the analogy of the speech heading 'Menaechmus Surreptus' which occurs in a number of Renaissance editions. In these editions the other twin is often called Menaechmus 'Sosicles' (or 'Sosides' or even 'Advena').[25]

The Folio word 'Erotes', or 'Errotis', as the cognomen of the traveller twin, is more difficult to account for. It has been unconvincingly explained as an indirect reference to Erotium in *Menaechmi*; it is argued that Shakespeare may have 'thought initially of the Antipholus who was to be entertained in mistake for his brother by Adriana as identified with Erotium's Menaechmus; or, alternatively [. . .] the name of the Courtesan prompted Shakespeare to think of Eros, and to mark off Antipholus of Syracuse as the one who falls in love.'[26] The interpretation generally accepted today is still less plausible: 'Erotes' is taken to have been derived from 'erraticus' or 'errans', meaning the traveller, 'errant' twin, who is thus contrasted with the stolen twin ('surreptus'). However, Foakes correctly notes that it is hard to explain how 'Erotes' could be derived from 'Erraticus'.[27] On the other hand, the name Erotes really does make sense if it is derived from the Greek word 'ερωταω' 'to ask', 'to try to find out'. The proper form of the name would then be 'Erotetes', but the contraction may be explained as a case of haplology. Thus the Greek name 'Sosicles' for the Plautine twin is here replaced by another Greek word, a defining attribute, which characterizes him as a Quester and distinguishes him from the other twin on account of his specific function in the play. This cognomen has to be seen in the light of other Shakespearean names of Greek

---

[24] Cf. chapter IX, note 24.
[25] Cf., for example, the editions *M. Accii Plauti Sarsinatis Comici Festiuissimi Comoediae XX* (Basel, 1535), *Plautus Poeta Comicus* (Strasbourg, 1508), and Baldwin, *Five-Act Structure*, p.695.
[26] Foakes, op. cit., p.xxvif.
[27] Foakes, op. cit., p.xxviif. Baldwin is not helpful either when he points out that the name Erotes recurs in an obscure work, Nicolaus Wyman's *Colymbetes sive De Arte Natandi*; he fails to establish any connection between this text and Shakespeare's *Errors*. (*Shakspere's Five-Act Structure*, p.697).

origin, such as, for example, Ophelia and Sycorax.[28] In any case, it is an astonishing instance of Shakespeare's erudition.

As far as the name 'Dromio' is concerned, most critics hold the view that it is formed from the slave name 'Dromo', which occurs in Terence. However, the Dromos in Terence are particularly insignificant figures, being almost supernumeraries who have nothing to do with the *servus currens* or *servus callidus* types. Indeed, to Erasmus the name simply suggests a dull character, for he speaks of the 'Dromonem stupidum atque hebetem',[29] and he frequently uses it in his *Colloquia Familiaria*. There can be no doubt, however, that, as we have seen, the immediate source of the name is Lyly's *Mother Bombie*, since Lyly's Dromio bears a considerable resemblance to Shakespeare's twin servants. Whereas the original meaning of the name Dromo is 'a runner', Lyly and Shakespeare, by introducing an extra 'i', slightly modify it so that it acquires a lively rhythm; it thus nicely suggests the nervous activity of these servants. The minor character of the goldsmith is given the name Angelo, an appropriate tag name in Elizabethan times, because an 'angel' was a gold coin with the figure of Saint Michael stamped upon it.[30]

In his book on Shakespeare's names, Levith claims that 'Adriana' contains an implication of 'darkness',[31] but to me it is not clear how this meaning should suggest itself by way of a Latin etymology. One could argue that, since it recalls the male name Hadrian, it implies a certain 'maleness', and therefore 'Adriana' seems just the right name for the shrewish wife of Antipholus. However, the key to the significance of this most unusual name lies elsewhere. No one has noticed that the name Adriane occurs several times in Chaucer as well as in Gower — as a variant of the classical Ariadne. Wherever we look in medieval vernacular literature, be it the poetry of Machaut, Boccaccio, or the Italian translation of Ovid's *Heroides*[32] which contain Ariadne's letter to Theseus, we find the name Adriana which may go back to a medieval Latin form 'Adriagne'.[33] That Shakespeare knew Ovid's retelling of Ariadne in the original Latin of his *Heroides* is confirmed by the fact that in *III Henry VI* (I, iii, 48) as well as in *The Taming of the Shrew* (III, i, 42) he quotes lines from this

---

[28] On Greek names in Shakespeare cf. J.W. Hales, 'Shakespeare's Greek Names', *Notes and Essays on Shakespeare* (London, 1884), p.105 – 119.

[29] Erasmus, *De Ratione Studii*, in: *Opera Omnia Desiderii Erasmi Roterodami*, ed. J.C. Margolin (Amsterdam, 1971), I,2,144,9.

[30] Levith, op. cit., p.69.

[31] Levith, ibid.

[32] Machaut, *Le Jugement du Roy de Navarre*, quoted in E.F. Shannon, *Chaucer and the Roman Poets* (Cambridge, 1929), p.68. Boccaccio has Fiammetta compare her tears to those of 'Adriana' in: *Elegia di Madonna Fiammetta*, ed. F. Erbani (Milano, 1988), p.146f. On the Trecento translation of *Heroides* cf. S. Brown Meech, 'Chaucer and an Italian Translation of the *Heroides*', *PMLA*, 45 (1930), 116. On Shakespeare's knowledge of Chaucer see A. Thompson, *Shakespeare's Chaucer* (Liverpool, 1978).

[33] Cf. J. Gower, *Confessio Amantis* in *The English Works of John Gower*, ed. G.C. Macaulay (Oxford, 1901), II, 89.

Ovidian text. He will then also have consulted Chaucer's *Legend of Good Women* which is based on Ovid. In Chaucer's version, as we have already seen, Ariadne is always mentioned as Adryane.[34] He shows how Ariadne/Adryane and her sister at first feel pity for Theseus, who is to be killed by the Minotaur. By using her famous thread, Ariadne shows him the way out of the labyrinth. He swears that he will ever be faithful to her, and they become husband and wife. Having entered the labyrinth with the gaoler, they secretly make their escape. Suddenly, however, Theseus becomes enamoured of Ariadne's sister because, in the words of Chaucer, she 'fayrer was than she' (*Legend of Good Women*, 2172);[35] he steals away from Ariadne while she is asleep. Then she complains about having been 'betrayed' (*Legend of Good Women*, 2188), and this is where her Letter to Theseus starts in Ovid's *Heroides*. Ariadne's complaint culminates in the following lines:

> quid faciam? quo sola ferar? . . .
> Cum mihi dicebas 'per ego ipsa pericula iuro
> Te fore, dum nostrum vivet uterque, meam.'
> Vivimus, et non sum, Theseu, tua; si modo vivis,
> Femina periuri fraude sepulta vivi . . .   59ff

> What am I to do? Whither shall I take myself? [. . .] you said to
> me: 'By these very perils of mine, I swear that, so long as both of
> us shall live, thou shalt be mine!' We both live, Theseus, and I am
> not yours! — if indeed a woman lives who is buried by the treason
> of a perjured maid . . .

> Morsque minus poenae quam mora mortis habet.   82[36]

> and death holds less of dole for me than the delay of death.

In Shakespeare's *Errors*, the name Adriana, being a vernacular form of Ariadne, opens up an interesting mythological parallel and is at the same time an inversion of the classical Ariadne. In both Ovid and Chaucer Ariadne is the victim of Theseus's infidelity;[37] in some dramatic moments of the play, Shakespeare's Adriana, too, complains about her husband's suspected betrayal:

> The time was once when thou unurg'd wouldst vow
> That never words were music to thine ear . . .   II, ii, 113ff

> I'll weep what's left away, and weeping die.   II, i, 115

---

[34] On Chaucer's version of the myth cf. S. Brown Meech, op. cit., 110−28 and B. Harbert, 'Chaucer and the Latin Classics' in: *Geoffrey Chaucer. Writers and their Background* (London, 1974), p.133−53.

[35] *The Works of Geoffrey Chaucer*, ed. F.N. Robinson (London, ²1957), p.512.

[36] *Ovid. Heroides* and *Amores*, ed. and transl. G. Showerman (Cambridge, Mass./ London, 1963).

[37] Cf. Shannon, op. cit., p.67.

Whereas, however, in the classical myth and in Chaucer's retelling of it, the faithful and 'good' woman helps Theseus out of the labyrinth in which death awaits him, Adriana involuntarily contributes towards entangling her husband deeper and deeper in a maze of confusions which makes him afraid of losing his life (IV, iv, 107). Yet like her mythological prototype, Adriana is compelled to think that her husband wants to make love with her sister, a suspicion that is, however, unwarranted because she takes the twin for Antipholus E. Whereas in Chaucer, Theseus by his infidelity, becomes a real 'traitour' (*Legend of Good Women*, 2174), Adriana's husband merely *intends* to become unfaithful as an act of revenge, while the other Antipholus realizes that, by falling in love with Luciana, he had almost become a 'traitor', yet not to her, but to himself (III, ii, 161).

Shakespeare's early plays in particular show that the Ariadne myth must have left a deep impression on Shakespeare. While in *1 Henry VI* the married Suffolk, who has fallen in love with Margeret, refers to the Minotaur and his labyrinth (V, iii, 189), in *The Two Gentlemen of Verona* a direct analogy is established between Julia's diappointment about her philandering Proteus and Ariadne's complaint; being confronted with her rival Silvia, Julia claims that she 'did play a lamentable part. / Madam, 'twas Ariadne passioning / For Theseus' perjury and unjust flight' (IV, iv, 167ff.). We also remember the fact that in *A Midsummer Night's Dream* Theseus' proneness to infidelity is expressly commented on by Oberon who refers to his betrayal of Ariadne (II, i, 79f.). If Shakespeare in *Errors* preferred the variant 'Adriana' to 'Ariadne', he wanted to achieve the effect of subtle allusion so that the educated members of his audience could discover for themselves both the paralleling and inverting of the Ariadne myth. Shakespeare is, then, indeed doing much to provide his comedy with intellectual depth: he first adds a mythological perspective to the confusions of identity by transforming the Amphitruo myth, and then he combines the confusions with the mythological motif of the labyrinth, with the effect that Adriana's behaviour, which is the opposite of that of Ariadne, is indirectly criticized. Moreover, the reminiscences of the classical myth of Ariadne and the labyrinth serve as a beautiful symbolic suggestion of the mysteries of human life. And Shakespeare adds a further mythological perspective by choosing the Phoenix image as a name for Adriana's house; Foakes comments on it as follows: 'The image of this mythical bird, rising out of its own ashes to renewed youth, is appropriate to the story of Antipholus and Adriana, whose love is finally renewed out of the break-up of their marital relationship.'[38] This comment hits the nail on the head and should not be omitted in any future edition of the play.

As regards the sign of the house of the Courtesan, Foakes is less convincing because he only quotes Sisson: 'there was an inn called the Porpentine "on

---

[38] Foakes, op. cit., p.16, n.75.

Bankside . . . Shakespeare's audience probably knew it well'' '.[39] The point is, of course, that the Porpentine is not just an inn but a brothel. As no one would associate a courtesan with a porcupine, the sign functions, as it were, *e contrario* and bears an ironical implication. The name of the inn where Antipholus S stays bears the name (and sign) of the Centaur, which the editions do not comment on. It is true that this tavern is not directly present or visible in the play, nevertheless its role is not unimportant, for Antipholus S arrives there between Acts I and II in search of his Dromio. Like the motif of the Phoenix, the Centaur could be interpreted in Christian terms and said to signify Man's twofold nature, his animal instinct and his human intellect; it is used in this way in *Titus Andronicus* (V, ii, 203) and *King Lear* (IV, vi, 124). Seen in this light, the image well suits Antipholus S, who in search of his own identity has to undergo a process of transformation. Likewise, the fact that the Centaur is half man and half animal links Antipholus with this same thematic strand of transformation, which culminates in the reference to Circe in the final Act of the play.[40]

The sinister person whose task it is to turn a human being transformed by the devil back into his original condition is the exorcist Dr Pinch. We could not easily think of a name more suitable for an exorcist than 'Pinch'. First, it perfectly 'depicts the character's physical appearance',[41] as described in the last Act (V, i, 238 – 242). Then, it is well known that the Elizabethans liked to think that elves and spirits 'pinched' human beings, an idea which we find in Shakespeare, too.[42] This is what Dromio fears when he says that if he and his master do not obey the spirits which they believe surround them, 'they'll [. . .] pinch us black and blue' (II, ii, 192). 'Pinching' thus amounts almost to 'a spirit taking possession of somebody'. If an exorcist wants to expel evil spirits from the human being in whom they dwell, he has to 'pinch' them in return, and therefore Dr Pinch's name suggests part of his activity as an exorcist. The name further implies violence, and his appearance on stage should indeed have a menacing effect.

It appears, then, that in the naming of his characters Shakespeare pursues a threefold aim. He takes great care that the sound effect of a proper name suitably evokes the character of the bearer. Levin has already observed this suggestive quality in some of Shakespeare's names, such as that of Shylock, of which he remarks: 'Shakespeare makes the sound convey a meaning of its own, compounded of sharpness and harshness, so that the name evokes the character by a kind of psychological onomatopoeia.'[43] The second function of names in Shakespeare is then, as we have seen, the direct indication of the

---

[39] Foakes, op. cit., p.49, n.116.
[40] On the important motif of transformation in *Errors* cf. W.C. Carroll, *The Metamorphoses of Shakespearean Comedy* (Princeton, 1985), p.63ff.
[41] Levith, op. cit., p.68.
[42] Cf. *Merry Wives of Windsor*, IV,iv,58 and passim.
[43] Levin, op. cit., p.65.

nature of a character. Names in *Errors* such as Antipholus, Dromio, Egeon, Pinch and Angelo can be best described as 'characteronyms'. However, Levin, who discusses this term, is unaware of the fact that the tradition of New Comedy, which contributed greatly to the frequency of such names in Shakespeare's works, is nowhere clearer than in the Latin names Fidele, Perdita, Marina and Miranda in his last plays. Levin merely makes the general remark that the device goes back at least as far as Homer, and then he turns to the morality tradition and to Restoration Comedy.[44] The third function of Shakespeare's name-giving in *Errors* is to open up a mythological or classical-humanist perspective in a most subtle way.

If the name Solinus contains specifically humanist implications, then the same is true of Luciana, perhaps the most interesting name in the whole play. I find Levith's attempt to derive 'Luciana' from 'lux' and to define its meaning as 'the shining one'[45] entirely unconvincing; as we shall see, her character in fact is incorrectly described as bright and shining. As the metrical context suggests, the name is to be pronounced Luc-i-ana and not trisyllabically, as in the Italian pronunciation. In his edition, Foakes suggests that Shakespeare may have derived the name from the word Lucina, which, he says, is the name of Apollonius's wife in the medieval romance.[46] It is true that she is given this name in the title of the *Apollonius* edition of 1576. Yet we have to be aware of the fact that 'Lucina' in classical literature had a precise meaning and could not readily be transferred to another character: it was the cognomen of Juno as the goddess of childbirth, and as such it occurs in the Plautine *Aulularia* (692) and *Truculentus* (476) as well as in the Terentian *Andria* (473) and *Adelphoe* (478), or to give an example from Renaissance poetry, in Poliziano's *Rime Varie*.[47] Shakespeare was certainly aware of this because in his *Pericles*, based on the romance of *Apollonius*, he uses this cognomen in its correct sense, when Pericles addresses Juno with these words: 'Lucina, o / Divinest patroness and midwife gentle' (III, i, 10 – 11). It is therefore most unlikely that Shakespeare would have derived 'Luciana' from 'Lucina', especially because Luciana's status as an unmarried woman does not in the least remind us of 'Juno Lucina'.

The reason for Shakespeare's choice of this name seems to lie elsewhere. In an age which was particularly language-conscious, it is simply inconceivable that this name was not meant as a deliberate allusion to Lucian, who was esteemed by the Renaissance humanists as one of their favourite authors of late antiquity. It is therefore hardly surprising that Shakespeare included a clear allusion to him in his 'classical' comedy. What Lucian meant to Renaissance humanism can only be assessed if his reception by Erasmus and

---

[44] Levin, op. cit., p.55f.
[45] Levith, op. cit., p.69.
[46] Foakes, op. cit., p.xxxi.
[47] Angelo Poliziano, *Poesie Italiane*, ed. S. Orlando (Milano, 1976), p.235.

Thomas More is taken into account; and in order to understand the full implications of the direct reference to Lucian, it is necessary to present an outline of the intertextual links between Lucian, the humanists Erasmus, Thomas More, and Shakespeare.

VIII

Erasmus, Thomas More and the Lucianic Tradition

There is an increasing awareness among critics that the writings of the humanists Erasmus and More are essential for the understanding of Elizabethan, especially Shakespearean drama, although in most cases the works referred to are merely *The Praise of Folly*, the biography of *Richard III*, or *Utopia*. Thomas More, and in particular his friend Erasmus, did much, as it were, to prepare the intellectual climate in which Shakespeare's art could be created; indeed, 'Without Erasmus, no Shakespeare'.[1] As, for example, a recent study has shown, Erasmus was of opinion that 'thoughts require images in order to be persuasive' and that these images are 'the prime source of delight;' this provides his writings with a certain poetic quality.[2] Erasmus was by nature inclined to the dialogic method; he knew that stating the truth is never a simple affair and that there are often two sides to a problem, or, as Huizinga has put it: 'He knew [. . .] how to avoid direct decisions [. . .] because he saw the eternal ambiguity of human issues'.[3] He liked to qualify his statements with a 'perhaps' or a 'protective reservation irritating to those critics to whom the propositions disputed were either right or wrong, good or bad.'[4] Thus it was impossible for him to join Martin Luther's Reformation. In fact he frequently called the Reformation a 'tragedy';[5] and tragedy was something which he preferred to shun. If there are strong affinities between Erasmus and Shakespeare, then there is, of course, also a world of difference between the Erasmian ideal of moderation and the uncompromising passion of the great Shakespearean tragic hero.

Erasmus's comparison of life with a stage play runs through his whole

---

[1] E. Jones, *The Origins of Shakespeare* (Oxford, 1977), p.13.

[2] J.D. Tracy, *Erasmus. The Growth of a Mind* (Genève, 1972), p.81.

[3] J. Huizinga, *Erasmus and the Age of Reformation*, transl. F. Hopman (Princeton, 1984), p.127.

[4] C.R. Thompson, ed. and transl., *The Colloquies of Erasmus* (Chicago/London, 1965), p.xxxxi.

[5] Cf., for example, Huizinga, op. cit., p.137.

work.[6] In his *Praise of Folly* he has Folly say that 'the whole life of men [is] but a sort of play'.[7] Yet it is clear that his concept of drama was essentially derived from comedy. We have seen that he prefers Terence, but, for example, in his satire *Julius Exclusus de Coelis*, he adopts 'many of the more colourful words and phrases' of Plautus, too.[8] In his educational treatise *De Ratione Studii* he presents a detailed discussion of how the comedies by Terence and by Plautus should be taught and interpreted at school in order to achieve the maximum educational effect.[9] Having a good knowledge of young people's psychology, he knew very well that comedy appeals to them much more than tragedy. His famous *Colloquia* are a major result of his reception of Roman comedy; in them he availed himself of the Roman comic and dialogic method for his discussion of vital moral and intellectual issues of his own time. They reveal very clearly 'that Erasmus had the dramatist's eye; he saw everything and could re-create these scenes with his pen'. 'Situation, plot, and characterization make them more than mere dialogues; they are incipient dramas or novels.'[10] We know that several *Colloquies* were even performed by students in Freiburg in Southern Germany in 1529.[11] One of his favourite characters is the swaggering soldier, partly modelled on the stock character of the *miles gloriosus* in Menander, Terence and Plautus; yet in creating this character he also added elements from real life as he saw it.[12]

How close he sometimes comes to the themes and atmosphere of Roman Comedy can be seen from the *Colloquy* about the young man and the harlot (*Adolescentis et scorti*).[13] Occasionally he even increases the effects of comedy by means of puns and quibbles, thus again continuing the classical comic

---

[6] In one of his letters, for example, he rebukes his friend Guillaume Budé in the following manner: 'In any case you act the indignant man; you are not angry. Granted that it is an act, it is certainly a very clever one, like that of the actor in Lucian playing Ajax, who broke two or three people's heads wearing an actor's mask; you are not in character, and you are dealing with a friend.' (*The Collected Works of Erasmus*, vol. 6. *The Correspondence of Erasmus*, transl. R.A.B. Mynors and D.F.S. Thomson [Toronto, 1982], p.204).

[7] *The Praise of Folly*, transl. B. Radice in: *Collected Works of Erasmus*, vol. 27. Literary and Educational Writings 5, ed. A.H.T. Levi (Toronto, 1986), p.103.

[8] *Julius Excluded from Heaven: A Dialogue*, transl. M.J. Heath, in *Collected Works of Erasmus*, vol. 27. Literary and Educational Writings, 5, p.167.

[9] *On the Method of Study (De Ratione Studii)*, transl. B. McGregor in *Collected Works of Erasmus*, vol, 24. Literary and Educational Writings, 2, ed. C.R. Thompson (Toronto, 1978), p.682.

[10] C.R. Thompson, *The Colloquies of Erasmus*, p.xxvi; cf. also Huizinga, *Erasmus*, p.114; W. Kaiser, *Praisers of Folly* (Cambridge, Mass., 1963), p.99.

[11] Cf. H. Rädle, ed. Erasmus von Rotterdam, *Colloquia Familiaria. Vertraute Gespräche* (Stuttgart, 1982), p.78.

[12] Cf. Thompson, *Colloquies*, p.12.

[13] Thompson, *Colloquies*, p.153 – 158.

tradition.[14] The overall style, like that of Roman comedy, is rhetorical as well as conversational. Erasmus justified his playful *Colloquies* by remarking that 'Socrates brought philosophy down from heaven to earth; I have brought it even into games, informal conversations, and drinking parties'.[15] The *Colloquia* became almost as widely influential as *The Praise of Folly*. George Saintsbury was the first to suggest that these *Colloquies* may have contributed more to the development of drama and prose fiction than is usually assumed.[16] It should also be expressly mentioned that Erasmus had a special sympathy for the social condition of women, and only occasionally is there an antifeminist echo in his works.[17]

Thompson even considered that the character of Maria in the Colloquy *On Courtship (Proci et Puellae)* might be compared 'in poise, intelligence, and wit to the women of Shakespeare's romantic comedies'.[18] Let us look at another colloquy, that *On Marriage (Coniugium)*, in which the two women Eulalia and Xanthippe discuss the right way for a wife to behave towards her husband. Xanthippe, who has been complaining about her husband, is reminded by Eulalia (the 'woman of good advice') that 'Paul teaches that wives should be obedient to their husbands in all subjection', to which Xanthippe retorts: 'But this same Paul teaches that husbands should cherish their wives as Christ cherished his spouse the church. Let him remember his duty and I'll remember mine.' Erasmus stresses the equal duties of husband and wife, yet he also implies that the wife has essential rights too. This results from his *balanced* consideration of the two sides of a problem. He would have had some sympathy with Adriana's question why the 'liberty' of husbands should be greater than that of wives. And on several occasions his colloquy *On Marriage* reminds us of *Errors*. In the following dialogue, Xanthippe finds fault with her husband:

XAN.   Hope to die if I wouldn't rather sleep with a brood sow than with such a husband!

EUL.   Don't you welcome him with abuse then?

XAN.   Yes — as he deserves. He finds I'm no mute.

EUL.   What does he do to counter you?

---

[14] For example in the colloquy *De Captandis Sacerdotiis (In Pursuit of Benefices)*, Thompson, *Colloquies*, p.11.

[15] Thompson, *Colloquies*, p.xxvii.

[16] Cf. Thompson, op. cit., p.xxvi.

[17] Cf. *De Pueris Instituendis (On Education for Children)*, Collected Works of Erasmus, 26, Literary and Educational Writings, 4, ed. B.C. Verstraete (Toronto, 1985), p.325: 'Erasmus' views on the education of girls and women were decidedly progressive for his day' (p.575); cf. also W.H. Woodward, *Desiderius Erasmus Concerning the Aim and Method of Education* (New York, 1964), p.148 – 53; on the concept of women in the Renaissance cf. E.V. Beilin, *Redeeming Eve* (Lawrenceville, Princeton, 1987).

[18] Op. cit., p.87.

XAN.   At first he used to talk back most ferociously, thinking he'd drive me away with harsh words.

EUL.   The bickering never came to actual blows?

XAN.   Once, at least, the argument grew so hot on both sides that it very nearly ended in a fight.[19]

Xanthippe's complaints are similar to Adriana's arguments and, as we proceed, Eulalia increasingly resembles the Abbess in *Errors*. The following short excerpts document the striking similarity with the great scene between Adriana and Aemilia. Like the Abbess, Eulalia explains how a good wife should behave:

XAN.   Wives have an unhappy lot for sure if they must simply put up with husbands who are angry, drunk, and whatever else they please.

EUL.   As if this putting up with things didn't work both ways! Husbands have much to endure from our habits as well. On occasion, however − in a serious matter, when something important's at stake − it's right for a wife to reprove her husband [. . .] (cf. with this the Abbess's criticism: 'You should for that have reprehended him' V, i, 57).

EUL.   . . . Despising his wife, he doted on a mistress with whom he would often enjoy himself away from home. He seldom *lunched or dined at home*. What would you have done in this situation?

XAN.   What? I'd have flown at his sweetheart's hair [. . .]

EUL.   But how much more sensible this woman was! She invited the girl to her own home and received her cordially. Thus she enticed her husband home too, without sorcery [. . .]

XAN.   I'd rather die than be bawd to my husband.

EUL.   But consider the case. Wasn't this far better than if she had simply alienated her husband by her fury and spent her whole time in brawling? [. . .]
       [. . .] There are even some failings you ought to wink at. Above all, in my judgment, you must be careful not to start an argument in the bedroom or in bed [. . .] (cf. Adriana's: 'In bed he slept not for my urging it' V, i, 63 (italics mine)[20]

These passages not only serve to demonstrate Erasmus's talent for dialogue, but they are also very similar in spirit to Shakespeare's treatment of the marital relationship of Adriana and Antipholus. We again find how important the humanist background to Shakespeare's classical comedy really is. Whereas Erasmus directly *refers* to St Paul's teaching on marriage in the *Letter to the Ephesians*, Shakespeare does not! What Erasmus tries to convey in these

[19] Op. cit., p.116.
[20] Op. cit., p.119ff.

Colloquies is not a rigid Christian dogma, but simply *pietas*. As he himself
explains in the *Declarationes ad censuras colloquiorum*, their purpose is that his
readers 'ad Rhetoricam preparentur denique et pietatis elementa quaedam
imbiberent'.[21] This virtue of piety is not basically different from the
'humanist' attitude of classical antiquity, as we find it in the plays of Terence
and in the best works of Plautus and as it is extensively discussed in Scaliger's
Poetics.[22] As we shall see, it is precisely this idea that assumes an essential
function in Shakespearean drama.

A further quality which distinguishes the Erasmian *Colloquies* is their
satirical tone. Erasmus uses satire, which is by no means alien to the classical
comic tradition, as a strategy in order to expose human folly. He inveighs
against abuses and superstitious practices of all kinds. This is familiar to us
from his *Encomium Moriae*, a text which is conceived as a speech by personified
Folly to her listening audience. This famous work also articulates the favourite
Erasmian paradox that the 'alazon', the braggart who thinks himself wise, is
the real fool, and the inversion of this paradox, as it was first expressed by St
Paul, becomes even more important: what appears to be folly in the eyes of the
world may turn out to be the workings of divine wisdom and grace.[23]

It is in this context that the impact of Lucian on Erasmus becomes
important. As Erasmus himself indicates, the satirical element in his reception
of New Comedy was considerably influenced by the model of Lucian's
satirical strategy. It is strange that Lucian should be remembered almost
exclusively for his works in the tradition of Menippean satire, because he is
certainly no less important as an author of comic dialogues. Urbanity and
elegance are qualities of his style that are also prominent in the works of
Erasmus. Lucian's influence on European culture, particularly from the 16th
to the 18th century, can hardly be overestimated.[24] Some of his dialogues
might be compared to small plays, and he has justly been called a dramatist in
his own right.[25] He, too, viewed life as a great stage of fools,[26] and his works
abound in references to the theatre. As an admirer of Old and New Comedy,

---

[21] Quoted by L. Wirth-Poelchau, ed. and transl., *Familiarum Colloquiorum Formulae. Schülergespräche* (Stuttgart, 1982), p.82.; cf. Huizinga, op. cit., p.104.

[22] Julius Caesar Scaliger, *Poetices Libri Septem*, ed. A. Buck (Stuttgart-Bad Cannstatt, 1964), p.32.

[23] Cf. W. Kaiser, *Praisers of Folly*, p.84ff.

[24] Cf. D.J.D. Cast, *Lucianic and Pseudo-Lucianic Themes in the Renaissance: A Study in Renaissance Humanism* (Diss. Columbia Univ., 1970); C. Robinson, *Lucian and his Influence in Europe* (London, 1979) and D. Duncan, *Ben Jonson and the Lucianic Tradition* (Cambridge, 1979); cf. also J. Martindale, *English Humanism* (London, 1985), p.28ff.

[25] Cf. e.g., W.M. Gordon, 'The Platonic dramaturgy of Thomas More's Dialogues', *JMRS*, 8 (1978), 196.

[26] For example, in his dialogue *Peregrinus* in: *Lucian*, ed. A.M. Harmon, The Loeb Classical Library (London/Cambridge, Mass., 1962), V,5; cf. also Salingar, *Traditions of Comedy*, p.154.

he adopted a number of comic elements in his dialogues: these are indeed replete with the 'familiar range of characters and situation'[27] of New Comedy. If Lucian drew suggestions for his dialogues from classical comedy, he also extended and transformed them in interesting ways: he emphasized the festive and saturnalian element and introduced, as it were, the aesthetic principle of variation. Furthermore, in contrast to classical comedy, which usually has three people simultaneously present on stage, he filled his 'stage' with seven or eight characters, preferably appearing in public places, and he invented lively actions and enriched the dialogue with rapid repartee. He employs the comic strategy of dialogue in order to expose people's manners and morals to satire and ridicule. The comic exposure reaches its climax when the 'alazon' unwittingly reveals his own folly. Thus, his *Dialogues of the Courtesans* are a satirical 'imitation' of the world of Plautine comedy. His frequent allusions to works of literature provide his texts with an almost unique quality of intertextuality. They rely on 'the previous existence of myth, romance, tragedy, comedy, the hellenistic novel, all of which they absorb into their own pattern'.[28]

Although it is not easy to give an impression of the charm and elegance of a Lucianic dialogue in a brief quotation, we shall here offer a survey of his famous dialogue *Philopseudes, The Lover of Lies*. It opens with the discussion of a problem which also concerned the humanists: are the tales of the poets mere lies, or are they true in spite of their fictionality? Lucian's implied answer is a humanist one: as they serve the purpose of utility in an entertaining way, their fictional, 'lying' quality can be excused. Lucian's dialogue then goes on to satirize people's credulous belief in all sorts of lies. The dialogue does not itself develop into action, but it does contain a number of narrated stories. A particularly Lucianic situation occurs in the story told by 'Arignotus, a man of superhuman wisdom', who tries to prove that apparitions are *true*. However, Tychiades, rather than praising Arignotus's wisdom, refutes this story as mere folly.[29] Then follows Eucrates's story of The Sorcerer's Apprentice, made famous by Goethe's poem. Note the brilliant elegance and sense of drama with which this tale is told:

> At last he [Pancrates] persuaded me to [. . .] go with him quite alone [. . .] But whenever we came to a stopping-place, the man would take either the bar of the door or the broom or even the pestle, put clothes upon it, say a certain spell over it, and make it walk, appearing to everyone else to be a man. It would go off and draw water and buy provisions and prepare meals and in every way deftly serve and wait upon us. Then, when he was through with its services, he would

[27] Robinson, *Lucian*, p.11.
[28] Robinson, op. cit., p.44.
[29] *Lucian*, ed. and transl. A.M. Harmon, The Loeb Classical Library (London/ Cambridge, Mass., 1960), III, 369ff.

again make the broom a broom or the pestle a pestle by saying another spell over it. [. . .] But one day I secretly overheard the spell — it was just three syllables — by taking my stand in a dark place. He went off to the square after telling the pestle what it had to do, and on the next day, while he was transacting some business in the square, I took the pestle, dressed it up in the same way, said the syllables over it, and told it to carry water. When it had filled and brought in the jar, I said, 'Stop! don't carry any more water: be a pestle again!' But it would not obey me now: it kept straight on carrying until it filled the house with water for us by pouring it in! At my wit's end over the thing, for I feared that Pancrates might come back and be angry, as was indeed the case, I took an axe and cut the pestle in two; but each part took a jar and began to carry water, with the result that instead of one servant I had now two. Meanwhile Pancrates appeared on the scene, and comprehending what had happened, turned them into wood again, just as they were before the spell, and then for his own part left me to my own devices without warning, taking himself off out of sight somewhere.   p.373ff

Eucrates has not succeeded in defeating Tychiades's scepticism. The dialogue comes to an end with one of Lucian's fascinating 'twists'. Tychiades, the un-believer, wishes to obtain 'a dose of forgetfulness', because he thinks he sees 'apparitions and spirits and Hecates!' (p.379). His dialogue partner Philocles replies: 'It is likely [. . .] that having been bitten yourself by a multitude of lies in the house of Eucrates, you have passed the bite on to me; you have filled my soul so full of spirits!' (p.381) The concluding remark by Tychiades sums up the whole dialogue and articulates the 'moral': 'Well, never mind, my dear fellow; we have a powerful antidote to such poisons in truth and in sound reason brought to bear everywhere. As long as we make use of this, none of these empty, foolish lies will disturb our peace.' (p.381) However, the paradox remains that we enjoy the dialogue not so much because of its content, but because of the artistic skill with which the fictional stories are told.

Erasmus was so attracted by Lucian's brilliant wit and satire that he translated 28 of his dialogues into Latin.[30] In our context, the most interesting work is perhaps the Colloquy *Exorcismus sive Spectrum*. In a manner surprisingly similar to Lucian's *Philopseudes*, Erasmus sets out here to satirize the human folly of credulity and superstition. In this *Colloquy* too, we have a long narration: we are given the account of the performance of a very funny five-Act comedy in which a character is cured of his superstitious belief in spectres by a practical joke: the 'appearance' of a ghost is performed by a group of actors, and one of them can be recognized as Thomas More. It is significant that this *Colloquy* not only indirectly refers to the famous *Philopseudes* by Lucian, but that it also expressly alludes to the tradition of New Comedy by a

---

[30] Cf., for example, U. Baumann and H.P. Heinrich, *Thomas Morus. Humanistische Schriften* (Darmstadt, 1986), p.42.

metadramatic reference: the character called Thomas remarks that 'This play
[. . .] beats Menander's *specter.*'[31]

Thomas More, too, was a great lover of plays and, like Erasmus, he had a
keen sense of comedy, especially of New Comedy. In his early youth he took
part in the production of plays.[32] With his 'iesting rhetorike',[33] he opposed the
self-assuredness of Martin Luther, and among his contemporaries he acquired
the image of a 'wise foole'.[34] He too was an admirer of Lucian. In an
important but neglected essay J.A.K. Thomson goes so far — and I think
rightly — as to state that Lucian taught both Erasmus and More 'a lesson in
the art of applying irony to literature. The *Moria* [The Praise of Folly] now
becomes possible, the *Utopia* becomes possible.'[35]

All this is remarkably reflected in the play *The Book of Thomas More*, in which
Shakespeare had a hand; this is, therefore, a very important document in our
context. Here a history play is mixed with touches of a comic Lucianic spirit.
For example, More spontaneously takes part in a play within the play entitled
The Marriage of Wit and Wisdom, which is really part of the Morality Play *Lusty
Juventus*. In the role of 'Good Counsel' he combines 'wit, wisdom, and
theatricality', and this perfectly reflects the nature of his personality.[36] In the
eyes of the world the humanist Thomas More is, of course, a fool because he
gives up his high social and political position and finally even risks his life by
resisting the will of the king. Yet, paradoxically, in the eyes of God he is the
truly wise man because he has accorded his will to the will of God; thus his
tragedy is converted into a 'divine' comedy, and he stages his own end in the
manner of a comedy by his playful jests and puns. We recognize in Thomas
More the 'wise fool' of the Lucianic tradition, particularly in a scene in which
he acts in the 'foolish' but human defence of a cutpurse. Lifter, the
pickpocket, has been caught and judgement has been passed on him.
However, Suresby, the judge, has some sympathy for the criminal; he argues

[31] Thompson, *Colloquies*, p.233. The play *Spectre* is, in fact, by Philemon, another New
    Comedy author.

[32] *The Life of Syr Thomas More by Ro. Ba.*, ed. E.V. Hitchcock and P.E. Hallett
    (London, 1950), p.63 and esp. W. Roper's Life of Thomas More (London, 1935),
    p.5.

[33] Ibid., p.63.

[34] Ibid., p.266.

[35] 'Erasmus in England' *Vorträge der Bibliothek Warburg*, 9 (1930/1), 64 – 82; 75; on
    Lucian's influence on More's *Utopia* cf. T.S. Dorsch, 'Sir Thomas More and
    Lucian: An Interpretation of *Utopia*', *Archiv*, 203 (1967), 345 – 363; W.W.
    Wooden, 'Thomas More and Lucian: A Study in Satire, Influence and Technique',
    University of Mississippi Studies in English, 13 (1972), 73 – 57; Duncan, op. cit.,
    p.66 – 74; Robinson, op. cit., p. 130 – 133 and G.M. Logan, *The Meaning of More's
    'Utopia'* (Princeton, 1983), p.144 – 145.

[36] Cf. C.R. Forker and J. Candido, 'Wit, Wisdom, and Theatricality in *The Book of Sir
    Thomas More*', *Shakespeare Studies*, 13 (1980), 85 – 104, esp. p.89; cf. also A. Fox,
    'The Paradoxical Design of *The Book of Thomas More*', *Renaissance and Reformation
    Studies*, 17 (1981), 162 – 173.

that these 'lifters' are often tempted by thoughtless men who irresponsibly carry with them large sums of money. Thomas More, who has listened to the judge's argument, goes one step further, and, in a typical act of unmasking, proves, with the help of the cutpurse, that the judge is himself carrying with him a large sum of money. By his joke More has achieved his purpose: he has been able to demonstrate to the judge that he is guilty of the very offence which he has condemned in others. In other words, while exposing folly in another person, the judge has been forced to reveal his own foolishness.[37] It is very fitting that in this anonymous drama Thomas More is made the protagonist of an entire Elizabethan play.

As R.S. Sylvester, in his excellent edition of More's *History of King Richard The Third*, has shown, More presents the English King not with historical accuracy, but as a humanist skilfully transforming ideas from classical historians such as Tacitus, Suetonius and Sallust and maintaining an ironic tone.[38] We may well call this Lucianic. Given this connection and More's strong histrionic foible, it is no wonder that Thomas More conceived of Richard III as a skilful actor in a drama with a sense of comedy, and this may have 'encouraged Shakespeare to add to Richard that touch of comedy that makes him so distinguished a villain.'[39] For More, Lucian ranked among the foremost authors who ideally combined the 'utile' with the 'dulce'. He believed that, in the final analysis, Lucian wrote for the propagation of the four Christian cardinal virtues and that he thus provided guidance for the Christian life.[40] More translated four of Lucian's dialogues, including the important *Tyrannicida*. This is a condemnation of tyrants; the killing of the tyrant is described in terms of performing a tragedy,[41] and ideas from it went into his biography of *Richard III* and from there into Shakespeare's play.[42] Thus we see how a certain indirect relationship between Lucian and Shakespeare's early work can be established.

For a long time, scholars have been unwilling to accept that there is indeed a Lucianic element in Shakespeare. This is surely a reflection of the general reluctance to recognize a satirical tone in Shakespeare. It has been held that Shakespeare, as opposed to Ben Jonson, had no genuine interest in satire. However, Bevington has shown that this is not entirely true; he rightly, for one, maintains that Shakespeare 'experimented' with satire and that his

---

[37] *The Book of Thomas More* in: *The Shakespeare Apocrypha*, ed. Tucker Brooke (Oxford, 1908), p.389.

[38] R.S. Sylvester, ed., *The Complete Works of St. Thomas More* (New Haven, London, 1963), II, esp. p. lxxxviiff.

[39] Tillyard, *Shakespeare's History Plays* (London, 1961), p.215; cf. also E. Story Donno, 'Thomas More and Richard III', *RenQ*, 35 (1982), 401 – 47.

[40] Cf. Baumann, op. cit., p.48 – 50.

[41] *Tyrannicida* in: *Lucian*, ed. A.M. Harmon, V, 445ff.; esp. p.469.

[42] Baumann, op. cit., p.54; on Erasmus's and More's translation of Lucian see R. Thompson, *The Translations of Lucian by Erasmus and Sir Thomas More* (Ithaca, 1940).

'fascination with satire [. . .] was by no means simply negative'. Although 'Shakespeare's attitudes [towards satire] are harder to pin down'[43] than those of Jonson, Bevington finds that Shakespeare begins to concern himself with 'the question of satire in drama with some intensity during the years from 1598 to 1602'.[44] He mentions Jaques, Thersites, Parolles and Lucio, and from these it seems possible to 'piece together an impression of Shakespeare's view of the satiric scene.'[45] Yet with regard to the earlier comedies he claims that 'Shakespeare's apprenticeship to neoclassical forms of comedy during his experimental years did not extend to satire'.[46] We shall argue here that this view is incorrect, it is possible only from a modern, rather than from a historical perspective. If Jonson 'describes art's highest purpose as the taxing of human follies',[47] then this basically humanist concern is no less present in Shakespeare's works — beginning with his early comedies, not least *Errors*, which is so much more than a farce; and Shakespeare appears to have been fully aware of the fact that, beginning with Menander, there is a satirical element in the New Comedy tradition which was reinforced by the humanist reception of Lucian. If Shakespeare's comedies differ essentially from those of Ben Jonson, it is not because they are devoid of satire, but because they are most complex works of art in which a satirical perspective is always *one* dramatic constituent.

More recently, a Lucianic tone in Shakespeare has occasionally been recognized. Even if very little of Lucian was translated into English, 'one or two dialogues read at school in Erasmus's Latin [. . .] could have provided him with all the Lucian that he needed to remember'.[48] As Baldwin, in his book on *Shakspere's Small Latine and Lesse Greeke* shows on many occasions, Lucian counted among the most frequently read school authors. Furthermore, we shall see that Shakespeare was familiar with the Lucianic *Timon* comedy, and he may have known more Lucianic texts either in Latin or French.[49] Duncan, who has suggested that there is a more frequent echo of Lucian in Shakespeare than is generally assumed, first refers to the famous overhearing situation in *Love's Labour's Lost* (IV, iv). He calls this 'a distinctively Lucianic

---

[43] D. Bevington, 'Shakespeare versus Jonson on Satire' in C. Leech and J.M.R. Margeson, eds., *Shakespeare 1971. Proceedings of the World Shakespeare Congress Vancouver, August 1971* (Toronto/Buffalo, 1972), p.107 – 122; cf. also R. Stamm, 'Shakespeare und die Satire', in: Zwischen Vision und Wirklichkeit. Zehn Essays (Bern, 1964), p.45 – 62, and A.L. Birney, Satiric Catharsis in Shakespeare. A Theory of Dramatic Structure (Berkeley, 1973).

[44] Ibid., p.114.

[45] Ibid.

[46] Ibid.

[47] Ibid., p.112.

[48] Duncan, op. cit., p.91.

[49] W.H. Clemons, 'The Sources of "Timon of Athens"', *Princeton University Bulletin*, 15 (1904), 208 – 23.

variant of the world-upside down *topos*.[50] Yet it is more significant than that: it
is a splendid example of the humanist reception of the New Comedy tradition.
The eavesdropping situation, like the motif of disguise a most characteristic
element of this tradition, is not only used in a dramaturgically far more
brilliant way than in Plautus or Terence, it is also *combined* with the
characteristically Lucianic exposing of sham wisdom. The scene contains the
comically teasing exposure of universal folly, in the Lucianic manner, because
not only does each eavesdropper reprove his victim merely to be reproved in
turn, but Berowne, who chides them all because of their hypocrisy, is
recognized by the audience as being affected by the same weakness himself.
Everyone involved becomes a kind of 'alazon', and indirectly they all reveal
themselves for what they are.

After describing Puck's comment: 'Lord, what fools these mortals be!' (*A
Midsummer Night's Dream*, III, ii, 115) as Lucianic, Duncan goes on to show
how Shakespeare in *As You Like It* plays with the possibilities of satire, and he
shows how Jaques refers to Erasmus's defence of general satire. Jaques's
soliloquy on the Seven Ages of Man, while not directly derived from Lucian,
is nevertheless reminiscent of the Lucianic mode. 'This is satire wittier than
the complaint, less vindictive than the Juvenalian, and persuasively
comprehensive in seeming to range over the whole of human life.'[51] After
commenting on *Timon of Athens*, which, as we shall see, has special Lucianic
connections, Duncan concludes that 'With a little ingenuity, other puzzling
plays like *Troilus and Cressida* and *Measure for Measure* might be similarly related
to the Lucianic mode.'[52] This is a very valuable suggestion, and we shall find
how worthwhile it is to examine plays like these from this unusual perspective.

It seems, though, that there is a special Lucianic element even in *Hamlet*,
whose date of composition is close to that of *Troilus and Cressida*. It can hardly
be purely accidental that a character in 'The Murder of Gonzago', the 'play
within the play', should bear the name 'Lucianus'. Its plot goes back to an
actual Italian murder case. As one of the persons involved was called 'Luigi',
it has been assumed that it was this that suggested the name Lucianus to
Shakespeare.[53] This, however, seems most unlikely, because there is not the
slightest onomastic connection between 'Luigi' and 'Lucianus'. Shakespeare's
use of the name Lucianus must have been very deliberate, because the
Elizabethans would certainly have been reminded of the famous author
Lucian. We therefore have to enquire as to the reason why Shakespeare
thought fit to include this literary allusion, why, in other words, he added this
intertextual perspective to his play. As a great lover of drama, Lucian wrote
some short plays himself, and he even took part in some of his dialogues, such

---

[50] Duncan, op. cit., p.92.
[51] Ibid., p.92 – 93.
[52] Ibid., p.94.
[53] Cf. H. Jenkins, ed., *Hamlet*, The New Arden Shakespeare (London, 1982), p.102.

as *Nigrinus*,[54] under the name of 'Lycinus'. Here, Lycinus tells his friend that he wants to be an actor and to prove that his memory is powerful and reliable, and he informs his friend that he has to take over the role of a messenger in tragedy. More importantly, this dialogue contains a number of detailed comments on acting, which show a remarkable similarity to Hamlet's extensive discussion of the theatre and its actors. Lycinus's complaint is directed in particular towards tragic and comic actors who are used to being hissed and who, having destroyed the dramatic effect of a play, are chased off the stage. Lycinus emphatically denies that he has anything in common with those bad actors (!) who, having chosen the part of Agamemnon, Creon or Hercules, strut onto the stage in the apparel of a king or with the grim face of a hero, and who open their mouths wide only to produce a high, feminine voice that would be far too weak even for a Hecuba or Polyxena.[55] It thus seems possible that with his own comments on the stage in *Hamlet* Shakespeare places himself deliberately in a literary tradition of theatrical satire that derived from Lucian. Erasmus contributed to the spreading of this Lucianic theatrical criticism by including it in his own *Parabolae*.[56]

Furthermore, Hamlet's repeated comments on Fortune find their parallels in Lycinus's comments on the whims of Fortune.[57] And finally, in his speech as messenger, Lycinus delivers a remarkable satire on Rome that would be equally fitting to Hamlet's Elsinore. He states that Rome is the right place for someone wanting to live in luxury. Here the soul is able to devote itself to luxury with all the senses. All the vices, including adultery, perjury and avarice, grow to such proportions that they sweep away all feelings of shame, justice and virtue. We are then reminded of Osric in *Hamlet* when he describes a fop and says that it is hardly possible not to laugh at the affected way in which he performs his role.

Although these analogues are surprisingly numerous, I would not wish to suggest that all of them point *directly* to Lucian. What is surprising, however, is the similarity between the satirical tone of Shakespeare and Lucian. Shakespeare's calling one of the actors in 'The Murder of Gonzago' Lucianus indicates a subtle and significant intertextual relationship that can no longer be disregarded. The 'Mousetrap' play as a whole is given the typically Lucianic and humanist function of revealing the truth and exposing lies and pretence as well as of satirizing human passions.

There is a further situation in *Hamlet* which should also be viewed in this context. When in II, ii Hamlet appears reading a book whose author he refers to as a 'satirical rogue' (196), he probably does not have Juvenal in mind, as

---

[54] *Nigrinus* in: *Lucian*, ed. A.M. Harmon, V, 98 – 139.

[55] Ibid., p.109 – 111.

[56] *Parabolae* in *Collected Writings of Erasmus*, vol. 23, Literary and Educational Writings, 1, ed. C.R. Thompson (Toronto, 1978), p.218.

[57] *Nigrinus*, p.119 – 121.

Baldwin would have us believe.[58] It is far more plausible to assume that Hamlet means Lucian, who achieved his satire through his art of *comic dialogue*: is it not this same strategy of comic and satiric dialogue which Hamlet is directing in this situation towards Polonius?

Having recognized the significance of Lucianus in *Hamlet*, we would do well to assume that Shakespeare introduced the name Luciana deliberately into his *Errors*. If in Solinus he is referring to a 'humanist' author of the third century A.D., in Luciana he is alluding to another famous 'humanist' author of the second century. Although Luciana's role is considerably shorter than that of Adriana, she is an interesting character, whose nature becomes fully apparent only when she is played on stage. One of her functions in the play is clearly the Lucianic exposure of the folly and misbehaviour of human beings. On several occasions she wonders at the foolishness of her partners Antipholus, Dromio and Adriana. Scene II, i is particularly interesting in this respect: when Adriana, who has just complained about her marriage problems, leaves the stage, Luciana comments on her exit with the Lucianic remark: 'How many fond fools serve mad jealousy?' (II, i, 116). This is comparable with Puck's Lucianic comment, quoted above: 'Lord what fools these mortals be'. It is significant that Folly in Erasmus's *Encomium Moriae*, which strongly reflects the spirit of Lucian, includes jealousy, Adriana's problem, in her list of human follies.[59] There is a certain flippancy and frivolity in Luciana's nature, which agrees well with her Lucianic associations, but, very strangely, this aspect of her character is usually ignored by the critics. She encourages her sister's supposed husband to woo her and advises him to deceive his wife by wooing 'by stealth' (III, ii, 7). On the other hand, like all the other characters, Luciana, too, is liable to deception. It is highly ironic in the best Lucianic sense that Luciana, who in Act II revealed the folly in others, should in scene III, ii herself be made a complete fool by totally confusing the identity of her partner. She is unable to perceive that, behind the outward appearance of the twin Antipholus, there is not her brother-in-law but his twin, who is a different person.

The Lucianic touch in this early Shakespearean comedy is not confined to the characters, their proneness to deception, or to Luciana. On one level, the whole comedy may be interpreted as a process during which the follies of the major characters are exposed in a way reminiscent of Lucian. As our survey has shown, we cannot merely speak of Shakespeare's reception of New Comedy and its adoption by Plautus without paying attention to the way in which Erasmus and Thomas More favoured Lucian and emphasized the satirical Lucianic element in the comic dialogue. The further implications for the full understanding of *Errors* will have to be discussed in the next chapter.

---

[58] *Shakspere's Small Latine and Lesse Greeke*, II,526.
[59] *The Praise of Folly, Collected Works of Erasmus*, 27, p.98.

IX

The Significance of
Shakespeare's 'Classical' Comedy

Errors is a play in which a number of themes that were to become increasingly important in Shakespeare's work are dramatized. Very early in the play, the 'cosmic order', the 'cosmic reality behind appearance'[1] is envisaged, and the contrast between appearance and reality becomes fundamental. H.F. Brooks has rightly maintained that 'At the centre is relationship: relationship between human beings, depending on their right relationship to truth and universal law.'[2] The necessity of justice as well as of mercy is emphasized. All this, except for the theme of cosmic order, is fully in line with the spirit and tone of Menandrian New Comedy, which centres around the humanism of true relationships. There is, of course, no denying the impact of English late medieval drama on Shakespeare, yet as far as *Errors* is concerned, it is wrong to argue that, rather than being a play inspired by classical comedy, it is firmly rooted in the popular tradition of the Mystery and Morality Plays.[3] *Errors* is the result of Shakespeare's intensive study of the classical tradition, and this is what makes the play so important.

Not only is it wrong to see major reflections of the Mystery Plays and Moralities in *Errors*, the play is also less Christian in tone than is generally assumed. The Christian elements, rather than being essential, have the primary function of providing colour and a touch of realism; they make the audience feel that they are in a familiar world. If Antipholus S calls himself a 'Christian', then he does it merely in the context of an oath-like emphasis: 'As I am a Christian' (I, ii, 77), and when, at the appearance of the Courtesan, Dromio asks whether she is 'mistress Satan' (IV, iii, 47), such a reference remains entirely on the surface and cannot be taken as proving a specifically Christian *outlook*. The notion that husband and wife are 'incorporate' as one flesh, is, of course, a common Christian concept, yet in *Errors* it is not emphasized in a specifically Christian way. Of course, there are a number of

---

[1] H.F. Brooks, 'Themes and Structure in "The Comedy of Errors"', in: *Early Shakespeare* (London, 1967), p.67.

[2] Ibid.

[3] Cf. especially A.F. Kinney, 'Shakespeare's Comedy of Errors and the Nature of Kinds', *SP*, 85 (1988), 29 – 52.

allusions to Hell; they occur most frequently in Dromio's report of Antipholus E's imprisonment (IV, ii, 32 – 40). Yet, as we saw in an earlier context, their function is not so much to produce comic effects as to reinforce the element of threat. As the motifs of Hell and Satan are among the most common Christian notions and at the time when Shakespeare wrote were almost omnipresent, they can certainly not be seen as proving Shakespeare's alluding to the hell scenes and the presentations of Satan in the medieval Mystery Plays, as a recent interpretation would have it.[4] Nor should we overlook the fact that Dromio begins his series of hell metaphors by a reference to the classical Tartarus, calling this place 'worse than hell' (IV, ii, 32). The only reference, and a very brief one at that, to the medieval theatre which I can find in the play is Egeon's report of his adventurous life, the structure of which resembles a *de casibus* tragedy. There is nothing else in the play to medievalize its atmosphere in any essential way. That the play was performed on Holy Innocents' Day in 1594, and a second time at Court, exactly ten years later, certainly should not be seen as reflecting a connection between the supposed baptismal theme of *Errors* and this Christian feast;[5] on the contrary, the Gray's Inn report of this performance and the audience's response to it shows very clearly that the play was used as part of the Christmas *Revels*.[6]

A further argument put forward in order to prove the supposedly Christian quality of the play is the fact that Shakespeare chose Ephesus as its locality. It is claimed that he made this choice deliberately because this city was familiar to the Elizabethan audience from its description in the Acts of the Apostles, where its superstitious and mercantile atmosphere is evoked; and it is further argued that this gave Shakespeare the chance to include St Paul's admonition to husbands and wives in his *Letter to the Ephesians*.[7] At first sight, these arguments seem to be more substantial than the ones first mentioned, yet they, too, are deceptive. It is, of course, very likely that Shakespeare reckoned with the Elizabethans' being 'familiar' with Ephesus and its reputation of being a place of witchcraft and superstition, yet I would like to suggest that this was not the major reason for his choice of locality. This lies rather in the fact that Ephesus was a favourite and important locality for the plots of New Comedy which already made use of its mercantile atmosphere, as in *Bacchides* or in the famous *Miles Gloriosus*. Merchants are among the more prominent characters of the plays of classical comedy, and this points to the circumstances which gave rise to Greek New Comedy, the new shift in interests from the common concerns of the Athenian people to private life in Athenian

---

4 Kinney, op. cit., p.47 – 48.
5 Kinney, op. cit., p.32.
6 Cf. the recent study by M. Knapp and M. Kobialka, 'Shakespeare and the Prince of Purpoole: The 1594 Production of *The Comedy of Errors* at Gray's Inn Hall', *Theatre History Studies*, 4 (1984), 71 – 82.
7 This argument is contained in most interpretations of *Errors*.

society.[8] It is very interesting that in *Errors* Shakespeare preserves something of this original background, or rather he adapts it to the conditions of his own time when, particularly in the second scene of the play, he creates a specifically 'mercantile' atmosphere. It would therefore be wrong to claim that this business world was meant to show the Marxist 'alienation' among the play's major characters.[9]

Among the Christian aspects of the play, there is, of course, the character of the Abbess. Yet it is quite remarkable that, apart from her position, there is no specifically Christian quality to be found in her. She never refers to the Christian God (nor, by the way, does any other character). She mentions, it is true, her 'holy prayers' (V, i, 104) and she refers to her 'oath' (106), but these are the only indications of her spiritual life, which she gives. When she teaches the Duke the superiority of mercy over justice, we are inclined to interpret this as a Christian theme, and yet the 'clementia' of a governor had been a humanist virtue ever since classical antiquity – we need only think of Cicero, Seneca and Stoicism in general, or, as we have seen, of Solinus.[10] If Shakespeare had wished to make the Abbess a Christian character, and to introduce questions of Christian *belief* in his play, he would certainly have used this opportunity in a different way. (Let us remember that the Act of Parliament which forbade the use of the name of God was not passed until 1606.) The constant repetition of critics that the Ephesian Abbess pronounces views on marriage which St Paul first addressed to the Ephesians does not add credibility to their claim. We remember our comparison in the last chapter between Adriana's dialogue with the Abbess and the Erasmian Colloquy *On Marriage*. The interesting difference between the two lies in the fact that, while Erasmus (who is himself an undogmatic Christian humanist) directly mentions St Paul's teaching on marriage, Shakespeare does not. The view expressed by Luciana that the wife has to submit herself to the authority of her husband is part of a brief sketch of the Elizabethan view of the cosmic order and cannot therefore be interpreted as specifically Pauline. We should further note that the Abbess never adopts St Paul's idea of female subordination; *on the contrary*, she argues from the point of view of female self-assertion and first suspects that Adriana has not 'reprehended' her husband 'rough enough' (56f.). In any case, the Abbess's advice to Adriana is based on *common sense* or reason, rather than on any specifically Christian principles. The way in which

---

[8] Cf., for example, S.M. Goldberg, *The Making of Menander's Comedy* (London, 1980), p.1ff., and Salingar, *Traditions of Comedy*, p.105.

[9] For a Marxist interpretation cf. A. Schlösser, 'Das Motiv der Entfremdung in der Komödie der Irrungen', *ShJ*, 100/1 (1964/5), 57 – 71.

[10] Cf. Cicero, *De Re Publica*, e.g., II, 14 (27); Seneca, *De Clementia*. On the opposition between law and the Church as discussed at the Inns of Court, cf. W.R. Prest, *The Inns of Court under Elizabeth I and the Early Stuarts 1590 – 1640* (Totowa, New Jersey, 1972), p.209. I fail to see the 'Christianity' and 'inner life' of which A. Barton speaks (*The Riverside Shakespeare*, p.81).

she tackles Adriana's problem is simply motivated by her desire to make Adriana aware of her possessive jealousy.

The fact that Aemilia and her family had been separated for 33 years has reminded one critic of the 33 years of Christ's life.[11] But what point could there be in any such association? Since in the entire play there is nothing which directly refers to Christ's redemption, an attempt of this kind to prove the medieval and Christian spirituality of this comedy is well-nigh absurd, and one is almost forced to say that criticism of Shakespeare's *Errors* is, to some extent, itself a 'comedy of errors'. But what are we to make of the fact that, after the unravelling of the plot and after the various mutual recognitions, the Abbess invites all to a 'gossips' feast' (405), where the family reunion is to be celebrated? First, it has to be seen that the emphasis is clearly on 'feast' rather than on 'baptism'. Then, the theme of rebirth is not an exclusively Christian one. In fact, it has been subtly prepared for by including the motif of the Phoenix, which, as we have seen, is the appropriate name for Antipholus's house. (In *The Winter's Tale* Shakespeare shows another classical 'rebirth' – Hermione's reunion with her husband.) At any rate, the 'gossips' feast' in *Errors* is alluded to in a metaphorical way, and Shakespeare deliberately avoids any 'sacramental' or 'liturgical' associations. Let us remember the fact that both Antipholi retain their names, whereas in *Menaechmi* the traveller Menaechmus becomes Sosicles again after he has found his twin.[12] What bring about the final reunion are the humanist qualities of love, patience, and endurance, rather than divine interference. Is it not strange that the Abbess, before she invites the newly-found family members, omits all references to the godhead? Instead she suggests the human solidarity of sympathizing (397) as the prerequisite of the final reunion.[13] Whereas in Shakespeare's late plays the belief in divine guidance becomes a central theme, in *Errors* the idea of providence is, as it were, only subliminally present in the frequency with which characters experience situations they cannot account for, so that they

[11] B. Freedman, 'Egeon's Debt: Self-Division and Self-Redemption in The Comedy of Errors', *ELR*, 10 (1980), 379.

[12] This has been rightly observed by D. Haberman, 'Menaechmi: A Serious Comedy', *Ramus*, 10 (1981), 136.

[13] I am inclined to assume with Foakes that the Folio line 'After so long grief, such Natiuitie' (V, 406) erroneously repeats the term 'nativity' from two lines above and that Hanmer's emendation to 'felicity' is convincing and even brilliant. 'Felicity' is the appropriate and expected contrast to grief: 'After so long grief, such felicity'; 'felicity' is even preferable to 'festivity', yet not 'only because it does not simply echo the word "feast", ll. 405 and 407' (Foakes), but because 'felicity' is an eminently characteristic humanist term, which not only occurs frequently in English humanist drama; it also occupies a central position in a work like Thomas Morus's *Utopia*, where it expresses the final stage of human well-being, which Man achieves if he lives in harmony with himself and if he enjoys the support of human solidarity (*Utopia and a Dialogue of Comfort*, ed. J. Warrington [London, ²1951] p.39.

think they are dreaming.[14] Again, this sense of wonder is developed much
further in the later plays.

The Egeon overplot, of which the Abbess is a part, and which is based on
the *Apollonius of Tyre*, has usually been taken as a specifically medieval
element, or to be more precise, as an element of medieval romance. This
again is a misunderstanding of Shakespeare's intentions. The *Apollonius* story
is not just a typical example of a medieval romance, not even if it is Gower
who retells it. True, in Gower the hero is called a knight, and Apollonius's
wedding is described as a courtly feast, but Gower uses this tale of antiquity,
in which Diana and Neptune dominate the world, as a deterrent against the
sexual aberration of incest. Chaucer refused to include *sujets* of this kind
because he considered them too distasteful[15]. Not so Shakespeare: incest
occurs in his work in a number of forms; we think, apart from *Pericles*, above
all of *Hamlet*, where Gertrude's remarriage is considered incestuous. And in
Errors, as Ralph Berry has observed, incest becomes a '*theatrical* possibility'[16] in
the very pivot of the play: if Adriana had 'marital' intercourse with the twin,
she would have unwittingly committed the sins of both adultery and incest. It
is certainly true that not much is made of this theme in *Errors*, but its presence
as a dramatic possibility cannot be denied; it certainly does not contribute to
the allegedly 'Christian tone' of the play. Hence it really makes no difference
whether Shakespeare read the *Apollonius* in Gower's version or as a late
classical romance. Egeon, far from being a Christian character, tells his
romance story not so much in a medieval but rather in a classical tone, and
Shakespeare seems to wish to emphasize this point because Egeon is the only
character in the play who refers to 'the gods' (whom he calls 'merciless') (I, i,
99).

A further reason why the Egeon overplot produces a classical impression is
the intertextual links between Apollonius and the world of the New Comedy
tradition, as it is reflected in the refined Plautine *Rudens*. A brief consideration
of these texts must suffice here because we shall have to return to them in our
final chapter. In both texts, family members are separated and happily
reunited through divine providence as well as through the virtue of human
piety (*pietas*), a virtue which, as we have seen, Erasmus also strongly
emphasized in his own work. In the *Apollonius* this piety causes the
protagonist's wife to become a priestess in the temple of Diana, while in *Rudens*
a priestess of the temple of Venus helps to bring about the final reunion. Just
as in *Rudens* the virtue of *pietas* has a central role – and its importance is
strongly emphasized as early as the Prologue – so Egeon, by his piety and

---

[14] Cf. W. Babula, 'If I dream not: Unity in "The Comedy of Errors" ', *South Atlantic
   Bulletin*, 38 (1973), 26 – 33.
[15] Chaucer, *Canterbury Tales*, Introduction to *Man of Law's Tale*, 80ff.
[16] R. Berry, *Shakespeare and the Awareness of the Audience*, p.40.

patience, is able to withstand his tragic fate. This theme of human piety is, as it were, made to replace a specifically Christian attitude.[17]

The final piece of evidence usually adduced by those claiming that there are essential medieval constituents in *Errors* is, of course, the 'romantic' love between Luciana and Antipholus. However, if we look closely at scene III, ii, we observe clearly that this situation is very different from the typical romantic wooing scene. The sooner we give up the common notion that Shakespeare's romantic comedy originated in his early *Errors*, the better. It seems that the sheer poetry of the scene has distracted critics from observing what is really going on. Before we begin our analysis, we must bear in mind two things: first, that Shakespeare wanted us to experience the scene from the point of view of Antipholus as the central character, and, second, the fact that, from first to last, Luciana believes that she is addressing her own brother-in-law.

What happens in this scene is indeed a far cry from a genuine romantic wooing. Whereas normally the active part in a wooing scene is assigned to the wooer, the initiative here clearly lies with Luciana, who opens the scene by addressing Antipholus in a speech comprising almost 30 lines. We are, of course, to assume that he had already spoken to her in Adriana's house, and that she is now responding to his 'advances'. But in a play it is what we *see* on stage that has the decisive effect. And we are shown Antipholus not so much as an active wooer, but as one *responding* to Luciana's suggestions and to the signs of encouragement which she gives him. The first thing he says is that he acknowledges her as his teacher: she is to teach him 'how to think and speak' (III, ii, 33). He then goes on to say that she has charmed him and that he has come entirely under her spell, so much so that he is speaking as though in a state of rapture; his adoration culminates in his claim that his identity and hers are one: 'I am thee' (66). He feels so attracted to her that he forgets the quest for his brother. One might argue that there are other romantic lovers who react in a manner similar to Antipholus. The point, however, is that Antipholus himself very early on experiences his falling in love with Luciana not as being enchanted by her beauty, but rather as succumbing to the bewitching temptations of a 'siren'.

What can hardly have escaped the notice of either Antipholus or the Elizabethan audience is the bafflingly immoral tone of Luciana's initial advice to him. It is most strange that nevertheless almost all critics admire the alleged wisdom of her advice;[18] she is even called an impersonation of 'virtue' as opposed to the 'vice' of the Courtesan.[19] And one critic surprises us with a most daring inversion of what we find in the text: whereas Luciana advises

---

[17] This has been overlooked by J.L. Sanderson, 'Patience in *The Comedy of Errors*', *Texas Studies in Literature and Language*, 16 (1975), 610.
[18] Tillyard, for example, called her 'worldly wise' (*The Nature of Comedy and Shakespeare*, The English Association, Presidential Address 1958 [Oxford, 1958], p.8).
[19] Freedman, op. cit., p.380.

Antipholus to 'become disloyalty', he ventures to claim that one of her qualities is 'loyalty'![20] Occasionally, a critic has felt some uneasiness about her words but has made light of it; her 'slightly disconcerting' moral views were, on one occasion, explained away as reflecting the influence of Ovid's *Amores*.[21] In our production of the play, the actress who played Luciana became more and more uneasy about her role during rehearsals, and gradually the evasive ambiguity of Luciana's character emerged. Her advice is indeed difficult to account for: she suggests to the supposed husband of her sister that he should betray her by 'stealth' (III, ii, 7). The advice she gives here corresponds exactly to that of Folly in Erasmus's *Praise of Folly* on achieving peace in marriage: 'Goodness me, what divorces or worse than divorces there would be everywhere if the domestic relations of man and wife were not propped up and sustained by the flattery, joking, complaisance, illusions, and *deceptions* provided by my followers!'[22] Luciana, as we have seen in an earlier context, is herself a typically Lucianic character who, in advising her partner to be foolish-wise, reveals her own folly because she mistakes Antipholus S for her brother-in-law. At the end of the situation she is prepared to ask her sister for her 'good will' (70). For what? one must ask. Even for a present-day audience with their much more liberal moral standards, Luciana's views are rather daring. It is therefore all the more difficult to understand that critics have been 'caught' by the *poetry* of this love situation and have even claimed that the purpose of the scene is to enable Antipholus to find a new identity in Luciana.[23]

It is important for a more profound understanding of *Errors* to see that here, in contrast to later comedies, especially *Twelfth Night*, a young man does not find his identity in his love for a woman or in the love for a female partner together with the friendship with a male friend. *Errors* is *solely* concerned with a young man's search for his social integration in his family and especially for his male counterpart. Finding each other, the twins become a symbol of male friendship because they best embody the way in which true friendship is defined by classical authors, above all by Cicero as well as by Renaissance humanists.[24] Love between friends is seen as an attraction between two similar

---

[20] B.O. Bonazza, *Shakespeare's Early Comedies. A Structural Analysis* (London, 1966), p.42.

[21] S. Wells, ed. *The Comedy of Errors*, p.27, 153.

[22] *The Praise of Folly*, transl. B. Radice, in: *Collected Works of Erasmus*, 27. Literary and Educational Writings, 5, p.97 (italics mine).

[23] Cf., for example, Foakes, op. cit., p.xliii.

[24] Cicero, *De Amicitia*, ed. W.A. Falconer (London/Cambridge, Mass., 1964), p.160: 'nihil esse quod ad se rem ullam tam illiciat et tam trahat quam ad amicitiam similitudo.' On this idea in Erasmus cf. his *Adagia* transl. M. Mann Phillips ('Simile gaudet simili'), *Collected Works of Erasmus*, 31 (Toronto, 1982), p.167f., and especially *De Ratione Studii*, transl. B. McGregor in: *Collected Works of Erasmus*, 24, Literary and Educational Writings 2: 'Friendship can exist only among similar people, for similarity promotes mutual good will, while dissimilarity on the other

minds, between two people of similar qualities and feelings, so that the friend is considered as the *alter ego*, the 'other I', as Sir Thomas Elyot directly translates it.[25] Antipholus finds himself by transcending himself through his love for his twin. The Duke hints at this by using a word with particularly classical and humanist connotations: when he sees the twins together, he observes that 'one [. . .] is *genius* to the other' (V, i, 332). The implications of this term have not been fully recognized; it is not just that the one is the 'attendant spirit'[26] of the other; the term 'genius' also meant the personification of the higher self to which one aspires.[27]

Antipholus S wants to find his mother and in particular his brother in order to discover who he is himself. Adelman was on the right track when she claimed that 'the love plot exists largely to add to the confusions of identity'[28], except that there is in fact no love plot, but just one scene; thereafter, the motif of courtship is dropped. In the final situation the idea of Luciana and Antipholus becoming a couple is only very vaguely hinted at and does no more than serve a convention. What we do see is that Antipholus, while he is alone on stage, suddenly realizes that he has been on the point of abandoning his essential task, his quest for his twin as his *alter ego*. As a consequence, he immediately revokes his behaviour towards Luciana; it appears to him that he was about to commit a serious mistake by succumbing to the charms of a 'mermaid' (163). He says that her 'enchanting presence and discourse, / Hath almost made me traitor to myself' (160f.). The word 'traitor' in Shakespeare has to be taken very seriously; we are by no means justified in passing over it lightly. The sentence suggests nothing less than that Antipholus, by being 'seduced' by Luciana's charms, almost gave up his quest for his brother and thus, implicitly, for his real self, too. Just as he thinks that he has met a 'witch' (143), so Antipholus in retrospect thinks that he was enchanted by witches. Antipholus, in his rapture, asks Luciana to 'transform' him (40), while Dromio believes that he was 'transformed' by the 'witch' Nell (145). Karen Newman thus comes very near the truth when she states that 'Words such as *dote*, *siren*, *mermaid* and the like seriously undermine a wholly positive interpretation of the twin's love at this point.'[29] Indeed, Shakespeare here

hand is the parent of hatred and distrust [. . .] the greater, the truer, the more deeply rooted the similarity, the firmer and closer will be the friendship.' (p.683 – 4); 'The deepest form of love coincides with the deepest resemblance [. . .] each is drawn to nothing other than his own character as reflected in another person, that is, to himself in another form.' (p.686).

25 *The Book Named the Governor* (London, 1962), p.134.

26 Foakes, op. cit., p.103, n.332.

27 On the significance of 'genius' cf. D.T. Starnes, 'The Figure Genius in the Renaissance', *Studies in the Renaissance*, 11 (1964), 234 – 244.

28 J. Adelman, 'Male Bonding in Shakespeare's Comedies', in: *Shakespeare's Rough Magic*, ed. P. Erickson and C. Kahn (Newark/London/Toronto, 1985), p.75.

29 K. Newman, *Shakespeare's Rhetoric of Comic Character* (New York/ London, 1985), p.143, n.10.

deliberately inserts references to the *Odyssey*, as Ralph Berry has recently observed.[30] When Antipholus stops his ears 'against the mermaid's song' (III, ii, 163), he has the Calypso episode of Book XII in mind. As Ulysses later encounters Circe, so Antipholus next meets the Courtesan whom he thinks to be another siren. The last direct allusion to the *Odyssey* occurs immediately before the situation of *anagnorisis*, when the Duke says of the total confusion: 'I think you all have drunk of Circe's cup' (V,i,271).

However, Antipholus, although he has become aware of the powers which, as he thinks, are distracting him from his quest, nevertheless loses himself ever more deeply in a labyrinth of confusions. The same happens to his brother; he has first to taste the fear of being murdered and to approach the verge of insanity before he finally finds himself through the recognition of his brother. By means of Adriana's subtle name, which, as we have seen, is a variant of Ariadne, Shakespeare alludes to the famous Renaissance (and particularly mannerist[31]) concept of the labyrinth and opens up a further mythological perspective. These mythological associations provide the play with a universal, symbolic significance. At the same time the critical view of Adriana is reinforced: she does not possess the perfection of Ariadne, and consequently, rather than helping her husband out of the labyrinth, she in fact causes him – and indirectly his twin brother, too – to become more and more entangled in a maze.

To a Renaissance audience the problem of the confusing and transforming of identities was not, however, confined to the world of poetry or mythology; it could become a fact in real life too, and we find it even in the guise of a practical joke. There is an Italian anecdote according to which the famous Brunelleschi once tried to convince a fat carpenter that he had changed into another person, a certain Matteo. Some of Brunelleschi's friends, including Donatello, who were present, all 'confirmed' to the poor carpenter that he had become Matteo until he finally believed it and asked himself: 'What shall I do now, since that I have become Matteo?'[32] In a superstitious age, the carpenter has become the victim of his own credulity.

Here Shakespeare's *Errors* reveals, as it were, an additional level of meaning. Because of his own prejudiced credulity, Antipholus S interprets all the hindrances on his quest as dangerous 'mermaids' and 'sirens'. His brother, too, is almost ruined by the Ephesian belief in witchcraft. Shakespeare not only makes a laughing-stock of exorcism, but he is also concerned about the inhuman effects which may arise from superstition. Just as Antipholus E is taken to be possessed, just as the Courtesan and the other

[30] R. Berry, *Shakespeare and the Awareness of the Audience*, p.32 – 33.

[31] Although Shakespeare's art greatly excels mannerism, there are some interesting points of contact which have been discussed in a number of publications; cf. e.g. A. Hauser, *Mannerism: The Crisis of the Renaissance and the Origin of Modern Art* (London, 1965).

[32] Quoted in P. Burke, *Die Renaissance in Italien* (München, 1988), p.230.

women are taken to be witches, so in Elizabethan everyday reality innocent men and women were condemned as real witches. In both cases the same mechanism of misinterpreting 'reality' through a prejudiced imagination is at work. It seems to me that we have not considered seriously enough the fact that, on one level of meaning, *Errors* also reflects the witch craze, which reached a first climax in the last decades of the 16th century.[33] *Errors* is written in the same spirit as Erasmus's and Lucian's fight against superstition and exorcism, against the blinding of man's reason by foolish credulity. Shakespeare's intention can in particular be compared to that of Erasmus in his Colloquy *Exorcismus sive Spectrum* and of Lucian in his *Philopseudes*, which we examined in the previous chapter. The play, narrated in the Erasmian dialogue, shows a character who is made a dupe, and as a result suffers such ill effects that he 'would have been close to real insanity, had not relief come through a quick cure.'[34] Erasmus tries to show that calling a person a witch or considering someone to be possessed by a demon is not merely a matter of human misjudgement, but may even, as in the case of Shakespeare's Antipholus E, destroy the victim's very identity.

There is, then, even a satirical level in the complex play of Shakespeare's *Errors*. All the major characters are made fools of because they are deceived into accepting appearance for reality. We have already seen that even Luciana is satirized as a fool because she is totally mistaken about the real identity of the traveller Antipholus, and he in turn becomes a fool when he allows himself to be ruled by the common prejudice against Ephesus and sees witches in all the women he meets. When, towards the end of the great second scene of Act II, he decides to act the man all the others take him for: 'I'll say as they say and persever so, / And in this mist at all adventures go', then this counsel might easily have been suggested to him by Erasmus's Folly.[35] And then there is the critical light cast on Adriana's problematic relationship with her husband and the way in which the Abbess tries to cure it. Let us recall that in *Menaechmi* the theme of routine in marriage and the problems arising from it are also articulated, and Menaechmus is seen to struggle for freedom until finally the game of the auction is announced; yet these problems are simply mentioned as the cause of a turbulent action, and no attempts are made to overcome them. In *Errors*, the Abbess tries to correct Adriana's exaggerated jealousy, which is a clear symptom of her possessiveness. As we have seen,

---

[33] This claim has also been made by T. Hawkes, 'Shakespeare and new critical approaches', in: *The Cambridge Companion to Shakespeare Studies*, ed. S. Wells (Cambridge, 1986), p.297.

[34] *The Colloquies of Erasmus*, transl. by C.R. Thompson (Chicago, London, 1965), p.230 – 237.

[35] 'A man's conduct is misplaced if he doesn't adapt himself to things as they are, has no eye for the main chance [. . .] and asks for the play to stop being a play.' (*The Praise of Folly*, op. cit., p.103).

even Shakespeare's early comedy is, among other things, 'corrective comedy'.[36]

This corrective aspect is already fully developed in New Comedy. For example, in the Menandrian play *Perikeiromene* the jealousy of a character is exposed to laughter.[37] The comedy of Menander is concerned with a right sense of values and with the 'educational problem' to propagate these values in a play which does not totally dispose of satire.[38] Although Menander's plays were unknown in the Renaissance, there was a collection of his moral sentences which Erasmus frequently quoted.[39] 'Error' in New Comedy is, then, not only a matter of identities being concealed by disguise, and confusions resulting from deceit or the vicissitudes of life; it also implies misguided attitudes towards life or towards one's inner self. As early as the comedies of Menander we find the admonition of γνῶθι σεαυτον by the Delphic Apollo.[40] The dramatic process of Menandrian comedy from *agnoia* to knowledge also comprises the losing and finding of one's self, the achieving of self-knowledge. Although Shakespeare can have had only a vague notion of Menandrian comedy, he nevertheless became familiar with practically all the dramaturgic and thematic possibilities which this tradition had to offer because, as we have seen, some of Plautus's comedies have faithfully preserved Menander's comic dramaturgy. In some plays of Plautus too, the problem of identity is made dramatic use of, as in *Miles Gloriosus* (169). In *Menaechmi* we have the quest of Menaechmus S for his *alter ego*; 'he knows in some fashion that his own true identity is dependent upon the discovery of his brother',[41] yet in this play, the problem is entirely made subservient to the achieving of comic effects. However, in *Amphitruo*, this theme is treated in a much more profound way. Here the loss of identity brings the human characters on the verge of tragedy, and comic as well as tragic emotions are released in a 'tragicomoedia', which has now been recognized as Plautus's original creation.

It is, I think, Shakespeare's greatest triumph in *Errors* that he fulfils the 'educational' task of comedy by brilliantly combining the *Menaechmi* with the *Amphitruo*. The latter play, almost more than *Menaechmi*, inspired him to write his own 'classical' comedy about identity without ever becoming didactic in a non-dramatic sense. In his mixing of tragic and comic emotions he went far

---

[36] This point has also been made by S. Wells, *The Comedy of Errors*, p.28.

[37] *Perikeiromene* in *Menander*, ed., N. Miller (London, 1987), p.113f.; cf. Sandbach, *The Comic Theatre of Greece and Rome* (London, 1977), p.81. Jealousy is also attacked by Lucian, e.g. in his *Charon*, or *The Inspectors* in: *Lucian*, ed. A.M. Harmon, II,429.

[38] Cf. T.B.L. Webster, *Studies in Menander* (Manchester, ²1960), p.116f.

[39] Cf. J.C. Margolin in: *Opera Omnia Desiderii Erasmi Roterodami* (Amsterdam, 1917), I,ii,115, n.11.

[40] Cf. Daos in *Aspis*, Menander, ed. W.G. Arnott (Cambridge, Mass./ London, 1979), p.35.

[41] Haberman, op. cit., p.133.

beyond *Amphitruo* and he, too, for the first time, experimented with the possibilities of tragicomedy.[42]

Since *Errors* is a most accomplished achievement, it is improbable that it is a *very* early play or even Shakespeare's very first comedy. He obviously completed his *Errors* under the fresh impact of William Warner's translation of *Menaechmi*, although Shakespeare also worked with the Latin text of the play.[43] If *Errors* will not have originated before 1594, it becomes possible and even likely that it was specially written for Gray's Inn, where it was performed on December 28, 1594. It is tempting to speculate here a little and to assume that there might have been an additional reason for the connection between *Errors* and Gray's Inn. In 1594 Shakespeare dedicated his *Rape of Lucrece*, an epic poem based on a classical myth, to Henry Wriothesley, the third Earl of Southampton, who is possibly the male friend to whom Shakespeare also dedicated his *Sonnets*.[44] It may well be that Henry Wriothesley, who had been a student of Gray's Inn, requested Shakespeare to write a 'classical' comedy for 'his' Inn.

It is particularly remarkable that there is a close thematic connection between *Errors* and the *Sonnets* (which, in the view of modern scholarship, were also written in the first half of the nineties).[45] First, some very unusual phrases are to be found in both works. Adriana reminds her supposed husband that her body is 'consecrate to thee' (II, ii, 132); similarly, in sonnet LXXIV the speaker assures his friend that his life was 'consecrate to thee' (6). Adriana complains to her sister that she 'at home starves for a merry look' (II, i, 88), while in sonnet LXXV the speaker speaks of himself as 'clean starved for a

---

[42] If Shakespeare opens his comedy with a tragic scene, so does Menander in his *Aspis*. There, too, the audience are first confronted with the narration of the tragic event. The slave Daos reports that the shield which he has brought back from battle has not saved his master from a tragic fate; then he narrates in detail the battle in which he believes his master to have died, and tragic emotions are released. But then suddenly the stage is cleared and Tyche appears, telling the audience that Daos and the others have been deceived into believing that the owner of the shield is dead; since he is in fact still alive, the comedy can take its course. The difference between Menander's and Shakespeare's opening is important: whereas in *Aspis* the tragic beginning gives way to an entirely comic development of the plot, in *Errors* comic and potentially tragic developments run parallel, or rather they appear as *either* comic *or* tragic according to the perspective from which they are viewed.

[43] For a further argument that *Errors* may have originated in 1594, cf. K. Tetzeli v. Rosador, 'A Suggestion for Dating The Comedy of Errors', *Archiv*, 217 (1980), 347 – 349.

[44] On Shakespeare's Patron cf. C. Carmichael Stopes, *The Life of Henry, Earl of Southampton, Shakespeare's Patron* (Cambridge, 1922).

[45] Cf. on this problem L. Fiedler, 'Some Contexts of Shakespeare's Sonnets', in E. Hubler, *The Riddle of Shakespeare's Sonnets* (New York, 1962), p.52 – 90; W.T. McCary, 'The Comedy of Errors: A Different Kind of Comedy', *NLH*, 9 (1977/8), 525 – 536; M. Krieger, *A Window to Criticism. Shakespeare's Sonnets and Modern Poetics* (Princeton, 1964), p.86f.

look' (10). Most of the parallels, however, are between Antipholus S and some
of the sonnets. In his dialogue with Luciana his language reminds us not only
of the Elizabethan love lyric in general, but particularly of Shakespeare's
sonnets; yet, interestingly enough, of those addressed to his *male friend*. When
he declares his 'love' to Luciana, he says that he is calling her 'love' because
'It is thyself, mine own self's better part' (III, ii, 61); in a similar way, the
speaker of sonnet LXXIV assures his male friend that 'My spirit is thine, the
better part of me'. (8). In these sonnets to the male friend the speaker
expresses the idea that he finds his identity because it is revealed to him in his
male partner as in a mirror, and that it is by him that he becomes capable of
conquering his 'sin of self-love', as in Sonnet LXII:

> Sin of self-love possesseth all mine eye,
> And all my soul, and all my every part;
> And for this sin there is no remedy,
> It is so grounded inward in my heart.
> Methinks no face so gracious is as mine,
> No shape so true, no truth of such account,
> And for myself mine own worth do define,
> As I all other in all worths surmount.
> But when my glass shows me myself indeed,
> Beated and chopp'd with tann'd antiquity,
> Mine own self-love quite contrary I read;
> Self so self-loving were iniquity.
>   'Tis thee (myself) that for myself I praise,
>   Painting my age with beauty of thy days.

As we know, it is this idea that lies behind Antipholus's quest for his brother,
yet he commits the temporary 'error' (a *leitmotif* in the *Sonnets*, too) of looking
for 'his glass' in an unknown woman, before finding it by the recognition of
his *male* twin. This theme is subtly and beautifully echoed in the play's coda,
where Dromio E addresses his twin as 'my glass, and not my brother' (V, i,
417), because he is able to see his own image in his brother.

Shakespeare has been blamed for increasing the improbability of the
confusions by doubling the twins; nevertheless, he has admirably succeeded in
achieving credibility, a quality which the humanists demanded from art. In a
sense, it could be maintained that with his *Errors* Shakespeare created a kind of
Utopia through art, a concept so dear to the humanists: in this utopian world
it becomes possible for an impending tragedy — Egeon awaiting his execution
and Antipholus E about to lose his identity — to be averted at the last moment
and for four twins and two parents to be reunited on one and the same
occasion. This relatively early play seems to anticipate the intrinsic utopian
quality of all great art, which Shakespeare then realizes in much more
complex ways in his mature and late plays.

It should have become clear from our close comparison between the
Roman and the Elizabethan comic playwrights that Shakespeare's greatness is

by no means diminished through the recognition of how he was familiar with the art of Plautus and its humanist reception. Only a superficial view of his achievement could lead one to say, as a recent critic has done, that Shakespeare's drama is lacking in greatness because by its concern with moral 'wholesomeness' it loses the quality of 'fantasy'[46], of presenting the world upsidedown and defamiliarizing the familiar. Quite the contrary is true. It is this very quality of fantasy[47] which manifests itself in Shakespeare's almost incredible intensification and transformation of the New Comedy tradition. It is critics who have tried to make Shakespeare more morally 'wholesome' than he really is: we have seen in *Errors* elements of an antique 'paganism' to which we should not be blinded by the recognition of the play's general moral soundness. And the familiar world could scarcely be more completely defamiliarized than it is in this 'classical' play. In his process of transformation Shakespeare reaches into the deep recesses of human existence, and even *Errors*, which has so often been considered as a mere farce, becomes a document of his inexhaustible richness.

---

[46] G. Taylor, *Reinventing Shakespeare. A Cultural History, From the Restoration to the Present* (London, 1989), p.395 – 404.
[47] Cf., for example, A. Leggatt, *Shakespeare's Comedy of Love* (London, 1973), p.18, and R. Berry, *Shakespeare and the Awareness of the Audience*, p.37.

X

The Continuation of the New Comedy Tradition in the Shakespearean Canon

1. *Early and middle comedies*

The fact that *Errors* is the accomplished result of a careful humanist reception of New Comedy forces us to see its affinity with *The Taming of the Shrew*, which has often been noticed, in a different light. Compared with *Errors*, *Taming* is a comedy with a less profound intellectual background, despite the fact that the young gentlemen have studied at a university and have read their classical authors. *Taming* is a comedy with a native English as well as an Italian quality.[1] Therefore it necessarily differs in tone and character from *Errors*, and reflects the influence of Roman comedy to a lesser degree. Of course, by the time Shakespeare composed *Taming*, he had read Plautine and Terentian comedies at school, and he remembered the names Tranio and Grumio from the Plautine *Mostellaria*,[2] yet he did not develop Tranio from the model of the *servus* of Roman comedy. It is symptomatic that the very first words he speaks are Italian. Although Tranio calls himself 'cunning' (II, i, 404), the first intrigue in this play is not devised solely by him, but also by his master Lucentio, who prefers to carry out his own strategy.

It seems to me that the relationship between *Taming* and *Errors* has been well described by M. Mincoff, who is probably right when he says that in composing *Taming* 'Shakespeare is aware of Roman drama [. . .] but his deeper exploration [. . .] is part of his development as a comic dramatist, and we find it not here but in the more 'classical' comedy, *Errors*'.[3] If we assume that Shakespeare's reception of the humanist tradition of comedy sets in fully only with his study of *Menaechmi* and *Amphitruo*, then the reason for the difference of style between the two Shakespearean plays also becomes clear. The verse of *Errors* is rhetorically organized in a way that of *Taming* is not. Nor

---

[1] Cf. especially B. Morris in the excellent introduction to his New Arden edition of the play (London, 1981), p.72ff.

[2] The arguments put forward by W.E. Harrold for a direct influence of the *Mostellaria* on *Taming* ('Shakespeare's Use of *Mostellaria* in *The Taming of the Shrew*', *ShJW*, [1970], 188 – 194) do not strike me as really convincing.

[3] M. Mincoff, 'The Dating of *The Taming of the Shrew*', *ES* (1973), 554 – 565.

does *Taming* manifest the same game-playing with language as *Errors* and later Shakespearean comedies, and it contains fewer puns and quibbles than *Errors*.[4] The echoes in both works of Ovid's *Heroides* also suggest that the two plays were written within a short space of time. We have seen, that, when composing *Taming*, Shakespeare read the *Heroides* in the original and that this text was still in his mind when he set about writing *Errors*.

As far as the subject matter is concerned, it has rightly been pointed out that '*Errors* [. . .] begins where *The Shrew* ends',[5] namely with the problem of husband and wife living together after their wedding. Katherine's final address to the wives, in which she reminds them of their duties towards their husbands, is, as it were, anticipated by Luciana's description of the cosmic order. Yet Adriana is seen to *revolt* against the established order and Luciana, too, is not willing to accept this view wholesale. In II,i she concludes her teaching with a remark which implies that she herself seems to have some reservations against female subordination.

Contrary to a widespread view, Shakespeare's *Taming* is not a mere farce. Instead, it proves to reflect a humanist corrective purpose.[6] What seems so genuinely farcical, namely the process of taming itself, is motivated by Petruchio's intention of showing Kate, as in a mirror, the social misconduct that produces her shrewishness. As this, ultimately, serves the purpose of making Kate 'at one' with her real identity, one could say that in this comedy Shakespeare is moving in the direction of the humanist comedy of identity. But this pattern did not fully develop until his intensive reception of the tradition of New Comedy. It would seem that Shakespeare, starting his career as a comic playwright with *Taming*, first turned to the native tradition, with its folk motif of the shrewish wife, and for the second plot of this play took suggestions from Italian comedy, which was much discussed at that time and easily available through George Gascoignes's skilful translation of Ariosto's *I Suppositi*.[7] If this plot in some respects seems to resemble classical comedy, it is because Italian comedy itself developed from Roman comic drama.

It has long been recognized that *Errors* has close connections with *The Two Gentlemen of Verona*, and attention has been drawn to some thematic correspondences as well as to a similarity in the rhetorical stylization;[8] this is of

---

[4] Cf. Mincoff, op. cit., p.559.

[5] Cf. Mincoff, op. cit., p.558 and Morris, op. cit., p.61.

[6] R. Hosley, 'Sources and Analogues of *The Taming of the Shrew*', *HLQ*, 27 (1963 – 4), 289 – 308. The connections with Erasmus's *Colloquia* on marriage which Hosley tries to establish and which we quoted earlier are too general and even proverbial to be really convincing, and this objection was also raised by Morris, op. cit., p.86 – 87.

[7] B. Morris, following Mincoff, comes to the same conclusion, op. cit., p.61.

[8] Cf. C. Leech, ed., *The Two Gentlemen of Verona*, The New Arden Shakespeare (London, 1969), p.xxiii; he points out further correspondences between the two plays, p.xxiii, xxxiii – xxxiv.

particular interest in our context. In contrast to *Taming*, but like *Errors*, *The Two Gentlemen of Verona* is firmly rooted in the humanist tradition. The question arises which of the two plays was written first. Wells and Leech, who consider *The Two Gentlemen of Verona* as not an altogether satisfactory play, assume that it was therefore composed before *Errors*.[9] Yet this need not be so, because it would be simplistic to suppose that each succeeding work must necessarily be superior to those before it. Besides, I think that, viewed from the perspective of Shakespeare's growing humanist interest, *Two Gentlemen* appears a far more accomplished work than it is usually considered. As the play bears close structural and dramaturgic resemblances to New Comedy, it must have been written immediately after *Errors* or shortly before it, at a time when Shakespeare had begun his intensive study of Roman comedy for the project of his *Errors*. The formal weaknesses which Wells has found in some dramaturgic features of *Two Gentlemen* can be explained by this very assumption. Wells finds fault with the play's dramatic technique because it is limited 'almost exclusively to three devices',[10] namely dialogue, soliloquy, and aside. These are, however, precisely the dramaturgic devices used in a Plautine play, where the dialogue is established between two or at most three characters. If Wells complains that sometimes 'a character is left in unnatural silence when the dialogue switches from him to someone else',[11] then this looseness is again especially characteristic of Plautus. Working under the direct influence of Plautus, Shakespeare was obviously not concerned to avoid dramaturgic weaknesses of this kind. In addition, the use of aside-chains evokes Plautine associations, and so does the remarkable preference for entrance soliloquies, which are extremely popular in Roman, especially Plautine comedy; they are also 'Plautine' in that they partly address the audience and partly express the speaker's thoughts and feelings. What further strongly reminds us of Plautine dramaturgy is that a character sometimes enters the stage soliloquizing or commenting aside while other characters are already present. This specifically Plautine feature of simultaneous acting by different groups[12] becomes less prominent in Shakespeare's later plays, but in *Two Gentlemen* it contributes to the overall character of the play.

Wells rightly speaks of a 'surplusage of word-playing' which in *Two Gentlemen* 'sometimes takes on anticipatory depths'.[13] This, to me, is further and important evidence of a Plautine impact which, in its range, reminds us of Plautus's dramatic use of comic word play. There is, first, mere verbal

[9] S. Wells, ed., *The Comedy of Errors*, p.11; Leech, op. cit., p.xxxiv.
[10] Wells, 'The Failure of The Two Gentlemen of Verona', *ShJW*, 99 (1963), 161 – 173; 163.
[11] Wells, ibid.
[12] Cf. our discussion of this aspect in chapter III, p.80ff.
[13] Wells, op. cit., 171.

chiming, as in the opening scene. After a long passage between Proteus and Speed,[14] Speed answers Proteus's question as to how Julia received his letter:

Pro. But what said she?
      [*Speed nods . . .*]
Spe. Ay.
Pro. Nod-ay -why, that's 'noddy.'
Spe. You mistook, sir: I say, she did nod; and you ask me if she did nod, and I say, 'Ay'.
Pro. And that set together is 'noddy.'
      [. . .]
Spe. Marry, sir, the letter, very orderly, having nothing but the word 'noddy' for my pains.   I, i, 110 – 124

This kind of language play, which occurs in *Errors*, too, is very reminiscent of the Plautine penchant for verbal pyrotechnics. In the first scene of Act II there is an example of the *paronomasia*-like pun, the most common type in Plautus:

Spe. That's because the one is painted, and the other out of all *count.*
Val. How painted? and how out of *count?*
Spe. Marry, sir, so painted to make her fair, that no man *counts* of her beauty.
Val. How esteem'st thou me? I *account* of her beauty.
                                                II, i, 56 – 61

This 'volley of words' (II, iv, 32), the reflection of a 'quick wit' (I, i, 125), reminds us of the fact that the Elizabethans preferred Plautus precisely because of the great variety of his 'wit'. A further type of Plautine pun which occurs in *Two Gentlemen* is the purposeful mistaking of a word by a servant, as for example in this dialogue between Speed and Launce:

Spe. How now, Signior Launce? what news with your mastership?
Lau. With my master's ship? why, it is at sea.
Spe. Well, your old vice still: mistake the word.
                                                III, i, 280 – 284[15]

Yet word-play in *Two Gentlemen* is above all the hall-mark of Speed. For Leech, 'Speed is the Lylyan page'.[16] However, it does not seem to me to be as simple as that. Even if there is some truth in what Leech says, we have seen how behind a Lylyan page like Dromio in *Mother Bombie* there are the Plautine slaves. Moreover, Speed is Shakespearean in the sense that he looks like an

---

[14] Cf. Leech, note I,i, 73; 82ff. The favourite pun with 'sheep' and 'ship' recalls *Errors*, IV,i,94f.
[15] Cf. our discussion of Weimann's interpretation of this passage, chapter V, p.153, and B. Spivack, *Shakespeare and the Allegory of Evil* (New York, 1957), p.202.
[16] Op. cit., p.xxviii.

'offshoot' of his own Dromio. This is made abundantly clear by the various echoes of Dromio in the words of Speed; not all of them have so far been recognized. The following passage is particularly interesting:

Spe. Why then, how *stands* the matter with them?
Lau. Marry, thus: when it *stands* well with him, it *stands* well with her.
Spe. What an ass art thou! I *understand* thee not.
Lau. What a block art thou, that thou canst not! My *staff understands* me.
Spe. What thou say'st?
Lau. Ay, and what I do too. Look thee, I'll but lean, and my *staff understands* me.
Spe. It *stands under* thee indeed.
Lau. Why, *stand-under* and *under-stand* is all one.   II, v, 20 – 33

This passage, with the obscene connotations of 'staff' and 'understand', reads like an extension and fusion of two comic situations in *Errors*. The first occurs when Adriana rebukes Dromio for not having brought her husband home:

Adr.   Say, didst thou speak with him? knowst thou his mind?
Eph. Dro. Ay, ay, he told his mind upon mine ear,
           Beshrew his hand, I scarce could *understand* it.
Luc.   Spake he so doubtfully, thou couldst not feel his meaning?
Eph. Dro. Nay, he struck so plainly I could well feel his blows
           – and withal so doubtfully that I could scarce *understand* them.   I, i, 47 – 54

The second passage, which we discussed earlier, comes in III,i of *Errors* in the course of a verbal exchange between Luce and Dromio E:

Eph. Dro. O Lord, I must laugh;
           Have at you with a proverb – shall I set in my *staff*
                                    50 – 51 (italics mine)

If, as we have seen, the situation where Antipholus waits in front of the locked door of his house has strong sexual connotations and serves the comedy's function of a release of sexual energy, then this same purpose is also strongly present in the dialogue between Speed and Launce.

Apart from dialogue, soliloquy, aside and word-play, Shakespeare in *Two Gentlemen* employs other elements of New Comedy as well, such as eavesdropping, disguise and trickery (although the intrigue itself is not carried out by the servant). Like *Menaechmi* and like Shakespeare's *Errors*, *Two Gentlemen* is organized according to a structural symmetry of parallels and contrasts. Furthermore, the five-Act convention corresponds to the definition given by Evanthius; and the plot may be described as an extended 'nodus erroris'. It is remarkable that the plot is built around a double concept of error — error as deception by outward appearance caused by intrigue, and error as perverse conduct arising from immaturity of character. What makes the structure of this plot so intricate is the fact that Valentine's erroneous concept of romantic love, his excessive praise of Silvia, which becomes sheer 'braggardism' (II, iv, 164) and which culminates in his promise to Proteus: 'I will help thee to prefer her too' (157), triggers off Proteus's New Comedy-like intrigue by which he tries to win Silvia for himself. Simultaneously, Proteus's decision to deceive his best friend by his intrigue is caused by his wrong concept of love and by his own self-deception. He deludes himself into thinking that, unless he is able to possess Silvia, he will 'lose' himself (II, iv, 207), and this echoes Antipholus's soliloquy in *Errors* (I, ii, 40). He thinks he can remain true to himself only by falling in love with Silvia and abandoning his love for Julia and his friendship with Valentine. He is thus under the misconception that the way to self-discovery involves turning one's back on one's existing social bonds.

Valentine's behaviour in the final scene, where he tells Proteus 'All that was mine in Silvia I give thee' (V, iv, 83) has often met with the critics' disapproval.[17] Yet the situation does make sense if it is viewed from the humanist background, and particularly in the context of the conflict between friendship and love. This approach was used by R.M. Sargent in a perceptive article[18] which has received far too little attention. Sargent demonstrates that a humanist text like Sir Thomas Elyot's famous *Book Named The Governor* goes a long way to explain what Shakespeare is about in the much-disputed final scene. Like other humanists, Elyot was looking for a way to combine the classical ideal of friendship with the medieval concept of romantic love; and the humanist solution to the problem is that 'if the claims of friendship are first fully lived up to, then, and only then, is it possible also to achieve the rewards of true love'.[19] Elyot explains the nature of 'perfet amitie' by narrating the story of Titus and Gisippus. The latter, who has become engaged, makes the mistake of extolling his fiancée to his friend Titus, and then introducing her to him. Titus falls deeply in love with her, and inner turmoil results for him. Finally, upon learning of the situation, and the struggle within Titus, Gisippus in a supreme gesture offers his fiancée to his friend. And the offer is made in almost the exact terms which Shakespeare's Valentine uses in making

---

[17] Cf., for example, D. Traversi, who calls the situation 'realistically absurd', but he justifies it rather vaguely 'in terms of the comic convention' (*An Approach to Shakespeare* [London, 1968] I, 94).

[18] R.M. Sargent, 'Sir Thomas Elyot and the Integrity of *The Two Gentlemen of Verona*', *PMLA*, 65 (1950), 1166–1180. The recent article by R. Morse ' "The Two Gentlemen" and the Cult of Friendship', *NM*, 84 (1983), 214–224, takes no account of Sargent's important study.

[19] Quoted from Sargent, p.1169.

a similar gesture to Proteus.[20] Sargent is also right in pointing out that, by overdoing his praise of Silvia, Valentine 'unwittingly, but unwisely leads Proteus directly into temptation'.[21] As Proteus shows repentance, Valentine forgives him. This forgiveness, as Sargent rightly maintains, has to be taken seriously. It is basically Stoic in tone. *Two Gentlemen* articulates a number of Stoic concepts and ideas which are frequently expressed in maxims and *sententiae*.[22] By forgiveness the renewal of friendship is made possible. Valentine's offering of Silvia to Proteus has the function of putting true friendship to the test; by renouncing Silvia and by returning to his own Julia, Proteus stands the test and in the end proves himself a true friend.[23]

As early as *Two Gentlemen*, romantic love is presented not only in a sentimental way but also from a critical and sometimes even a satirical perspective, as Ulrici and Leech[24] have recognized. Leech is right in pointing out that the play can be properly understood only if its characteristic 'friendly mockery'[25] is perceived. Satire here concentrates on the closeness of love and folly. As the satirical method is dialogic and dramatic and as it occurs within a context based on New Comedy, it may be called 'Lucianic'. As early as the second scene of the play, Lucetta strikes a 'sardonic'[26] and satirical tone when she makes her 'saucy' (I, ii, 89) comments about Julia's romantic love. The same satirical tendency can be observed with the clowns, who with their comic punning offer a satirical comment on the lovers Proteus and Julia. They add to the criticism implied in the play by pointing out that sexuality is the ultimate driving force behind even the yearnings of a romantic lover. Leech perceptively argues that *Two Gentlemen* 'gives us a clue to the interpretation of Shakespeare's writing as a whole'.[27] While I would not go along with his claim that Shakespeare had it in mind to expose 'the fragility, the minor quality, of both love and friendship',[28] I do agree with the point that he aimed at exposing the immaturity and folly of his characters. And this closely corresponds to the humanist intention of both Erasmus and Thomas More.

Since in *Two Gentlemen* romantic love is added to the theme of male friendship, thus giving the problem of friendship far greater complexity, I would argue that this play marks the real beginning of Shakespeare's romantic comedy, whereas in *Errors* 'romantic' love is recognized by Antipholus himself

---

[20] Ibid., p.1172.

[21] Ibid., p.1174.

[22] These maxims have also been observed by Wells, 'The Failure of *The Two Gentlemen of Verona*', 173.

[23] Cf. Sargent, op. cit., p.1168.

[24] H. Ulrici, *Shakespeare's Dramatic Art: and his Relation to Calderon and Goethe* (London, 1846), p.286; Leech approves of Ulrici's satirical assessment, op. cit., p.lii.

[25] Leech, op. cit., p.lxix.n

[26] A. Leggatt, *Shakespeare's Comedy of Love* (London, 1973), p.34.

[27] Leech, op. cit., p.lxxv.

[28] Leech, ibid.

as a temptation to abandon his search for the male partner. If *Errors* is a play focusing on two young men who undergo a process of coming to themselves by finding their family, particularly their male twin partners in 'perfet amitie' (Thomas Elyot) and who thus discover their true place in society, then in *Two Gentlemen* a further aspect is added: two young men approach self-knowledge by coming to know the nature not only of male friendship but also of love between the sexes together with the problems which the latter brings with it.

We should also note that the structural element of travel is common to both plays: in *Errors*, the travels of Antipholus S are ultimately a quest for identity, and in *Two Gentlemen* the travels of Proteus and Valentine are similarly a means to 'A sorting out of their tangled patterns of life'.[29] It was Northrop Frye, who in 1948 pointed out that *Two Gentlemen* 'is an orthodox New Comedy except for one thing'[30] — the fact that Valentine is made the Captain of a band of outlaws in a forest in which all the other characters assemble. The central motif of the disguised woman, too, invokes Plautine associations and reminds us in particular of the play *Casina*.

How skilfully elements of romantic comedy and a basic New Comedy structure have been fused becomes abundantly clear by a comparison with the Plautine *Bacchides*, which is a close rendering of a Menandrian comedy. In this strictly symmetrical and artfully contrived play which contains both coarse comedy and very witty language, we have two young men, two women, two parents and two further characters. Both young men are in love with a girl called Bacchis, and for this reason a shadow has been cast on the friendship of the two. Mnesilochus becomes desperate about his friend's supposed faithlessness. Yet soon the two friends meet and begin to discuss the nature of friendship and truth in general terms, until Pistoclerus throws light on the present situation by informing them that there are in fact *two* girls with the name of Bacchis, and the problem which had come between the two friends and seemed about to destroy their friendship is thus removed.[31]

Seen in the light of *Bacchides*, the central event of *Two Gentlemen* appears as a most skilful transformation and intensification of the Plautine framework. Whereas Plautus prevents the situation from developing towards tragedy, although the possibility of a tragic ending is not excluded from the play,[32] Shakespeare goes much further. In his comedy it is one and the same girl with whom both friends fall in love, and his interest lies in the development of the characters' feelings and emotions and in the way in which the plea for pardon of the one friend is answered by the other. The impressively clear New

---

[29] Leech, ibid., p.lviii.
[30] N. Frye, 'The Argument of Comedy', *English Institute Essays*, 48 (1948), 67f.
[31] On this play cf. e.g. W. Kamel, 'The "Bacchides" of Plautus. Its Plot and Origin', *Bulletin of the Faculty of Arts*, Cairo, 15 (1953), 101–112.
[32] *Bacchides*, 1699.

Comedy basis of *Two Gentlemen* was then further extended by native romance structures.

It seems that among the numerous impulses that were transformed by Shakespeare into his unique world of *Love's Labour's Lost*, the humanist reception of classical comedy, and especially of Plautus, also had its share. In the character of Holofernes, the play even contains a 'perverted' representative of the world of the humanists.

The *dramatis personae* exhibit a 'performing instinct which affects the characters' normal behaviour',[33] and this fact has an interesting parallel in the basic 'theatrical' atmosphere of Plautine comedy. Then there is a pervading 'language consciousness', the awareness of the uses to which language can be put. This, of course, marks the play as decidedly Elizabethan, yet it will certainly not do to refer to numerous kinds of influence that contributed to this 'language consciousness', while neglecting the obvious connections with the great variety and range of Plautus's comic and dramatic language. Already in Plautus we quite frequently have a 'self-conscious dance of language.'[34] In practically all of his comedies, Plautus exhibits an enormous delight in experimenting with the creative possibilities of language, culminating on many occasions in punning. The same is even more true of *Love's Labour's Lost*; it has been said that here 'the urge to pun reaches epidemic proportions' and that 'language reveals [. . .] the innate poetic instinct, at work'.[35] It can hardly be coincidental that the most frequent form of pun in Plautus and in *Love's Labour's Lost* is *paronomasia*. Furthermore, it is a major occupation of the characters both in Plautus and in *Love's Labour's Lost* to 'manipulate or misconstrue sounds into new words'.[36]

Yet apart from celebrating the power of language, this play also points the finger at various linguistic abuses. In particular, almost all the *commedia dell'arte* figures use language in various 'erratic styles'.[37] In critically exposing these abuses of language, Shakespeare is not content merely to present *commedia dell'arte* characters, he also goes far beyond some Plautine attempts at satirizing a character's exaggerated language. In *Stichus*, for example, there is the parasite Gelasimus, who, lacking any imagination of his own, collects puns and aphorisms from books and then learns them by rote in order to produce a favourable effect on his patron (V, 454). The best known example is the

---

[33] Leggatt, op. cit., p.63.
[34] Leggatt, ibid. On language as a game in this comedy cf. also W. Matthews, 'Language in *Love's Labour's Lost*', *E&S* (1964), 1 – 11; J.L. Calderwood, '*Love's Labour's Lost*: A Wantoning with Words', *SEL*, 5 (1965), 317 – 32;
[35] W.C. Carroll, *The Great Feast of Language in 'Love's Labour's Lost'* (Princeton, 1976), p.22; cf. also H.A. Ellis, *Shakespeare's Lusty Punning in 'Love's Labour's Lost'* (The Hague, 1973).
[36] Carroll, op. cit., p.21.
[37] Carroll, op. cit., p.39.

satirical exposure of the bombastic language of Pyrgopolynices, the *miles gloriosus*. Shakespeare's own Don Armado, who certainly cannot be traced back to any one individual model, although he is referred to as 'thrasonical' (V, i, 12), bears a far closer resemblance to the Plautine *miles gloriosus* than to the Terentian Thraso.

The difficulties some characters have with language are, however, surpassed by those they have with love. Both difficulties derive from what Erasmus, following Aristotle's *Ethics*, calls *philautia*, self-love, and thus *Love's Labour's Lost* becomes another 'comedy of errors', though this time the play concentrates on criticizing the characters' erroneous behaviour. Satire, then, becomes the play's predominant tone when erroneous forms of love are being criticized. Berowne, the *alazon* who in the great eavesdropping scene satirizes folly in others, must himself come to recognize his own folly before he is able to receive grace through his beloved, Rosaline. Yet here, Shakespeare is not content with satirizing both the observer and the observed; in this play we also meet the humanistic concept of fortunate folly: for Erasmus, as Chris Hassel shows, true wisdom and knowledge can be obtained only through an awareness of folly — not so much that of others as one's own.[38]

Shakespeare's *Midsummer Night's Dream* has often been praised for the most brilliant way in which four different strands of action are conjoined together in a work of exceptional artistic unity, and we admire the way in which he invented a unique plot of his own. Yet it does not diminish Shakespeare's achievement if we realize with Salingar[39] that the unifying structural principle is the concept of deceit of the New Comedy tradition, and that behind the outward deception there is the far more profound idea of error as deception about the nature of one's own emotions. A *Midsummer Night's Dream* is another 'comedy of errors' in which deceptions arise both from a mistaking of appearance for reality and from the characters' incomplete and false preception of their own selves and their innermost feelings; thus the play's *epitasis* verges on the tragic and, as we have seen, in a way common to the New Comedy tradition, tragedy itself is parodied in the play. The human proneness to error is at the same time pointed out in Puck's Lucianic and Erasmian comment:[40] 'Lord, what fools these mortals be' (III, ii, 115). It is in the woods that the four lovers cease to be fools and arrive at a fuller knowledge of themselves. Hassel is right in pointing out that Shakespeare's perfect

[38] R.C. Hassel, *Faith and Folly in Shakespeare's Romantic Comedies* (Athens, Georgia, 1980), p.51. However, since Hassel, like many Shakespeareans, has not looked in sufficient depth at Erasmus (he considers only his *Praise of Folly* and his *Adagia*), he fails to observe how close the parallel with the Erasmian reception of New Comedy really is.
[39] Salingar, *Traditions of Comedy*, p.128.
[40] T.N. Greenfield, '*A Midsummer Night's Dream* and *The Praise of Folly*', CL, 20 (1968), 236–44.

'blending of the comic, the romantic, and the Christian contexts'[41] reminds us
forcefully of a similar procedure in Erasmus.

When discussing the New Comedy tradition in Shakespeare, it is impossible to
omit mention of *Much Ado About Nothing*, a play whose place within this
tradition has not been fully recognized. Its structural organization, its use of
eavesdropping and disguise, its play with mistaken identity[42], and its complex
use of the 'error' concept, all point in this direction. Yet it is very significant
that Claudio's obvious error, his mistaking of identity, results precisely from
his 'inward' deception, his inability to place his unconditional trust in the
woman he loves and his failure to recognize her true nature, which would have
saved him from accusing her of infidelity. In this, *Much Ado*, far more than the
earlier *Errors*, approaches tragedy in the very moving Church scene, and
again, long before the so-called tragicomedies and the romances, Shakespeare
here aims at invoking tragicomic emotions. The title of the play is, of course,
ironic in its denial that serious moral issues, almost developing into tragedy,
are at stake. Yet it does point to the frequency of errors in the various strands
of the play, which are most subtly intertwined. Thus, Beatrice and Benedick
are cured of the 'error' of pride and self-love in the course of the intrigues
centring around two brilliant eavesdropping scenes, the New Comedy
connections of which we have already discussed in another context (cf. p. 82).

Beatrice and Benedick finally find each other by trying to help Hero and to
restore her violated honour. The love between Hero and Claudio is repaired
only by an act of forgiveness. This forgiveness has been commented on
extensively, and its quality has been claimed to be decidedly Christian. Some
critics therefore deny that this play is to be seen in the New Comedy tradition
at all. In his widely acclaimed book, Robert G. Hunter goes so far as to argue
for the existence of a distinct type within the canon of Shakespearean comedy,
the 'comedy of forgiveness', the first play in this group being, in his view,
Much Ado.[43] For Hunter, this type of comedy has developed from the native
tradition of the Mystery Plays and the Moralities; characters like Claudio,
Bertram, Posthumus, Leontes and Angelo are seen as the descendants of the
humanum genus figure. Hunter's theory presupposes a belief in a strongly
evolutionist process in literature and, moreover, fails to consider the
importance of the New Comedy tradition. For Hunter − and Howard
Felperin, in his book on Shakespearean romance,[44] seems to take a similar

---

[41] Hassel, op. cit., p.60.

[42] Salingar thinks that Shakespeare borrowed 'from Terence [. . .] in the [. . .]
scenes of gossip and eavesdropping and true or misleading report which are added
to Don John's intrigue in *Much Ado About Nothing*', *Traditions*, p.172; on the play's
complex structure cf., for example, J.R. Mulryne, *Shakespeare. Much Ado About
Nothing* (London, 1965), p.48ff.

[43] R.G. Hunter, *Shakespeare and the Comedy of Forgiveness* (New York, 1965).

[44] *Shakespearean Romance* (Princeton, 1972).

view — the New Comedy tradition is basically simple and superficial, it is a 'comedy in which boy wants girl, girl wants boy, and external forces are to keep them from getting what they want'.[45] We have seen that the New Comedy tradition has much more to offer than Hunter wants his readers to believe. Unless we are ready to see that the plays of New Comedy are by no means sufficiently characterized as presenting light 'amusement',[46] and unless we take into account that the humanists used them as a mirror, a 'speculum consuetudinis', in which manners and morals are shown in order that they may be corrected, we will never be able to assess properly what Shakespeare owes to this tradition.

In many of these plays, this correction implies an act of human forgiveness, as for instance in the Plautine *Captivi*, a play Lessing considered to be the finest comedy ever written.[47] In this play final harmony is achieved by the characters' readiness to pardon. Given the fact that the dramatic links between *Much Ado* and classical comedy are incomparably stronger than with the native morality tradition there can be no doubt that the Shakespearean forgiveness in this play is by no means exclusively Christian and does not need to be explained by references to Christian belief and dogma. Shakespeare himself seems to emphasize this because, the more the canon of his plays unfolds, the more he provides them with a classical colouring, which he especially achieves by frequently invoking the pagan gods.

This tendency already makes itself felt in another play which has too often been neglected. *The Merry Wives of Windsor* is usually considered as a mere farce, and this has prevented critics from recognizing its true significance. That it goes far beyond farce has been shown by J.A. Roberts.[48] We are certainly no longer entitled to exclude it from a discussion of Shakespeare's middle comedies. The more one examines this play, the more one becomes aware of its many classical elements; these have been transformed into a comedy which from first to last appears to be thoroughly English. If the tradition is correct according to which *Merry Wives* was commissioned by the Queen,[49] we may interpret Shakespeare's inclusion of abundant classical elements, which so far have been played down by the critics, as a compliment on his part to Elizabeth's classical erudition.

This classical emphasis is even made the occasion for a joke when, at the request of Mrs Page, a Latin lesson at an English Grammar School is

---

[45] Hunter, op. cit., p.4.

[46] Hunter, op. cit., p.102.

[47] G.E. Lessing, *Beiträge zur Historie und Aufnahme des Theaters* in: *Sämtliche Schriften* (Stuttgart, ³1889), IV, 191.

[48] J.A. Roberts, *Shakespeare's English Comedy. 'The Merry Wives of Windsor' in Context* (Lincoln/Newark/London, 1979).

[49] Cf. H.J. Oliver, ed., *The Merry Wives of Windsor*, The New Arden Shakespeare (London, 1971), p.xliv.

performed. Scene IV, i, which is partly anticipated by the activities of the schoolmaster Holofernes in *Love's Labour's Lost* (IV, ii), has not received the attention it deserves.[50] Does it not seem as though Shakespeare is here putting on stage his own schooldays when he himself first became acquainted with the plays of Plautus? Or is the fact that the name of the boy who plays the school lesson is William merely coincidental? William has to answer typical questions from a Latin lesson: 'What is *lapis*, William? [. . .] And what is "a stone" William?' And then he receives praise for his correct answers: 'That is a good William.' The comic effect of the scene increases as it proceeds. William's declension of the pronouns: '*Singulariter, nominativo, hic, haec, hoc*' is repeated by the Welshman Hugh Evans who pronounces the words as '*Nominativo, hig, hag, hog*' and the accusative pronouns as '*[hung], hang, hog*'. The joke is then extended in that '*hang hog*' is humorously 'translated': ' "*Hang-hog*" is Latin for bacon.' (31 – 49). What is interesting in our context is that Shakespeare here indulges in a play with the sound of mispronounced Latin words evoking associations with English ones with an entirely different sense. This play with language in the manner of *paronomasia* bears strong resemblances with the very frequent comic punning of Plautus, and the Plautine associations are reinforced by the fact that Plautine comedy introduces other languages for comic effects (e.g. *Casina* and *Miles Gloriosus*). Greek words are sometimes made part of a pun, and in *Poenulus* the integration of the Punic language is a vital part of the play's overall comic design. In *Merry Wives* Shakespeare extends and transforms this tradition with the Welshman Evans and the Frenchman Dr Cajus. Thus there is a subtle point in the play's comic Grammar School lesson. It makes use of precisely those comic effects of language which Shakespeare in his own Grammar School day had learnt in Plautus, as well as in other authors.

J.A. Roberts has correctly observed that the use of intrigue and of stock characters (many of them bearing characteronyms) places the play in the tradition of New Comedy.[51] As in his most mature comedies, Shakespeare redoubles major structural elements; he employs two central intrigues which provide the play's structural brilliance.[52] Critics of earlier times saw more clearly than some more recent ones that, with the exception of the introductory scene, the plot is tightly and very skilfully knit.[53] In fact, the structure corresponds closely to the Evanthian definition of the 'nodus erroris'. Furthermore, the play observes the three unities. The five-Act division of the Folio makes good sense: we have the *protasis* in Act one, the *epitasis* in Acts II – IV, followed by the comic catastrophe in the last Act, and,

---

[50] Sr Miriam Joseph refers to it without comment (*Shakespeare's Use of the Arts of Language*, p.45).

[51] J.A. Roberts, *Shakespeare's English Comedy*, p.64.

[52] Ibid., p.6667.

[53] Dryden spoke of 'the mechanic beauties of the plot', and some eighteenth-century critics were of the same opinion (cf. Oliver, ed., *Merry Wives*, p.lxxiv).

interestingly enough, the concluding scenes of Acts II, III, and IV are alike in that each prepares a further intrigue. This similarity between the scenes concluding the Acts helps to achieve a sense of the Acts as rhythmical units.

Whereas the attempt to establish connections between *Merry Wives* and Italian sources has not been successful, it has been shown that Shakespeare developed the love plot between Anne Page and Fenton from the Plautine *Casina*;[54] these connections need not, therefore, be discussed in detail here. A character like Falstaff has always 'provoked' critics to regard him as an example of traditional character types, particularly those of New Comedy. Yet it is by no means sufficient to describe him as a specially effective example of just *one* traditional type. Surely, the Falstaff of *Merry Wives* bears greater resemblance to the Parasite than to the *miles gloriosus*, but he also has something of the *senex amans*. In his introduction to the New Arden edition of the play, Oliver maintains that Shakespeare 'sidestepped' the Queen's desire to see Falstaff in love by showing 'Falstaff pretending to be in love *because* he was hard-up'.[55] Yet this is true only up to a point; in the first part of the play Falstaff decides to play the role of the Plautine *senex amans* for his own material profit; however, in the final part he does indeed remind us of the *senex amans*, otherwise there would be little point in his 'punishment' (III, iii, 196) for his 'lust and luxury' (V, v, 94). Yet a consideration of the different dramatic models that contributed to his making shows clearly that Falstaff is nevertheless a most original character who is so much more than the sum of his antecedents. Therefore, it is well to recall M. Doran's sound warning that 'The very number of the models that can be claimed for Falstaff reveals the absurdity of the attempt to fit him into any pattern'.[56]

However, the true relevance of *Merry Wives* can be appreciated only if the strong humanist basis of the play is recognized. This becomes especially evident in the significant references to classical mythology. Here Oliver gives a wrong impression when he claims that classical allusions in the play are relatively rare.[57] His quantitative assessment of these elements does not do justice to their real significance. For example, it is a splendid idea of Shakespeare's to turn Mrs Quickly into a 'she-Mercury' (II, ii, 80), who at the same time is no longer merely a woman of Windsor, but becomes the 'archetypal' go-between and female pander who provides opportunities for sexual adventure. Her real name suggests Mercurian swiftness, and she is also sly and cunning; as is well known, these, too, are particularly Mercurian

---

[54] R.S. Forsythe, 'A Plautine Source of *The Merry Wives of Windsor*', *MP*, 18 (1920), 401 – 21, and A.L. Bennett, 'The Sources of Shakespeare's *Merry Wives*', *RenQ*, 23 (1970), 429 – 33.

[55] Op. cit., p.lxviii.

[56] *Endeavors of Art*, p.159. Thus W. Kaiser's attempt to 'explain' Falstaff by a comparison with the Erasmian *Stultitia* is unconvincing (W. Kaiser, *Praisers of Folly: Erasmus, Rabelais, Shakespeare* [Cambridge, Mass., 1963], p.267 – 75).

[57] Op. cit., p.lxxvii.

qualities. She succeeds in deceiving Falstaff by making him believe that he is about to experience a love adventure, whereas in fact he is going to be made the dupe. Thus Shakespeare employs his 'she-Mercury' in a way different from Plautus in his *Amphitruo*, where Mercury, by his competence, helps Jupiter to succeed in satisfying his desire for Alcumena. In another sense, however, Mrs Quickly's nickname as 'she-Mercury' is also most comically inappropriate, because her linguistic insufficiency and lack of education are in stark contrast to the messenger god of classical antiquity and of *Amphitruo* in particular.

It is interesting that, before embarking upon his final adventure, Falstaff invokes Jupiter and reminds him of some of his metamorphoses into animal forms for the purpose of his erotic adventures. On the one hand, these invocations to the god have a comic effect, yet on the other hand they also implicitly suggest that 'love' may indeed turn man into a 'beast'. Here the humanist, corrective intention of the New Comedy tradition is particularly evident. Falstaff himself becomes an 'animal' too. By being transformed into a horned deer he also 'becomes' the classical Actaeon. The allusion, however, is not to the traditional Actaeon theme from the Diana myth, but to a reduced form, in which a man, without having seen the bathing Diana, is transformed into a horned animal which is then hunted. This very transformation is done for 'educational' purposes: it serves as a visual image of a man falling into folly. Falstaff, the horned fool, becomes a hunted deer. How admirably in Shakespeare's reception of Roman comedy the classical *and* native elements have been fused can once more be seen in the way in which Falstaff as Actaeon is also called upon to perform Herne the Hunter, a famous figure from the native folklore tradition. While he appears in the role of the hunter, he becomes at the same time, ironically, the hunted victim of society. Falstaff is punished, not because he is 'sexually threatening',[58] as Roberts claims (the Windsor wives know very well how to cope with the old and unattractive Falstaff), but because of his self-centredness and self-sufficiency.

It would be wrong to view the play merely from Falstaff's point of view. He is right in his final comment that in the night 'all sorts of deer are chas'd' (V, v, 235), meaning that the deceived appear in all shapes and sizes. In this play, 'nobody can afford to laugh at anybody else'[59] because all are made fools of – in a humanist and typically Lucianic sense. Just as Falstaff is made the dupe, so are Ford, the Pages, Dr Cajus and Slender. If Verdi's *Falstaff* ends with the wise insight of old age that in this world we are 'tutti gabbati', then the characters of *Merry Wives* have been made to see fundamentally the same truth. Yet the play's ultimate intention to 'dis-horn the spirit' (IV, iv, 64) culminates

---

[58] Roberts, op. cit., p.76; on the use of the Actaeon motif cf. J.M. Steadman, 'Falstaff as Actaeon: A Dramatic Emblem', *SQ*, 14 (1963), 231 – 44 and Roberts, op. cit., p.75 – 77.
[59] Oliver, op. cit., p.76.

in the final intrigue against Falstaff, which is as well a scene of 'scapegoating'[60] as a scene of exorcism.[61] Whereas in *Errors* we were confronted with the mock exorcism by Dr Pinch, here the pinching fairies perform an act of true exorcism in the sense that a perverted mental attitude is corrected. After this Falstaff is not excluded from society; instead his faults are pardoned.

Here a brief consideration of Falstaff in *Henry IV* becomes necessary. As Shakespeare wanted to integrate a comic subplot into this history play, he decided to avail himself of strategies which he had developed in his comedies. The Falstaff of *Henry IV* became his most original comic character, despite the fact that particularly the traditions of the Vice, the Lord of Misrule, Gluttony, the *miles gloriosus* and the parasite have been fused together in his making.[62] It seems to me that Shakespeare's achievement turns out to be even greater if we realize that two rival traditions, the native and the classical, are present here with almost equal force and have been most harmoniously blended in this character. There is, however, a marked tendency in recent criticism to overemphasize the Vice elements in Falstaff. Of course, these are directly referred to in the play (*1 Henry IV*, II, iv, 459), and Falstaff shares the most characteristic trait of the Vice, namely his attempt to deceive his victim in order to bring about his downfall. Yet by merely concentrating on the Vice it is difficult to explain that, from the very beginning of *1 Henry IV*, Prince Hal refuses to be tempted because, as he tells his audience in his famous soliloquy, he knows the character of both Falstaff and his companions (I, ii, 195ff.). It is Hal, rather than Falstaff as 'Vice', who is given the superior awareness. More importantly, if Falstaff's major function may be compared to that of the Vice, there is no character who represents 'virtue' in any clear-cut way. All attempts to find such a character have been unconvincing, not least because they distort or even destroy the subtle system of multiple parallels and contrasts in the relation between the major characters. Even Hotspur is presented far too critically to be taken as a character representing 'honour' as a virtue.[63]

In his well-known book on Falstaff, J. Dover Wilson argued that Hal is not only the youth tempted by the Vice but also the Prodigal Son Prince and, as such, continues the tradition of the humanist plays which are usually seen as specimens of a 'Terentius Christianus.'[64] Yet is is far more important to see

[60] Roberts, op. cit., p.82.
[61] Roberts, op. cit., p.82 – 83.
[62] On Falstaff's classical 'forebears' cf. especially E.P. Vandiver, 'The Elizabethan Dramatic Parasite', *SP*, 32 (1935), 411 – 27; D.C. Boughner, 'Vice, Braggart and Falstaff', *Anglia*, 72 (1954), 35 – 61; J.W. Draper, 'Falstaff and the Plautine Parasite', *CJ*, 33 (1938), 390 – 401; D.B. Landt, 'The Ancestry of Sir John Falstaff', *SQ*, 17 (1966), 69 – 76; on interpreting the character of Falstaff cf. also especially W.H. Auden, 'The Prince's Dog' in: *The Dyer's Hand* (New York, 1948).
[63] Cf., e.g. C.W.R.D. Moseley, *Shakespeare's History Plays* (London, 1988), p.88.
[64] *The Fortunes of Falstaff* (Cambridge, 1943), p.19.

that the game-playing and theatrical elements strongly recall the comic dramaturgy of Plautus and the way in which it was used by the humanists for educational purposes. A case in point is the improvised role-playing scene in *1 Henry IV*, II, iv, in which, for example, Falstaff impersonates Hal's father and thus exercises his function as Hal's 'alternative' father figure. This scene is anything but the tempting or deceiving of the Vice. Furthermore, as the action proceeds, Falstaff and his companions are made the dupe in a way that recalls the unmasking strategies of the duper duped of Plautine and Lucianic comedy. Falstaff's braggardism is uncovered as a *vice* in his *character*, and the intriguers define the purpose of their scheme as a decidedly corrective one (I, i, 180). It has often been observed how masterfully Shakespeare contrives to make a character whose vice is exposed so intensely likeable. The ultimate reason for this is that Falstaff is so utterly human and so unashamed of his complex humanity. With this he continues, as it were, the humanism of Menandrian comedy.

Henry IV is again a play in which human folly is exposed to criticism. Yet Falstaff's folly is folly in the 'salutary', Erasmian sense: there is often deeper wisdom expressed in his apparently foolish comments on the action of the main plot.[65] Moreover, his very presence on the battlefield of Shrewsbury implies an indirect criticism of war. Here the subversive potential of Falstaff becomes most clearly noticeable, and it is significant that this subversive function culminates in a pun. Falstaff pretends that he will help Hal to 'sack a city' with his pistol, yet when Hal 'draws it out' he 'finds it to be a bottle of sack' (V, iii, 54). Greenblatt rightly claims that the Elizabethan notion of power also contains within it the possibility of its subversion, and he goes on to demonstrate this by referring to the dramatic function of Falstaff.[66] I believe that it becomes clear that this subversion is closely connected with the humanist background to this play and in particular with Erasmian and Lucianic satire. The criticism of war which is expressed by Falstaff's activity on the battlefield is in the same spirit as Erasmus's *Querela Pacis*.

But what are we to make, then, of the Henry of *Henry V*, who has often been interpreted as a great warrior and even a national hero? Well, as early as the romantic age Hazlitt questioned the view that military strength is the main concern of this play. And in our own days these doubts are increasingly being articulated. It is becoming more and more evident that there are many things in the play which contradict such a simplistic view. And, given the importance of the humanist background for the *Henry IV* plays, it is hardly conceivable that this should be any less relevant when we come to *Henry V*. Roy Battenhouse has shown recently that Henry V must be understood as an

---

[65] Cf. esp. W. Kaiser, op. cit., esp. p.252ff.

[66] S. Greenblatt, 'Invisible Bullets: Renaissance Authority and Its Subversion' in: *Shakespeare's Rough Magic*, ed. Erickson and Kahn (Newark/London/Toronto, 1985), p.293ff.

ironical distortion of Erasmian ideals of kingship, that he is far more a Roman than a Christian hero and that his decision to wage war against France lacks any serious justification. According to Battenhouse, rather than merely being prepared to avoid war, Henry actively tries to shirk responsibility wherever possible.[67] In an important article A. Hammond goes even further. Through a critical reexamination of the Chorus, he comes to the conclusion that it is only on a surface level that the Chorus meets the expectation of the audience by endorsing the Tudor ideology. As Shakespeare obviously saw further than his audience, so Hammond continues, he indirectly suggested to the critically minded spectator that Henry adopts a false policy by choosing war. Hammond bases his argument on the observation that the expectation aroused by the Chorus 'is *never* satisfied by action on the stage' and he points out that we never actually see Henry in military action. Instead, other surprising things happen. For example, immediately after Harfleur's surrender we find ourselves in the private rooms of Princess Katherine, who is engaged in a comic dialogue containing rather obscene puns which would fit well into the atmosphere of New Comedy. There is plenty of reason to assume with Hammond that the picture of Henry as the ideal king and patriotic hero is being ironically undercut and even mocked at by Shakespeare himself. What has not so far been noticed, however, is that there is no Shakespearean play in which the words 'mock' and 'mockery' occur as frequently as they do in *Henry V*. In the light of this, the final words of the Chorus introducing Act IV take on a subtle ironic connotation, a conclusion which Hammond similarly reaches: the audience are asked to 'sit and see / Minding true things by what their mock'ries be.' By this point in the play it must be clear to the audience that 'mockery' does not simply refer to the inadequacies of dramatic representation; at the same time it suggests that this very representation is itself being consciously mocked. Here, Shakespeare is directly hinting at his own ironic strategy. By interpreting his technique in this way we remain within the humanist tradition, because what we have described is the same mocking, ironic Lucianic spirit as, for example, in Erasmus's paradoxical encomium *The Praise of Folly*. In this way Shakespeare achieves his own paradoxical effect: he 'interprets and challenges ideology at once'.[68]

---

[67] R. Battenhouse, '*Henry V* in the Light of Erasmus', *Shakespeare Studies*, 17 (1985), 77 – 88; cf. also the important article by A. Gurr '*Henry V* and the Bees' Commonwealth', *ShS*, 30 (1977), 61 – 72; for Hazlitt cf. G. Taylor, ed., *Henry V* (Oxford, 1982), p.3.

[68] A. Hammond, ' "It must be your imagination then": the Prologue and the Plural text in Henry V and Elsewhere' in: *'Fanned and Winnowed Opinions'. Shakespearean Essays Presented to Harold Jenkins*, eds. J.W. Mahon and T.A. Pendleton (London/ New York, 1987), p.133 – 150, esp. p.138 and 145. W. Iser does not take full account of the play's mocking qualities because he concentrates too much on its 'affirmative' character (*Shakespeares Historien. Genesis und Geltung* [Konstanz, 1985], p.183 – 203).

But to return to the comedies: If we approach *Twelfth Night* from our perspective, we soon realize that the underlying classical pattern, although it has been enormously extended, enriched and transformed, is still recognizable. As Shakespeare's detailed use of the *Menaechmi* in this play has been extensively analysed by Salingar,[69] there is no need to repeat his findings. We shall therefore concentrate on some central and some additional points in order to show that the extent of the classical basis has often not been fully appreciated.

The major structural transformation which the pattern of the New Comedy tradition undergoes in *Twelfth Night* is the introduction of a subplot, and in this way Shakespeare develops native dramatic traditions. Yet, as in earlier comedies, he links the two plots by the ubiquity of the central New Comedy concept of 'error'; this kind of linking causes Salingar to speak of 'a single symmetrical pattern of errors in criss-cross'.[70] Interestingly enough, Shakespeare himself seems to hint at the 'nodus erroris' in Viola's great soliloquy, immediately after the beginning of the *epitasis* (II, i). In her soliloquy Viola reveals one major reason why the world of this play is so much more complex than that of *Errors*, and this is the different sex of the twins. Whereas it is obvious that *Twelfth Night* is another comedy about the quest for one's identity, the process of this quest is far more complicated because Sebastian and Viola are brother and sister and, what is more important, Viola is temporarily sexually ambiguous through her disguise as a man. In *Twelfth Night* Shakespeare uses disguise as an added complication to the problem of identity, which interested him from the beginnings of his reception of New Comedy. Very early in the play disguise is exposed to criticism and is called a 'wickedness' (II, ii, 27). This criticism is valid because, by putting on a disguise, Viola is indeed temporarily denying her own identity. Yet in the context of this comedy it also has, ultimately, a salutary function because it promotes the process of social integration for Viola, Olivia, the Duke and Sebastian. In the final analysis, her disguise is part of the search for self-fulfilment, which she undertakes by going on a quest for her brother and becoming the spouse of the Duke. By acting in men's clothes, Viola, in a sense, also undergoes a process of 'becoming' the brother whom she is trying to find. There is a certain truth in her statement: 'I my brother know / Yet living in my glass' (III, iv, 379 – 380); she temporarily adopts the nature of her brother. (With this comment, she unwittingly echoes the final situation in *Errors*, where Dromio E tells his twin brother: 'Methinks you are my glass,

---

[69] L.G. Salingar, 'The Design of Twelfth Night', *SQ*, 9 (1958), 117 – 139; reprinted in: *Dramatic Form in Shakespeare and the Jacobeans* (Cambridge, 1986), p.53 – 77. M. Doran first expressed the view that '*Twelfth Night* [. . .] may have seemed quite Plautine' to the Elizabethans (op. cit., p.174).

[70] Salingar, *Dramatic Form*, p.68.

and not my brother: / I see by you I am a sweet-fac'd youth' [V, i, 417 – 418]).

As Adelman has shown, by temporarily assuming an opposite identity, Viola performs an educational function for both Orsino and Olivia, and, we have to add, for herself too.[71] Adelman further argues that Viola allows the Duke to develop both homoerotic and heterosexual feelings for her, since she is Cesario *and* Viola, her twin brother *and* herself in one and the same person. Whereas Antipholus S found his identity by discovering his other male self, things are more complicated in *Twelfth Night* because here, the twins being of different sexes, Viola, according to Adelman, has first to experience the maleness of her twin brother before she can fully identify herself with her own femaleness. It is significant that she does not give up her male role 'until she is in the presence of the twin who becomes in effect her male self'.[72] She knows that 'she can become fully female only when she has in effect found a repository for her maleness'.[73] Adelman further suggests that ultimately '*Twelfth Night* allows for the fantasy that the self can literally be both male and female'.[74] It is thus that Shakespeare in *Twelfth Night* exploits the possibilities of the identity theme of New Comedy to the utmost degree.

Twelfth Night indeed presents a most subtle probing into the nature of love. This comedy once again dramatizes the Erasmian paradox that love is a kind of folly, and in this way the New Comedy concept of 'error' is given a very profound interpretation. The comedy becomes 'outspokenly' corrective, particularly in the Malvolio scenes with their direct exposure of love as self-conceit or 'selflove' (I, v, 90). By Maria's comic intrigue, Malvolio is made a fool of, and in the end is treated like a madman. These scenes have often been interpreted as 'Jonsonian elements';[75] yet to see them from the Jonsonian perspective is to overlook what Shakespeare is really aiming at. These Malvolio scenes, which, as has frequently been noticed, parallel the treatment Antipholus E receives from Dr Pinch, were suggested by the New Comedy tradition *itself* and not by a supposedly new dramatic technique developed by his colleague. Shakespeare himself emphasizes for us the classical associations and thus points to the context in which we have to see these scenes. The hints are the numerous references to classical mythology. The feigned letter in the gulling situation itself begins with the words: 'Jove knows I love' (II, v, 96). Having read it, Malvolio goes so far as to say: 'It is Jove's doing, and Jove make me thankful!' (III, iv, 74 – 75). This frequent reference to Jupiter

---

[71] J. Adelman, 'Male Bonding in Shakespeare's Comedies', in: *Shakespeare's 'Rough Magic'*, p.73 – 103; 85f.

[72] Ibid., p.90.

[73] Ibid.

[74] Ibid., p.89.

[75] Cf. Mueschke P. and Fleisher, J. 'Jonsonian Elements in the Comic Underplot of *Twelfth Night*', *PMLA*, 48 (1933), 722 – 40.

puzzled Halliwell,[76] but it does make sense if it is seen as a pointer to the 'classical' atmosphere and humanist function of these scenes. Furthermore, when Malvolio rehearses to himself the behaviour he intends to adopt in his encounter with Maria, he, like Hal before him, indirectly places himself in the New Comedy tradition. Just as Malvolio is overheard and exposed to ridicule, so, too, is Sosia in *Amphitruo* (I, i).

The Malvolio scenes evoke still further Plautine associations which do not seem to have been recognized. The gulling of a character is by no means uncommon in Plautus, who in his comedies can sometimes even be satirical. We need only think of the braggart Pyrgopolynices in *Miles Gloriosus* who, likewise, is made a gull of because of his self-conceit. He thinks all women fall in love with him at first sight, while in fact everyone detests him. He is gulled through an intrigue directed against him. Thus, in the Malvolio scenes there is a clear Plautine basis for the Erasmian and Lucianic exposure and correction of human folly.

Shakespeare by far surpasses the subtlety of all previous gulling scenes by making the Clown a party to the intrigue. Feste disguises himself and acts the part of Sir Topas, pretending to cure Malvolio. Yet Feste the Clown, who represents the Erasmian paradox of the Fool who is the truly wise man, and who here intends to cure a poor fool, himself becomes a fool (with a strong bent towards malice) because he is induced to overdo his cure; he thus becomes involved and commits a serious wrong. The victim Malvolio rightly feels that he has been treated most unjustly. We believe him when in his anguish he exclaims that he is no more mad than all the others. Thus Shakespeare has again arrived at the Erasmian and Lucianic notion of the ubiquity of folly.

It is fitting that, while Malvolio is being duped, Fabian should make his famous anti-illusionist remark: 'If this were played upon a stage now, I could condemn it as an improbable fiction.' (III, iv, 127 – 128). The audience are, of course, aware that this situation *is* indeed being played upon a stage. There is a surprisingly similar play with illusion in a gulling situation in the Plautine *Mostellaria*. Here Theopropides, after having been made the dupe, is advised by Tranio to tell Diphilus and Philemon – two authors of Greek New Comedy – how his servant has gulled him: 'You'll have furnished 'em with the best dupe scenes on the comic stage.' ('optumas frustrationes dederis in comoediis' III, 1151). Just as Fabian's comment suggests that what has happened is *real*, but would be considered as *fiction* if it were used in a comedy, so Tranio here suggests by his remark that Theopropides's *real* experience would provide good material for *comedies*.

---

[76] Quoted in *Twelfth Night*, ed. J.M. Lothian and T.W. Craik, The New Arden Edition (London, 1975), p.96, n.75.

It has been said of *Twelfth Night*, and rightly, that the 'saturnalian spirit invades the whole play'.[77] It would, however, be rash to claim that this delight in the saturnalian spirit points exclusively to the native tradition. We have already seen how this element in Shakespeare's reception of the Plautine *Menaechmi* was fully recognized by the Gray's Inn audience, who, after the performance, indulged in a 'night of errors', extending the confusions beyond the confines of the play. How well the saturnalian element in Elizabethan drama agrees with the Plautine form of New Comedy is reflected by the fact, first observed by Salingar, that the saturnalian character of the Parasite Peniculus in *Menaechmi* recurs in *Twelfth Night* transformed into the Epicurean character of Sir Toby.[78]

A saturnalian element enters the language of the subplot, too, and above all that of the Clown. Feste, who 'can have no real emotions of his own, and may only live in his quibbles',[79] exhibits a distinctly Plautine spirit. The more one becomes familiar with Plautus, the more one notices a 'Plautine' quality in Feste. His masterly command of the *dramatic* play with language has affinities with that of Plautus. First, there is the Clown's penchant for inventing new names; this evokes not so much Rabelaisian as Plautine (and Lucianic) associations,[80] as when in his dialogue with Olivia he calls a philosopher 'Quinapalus' (I, v, 35), or later on he invents a series of nonsense names. 'Pigrogromitus', 'Vapians', 'Queubus' (II, iii, 23 – 24). The name Pigrogromitus in particular looks as though it may well have been modelled on a typically Plautine characteronym compounded from two individual words, such as, for example, 'Theopropides' in *Mostellaria*. Furthermore, Feste's attitude towards language includes a nonsensical play with it, as, for example, in the following comment: 'I did impeticos thy gratillity' (II, iii, 26), which, again, is reminiscent of Plautus. As Salingar has pointed out, Feste is 'the only character in Shakespeare to take pleasure, or refuge, in fantasies of pure nonsense';[81] and this delight in the comic effects of pure verbal nonsense is, as we have seen, also strongly present in Plautine comedy.

Salingar has drawn our attention to a further connection between *Menaechmi*, *Errors* and *Twelfth Night*; he argues that 'Olivia and her household, in their actions towards Sebastian, reproduce very closely the actions of the courtesan, her servants, and the parasite'.[82] This is a valid observation concerning the structure of *Twelfth Night*, and one should add to it a further point. An examination of locality in *Twelfth Night* shows that the action requires only two specific locations or houses, namely the Duke's palace and

[77] Salingar, *Dramatic Form*, p.55.
[78] Ibid., p.76.
[79] Ibid., p.73.
[80] Duckworth has already drawn a parallel between Plautus and Rabelais, op. cit., p.324.
[81] Salingar, *Dramatic Form*, p.73.
[82] Ibid., p.767.

the house of Olivia (and her adjacent garden). Many scenes are performed in a neutral locality, such as a street. This implies that, in his last romantic comedy, Shakespeare chose a dramaturgic organization surprisingly similar to the plays written for the stage of classical comedy.

Although the design of *Twelfth Night* is both symmetrically balanced and intricately complex, it is organized upon a New Comedy basis which was then *extended* and transformed by the use of native as well as Italian traditions. It was the structural design Shakespeare acquired in composing his *Errors* which provided him with a starting point when he wrote *Twelfth Night*. I do not believe that Salingar has sufficient grounds to assume that Shakespeare first took suggestions from various sources and then used New Comedy as a means of linking them together. Salingar believed that Shakespeare first read the Viola story in Riche's *Apollonius and Silla*, or elsewhere; that, having found the concept of 'dame Error', he then conceived the characters of Orsino and Olivia and that this 'suggested the role of Sebastian, with its Plautine farce and its romantic overtones of sea-adventure prolonged from *The Comedy of Errors*'.[83] Whereas Salingar suggests that 'this conjecture does seem to account for the way the whole stage design of the play holds so beautifully together'[84], it seems to me to be the other way round. Shakespeare did not have to look for the additional suggestion of the structure of a Plautine 'farce', because he already had a firm and thorough knowledge of the structural pattern of the New Comedy tradition, as it was received by the humanists and in which 'error' was the central idea. This basic pattern lent itself to copious extensions as well as to detailed transformations. It could be adapted to the Elizabethan and Shakespearean delight in celebrating feasts of language, wit and saturnalian topsyturvydom. It could incorporate further native popular dramatic traditions as well as the intense emotions and the highly poetic language of Shakespeare's great comic characters.[85]

---

[83] Ibid., p.77.

[84] Ibid.

[85] In our survey, we cannot entirely neglect the tragedies, especially since recent criticism has increasingly commented upon some important structural links between Shakespeare's comedies and tragedies. There has always been an awareness of the structural linking of New Comedy to tragedy, from which it was ultimately derived. Susan Snyder has made the interesting point that the form of Shakespeare's early comedies served him as a matrix for his tragic plays, because 'by the time the great tragic phase was well under way he had behind him no fewer than ten successful comedies'. (*The Comic Matrix of Shakespeare's Tragedies* [Princeton, 1979], p.4). Although she is aware of the influence of New Comedy on Shakespeare, she pays no attention to *Errors* and adheres exclusively to the concept of 'romantic comedy'. Thus, for Snyder, *Romeo and Juliet* has the structure of romantic comedy, which only in its final stage is turned into a tragedy (op. cit., p.56ff.). Yet it is wrong to assume that, because the central theme of the play is romantic love, the entire structure must have been adopted from romantic comedy. We have seen how the theme of romantic love was integrated into a New Comedy design in *The Two Gentlemen of Verona*. The intrigue devised by Friar Laurence

2. The dark comedies

It is conceivable that, after the enormous success of *Errors* at Gray's Inn, Shakespeare may have been asked to write another comedy with a similar classical basis for this intellectual audience, and thus it was, perhaps, that *Troilus and Cressida* came into existence. The theory that this drama was originally an Inns of Court play was first put forward by Peter Alexander in 1928 and was supported even by Greg.[86] There is indeed a great deal to be said

resembles in its form and purpose that of the Lucentio-Bianca plot in *Taming*. It has been devised, as it were, for the purpose of 'comedy', because its intention is to enable the lovers to become happily united after the obstacles to their marriage have been removed. A. Harbage has made the interesting suggestion that the structural element of intrigue in tragedy was adopted from comedy (quoted by Hosley, 'The Formal Influence of Plautus and Terence' in: *Elizabethan Theatre* [London, 1966], p.136). Seen from a New Comedy perspective, the Nurse appears as a kind of female pimp, who has an antecedent in the Plautine Astaphium in *Truculentus* and who anticipates the later Mrs Quickly and Mrs Overdone.

There is a further reason why in a discussion of the structure of *Romeo and Juliet* we have to take into account the model of classical drama, and this is the device of the Prologue. Its presence influences the reception of the play in a decisive way. One could not claim that the play arouses comic expectations which are then thwarted by the later course of the action, because the Prologue presents a summary of the *entire* plot in the manner of an 'argumentum', rather than a Plautine Prologue; properly speaking, the audience can be in no doubt about the tragic ending, whereas the Plautine Prologue informed the audience merely of *part* of the action. Yet the play's predominantly comic structure nevertheless has the effect that the audience, against all reason, still nourish some hope that the lovers will in the end be happily united. In other words, what we have here is a most subtle interplay between tragic and comic responses, a technique which Shakespeare had already experimented with in his *Errors*.

Some time ago, B. de Mendonça was among the first to discover elements of comic structure in *Othello*, but she defined them too narrowly as resulting directly from the influence of the *commedia dell'arte* (' "Othello": A Tragedy Built on a Comic Structure', *ShS*, 21 [1968], 31 – 38). However, as there is a great difference between the zany and Iago, Mendonça's comparison remains unconvincing. She does not take account of the fact that the *commedia dell'arte* itself goes back in part to Roman and particularly to Plautine comedy. Hence the points of contact which she discovers do in the final analysis point to New Comedy itself. What reminds us particularly of New Comedy is the scheming character of Iago and the fact that the intrigue is performed by means of an eavesdropping scene. Furthermore, the attempt to arouse sexual jealousy is, of course, much more typical of comedy than tragedy. Iago is so like the trickster of Roman comedy or the implied stage director in Plautine comedy that the connections with the medieval Vice, which are usually commented on, appear by comparison to be of minor importance. (D.S. Stewart considers Iago as 'almost the perfect slave of comedy' and, unconvincingly, sees in Othello 'the *miles gloriosus* to almost absolute perfection': '*Othello*: Roman Comedy as Nightmare', *Emory University Quarterly*, 22 [1967], 252 – 76. A similar point has recently been made by F. Teague, who is unaware of Stewart's article, '*Othello* and New Comedy', *CD*, 20 [1986], 54 – 64.)

[86] Cf. K. Palmer, ed., *Troilus and Cressida*, The New Arden Shakespeare (London, 1982), p.307 – 310.

in favour of this assumption. Even if the play was not written for the Inns, it is likely that it was performed there and it must have been a success. Palmer, the New Arden editor of the play, is right in maintaining that 'it would suit what we know of the taste of an Inn of Court', and that it 'contains [. . .] discussions of topics [. . .] that would directly interest a lawyer',[87] just as in *Errors* legal terms are surprisingly frequent. If *Errors* in some way reminds us of the *Odyssey*, as Ralph Berry has pointed out,[88] then *Troilus and Cressida* takes the world of the *Iliad* as its theme, although this is further enlarged and transformed by the medieval tradition. Both plays provide a similar pleasure to the audience by the skilful transformation of the classical source material, although the content in the later play is far more profound.

The structure of *Troilus and Cressida* is too complex to permit of any clear and simple classification and we cannot discuss it here in greater detail. The fusion of the love plot with the political *sujet* of the Trojan War and the disillusioned, cynical and even despairing note of the ending prevent us from establishing any *major* connections with the New Comedy tradition. On looking more closely at this play we notice, however, that among the various impulses that went into its making there are also some suggestions from classical comedy. It is very interesting that the anonymous Epistle, 'found in copies of Q in the second state',[89] not only extols the play's 'wit' but frequently speaks of it in terms of 'comedy', and that for this 'comedy' it claims a position among 'the best Commedy in *Terence* or *Plautus*'.[90] Indeed, *Troilus and Cressida* does contain some thematic and structural elements which undoubtedly reflect the humanist reception of this comic tradition.

As in the earlier classical play, a young man is seen in search of his self-fulfilment, but whereas in the earlier play he finds his identity, in the later one the 'hero' comes to grief. For various reasons he cannot succeed in achieving his goal, his self-fulfilment in his love of Cressida. He becomes a victim of the antagonism between love and war, and he fails to know himself. Whereas he sees himself as a lover in the tradition of romantic, idealized love, he is really the most sensual lover in Shakespearean drama.[91] Furthermore, he fails to find his identity in Cressida's love because he is unable to recognize her real nature ('This is, and is not, Cressid.', V, ii, 146). More importantly, he does not realize that he himself has involuntarily contributed to her becoming faithless;[92] before she was handed over to the Greeks, he was so hysterically afraid of her infidelity that he did in fact anticipate her betrayal in an act of

---

[87]　Ibid., p.309.
[88]　Cf. chapter IX, p.206
[89]　Palmer, op. cit., p.95, note.
[90]　Ibid.
[91]　Cf., for example, J. Bayley, 'Time and the Trojans', *EC*, 25 (1975), 67.
[92]　I have developed this point in my article 'Zur Dramaturgie des "Love Plot" in *Troilus and Cressida*', *ShJW* (1982), 119 – 132.

what modern psychologists would call 'self-fulfilling prophecy'. His distrust of Cressida's love is a major cause of the final catastrophe.

In *Troilus and Cressida* Shakespeare has a pervading interest in 'verification, and the means by which one achieves a right judgement, whether of identity or value',[93] and he uses 'all the ways in which a character can be identified, or mistaken'.[94] Palmer's analysis makes it clear how the play reflects humanist interests. Human ideals and values are still envisaged as moral imperatives, yet they are far from being readily accepted; rather they are shown to be subject to human 'valuation' ('What's aught but as 'tis valued?' II, ii, 52).

Whereas Shakespeare usually tends towards the integration of tragic emotions into the world of comedy, in this play tragic emotions are, as it were, superseded by a satirical strategy reminiscent of Lucian and Erasmus. Especially in the case of Ajax and Achilles, satire brings out the folly of excessive pride and the 'error in *self*-identification'.[95] The romantic language in which Troilus expresses his love for Cressida is shown to be mere veneer. Like everything else in the play, it is exposed to satire. One could even argue that, by this de-romanticizing process, the presentation of love becomes more similar to the realistic and sensual love in Roman, particularly Plautine comedy. And certainly the pimp Pandarus with his go-between services invokes associations with New Comedy. Further classical connections are established by the splendidly organized eavesdropping situation in V, ii. This scene is the climax of the play's humanist exposure of human folly. Thersites (and, to some extent, Pandarus) is the Lucianic commentator of the play. He seems in the end to triumph with his comment that 'The common curse of mankind, [is] folly and ignorance' (II, iii, 27 – 28), yet he himself cannot be exempted from this universal verdict. Palmer does not fully recognize how much this play has grown out of the humanist tradition. In his notes to the text he makes, it is true, several references to Erasmus's *Adagia*, and on one occasion he mentions the *Colloquies*.[96] If Erasmus in his *Colloquies* has fused elements of Roman comedy with the satirical strategy of Lucian, then Shakespeare, too, combines aspects of Roman comedy with Lucianic satire, which amuses 'those with a taste for scepticism and scurrility'.[97] It seems that Shakespeare's reception of the New Comedy tradition undergoes a marked shift of emphasis in the first years of the new century, because the satirical element increases in importance, not to recede again until the final plays.

---

[93] Palmer, op. cit., p.71.
[94] Ibid., p.73.
[95] Ibid., p.74.
[96] Ibid., p.167, note 168.
[97] Ibid., p.92.

Measure for Measure is a play that cannot be ignored in our context[98] because, as recent critics have noticed, it reminds us of the much earlier *Errors* in more than one respect,[99] and thus offers ample proof of the deep impact which the neo-classical structure of *Errors* had on the development of Shakespeare's dramatic canon. Elements and ideas that occurred in *Errors* are now taken up again and employed in a much more profound and complex way.

The play's humanist concern finds expression in the very first line, when the Duke speaks of the 'properties' 'of government'. In both plays, characters are under threat of execution, in both there is a desperate cry for justice. It is interesting how in Act V Isabella's appeal for justice, which she addresses to the Duke, resembles that of Antipholus E. Both characters plead in a strikingly similar way and both have to defend themselves against the suspicion of madness. When in the end mercy and pardon prevail over justice, the basic differences between the situations emerge. In the later play, characters have become guilty by their own deeds, whereas in *Errors* the appeal to the Duke has become necessary only because of the confusions between appearance and reality. Yet it is also true to say that *Measure* is made more complicated by the introduction of further elements, some of them reminding us of the New Comedy tradition, and some of them invoking Erasmian associations. In *Errors*, the Duke is a comic figure[100] because he is as helpless as his subjects, whereas the Duke in *Measure* is in command of the development of the plot. He first acquires his superior awareness by eavesdropping and then acts as a stage manager, whose prototype we have seen in Plautine comedy. Yet whereas the stage manager in Plautus was always the slave, in *Measure* he occupies a place at the other end of the social scale. What further creates a Plautine atmosphere is the bawdy world of Mrs Overdone. The fact that these scenes abound in comic puns invokes particularly Plautine associations.

Whether we regard the play *Measure* from the perspective of the Duke, Isabella, Angelo or Claudio, we notice that its major theme is the 'quest for self-knowledge'.[101] Angelo and Isabella have to undergo a painful process which involves experiencing the paradox that moral rigour may be a disguise for an inhuman stance because it disregards human fallibility. Interestingly enough, the punning play with the double meaning of a single word is used to point to this paradox. Isabella, in her attempt to persuade Angelo, speaks 'sense', yet the sense of her argument arouses Angelo's 'sense', his sexual desire (II, ii, 142). The favourite humanist paradox that, in order to become

[98] K. Muir has suggested that Shakespeare may have received his background information on friars and nuns from Erasmus's dialogue *Funus* in his *Colloquia* and that he may also have found there the names Francisco, Barnardo and Vincentio (*Shakespeare's Sources* [London, 1961], I, 108).

[99] Cf., for example, Berry, *Shakespeare and the Awareness of the Audience*, p.30.

[100] Cf. C. Leech, 'Shakespeare's Comic Dukes', *REL*, 5 (1964), 101 – 114.

[101] J.W. Lever, ed., *Measure for Measure*, The New Arden Shakespeare (London, 1965), p.xciv.

really aware of life, one must first have an experience of losing it, is in *Measure* very effectively dramatized in the way Claudio and Angelo are ready to accept death before they are pardoned. Ambiguity and paradox are seen in the Duke too, who, although the dominating character, is not free from errors and misconceptions. He is wrong about his ideal of a Duke because he thinks that boundless mercy and mildness will prevent society from falling apart. He is at first mistaken about Angelo's hypocritical character, and he is deceived into thinking that he can simply confer his authority on his deputy with the command: 'be thou at full ourself' (I, i, 43). This expression reflects an astonishing lack of self-knowledge. Hence Escalus's remark that the Duke is 'One that, above all other strives, contended especially to know himself' (III, ii, 232), is only partly true. And if he sometimes assumes the guise of a friar, then this disguise is ambiguous, as it not only serves a positive purpose but also involves the Duke in deception and in temporarily denying his own identity. Whereas in *Errors* the New Comedy element of disguise is only indirectly present in that the double identities have effects similar to disguise, in *Measure* this device is employed for purposeful deception. We recall Viola's criticism of it as a 'wickedness'; yet it is also used as a 'healing power',[102] a means of redressing a former wrong. Furthermore, disguise in this play appears also as an acquired pose by which a character's true nature is concealed. The very name Angelo is part of the mask which this character wears[103] because it ironically conceals the fact that his nature contains elements which are far from angelic. *Measure* is, then, a further 'comedy of errors' and a much more mature one, in which characters do not simply mistake appearance for reality; what interests Shakespeare in particular is the inner moral aberrations rather than merely the outward confusions. The play shows that even values and ideals may be used as means of disguise and pretence.

Measure contains a strong element of satire, and this too reflects the play's humanist background. The satire is directed, as Hawkins has put it, against 'extremism in the pursuit of anything'.[104] Duncan was right when he suggested that *Measure* might on closer inspection reveal a Lucianic tendency in the ironic deflation of characters and their pretences.[105] The central temptation scene, in which Angelo makes a fool of himself and betrays his moral standards by succumbing to Isabella's charms, is typically 'Lucianic'. The character who has the strongest Lucianic associations, however, is the amusing Lucio, whose main function is that of 'unmasking'. He is, no doubt, a composite character, yet it is not enough to state that 'Elements of the

---

[102] Cf. on this aspect P. Edwards, 'Shakespeare and the Healing Power of Deceit', *ShS*, 31 (1978), 115 – 125.

[103] Cf. E. Schanzer, *The Problem Plays of Shakespeare* (London, 1963), p.94.

[104] H. Hawkins, *Likenesses of Truth in Elizabethan and Restoration Drama* (Oxford, 1972), p.75.

[105] R. Duncan, *Ben Jonson and the Lucianic Tradition*, p.94.

slanderous courtier of romance, and the typical Jacobean gallant and "fantastic" '[106] went into his making. Isabella senses his satirical force and complains about what she considers to be his unjust treatment of her: 'You do blaspheme the good, in mocking me' (I, iv, 38).

As the subsequent course of the play shows, Lucio's critical and satirical stance towards her is justified: the halo of her saintliness fades away. Lucio's disrespect for the Duke is of special interest in our context. The Duke is made the comic butt of Lucio, and he deserves it, because he cannot exempt himself from the charge of fallibility. He is, as we have said, a perfect stage manager, but not an ideal Duke. As H. Hawkins, for example, has pointed out, he consistently refuses to 'face up to the dilemmas and responsibilities of a governor, who, whether he likes it or not, is bound to enforce the law'.[107] He does in fact neglect Cicero's warning in his *De Re Publica* that excessive freedom ('nimia licentia') is very dangerous: it is the seed out of which a new tyrant grows. And then Cicero adds the humanist maxim that all extremes should be avoided by steering a middle course of moderation.[108] While I would not go so far as Hawkins who further claims that Shakespeare 'seems to treat the Duke with something like poetic contempt',[109] there can be no doubt that the audience are meant to sympathize with Lucio's satire, which has a subversive quality because it is directed against authority. Unaware that the Duke is standing in front of him in disguise, Lucio, in a sense, unmasks him with his comment: 'It was a mad fantastical trick of him to steal from the state and usurp the beggary he was never born to' (III, ii, 92 – 94). A few lines later, in a particularly Lucianic tone, he again directs his satirical comments towards the Duke and his deputy. But, as is often the case, the Lucianic figure himself is not immune to deception. We should perhaps not go so far as to see in the name of Lucio an allusion to Lucian; yet it is not impossible that Shakespeare may indeed have intended a subtle allusion. The name of Luciana, who introduced a satirical perspective into *Errors*, and the appearance of Lucianus in *Hamlet*, are direct allusions; furthermore, it is not without interest that in *Two Gentlemen* a satirical tone is added by the character of Lucetta. It is therefore possible that Lucio in *Measure* is the last instance of a number of playful references to the name of an author who obviously meant almost as much to Shakespeare as he did to Erasmus and Thomas More.

In view of these close humanist connections, the question of the play's tragicomic structure appears in a new light. It is usually assumed that *Measure* is a tragicomedy written under the strong Italian influence of Guarini or

---

[106] Lever, op. cit., p.xcvi.
[107] Hawkins, op. cit., p.64; cf. also R. Miles, *The Problem of 'Measure for Measure'* (London, 1976).
[108] Cicero, *De Re Publica*, I, 44, 68.
[109] Hawkins, op. cit., p.73.

Cinthio.[110] Yet is this assumption really convincing? Does not the play differ markedly from the Jacobean pastoral tragicomedies that appear to have been written under the direct influence of the new Italian concept of tragicomedy? It seems rather that the individuality of *Measure for Measure* can be better appreciated if the play is seen as part of the *unfolding* of a dramatic pattern, offering a full view of life by exploring comic as well as tragic emotions, a pattern which, under strong humanist influence, first appeared in *Errors* and then continued to fascinate Shakespeare to the end of his dramatic career. That the Italian influence may have reinforced these tendencies, is another matter.

All's Well that Ends Well is usually seen as having exclusively medieval origins. The thematic concern of Shakespeare in this play is, however, remarkably close to the humanism of the classical tradition. It is all very well to point to Boccaccio as the ultimate source and to claim that there are possible associations with Count Girart of Roussillion as well as a further connection with Christine de Pisan.[111] Yet these associations are correct only if the play's structural basis in the New Comedy tradition is also recognized. The plot is, as it were, an astute transformation of the motif of mistakings of identity, separations and reunions. The structural organization according to *protasis* and *epitasis* is clearly recognizable.[112] The *protasis* is strictly confined to the first Act; the complications beginning with Act II increase in intensity and culminate in the conclusion of Act IV, the bed-trick and Helena's 'stealing' of her own ring, so that preparations can be made for the comic catastrophe of Act V.

Moreover, it seems to me that the mythological opposition between Mars and Diana (and also Venus, of course) is meant to emphasize the classical perspective, and this opposition, with its symbolic implications, helps to establish the tone of the play at least as much as any possible connections with the *Psychomachia* or the Morality Plays. In any case, it is problematic to equate Helena with the good and Bertram as well as Parolles with the bad, and even Fraser, who makes this suggestion, has to add that 'the moral distinctions are blurred',[113] because Shakespeare here takes life to be a 'mingled yarn, good and ill together . . .' (IV, iii, 71 – 72), and this definition of the human condition exactly corresponds to the spirit of New Comedy. Bertram and

---

110 Cf. Lever, op. cit., p.lxlxiii.
111 R. Fraser, ed., *All's Well that Ends Well*, The New Cambridge Shakespeare (Cambridge, 1985), p.5 – 8.
112 On the overall structure of *All's Well* cf. R. L. Smallwood, 'The Design of "All's Well that Ends Well" ', *ShS*, 25 (1972), 45 – 61.
113 Fraser, op. cit., p.14; W.L. Godshalk has tried to establish connections with the Morality Play: '*All's Well that Ends Well* and the Morality Play', *SQ*, 25 (1974), 61 – 70.

Parolles are followers of Mars; as a consequence, Bertram decides to become a hater of love, and this already indicates the imbalance of his nature which has to be corrected. Helena is at first the virtuous woman, the paragon of virginity, a fact exemplified by her associations with Diana. What she has to realize, however, is that virtue in life may not be enough. She consequently betrays this ideal by acting in disguise as Bertram's paramour who, significantly, is given the very name 'Diana'. By deciding to win Bertram through the bed-trick, Helena comes to understand a more complex concept of love, personified by Venus.

Through his close links with Bertram, the important character of Parolles also acquires a structural function. He has long been recognized as a descendant not only of the parasite, but above all of the *miles gloriosus*; he has, indeed, much closer affinities with the Plautine *miles* than the Terentian *Thraso*. The characteronym 'Parolles' is a most appropriate one, because it suggests that he is nothing but words, and that he is completely devoid of any moral concepts.[114] Parolles's fascination with the power of words and his playful attitude towards language remind us very strongly of what we find in Plautus. His primary function in this play is clearly the exposing of folly, and therefore he is another instance of the Plautine as well as Lucianic strategy of satire through comedy. Besides, it is entirely in line with the tradition when the satirist himself exhibits the very vice he criticizes in others.

One of the dramatic highlights of *All's Well* is the scene in which the unmasking of the 'alazon', the exposing of Parolles's foolish braggardism, takes place. The way in which this is achieved evokes distinctly Plautine associations, in particular of his *Poenulus*. This is a play in which there is a very effective amalgamation of New Comedy and the Roman popular tradition and in which Plautus's linguistic creativity makes for dynamic theatre. Here the character Hanno, although he can speak Latin as well as his companions, starts to speak Punic. The superb joke then consists of the fact that Milphio, although he does not know a word of the Punic language, plays the interpreter. Plautus here succeeds in creating comic characters solely through language (V, ii; IV, 961ff.), and this is what Shakespeare does, even more

---

[114] To some extent he also reminds us of the parasite. Traces of the *miles* and the parasite seem to merge in Parolles's self-characterizing soliloquy:

> Captain I'll be no more,
> But I will eat and drink and sleep as soft
> As Captain shall. Simply the thing I am
> Shall make me live. Who knows himself a braggart,
> Let him fear this; for it will come to pass
> That every braggart shall be found an ass.
> Rust sword, cool blushes, and, Parolles, live
> Safest in shame! Being fool'd, by fool'ry thrive!
> There's place and means for every man alive.   (IV, iii, 331 – 339)

admirably, with Parolles. It almost seems that the famous unmasking of Parolles alludes to this Plautine scene, which, as usual, is transformed into a situation of far greater complexity. The Parolles scene is not only overwhelmingly comic and brilliantly effective; it also holds an important position in the whole context of the play because here the edge of the play's satirical commentator is turned against himself.

The apparently wise Parolles turns out to be utterly foolish − this famous Erasmian paradox is not the only one in this play, indeed the world of *All's Well* is in a sense made up of a web of paradoxes and ambiguities. This is the major reason why it has met with critical acclaim in recent years, whereas previously it was largely neglected. A paradox is revealed even in part of the play's structure: Bertram, lying with his own wife, yet believing her to be Diana, is both guilty and not guilty. In this play, the bad may appear as good and vice versa, according to the perspective from which it is considered. The paradoxical tenor of the play has deep roots in the humanist tradition. If it has been pointed out that Shakespeare here depicts life in its postlapsarian state,[115] then it has to be added that man's salvation comes mainly from himself and the faults of others have to be forgiven; Helena remarks: 'Our remedies oft in ourselves do lie' (I, i, 216). The divine guidance which is envisaged here is similar to that articulated in the plays of the New Comedy tradition. Therefore, when Helena refers to God, as in the phrase 'The greatest grace lending grace' (II, i, 160), she makes this reference in the context of the classical humanist tradition, which is emphasized by the invocation of Greek mythology:

> [. . .] The greatest grace lending grace;
> Ere twice the horses of the sun shall bring
> Their fiery torcher his diurnal ring,
> Ere twice in murk and occidental damp
> Moist Hesperus hath quench'd her sleepy lamp, [. . .]
> Health shall live free, and sickness freely die.   160 – 168

This *classicism* has to be borne in mind when one speaks of the predominant medievalism of the play.

Before turning to the so-called romances, it is necessary to consider briefly *Timon of Athens*. Here is another play which does not easily fit into any one dramatic genre: it is neither pure tragedy nor genuine comedy. It contains, however, comic as well as tragic elements, and in some important respects it even prepares the way for the final plays. Its major source is Plutarch's *Lives*, yet critics are now inclined to assume that Shakespeare also knew Lucian's

---

[115] Cf. Fraser, op. cit., p.9.

dialogue *Timon* or *Misanthropus*, possibly, even probably, by way of the anonymous *Timon* play.[116]

If we look at the sparse facts which Plutarch reports about Timon, it quickly becomes clear that the anonymous *Timon* comedy in all likelihood provided Shakespeare with many further suggestions for his *Timon of Athens*. Let us therefore start by considering briefly the anonymous comedy which has usually been condemned as 'wretched', although, or precisely because, it was thought to be 'the work of an academic'.[117] It must have been composed in humanist circles, at one of the Inns, if Bradbrook is correct, presumably in Middle Temple.[118] It contains interesting legal references and reflects a consciousness of the classical tradition, as far as the structure of comedy, rhetoric and philosophy are concerned. Its language is also worth considering because the play may then appear to us far less 'wretched'. We have to recognize how the author delights in playing games with language; he employs verbal pyrotechnics, and makes abundant use of *paronomasia* by playing with the similarity of different words and by perceptively altering their morphology, devices which seem to be deliberate attempts at imitating Plautus's verbal artistry.

The anonymous comedy *Timon* was used for the purpose of humanist teaching, although it also satirizes the pretentiousness of excessive learning. Like the works of, for example, Erasmus, it fuses elements of Roman comedy (on one occasion it draws on Plautus's *Aulularia*,[118] and the name Gelasimus stems from the Plautine *Stichus*), and Lucianic satire in order to instruct the audience by means of comic laughter.

The anonymous comedy is largely based on the *Timon* or *Misanthropus* of Lucian and, using his technique of ironic deflation, centres on the Lucianic paradox of a man being kind yet entirely lacking in wisdom.[120] Although the play expressly calls itself a 'comedy', on one occasion it describes Timon's own feelings even as 'tragicall'.[121] It also uses such comedy elements as a trickster figure and the technique of overhearing. The strongest argument for

---

[116] Cf. R.W. Bond, 'Lucian and Boiardo in *Timon of Athens*', *MLR*, 26 (1931), 52 – 68; R.H. Goldsmith, 'Did Shakespeare use the Old Timon Comedy?', *SQ*, 9 (1958), 31 – 38; W.A. Bonnard, 'Note sur les sources de *Timon of Athens*', *EA*, 7 (1974), 63 – 64; H.J. Oliver, ed., *Timon of Athens*, The New Arden Shakespeare (London, 1959), p.xxxii – xl, and especially J.C. Bulman, Jr., 'Shakespeare's Use of the "Timon" Comedy', *ShS*, 29 (1976), 103 – 116. M.C. Bradbrook's theory that the play is 'a law students' burlesque of Shakespeare's *Timon*' is unconvincing ('The Comedy of Timon: *A Reveling Play of the Inner Temple*', *RD*, 9 [1966], 83 – 103; 83); cf. also Duncan, *Ben Jonson*, p.93.

[117] Steevens, quoted by Bradbrook, op. cit., p.83.

[118] Cf. Bradbrook, ibid.

[119] Cf. Bradbrook, referring to Dyce, op. cit., p.96.

[120] Cf. Bulman, op. cit., esp. p. 105 – 111.

[121] I quote from the abbreviated reprint of the play in G. Bullough, *Narrative and Dramatic Sources of Shakespeare* (London, 1966), VI, 321.

Shakespeare's use of this play is the presence of a faithful Steward in both works.[122] As he is not only faithful but also wise and reasonable, we may see him as a descendant of the slaves in Roman comedy. It is in keeping with the didactic and educational function of this comedy that it abounds in rhetoric, and that this aspect is often expressly signalled by means of metapoetic comments.

It seems to me very significant that the anonymous *Timon* comedy uses 'romance' elements in its plot, and at the same time continues the New Comedy tradition. When Timon is in the midst of his wedding ceremonies, he is told that Fortune has withdrawn her favours from him: he is informed by a 'shippwrackte sayler' that his 'shippes are drown'd / In Neptune's waves'.[123] This sudden reversal of Fortune turns Timon into an uncompromising hater of mankind. It seems as though the comic structure of the play is thus turned into a tragedy; yet the play is not merely *called* a comedy, it is also made to end like one, although the ending seems artificially contrived: after Timon has struck his 'friends' with his spade, he is given a final monologue which he addresses to the audience as the play's Epilogue. Here he appears transformed, he suddenly becomes humble and mild, his 'fury doth abate' and his heart 'lays aside his hate'. As 'Timon doffs Timon', [124] the audience is asked to show true love towards him and receive him again as a member of the city. Like some major characters in Shakespeare's comedies, Timon in the anonymous comedy has passed from folly to humility. He has achieved this with the help of stoic virtues. The emphasis with which stoic virtues are proclaimed in this play is significant; by acquiring these virtues, Timon is finally re-integrated into society.[125]

In a sense, Shakespeare's own *Timon* can be seen as the very climax of his *humanist* reception of the New Comedy tradition, because here, more than in any other play of his, the educational and didactic concern is given free rein; here he has, as it were, allowed the strategy of Lucian or, for that matter, of Erasmus to 'prevail' over the impact of Plautine comedy. What Shakespeare does in his own *Timon of Athens* is something very radical: he turns the 'romantic' plot structure of New Comedy upside down and then fuses it with the pattern of the *de casibus* structure. The radical reversal of the plot pattern of comedy produces a play at whose beginning a man is shown in harmony with society, and only later does it become evident that this impression is deceptive. Unlike the traditional comedy pattern, the play does not begin with a situation of impending threat or of social conflict. Instead, we see Timon when he has already reached the climax of his reputation, and a little later the first signs of

[122]   This point has already been made by Bulman, op. cit., p. 114n.
[123]   Op. cit., p.317.
[124]   Op. cit., p.339.
[125]   Bullough recognizes only 'stoic commonplaces' (p.233) in the play. The philosopher Stilpo is an allusion to Stilpon of Megara who is mentioned in the ninth letter of Book I of Seneca's *Epistulae Morales*.

his imminent fall begin to appear. Yet, on the other hand, the play is no mere tragedy either, especially since the satirical and the comic elements form an essential part of its structure. Whereas in the anonymous comedy Timon's fall is caused by a malevolent Fortune, in Shakespeare's play it is Timon himself who brings about his fall, although the beginning of the play dramatizes the theme of the capriciousness of Fortune. Before beginning his journey (a romance element), he perverts all the values and virtues that uphold human society into their 'contraries' (IV, i, 20).

The plot of Shakespeare's *Timon* results from the failings of the hero himself. Timon is not only unable to recognize the world as it is, but he is also ignorant of his true self, of the ultimate motives of his actions and the real nature of values. Timon, who at the beginning of the play is reported to be wise, is revealed by his actions to be an utter fool. His kindness and generosity are shown to be sham, manifestations merely of his egotistic pride. As his love of mankind was so far from genuine, it degenerates at once into hatred.

Shakespeare's dramatic strategy in the opening part of his play is particularly close to that of Lucian. The Poet describes a work of his containing the moral that man should beware of fickle Fortune. The Painter replies: 'A thousand moral paintings I can show / That shall demonstrate these quick blows of Fortune's' (I,i,90 – 91), and he adds a major cause of the reversal of man's Fortune, namely his deception by flatterers, thus anticipating Timon's fortune. In his dialogue on *Slander*, Lucian, too, discusses the reversal of a man's fortune by flatterers and he demonstrates his 'moral' by a painting, reminding us of the discussion of art in Shakespeare's *Timon*. Lucian demonstrates his main points by describing the painting 'Slander' by the famous painter Apelles. The picture shows how Apelles was slandered by his rival Antiphilus through envy of his favour at court and jealousy. Lucian then continues the description of this painting in the following way:

> On the right [. . .] sits a man with very large ears [. . .] extending his hand to Slander [. . .] Near him stand two women – Ignorance, I think, and Suspicion. On the other side, Slander is coming up, a woman beautiful beyond measure [. . .] evincing as she does fury and wrath by carrying in her left hand a blazing torch and with the other dragging by the hair a young man who stretches out his hands to heaven [. . .] there are two women in attendance on Slander [. . .] According to the interpretation of them given me by the guide to the picture, one was Treachery and the other Deceit. They were followed by a woman dressed in deep mourning [. . .] Repentance, I think, her name was.[126]

---

[126] *Slander* in: *Lucian*, transl. by A.M. Harmon, Loeb Classical Library (London/ Cambridge, Mass., 1915), I, 363, 365, 367. On personification in Shakespeare's Plays cf. H. Zimmermann, *Die Personifikation im Drama Shakespeares* (Heidelberg, 1975).

This description is given a function which is strikingly similar to the painting described by Shakespeare's Poet. The dialogue, which was very popular in Renaissance Italy, is also referred to by Alberti in his treatise *Della Pittura*. He recommends Apelles' *Slander* as a 'bella invenzione' and claims that personifications are a subject where the painter may successfully vie with the poet. Sandro Botticelli relished the antique 'bella invenzione' as a welcome opportunity for developing his own masterful allegorical personifications.[127] Here we see the danger of focussing too exclusively on the Morality tradition in our search for the origins of dramatic personifications in Elizabethan drama.

By being unable to distinguish between a flatterer and a friend and by avenging himself on the whole of society with his hatred, Timon has discarded an essential aspect of humanist teaching. In the woods he meets not only the Banditti but also Alcibiades, who has been banished from the town of Athens. Whereas Alcibiades succeeds in becoming reunited with society, Timon refuses to establish contact with the Athenians and ends in his cave in utter isolation. It is, I think, a masterful stroke on Shakespeare's part that Alcibiades is accompanied by Courtesans, who are certainly meant to remind us of a favourite element in New Comedy plots and who are part of the society of comedy. Timon, however, cannot but hate the Courtesans, regarding them merely as bearers of disease and instances of moral perversion, and since he denies their being in any way human, they in return call him a 'monster' (IV, iii, 88). Apemantus, who clearly represents the satirical and Lucianic perspective, is right in his remark that Timon has never known 'The middle of humanity', but was familiar only with 'the extremity of both ends' (IV, iii, 300 – 302). We might say, in other words, that he refused to accept the virtue of moderation to which Erasmus, following classical humanism, subscribed.

In one way *Timon of Athens* is very similar to the anonymous *Timon* comedy: the ultimate purpose of both plays is, of course, a *corrective* one. The audience are not only made to see the immaturity of Timon's bounty, but they are also reminded of those basically stoic virtues by which the blows of Fortune can be withstood. If, in the anonymous comedy, Timon makes his peace with human society, in Shakespeare's *Timon of Athens* society makes its peace with him, albeit in a *post mortem* act of forgiveness which brings out the basic nobility of his character. This finds expression in Alcibiades' comments on Timon's epitaph: 'rich conceit / Taught thee to make vast Neptune weep for aye / On thy low grave, on faults *forgiven*. Dead / Is *noble* Timon . . .' (V, iv, 77 – 80, italics mine). Here Shakespeare is approaching the 'solution' of the final plays, where the same virtues emerge and where the healing power of art becomes a major theme.

---

[127] R. Lightbown, *Sandro Botticelli. Life and Work* (London, 1978), I, 124. L.B. Alberti, *Della Pittura*, ed. L. Mallé (Firenze, 1950), p.99.

8 Sandro Botticelli: *La Calunnia*

3. The 'romances'

If it may seem problematic to assume that after 1600 the so-called tragicomedies appeared as a new genre in the Shakespearean canon, then a similar reservation must be made with regard to the romances.[128] Of course, their distinctive tone, which is not easy to define, is somewhat different from that of the earlier plays. There is the frequently noted acquiescence in the will of the gods, who are directly invoked by prayers, and classical mythology is used abundantly. Human virtues such as patience and forgiveness are emphasized. The happy ending is brought about by the oracle of Apollo, the epiphany of Diana or Jupiter, by the help of some divine intervention, or by white magic. In her interesting book, Joan Hartwig makes the point that these plays have to be seen as Shakespeare's version of the genre of tragicomedy, and she thinks that this 'new' genre is also the cause of the great emphasis on art and artifice. Hartwig is right in pointing out that the last plays are presented as an artifice which at first 'seems more vital than life, more real',[129] and art becomes 'a focusing agent for reality',[130] so that 'we can accept, in Shakespeare's plays, the poetic lie as truth'.[131] Although these comments are correct, I am not so sure whether the tragicomic structure of these plays is *entirely* new, because Shakespeare started to move towards the tragicomic vision early in his development. And Calderwood has shown recently that Shakespeare in his *Henry IV* was much concerned with the relationship between the historical *sujet* and the fictional, 'lying' character of poetic drama.[132] Shakespeare knew that the tragicomic vision presents the most comprehensive view of man. And if for a moment we look back to *Errors*, we recognize that already in this play the theme of art as artifice is present, although it is not directly articulated. The world of *Errors*, with the most daring doubling of the twin motif, is artificial in the highest degree, and yet it appears 'more vital than life, more real', so that we can accept the illusion, the 'lie' as truth. The major difference between this comedy and his dramatic strategy in the late plays lies in the fact that in *Errors* the audience *are not made aware* of the artifice as art. Nevertheless, through this artifice, the healing effect of social re-integration is achieved, and in this there is an astonishing similarity to the 'romances'.

In recent times the question has increasingly been asked whether the last plays 'are really romances'.[133] One thing is certain: they clearly reflect the

---

[128] On recent research on the romances cf. F.D. Hoeniger, 'Shakespeare's Romances since 1958: A Retrospect', *ShS*, 29 (1976), 110.

[129] J. Hartwig, *Shakespeare's Tragicomic Vision* (Baton Rouge, 1972), p.25.

[130] Ibid., p.21.

[131] Ibid., p.32.

[132] J.L. Calderwood, *Metadrama in Shakespeare's Henriad* (London, 1979).

[133] C.T. Childress, 'Are Shakespeare's Last Plays Really Romances?', in: *Shakespeare's Late Plays, Essays in Honor of Charles Crow*, ed. R.C. Tobias and P.G.

humanist tradition and express the belief that a malevolent Fortune and the evil forces in man can be overcome by virtues such as faith, patience, forgiveness, and piety. As we have seen, these themes had been present in Shakespeare's plays from the beginning of his dramatic career. Thus *Errors* indirectly suggested the strength of patience and the superiority of mercy over justice, and *Two Gentlemen* demonstrated the necessity of forgiveness. It also seems that, when he composed his 'romances', Shakespeare returned to classical dramatic conventions and made abundant use of a dramaturgic insight he had acquired from his study of the New Comedy tradition, namely that the plot built around the 'nodus erroris' lends itself to a presentation of a comprehensive view of man, his proneness to being deceived by appearance no less than his liability to error in his character development. It has also been rightly pointed out that 'the identification of recovered children by clothing, jewellery, or special marks', as it recurs in *Pericles*, *Cymbeline*, and *The Winter's Tale*', is a characteristic motif of the plots of New Comedy.[134]

Let us begin with a brief look at *Pericles*, the last three Acts of which are undoubtedly from Shakespeare's own hand, while in the first two Acts he seems at least to have had some share.[135] Although it is the least satisfactory of the final plays, it is nevertheless very characteristic of them as a whole.

The occurrence of Gower as Chorus reminds us that Shakespeare draws on Gower's retelling of the *Apollonius* romance; yet with his own *Pericles* he has not just written a play about a medieval romance, because he must have been aware of the classical origins of this source. The choice of this *sujet* for a play is in itself significant because it has been known for a long time that 'Greek romances have a curious affinity to drama',[136] although the older theory of a common origin of Greek novel and New Comedy is incorrect.[137] Yet it has been shown by a critical analysis of the *Apollonius* romance[138] how this novel adopts suggestions of already existing literary types and how it is a mixture of

Zolbrod (Athens/Ohio, 1974), p.44–55; cf. also H. Castrop, 'Romanze, Tragikomödie und Satyrspiel in *The Winter's Tale*', *ShJW* (1987), 57ff.

[134] J.H.P. Pafford, ed., *The Winter's Tale* (London, 1963), p.xlix, note; cf. also C.C. Coulter, 'The Plautine Tradition in Shakespeare', *JEGP*, 19 (1920), 66–83.

[135] Cf. F.D. Hoeniger, ed., *Pericles*, The New Arden Shakespeare (London, 1963), p.liii–lvi.

[136] C. Gesner, *Shakespeare and the Greek Romance* (Lexington, 1970), p.83.

[137] For the old view see Tillyard, *Shakespeare's Early Comedies* (p.47), quoted in Gesner, op. cit., p.55; for the present state of scholarship see C.W. Müller, 'Der griechische Roman' in: *Griechische Literatur*, ed. E. Vogt, *Neues Handbuch der Literaturwissenschaft* (Wiesbaden, 1981), II, 377.

[138] The basic study on the romance of *Apollonius* is by E. Klebs, *Die Erzählung von Apollonius aus Tyrus. Eine geschichtliche Untersuchung über ihre lateinische Urform und ihre späteren Bearbeitungen* (Berlin, 1899). A modern critical interpretation has been offered by F.P. Waiblinger, ed. and transl., *Historia Apollonii Regis Tyri. Die Geschichte vom König Apollonius* (München, 1978), p.12–13.

different elements and traditions. The plot, made up of separations, adventures, misfortunes, recognitions, is basically similar to the error plot of classical comedy, and there are further parallels to classical historiography, to the epic and also to tragedy. As in Greek tragicomedies, the tragic ending is prevented only by a *deus ex machina*. There are above all some particularly close analogies between the *Apollonius* and New Comedy. The plot pattern of the romance and that of New Comedy have in common an initially disturbed society and the final restitution of social harmony. On several occasions the *Apollonius* itself refers to the performance of a comedy and thus provides a metapoetic comment on its own intrinsic quality. Thaisa's delivery into a brothel in particular creates a situation akin to New Comedy, with its comic potential and its stock figures of the wicked pimp who is finally punished. Shakespeare adopted this dramatic situation in his own *Pericles*.

Furthermore, it is interesting that in tone, spirit and in its 'dramatic' quality the *Apollonius* sometimes comes very close to the Plautine *Rudens*, a play which clearly reflects humanist attitudes and whose plot is itself entirely of a romance character. Its fisher scene (II, i) has interesting affinities with that of Shakespeare's *Pericles* (II, i). From a thematic point of view, too, there is a basic correspondence between *Apollonius* and *Rudens*, namely the similar faith of the characters in divine guidance and their love towards their fellow human beings, a love which in both texts is succinctly defined by the term 'pietas'. And in *Pericles* this essential humanist virtue is equally prominent and is presented in moving situations; the Epilogue expressly reminds the audience of other related qualities such as 'virtue', 'truth', 'faith', 'loyalty' (5ff.). What this very interesting blending in *Pericles* shows is that the important tradition of medieval romance is not something alien or new to New Comedy, but rather a development of a tendency that was already an essential constituent of classical drama. If, then, Shakespeare based one of his plays on the romance of *Apollonius*, it follows that he nevertheless remained within the New Comedy tradition.

Cymbeline is a play that has often been unduly neglected, yet it has many qualities of its own. The world of this romance is characterized by its intentional 'artificiality' and by a pervasive classical atmosphere. Wilson Knight correctly remarked that *Cymbeline* contains an 'immense wealth of classical and mythological allusions'.[139] For example, Imogen, before she falls asleep, prays to the gods to protect her. By the mythological associations the whole situation (II, ii, 34ff.) is, as it were, turned into a work of art. This has the effect that the audience will remain confident that Iachimo who, observing the sleeping Imogen, makes his notes in order to set his intrigue in motion,

---

[139] Quoted from J. Nosworthy, ed., *Cymbeline*, The New Arden Shakespeare (London, 1966), p.lxvii.

will not succeed in proving her adultery and in working out a tragedy. Nevertheless, the realm of tragedy is approached, and tragic emotions as well as comic ones are released before the final harmony is established. This is achieved by Jupiter's appearance, which Nosworthy has called a 'heavy weight thrown into the comic scale.'[140] However, the structural pattern of *Cymbeline* should be seen in the tradition established by Shakespeare's own classical *Errors* with its tragicomic 'ambiguity' resolved by the device of the *deus ex machina*, for which Shakespeare had a special preference in his last plays.

Let us recall that already in *Errors* the suspicion of adultery plays an important role. In *Cymbeline*, however, it becomes far more prominent. What seems remarkable is the fact that the epiphany of Jupiter, who prevents a tragedy and helps to achieve a comedy, had already occurred with the same function in *Amphitruo*,[141] Shakespeare's second source for *Errors*, the difference being that there he himself had been a party in the play and that by his own adultery he had himself caused the confusions of the human characters. Note that in *Cymbeline* he is invoked precisely because he is an expert in 'adulteries' (IV, iv, 33). I would claim that we understand far better Shakespeare's intentions in *Cymbeline* if we see that the plot, being of a 'romance' character, was developed within the dramatic tradition of New Comedy and not in analogy to Elizabethan prose romances, the *Faerie Queene* or medieval romances such as *Guy of Warwick*.[142]

In *Cymbeline* Shakespeare did not simply return to dramaturgic techniques of the native medieval 'presentational' drama, as Mowat claims. She starts from the correct observation that, whereas in the plays prior to the romances there is a tendency to a relatively sparse use of soliloquy and aside, in *Cymbeline* we find, by contrast, 'the burgeoning wealth of four hundred thirty lines of soliloquy' and she adds that this 'revival of the soliloquy' is accompanied by 'obtrusive entrance announcements and doggerel exit signals'.[143] The conclusion Mowat is inclined to draw from this is, however, unconvincing. Despite these more 'primitive' elements of scenic dramaturgy, *Cymbeline* is by no means more 'presentational' than earlier plays. It seems to me far more likely that Shakespeare is here resuming the less 'realistic' dramatic techniques he had employed in *Two Gentlemen*, a play that anticipates the 'romances' in a remarkable way. And for his *Two Gentlemen* he had adopted the conventions and devices not from 'presentational tactics', but from the comedies of Plautus as a means 'to effect sporadic audience disengagement'.[144]

---

[140] Op. cit., p.l.
[141] *Amphitruo* has already been suggested as a possible model for Jupiter's epiphany in *Cymbeline* by Salingar, although he ignores the important connection of the adultery motif: 'Time and Art in Shakespeare's Romances', *RD*, 9 (1966), 26.
[142] Nosworthy, op. cit., p.xlvii.
[143] B.A. Mowat, *The Dramaturgy of Shakespeare's Romances* (Athens/Georgia, 1976),p.43.
[144] Mowat, ibid.

Thus, in order to explain Shakespeare's new interest in 'taking [. . .] the audience in and out of the illusion of reality', we need not refer to medieval 'presentational spectacle',[145] which is not what Shakespeare is intending, but should instead look to the tradition of New Comedy. This tradition presents the 'classical frame'[146] of which Nosworthy rather vaguely speaks. Thus, we clearly have the tying and untangling of a *nodus erroris*, and 'error' in this play implies both outward deception and 'inward' aberration. We also find a five-Act structure that makes good dramatic sense and corresponds to the Evanthian rules, while the influence of the native tradition is reflected in the fact that Shakespeare has greatly extended the plot and does not observe the unities of time and place.

It has been said, and rightly, that the quality of *Cymbeline* 'lies beyond the romance orbit',[147] and this provides the play with its richness. One aspect of this richness is the humanist satire through New Comedy. The satire is used to expose the characters' foolishness, as, for example, in the case of Cloten. Yet the climax of this humanist satire, which we have called Lucianic, is the dramatically effective soliloquy of Posthumus, whose name is, by the way, also mentioned in Act II, scene iv, in Plautus's comedy *Aulularia* (I, 162 – 164). The first part of it is a linguistic reflection of his wild thoughts and emotions at the news of Imogen's supposed infidelity. With the words 'Could I find out / The woman's part in me' (II, v, 19 – 20), he changes over to listing a catalogue of all the traditional satirical charges against women, and he even satirizes this traditional satire as being far too mild. What he does not realize, however, is the fact that he is *falsely* accusing a woman, and that he, the man, is to be blamed for his own credulity and ignorance of the nature of his beloved, which has caused him to be deceived.

The play's ending in harmony and concord is not easily contrived. It is important that the epiphany of Jupiter, which happens as a 'real' dramatic event on stage, is nevertheless motivated by Posthumus's *dream*. The dream motif, which we have seen was already important in *Errors*, suggests nothing less than that, while on the one hand the characters experience the religious emotion of awe as they become aware of the benignity of a divine being, the impulses for the achievement of social harmony must come from the human beings themselves. What is required of them if they want to turn tragedy into comedy is the act of pardoning for which New Comedy, with its origins in Euripidean tragicomedy,[148] provides an appropriate frame.

---

[145] Mowat, p.58.
[146] Op. cit., p.xlix.
[147] Nosworthy, op. cit., p.lxxvii.
[148] For a more recent discussion of the dependence of New Comedy on Euripides cf. B. Knox, 'Euripidean Comedy' in: *The Rarer Action*, eds. A. Cheuse and R. Koffler (New Brunswick, 1970), p.68 – 96.

It is not altogether inconceivable that Shakespeare may have had some knowledge of Euripides,[149] and in particular of his tragicomedies. A good case has been made for the influence of the Euripidean *Alkestis* on *The Winter's Tale*, and there are indeed connections between Hermione and Alcestis, Leontes and Admetus, Paulina and Hercules.[150] The closest analogy is, of course, between Alkestis's rebirth into life and Hermione's symbolic rebirth through the device of the statue. The oracle of Apollo, a further motif from classical tragedy, has rightly been called the 'pivot' of the entire play.[151] Although these reminiscences of Euripidean tragedy are undeniable, it would certainly be a mistake to suggest that the classical influence is confined to just this tradition. *The Winter's Tale*, in particular, is a highly composite work of art, amalgamating and fusing different traditions.

If we compare *The Winter's Tale* with its source, we find that there is little in Greene's *Pandosto* that would account for the essential humanist dimension of Shakespeare's play.[152] Our special attention should focus on Autolycus, who has no real counterpart in *Pandosto*. It has been claimed that in creating Autolycus Shakespeare drew on Greene's description of cony-catching.[153] There have also been attempts to place him firmly in the native popular tradition.[154] No doubt his comic potential and his songs with their popular character as well as the fact that he sells ballads would tend to support this view. He has also been seen as having been derived 'from Shakespeare's knowledge of contemporary life'.[155] He is a strikingly original character, yet we must also ask: why did Shakespeare give him the name of the classical thief and cheat? I would prefer to interpret him as a further major example of Shakespeare's masterful blending of native and classical elements. Autolycus very much takes after his father, who is Mercury, the god of thieves. As we have seen, Mercury is important elsewhere in Shakespeare, and especially in the Plautine *Amphitruo*. There he acts as the god of thieves *par excellence*, as he has to assist Jupiter to steal the love of Amphitruo's wife. With his art of

---

[149] On Euripidean tragicomedy cf., for example, H.D.F. Kitto, *Greek Tragedy. A Literary Study* (London, 1961), p.311 – 329. Kitto points out that Euripidean tragicomedy tends towards 'sheer theatricality' (324) and 'artificiality of contrivance' (327); cf. also B. Seidensticker, *Palintonos Harmonia, Studien zu komischen Elementen in der griechischen Tragödie*, Hypomnemata, 72 (Göttingen, 1982).

[150] J.H.P. Pafford, ed., *The Winter's Tale*, The New Arden Shakespeare (London, 1963), p.lviii.

[151] Pafford, ibid.

[152] It is, however, interesting that even Greene's *Pandosto* reflects a minor detail of the humanist tradition. One of the characters in this work bears the seemingly unique name 'Capnio'. This is in fact the humanist name which the famous Johannes Reuchlin gave himself by translating the meaning of his German name (= 'smoke') into Greek.

[153] Cf. Pafford, op. cit., p.xxx.

[154] R. Weimann, 'Laughing with the Audience . . .', *ShS*, 22 (1969).

[155] Pafford, op. cit., p.lxxxi, note 3.

deceiving and gulling, his son Autolycus is a representative of a character type of Roman comedy. We should therefore not be surprised to find that in the Plautine *Bacchides* the character Nicobulus, suspecting that he has been cheated of his money, exclaims: 'I've trusted my gold to an Autolycus of a friend!' ('Deceptus sum, Autolyco hospiti aurum credidi' I, 275).[159]

The fact that Autolycus is temporarily a servant of Florizel and that he promotes the happiness of this disguised prince may furthermore be interpreted as reflecting the Plautine tradition of the *servus callidus*. Paradoxically, it is through Autolycus's deception that the reunion can be achieved, and so he can say of himself that he had done 'good [. . .] against my will' (V, ii, 124). His habit of deceit and trickery is used to bring about the comic harmony of the final design. Just as the 'lifting' situation in *The Book of Thomas More* (cf. p. 192) serves a satirical and specifically Lucianic function, so does Autolycus's purse-taking. In a way similar to the 'lifter', Autolycus exposes folly in another character. He pretends to be a man looking for pity after having been beaten up, robbed of his money and left lying on the ground. When the Clown tries to help him up, Autolycus has no difficulty in taking advantage of the Clown's naive foolishness. He then makes his satirical comments and says that he used to serve a prince but was whipped out of court. Whereas the Clown foolishly remarks that 'there's no virtue whipt out of the court' (IV, iii, 91 – 92), the audience know that the Prince as well as Hermione and Perdita have been similarly expelled from thence. Autolycus, who likewise becomes a dupe because he is unaware of the purpose of the disguise-intrigue, is the last major instance of Shakespeare's Lucianic colouring of elements taken from Plautine comedy. Given the considerable humanist implications of the Autolycus scenes, we no longer need to ask ourselves why Shakespeare has provided this character with a classical name. It is also significant that the Autolycus scenes in *The Winter's Tale* contain typical elements of Plautine comic dramaturgy such as disguise, eavesdropping, asides and brilliant role play, sparkling with comic vitality. Furthermore, one could demonstrate how the great scene IV, iv, with its strategy of observing and overhearing, of soliloquizing and of simultaneous acting on two separate parts of the stage, exhibits a decidedly Plautine dramaturgy.

In *The Winter's Tale*, where the opposition between nature and art plays a central role, we find the interesting reference to Giulio Romano, Raffael's favourite pupil, a reference which, to my knowledge, has not been commented on in any greater detail. It seems however, well worth asking why Shakespeare singled out Giulio Romano and why he praised him as 'that rare Italian

---

[156] Much earlier, M.Y. Hughes, too, had argued that the character of Autolycus may have been suggested mainly through the Plautine tradition, 'A classical vs. a social approach to Shakespeare's Autolycus', *Shakespeare Association Bulletin*, 15 (1940), 219 – 226. The *locus classicus*, where Autolycus's deeds are described, is the *Homeric Hymns*, IV,iii.

master [. . .] who, had he himself eternity and could put breath into his work, would beguile Nature of her custom, so perfectly he is her ape.' (V, ii, 97ff.). We shall soon see that a discussion of the individuality of Giulio's art will serve to illuminate more fully the humanist context in which Shakespeare worked. Giulio Romano has recently attracted renewed international attention through the 1989 Exhibition in Mantova. Studies by E.H. Gombrich and others written to mark this event show that the usual label 'mannerism' entirely fails to do justice to Giulio Romano's impressive work. A visit to the famous Palazzo del Te in Mantova, for example, overwhelms us with the intensity, the expressive force and richness as well as the originality of this artist.[157] Without refraining from including elements of cruelty and violence,[158] Giulio appeals to the whole gamut of human emotions.[159] One begins to realize that Shakespeare must have felt an affinity to this man and his work.

What Shakespeare and Giulio Romano had in common was not only a most profound creative power, but also an almost unlimited capacity for rapidly adopting ideas from various sources and traditions, and then transforming them into something 'rich and strange'.[160] This aspect of Giulio's genius was first commented on by Vasari when he described it as 'vario, ricco e copioso d'invenzione ed artificio'. To begin with a fact important for our comparison: as Giulio grew up in Rome, he became familiar with the revival of classical drama, especially of Plautus and Terence. In the Virgilian city of Mantova, at the court of Federico Gonzaga with its humanist atmosphere, Giulio was assigned the task of scenery and costume designer. His familiarity with the theatre and his profound sense of drama are amply reflected by the expressions, groupings, gestures and movements of the figures in his paintings.[161] Even emotions are expressed by his theatrical idiom.[162] Yet at the same time he is capable of great and intense pathos, as for example in the Sala dei Giganti in the Palazzo del Te, where the gestures and movements transcend all conventions and restrictions.[163] Here an illusion of reality is created which is, in the literal sense of the word, breathtaking.

The classical basis of Giulio's art, however, goes far beyond his familiarity with classical *theatre*. The name 'Julio Romano' is in itself a declaration of his

---

[157] On Shakespeare's knowledge of Giulio Romano cf. Pafford, op. cit., p.150, n.96.

[158] M. Tafuri, 'Giulio Romano: linguaggio, mentalità, committenti' in: E.H. Gombrich, M. Tafuri et al., *Giulio Romano* (Milano, 1989), p.29.

[159] E.H. Gombrich, ' "Anticamente moderni e modernamente antichi": Note sulla fortuna critica di Giulio Romano pittore', in: *Giulio Romano*, p.13.

[160] S.F. Pagden, 'Giulio Romano pittore e disegnatore a Roma', in: *Giulio Romano*, p.65; Vasari quoted from Gombrich, op. cit., p.11.

[161] H. Burns, ' "Quelle cose antique et moderne belle de Roma", Giulio Romano, il teatro, l'antico', in: *Giulio Romano*, p.237.

[162] Ibid.

[163] K. Oberhuber, 'Giulio Romano pittore e disegnatore a Mantova' in: *Giulio Romano*, p.157.

artistic orientation.[164] He grew up in Rome and from his infancy was confronted there with the great examples of classical, particularly Roman art, such as the great column of Trajan. He studied classical sculpture, and he personally owned a collection of classical sculptures.[165] This explains why his figures often have a sculpture-like three-dimensionality, although he was not a sculptor, as Shakespeare critics have wrongly assumed. Giulio, however, was far from being a mere imitator of the classics. It was his friend Pietro Aretino, himself an author of comedies inspired in part by Plautus, who was the first to notice that his art is a most skilful transformation of classical suggestions, that, in fact, it contains 'concetti anticamente moderni e modernamente antiche',[166] and in recent times this has rightly been called an achievement of assimilation.[167] In this respect Giulio goes beyond even Raffael because in this transformation he exhibits a greater freedom and inventiveness than his master. More importantly: this transformation is carried out with a strong sense of humour[168] and ironic playfulness. The most recent attempt to define this quality of humanist 'ludus' is by Tafuri, who states that Giulio displays a strong Lucianic strategy, that he 'sembra introdurre un personale lucianismo'.[169] Tafuri expressly compares him with the great Italian humanist Leon Battista Alberti, who himself wrote decidedly Lucianic texts.[170]

Part of this playful Lucianic quality is his foible for mixing different elements, styles, and motifs, and this tendency was no doubt enhanced by his extreme intellectual receptiveness. In particular, Giulio employs a poetics of contrast,[171] because he likes to oppose the sublime and courtly with the popular.[172] There is a plebeian element in his art; he requires it in order to provide his work with its bipolarity. Romano achieves another form of contrast by the juxtaposition of seriousness and playfulness in one and the same work. With this, he succeeds in creating the classical ideal of both *varietas* and *concinnitas*.[173] It might be objected here that other Renaissance artists also worked with the principle of contrast, yet it has been pointed out that hardly anywhere else are these elements used with the same radical, uncompromising consistency as in the work of Giulio Romano.[174]

---

[164] Burns, op. cit., p.227; his real family name was Pippi.
[165] Burns, op. cit., p.233.
[166] Quoted from Gombrich, op. cit., p.11.
[167] Cf. H. Burns, op. cit., p.242.
[168] Tafuri, op. cit., p.59.
[169] Op. cit., p.53.
[170] On Alberti's Lucianism cf. E. Garin, *Studi su Leon Battista Alberti* in: Rinascite e rivoluzioni. Movimenti culturali dal XIV al XVIII secolo (Roma, Bari, ²1976), p.133ff. and E. Mattioli, *Luciano e l'Umanesimo* (Napoli, 1980).
[171] Tafuri, op. cit., p.35.
[172] Ibid., p.37.
[173] Tafuri, op. cit., p.20.
[174] Tafuri, op. cit., p.59.

9 Giulio Romano: Mars and Venus pursuing Adonis; part of a fresco
in the Palazzo del Tel at Mantova

10   Part of a painting by Giovanni da Udine on the ceiling
of the Villa Farnesina, Rome

The number of similarities between the works of Shakespeare and Giulio is
very surprising: every single element that has been found to be essential to
Giulio's art is important for Shakespeare as well, although, of course, Giulio's
art does not acquire Shakespearean dimensions. This being the case, we are
again confronted with the greatness of the humanist basis on which these
artists worked. Rather than commenting on Giulio's art in detail, we shall
conclude our survey by singling out one feature of his work: its underlying
'pagan' sensuality which shines through even when the ostensible subject is
'spiritual'. This new feeling for the body is, of course, a side-effect of the
rediscovery of the classics and their works of art. In Shakespearean comedy,
this sensuality is often played down by the critics. We find this same tendency
even in tragedy (as a means of contrast), in his 'Italian' play *Romeo and Juliet*,
in which Mercutio talks about the romantically enamoured Romeo in the
following way:

> Now will he sit under a medlar tree,
> And wish his mistress were that kind of fruit
> As maids call medlars, when they laugh alone.
> O, Romeo, that she were, O that she were
> An open [-arse], thou a pop'rin pear!   (II, i, 34 – 38)

This violently sexual pun, forming a contrast to the courtly, romantic love of Romeo, finds its painted parallel in the artistic context of Raffael and Giulio, on the painted ceiling of the Farnesina Loggia in Rome, which was executed by Giulio Romano and others after a design by Raffael. The 'painted pun' to which I am referring, is by Giovanni da Udine.[175]

But to return to *The Winter's Tale*. From what we have seen, it appears that Shakespeare's direct reference to the art of Giulio makes sense not only in the final recognition scene; rather, the play in its entirety is based on artistic principles that have a lot in common with Giulio. There is a comparable artistic atmosphere at the courts of Shakespeare's Leontes and of Federico Gonzaga. The passionate, eruptive opening with its tragic pathos as well as the transformations of suggestions from classical mythology, from Plautine dramaturgy and from the Euripidean *Alkestis* bear a considerable resemblance to Giulio's art. The same is true of the strikingly picture-like quality of Act IV, where the opposition between art and nature is discussed for the first time in the play. Through the presence of Perdita in the rustic world of the peasants celebrating the feast of sheep-shearing, we have the element of contrast which is particularly important for the artist to whom Shakespeare seems to have been strongly drawn.

At the same time Shakespeare reaches beyond Giulio. It has been shown that Shakespeare here exploits the idea going back to Aristotle and Plato that 'art itself is nature'.[176] Perdita's 'role in the sheep-shearing is the creation of Art',[177] in that process she becomes a 'goddess' and 'queen'. Finally it will be seen that she *is* the queen by nature that she has become by art; yet, Shakespeare complicates the issue by suggesting that in the final analysis she is still a fictional character in a work of art, and the same, of course, holds true for Hermione, although with a difference. The statue 'performed' by Hermione is life itself in a higher sense than a figure in Giulio's painting because it has been refined by long years of suffering and patience, and by this quality Hermione is capable of acts of forgiveness and of rebirth. When she steps down from the pedestal, she destroys the artistic illusion of realism which she had

---

[175] Here Jones and Penny have suggested the possible influence of Aretino who, in defending his lascivious sonnets, which were illustrated with drawings by Giulio Romano and Marcantonio Raimondi, referred to a *classical* sculpture in the Chigi collection. (R. Jones and N. Penny, *Raffael* [New Haven/London, 1983], p.185).

[176] E.W. Taylor, *Nature and Art in Renaissance Literature* (New York/London, 1964), p.135.

[177] Ibid., p.137.

11 Giulio Romano from Vasari's Lives

created; her art has become nature, and yet she continues to be a fictional character in a play.

Because *The Tempest*, like *Errors*, strictly observes the classical unities, the play has often evoked classical associations. Indeed, it may be called Shakespeare's humanist 'summa', since specifically humanist themes which have interested him from the time of his early *Errors* now find their final resolution. He adds, however, a new theme in Gonzalo's vision of Utopia, and thus takes up, as it were, the challenge of the great humanist Thomas More. It is significant in this context how Shakespeare emphasizes Prospero's learning, how Prospero takes pride in his 'books' (I, ii, 166), and how he refers to his study of the 'liberal arts' (I, ii, 73). Much has been written on the complexity of this play, but one major aspect has been neglected, namely the way in which Shakespeare once more activates and draws upon the dramaturgy of New Comedy. However, most critics have failed to recognize the extent of this New Comedy basis, because they have been content merely to accept Baldwin's theory that Shakespeare took over the five-Act division from Terence. This has blinded them to the considerable impact Plautus has exerted on the structure and theme of *The Tempest*.[178] The play's structural organization into *protasis*, *epitasis*, and *catastrophe* corresponds to the Evanthian definition. The Act division of the Folio text makes very good sense: the *epitasis* proper starts with Act II, and the beginning of Act V coincides with the preparation of the catastrophe, because Prospero, who at the end of Act IV has left the stage, re-enters immediately, wearing his magic robes and trying to untie the knot.[179] *The Tempest* confirms our argument that, by his intensive study of Plautine plays, Shakespeare learnt how to make dramatic capital out of the convention of Act division; and it is significant that those plays which are particularly closely related to the Plautine tradition, such as *Much Ado About Nothing*,

---

[178] The widely known article by B. Knox on the Plautine background of *The Tempest* ('*The Tempest* and the Ancient Comic Tradition', *English Stage Comedy*, English Institute Essays, 1954) is too superficial when it seeks to establish a close connection between Ariel and Caliban on the one hand and two types of slaves on the other. This has been justly criticized as unconvincing by L.E. Barber ('*The Tempest* and New Comedy', *SQ*, 21 [1970], 207–212). Nevertheless Knox recognized that Ariel's constant plea for freedom is strongly reminiscent of the slave's desire to become a freedman so that this motif of classical comedy was possibly one of the suggestions that helped to create the world of *The Tempest*.

[179] There is no need to claim that, in his *Tempest*, Shakespeare used a Jonsonian structure (D.C. Boughner, 'Jonsonian Structure in *The Tempest*', *SQ*, 21 [1970], 310).

Measure for Measure, *The Winter's Tale* and *Cymbeline*, all have Act divisions in the Folio, which make good dramatic sense.

The Plautine play which Shakespeare studied thoroughly when he composed his *Tempest* was *Rudens*, which had begun to interest him when he wrote his *Errors* and to which he returned in the composition of *Pericles*. It is surprising that *Rudens*, a play so highly esteemed by the humanists, has not been generally accepted as a major source of *The Tempest*.[180] *Rudens* is a complex 'speculum consuetudinis', a mirror of human actions and aberrations, and it also articulates the humanist values which, from the times of Menander, had been thought necessary for a happy and successful life. Human wickedness is not allowed to triumph, but is overcome by divine providence and benignity in conjunction with human piety. What the wicked pimp Labrax destroys is made whole again by the intervention of the gods, the family bonds are restored once more. The exiled father Daemones is reunited with his daughter Palaestra, who had been stolen, and Palaestra is married to her lover Plesidippus.

Rudens opens with the Prologue spoken by the star-god Arcturus, who at Jupiter's behest raises a sea-storm in order to prevent Labrax from stealing Palaestra and taking her to Sicily, where he wants to make a fortune by selling her. He has broken the law by failing to keep the oath he gave to Plesidippus, who wanted to free Palaestra. Then Arcturus strikes the specifically humanist note of the play. He says that ' 'Tis Jupiter, the lord of gods and men, that doth assign us each our different posts among the peoples, that we may learn of the deeds and ways of men, their reverence and loyalty, and how well each doth fare.' ('qui est imperator divom atque hominum Iuppiter, / is nos per gentis alium alia disparat, / qui facta hominum, mores, pietatem et fidem / noscamus, ut quemque adiuvet opulentia.' 9 – 12). He advises his audience to be righteous for their own profit because only in this way can they find God's grace: 'The righteous man will find God's grace by prayer more readily than will the knave.' ('facilius si qui pius est a dis supplicans, / quam qui scelestust, inveniet veniam sibi.' 26 – 27). The play emphasizes the virtue of 'pietas' throughout. When Daemones has found his daughter again, he expresses his gratitude to the gods: 'Isn't it a fact that if the gods wish to help a man, it does somehow come about that the

---

180 But cf. Salingar, *Traditions of Comedy*, p.79 and 173, and especially J.T. Svendsen, 'The Fusion of Comedy and Romance: Plautus' *Rudens* and Shakespeare's *The Tempest*' in: K.V. Hartigan, ed., *From Pen to Performance. Drama as Conceived and Performed* (Washington, D.C., 1983), p.121 – 34. Most of the analogues which I shall discuss have already been observed by Svendsen.

prayers of the pious are answered?' ('satin si cui homini dei esse bene factum volunt, / aliquo illud pacto optingit optatum piis?' 1193 – 1194). He takes his good fortune as a reward for his piety.

Yet, on the other hand, the power of the impious is strong, and human beings have to make great efforts to overcome it. Trachalio, in his desire to help the innocent and wronged woman, addresses the inhabitants of Cyrene: 'Let not the power of the impious be more potent than that of the innocent creatures [. . .] Make an example of impudence and give pudency its recompense! See ye to it that men may live here under law, and not as objects of oppression!' ('[. . .] ne impiorum potior sit pollentia / quam innocentum [. . .] statuite exemplum impudenti, date pudori praemium, / facite hic lege potius liceat quam vi victo vivere.' 618 – 621). The dramatic presentation of Palaestra's despair is impressive because she expresses it most fittingly in a soliloquy in which, believing herself to be alone, she gives vent to her thoughts and feelings:

> hoc deo complacitumst, me hoc ornatu ornatam in incertas
>   regiones timidam eiectam? [. . .]
> hancine ego partem capio ob pietatem praecipuam?
> nam hoc mi haud laborist, laborem hunc potiri,
> si erga parentem aut deos me impiavi;
> sed id si parate curavi ut caverem,
> tum hoc mi indecore, inique, inmodeste
> datis, di; nam quid habebunt sibi signi impii posthac,
> si ad hunc modum est innoxiis honor apud vos? [. . .]
> sed erile scelus me sollicitat, eius me impietas male habet.
>
>   IV, 187 – 198

> Is it really the will of God that I should be cast on a strange shore in this pitiable plight and frightened so? [. . .] Is this my reward for trying my best to do right? Why, I can suffer this and not think it suffering, if I have sinned against a parent or against the gods. But if I have been careful as could be not to do so, then, gods, you are treating me unfittingly, unfairly, unjustly. For how will the guilty be marked out by you now, if this is the way you honour the innocent? [. . .] it is my master's wickedness afflicts me, his guilt that brings me misfortune.

Yet in this play, where Venus is present in and through her Temple, the plot, although 'full of traps that cheat and catch mankind' ('in aetate hominum plurimae / fiunt trasennae, ut decipiuntur dolis.' 1235 – 1236), ends in harmony and with the celebration of a feast.

The general tone of *Rudens*, as well as its theme of human temptation, is paralleled remarkably closely in Shakespeare's *Tempest*, a play which also tries to prove the necessity of 'pietas' as the appropriate attitude towards one's fellow human beings and God; here, however, the concept is contained not in the word 'piety' but by the more general term 'virtue'. The very first scene, in which the shipwreck has occurred, is concluded by Gonzalo's comment: 'The wills above be done!' (I, i, 67). Prospero and Miranda come ashore on the island 'By Providence divine' (I, ii, 159), and Fortune has also brought Prospero's enemies to this same place. Yet Prospero and his servant Ariel are themselves agents of Providence and so are the gods, who 'preside' in *The Tempest* as well as in *Rudens*. Like Arcturus, Prospero raises a storm in order to correct unlawfulness. In both plays, greed for material gain is a weakness which breeds human misery. In *The Tempest*, characters are affected by this greed; Caliban himself complains that Prospero has deprived him of his island: 'This island's mine [. . .] Which thou tak'st from me.' (I, ii, 331 – 332). Guilt and crime have to be vanquished and forgiven in both plays, and the natural bonds have to be re-established.

It is Caliban who, among other things, represents destruction, greed and the lack of any cultural education. There is hardly a doubt that among the influences which helped to create this important character there is the wicked pimp Labrax, the villain in *Rudens*, whose name means 'fish'; in the play he is called a 'dirty beast' and he appears as a perjured, parricidal monster, impudent, impure and impious. Note that Caliban is described as 'half a fish and half a monster' (III, ii, 29); he is a 'savage beast'. He and his men are as greedy for loot as is Labrax. He is confined to a 'rock', just as Labrax sits on a rock after the shipwreck. Just as Caliban complains of having been wronged, so Labrax feels 'robbed of my rights' (711). The thought of taking revenge on the villain who caused great wrong is in *Rudens* expressed only once, when Palaestra, in her distress, prays to the goddess Venus: 'Wreak vengeance on the wicked men who have scorned thy shrine, and in thy good grace let this altar be our refuge.' ('Fac ut ulciscare nosque ut hanc tua pace aram obsidere / patiare' 698 – 699). The idea of revenge is, however, abandoned completely, because what in the end prevails is *pietas* and *venia*. Strikingly enough, we find a similar process in *The Tempest*, where Prospero praises 'The very virtue of compassion' (I, ii, 27). The motif of revenge is referred to several times, and it is even made to form an essential part of the action, since Caliban's plot is motivated by his revenge. Yet Prospero knows that if he had answered this plot by his own revenge, he would have debased himself. Instead he pronounces the maxim that 'The rarer action is / In virtue than in vengeance.' (V, i, 27 – 28): it is piety that ultimately prevails.

To realize the close connections between *Rudens* and *The Tempest* may help to bring a major aspect of Shakespeare's play into sharper focus: the nature of Prospero's humanism, as it is reflected in his treatment of Caliban. Hans Mayer has shown that Prospero, rather than being an early instance of an 'enlightened' ruler, fully identifies with a mythical world ruled by white magic, and also that Prospero's humanism fails when he is faced with the 'inhuman' monster Caliban. Prospero not only calls him a 'beast' (IV, i, 140), but also 'A devil, a born devil, on whose nature / Nurture can never stick; on whom my pains, / Humanely taken, all, all lost, quite lost [. . .]' (IV, i, 188ff.). We do not find Prospero taking pains with educating Caliban 'humanely'. It is true, Prospero renounces his revenge, decides to follow 'reason' and to set his enemies free; yet he ignores the fact that he had wronged Caliban by depriving him of his island, and he wrongs him a second time by his assumption of his incorrigibility: Prospero had certainly not anticipated Caliban's intention to be 'wise hereafter, / And seek for grace.' (V, i, 295f.).[181] It seems that Prospero's decision to exclude Caliban from human society as unworthy of it is here indirectly criticised by Shakespeare. This view is confirmed by comparing the closing scene of *Rudens*: there, the monster Labrax is finally integrated into society. Plautus nicely suggests this when Daemones invites him to dinner and Labrax accepts the invitation (1417).

There is a further plot element which Shakespeare seems to have adopted from *Rudens* in the creation of the unique world of his *Tempest*, and that is the love between Palaestra and Plesidippus, a love that finally proves stronger than the obstacles it has to overcome. Shakespeare, of course, presents the love of Miranda (note the significance of the Latin name) and Ferdinand as something much more complex and refined than that of the lovers in Plautus − in fact, he refined the 'two most rare affections' (III, i, 75). Yet it seems that Plautus provided him with the suggestion to integrate this theme in this context. Prospero feels the need to test the rareness of Miranda's and Ferdinand's love. The love trials are entirely Prospero's own idea. It is interesting that when the 'contract of true love' is to be celebrated (IV, i, 84), we are shown a whole mythological pageant with Iris, Ceres and Juno. In a way typical of the last plays, the 'theophany' is presented in the 'guise' of the gods of classical mythology, the Greek gods are used as the visual expression of the general note of piety. Here Shakespeare is again close to the *Rudens*, where the references to the gods are frequent, and where Venus plays a major role; Plesidippus, having lost his beloved, arrives at Venus's temple, where he is at first mocked by those present, who say that, as he is hungry, it is Ceres he should invoke, not Venus.

The mythological pageant put on in celebration of the union of the lovers is, of course, a kind of 'play within the play', and Shakespeare's last romance, like his other plays, is marked by a strong element of theatricality, which, again, reveals an affinity with Plautus. In a sense, *The Tempest* is Prospero's

[181] Cf. H. Mayer, *Versuche über die Oper* (Frankfurt, 1981), p.67 − 69; he refers to L.A. Fiedler's interpretation of Caliban in: *The Stranger in Shakespeare* (New York, 1972), p.234.

own creation because he acts like an implied stage director who produces the play. The Plautine scholar Niall W. Slater was right to compare Prospero with the Plautine character Pseudolus.[182] In the comedy that bears his name, the slave Pseudolus, by his skill and ingenuity, 'stages' the action of the play in a way somewhat comparable to Prospero. Thus, both plays are given a prominent theatrical quality, culminating in *The Tempest* in Prospero's evoking and renouncing the power of dramatic art. It is interesting that, in *Rudens*, too, human life is equated to a play. Daemones exclaims, 'the gods do produce strange plays for us humans' ('Miris modis di ludos faciunt hominibus' 593), and on a later occasion a character ironically remarks that, whereas actors in the theatre are applauded for their wisdom and moral advice, no one remembers this and acts accordingly in real life, after the performance is over (1249 – 1253).

To sum up, we have seen that examining Shakespeare's plays from the perspective of the New Comedy tradition does not allow us to regard the romances as the entirely new dramatic genre they are often thought to be. There may, after all, be some sense in the fact that the Folio lists both *The Winter's Tale* and *The Tempest* with the comedies. That for his *Tempest* Shakespeare has, among other things, drawn on suggestions from *Rudens* as an example of the New Comedy tradition does not, of course, 'explain' or account for the wonderful richness and complexity of his last 'romance', a play in which all that has been adopted undergoes a creative 'sea-change'. Yet this classical basis seems once more to have been a starting point from which he began to build his own incomparably complex and coherent structure. The Roman, especially Plautine impact was then amalgamated with the native popular and Italian traditions.

What is so strikingly similar in *The Tempest* and *Rudens* is the general 'humanist' tone. We have tried to show throughout the present book that the frequently held view of Plautus as an author merely of entertaining farce is wrong. If Polonius in his famous dictum: 'Seneca cannot be too heavy, nor Plautus too light' (*Hamlet*, II, ii, 400f.) seems to take a similar view, he does not imply that Plautus is *always* light because he wrote plays differing considerably in character. A play like *Rudens* or the beautiful *Captivi* had much to offer to the humanists and to Shakespeare, too; they found there what they were looking for, namely a text arguing the need for human solidarity, and faith in divine guidance.

Yet it is precisely these concepts and ideas that have misled critics like Howard Felperin into interpreting the romances in exclusively Christian terms and claiming that they came into existence through Shakespeare's 'appropriation and secularization of the forms of the medieval religious

---

[182] *Plautus in Performance* (Princeton, 1985), p.146.

drama'.[183] I fail to see how the Christian medieval drama could have inspired Shakespeare to write his 'romances', which strongly point in the classical direction. Such a view presupposes a distortion of the facts; it is a grave oversimplification to contrast 'the Christian and romantic motive of forgiveness' with 'the Hebraic-Hellenic and tragic one of retribution'.[184] Have we not seen that in *Rudens* the thought of revenge is discarded and that guilt (*impietas*) is met with forgiveness (*venia*)? Pity and compassion are virtues that are not exclusively found in Christianity.[185] It was Cyrus Hoy who in his very fine book reminded us some time ago that it is part of the nature of comedy in general to restore the final harmony by an act of forgiving.[186] What we do find in the Romances is a view of man, of the world and of the divine that is closely related to the humanist tradition, in other words, Shakespeare's plays reflect a 'Christian humanism'. It is interesting in this context that in his *Poetics* Scaliger has included a comprehensive definition of the idea of *pietas*. He not only states that 'pietas' sometimes includes mercy ('misericordiam'), but he distinguishes mainly between 'pietas' against human fellow-beings ('parentes, uxorem, liberes, affines, amicos') and the gods, Virgil's 'pius Aeneas' being of course the greatest literary example. To draw the Christian analogies is entirely left to the reader.[187]

Our examination of Shakespeare's reception of the New Comedy tradition confirms the results which other critics have arrived at from a different approach, namely that Shakespeare's religious attitude is very similar to that of Erasmus who, too, was much more inclined to emphasize the elements Christianity had in common with the humanist (Epicurean and Stoic) tradition than to focus on specifically Christian dogma.[188] In the final analysis, the basic virtues and values occurring in Shakespeare's *late* comedies are those of Stoic philosophy. Stoicism in Elizabethan culture goes back mainly to the Senecan tradition, but it was reinforced by elements of the New Comedy

---

[183] *Shakespearean Romance* (Princeton, 1972), p.278.

[184] Felperin, op. cit., p.273.

[185] On the question of Shakespeare's Christianity cf. also R.M. Frye, *Shakespeare's Christian Doctrine* (Princeton, 1963), and E.M. Wilson, 'Shakespeare's Christian Doctrine: Some Qualifications', *ShS*, 23 (1970), 7989; P. Milward, *Shakespeare's Religious Background* (Bloomington/London, 1973).

[186] C. Hoy, *The Hyacinth Room. An Investigation into the Nature of Comedy, Tragedy, and Tragicomedy* (London, 1964): 'Comedy is nothing if not hard-headedly realistic about the nature of man and the nature of human life; but it can also be compassionate in its forgiveness and its acceptance of human failings.' (p.18).

[187] Julius Caesar Scaliger, *Poetices Libri Septem* ed. A. Buck (Stuttgart/Bad Cannstatt, 1964), p.92.

[188] Cf. C. R. Thompson in the introduction to his translation of the Erasmian *Colloquies*: 'However necessary the formularization of Christian beliefs in creeds, the main thing to Erasmus was religion, not theological statement.' (*The Colloquies of Erasmus* [Chicago/London, 1965], p.xviii.); and Thompson adds that Erasmus himself was convinced that 'Christ requires of us nothing but a pure and sincere life'. (ibid.).

tradition. The 'stoic' content of New Comedy is less surprising if we realize that stoicism has much more to offer than modern critics would have us believe; this philosophy is concerned with a lot more than 'that fashionable Renaissance doctrine of apathy.'[189] It concentrates on the attempts of the individual to recognize himself, his place in the world and his relationship with the divine being. Basically, New Comedy is a comedy about the confusion of identities and the final recognition and identification of the characters. Shakespeare's most significant transformation of classical comedy is perhaps the way in which he, basing himself on *Menaechmi* and particularly on the far more complex *Amphitruo*, developed this tradition into his own comedy of identity.

---

[189] Felperin, op. cit., p.183.

Conclusion

A major result of the present study has been to demonstrate that the importance of Plautus for the Elizabethans and particularly for Shakespeare is far greater than has so far been assumed. Whereas the continental humanists tended to prefer Terence, in England the choice fell upon Plautus, yet for quite some time this fact has been obscured by Baldwin's voluminous study on the five-Act structure, which through his strong bias *against* Plautus severely distorts the facts. Baldwin turns a blind eye to what Plautus really meant to Shakespeare and to many Elizabethans. There is abundant evidence for concluding that it was Plautus who introduced the Evanthian structure of comedy as well as the five-Act convention to many playwrights, including Shakespeare. Shakespeare's use of dramatic irony and further devices such as soliloquy and aside, eavesdropping and disguise (so very prominent in *Amphitruo*) shows interesting links with Plautus. Shakespeare, of course, did not 'study' Plautus as an academic; rather, he grasped the decisive suggestions firmly with his imagination, and one reason why this could happen is that there are so many correspondences between the dramatic 'temperament' of Shakespeare and Plautus, who, it has now become clear, 'deserves' to be compared with Shakespeare. We have very good cause to assume that one of Plautus's plays, and perhaps the most 'popular' *Menaechmi*, was performed during Shakespeare's schooldays and that Shakespeare himself played a part in the performance so that he acquired an intensive *practical* dramaturgic experience through Plautus. Both Plautus and Shakespeare are actor-playwrights with a profound sense of theatre. The great majority of the Elizabethan dramatists preferred Plautus because of the dramatic and linguistic variety of his comedies. Terence served as a secondary influence; it is significant that none of Shakespeare's plays is based on a Terentian comedy.

Both Plautus and Shakespeare usually base their plays on existing sources and, as a rule, they do not invent their plots themselves. Unlike other Renaissance authors, Shakespeare does not usually transpose his plots into a contemporary setting. While, for example, Machiavelli in his *Clizia* transferred the action of the Plautine *Casina* deliberately to the Florence of his own day, Shakespeare in his 'classical' play chose to *retain* the remote locality of his sources, while at the same time superimposing on it topical allusions to places familiar to his audience, so as to achieve the contrasting effects of 'engagement' and 'detachment', a dramatic technique which is so fundamental to his dramaturgy.[1] In doing so, he employed a strategy which has early and, of course, far cruder antecedents in Plautus: an important difference between Terence and Plautus lies in the fact that Plautus on the one hand retains the Greek settings of the comedies, yet on the other hand he is never content with merely adopting the Greek plots and Greek characters of New Comedy plays, but instead always includes some references to the Rome of his own time. Like Shakespeare, Plautus takes delight in establishing the illusion of the world of the play and then often temporarily suspending it again, yet it is clear that Shakespeare employs this technique with a far greater dramatic economy.

However, the greatest 'affinity' between Plautus and Shakespeare surely lies in the fact that both are constantly aware of the *performative* character of a comedy. Therefore their plays abound in theatricality and game-playing, and language, too, is employed in the spirit of game. Far more than Plautus, Shakespeare knows how to exploit the dramatic possibilities of language, particularly of word play. Yet, as our examination has shown, there is reason to assume that Shakespeare's study of the Plautine language games was a decisive impulse for his development of dramatically effective puns and skilful forms of word-play. Moreover, in Plautus's brilliant use of language, the Elizabethans recognized their own stylistic ideal of *copia*.

As Shakespeare's achievement in his *Errors* is based on an intensive reception of Plautus's dramatic art, it is hardly conceivable that this could have been his very first comedy, as is frequently maintained. As we have seen, *Errors* is certainly not the beginning of his romantic comedy, because the love theme integrated into the play cannot be seen in the context of romantic love. It has emerged from our analysis that the unfolding of Shakespeare's romantic comedy may have started with *The Two Gentlemen of Verona*; in this play, Shakespeare seems for the first time to have taken up the tradition of English romantic comedy and to have fused it with the structure of New Comedy which he had studied intensively during the composition of *Errors*. It looks as if Shakespeare, when he began to write his comedies, first took Italian comedy as his principal model, composing *Taming* before starting with his reception of the Plautine form of New Comedy which from then on continued to exert its influence on him. Whereas nothing speaks against the assumption that *Errors* was composed some time after *Taming*, there are indeed strong reasons that would support such a view. Notwithstanding T.S. Dorsch's recent objections,[2] *Errors* can hardly have been written before 1594, because it is a far more accomplished play than is usually assumed and because, as I demonstrate in

---

[1] M. Mack, 'Engagement and Detachment in Shakespeare's Plays', in: *Essays on Shakespeare and Elizabethan Drama in Honor of Hardin Craig*, ed. R. Hosley (Columbia, M., 1962).

[2] T.S. Dorsch, ed., *The Comedy of Errors*, The New Cambridge Shakespeare (1988), p.6.

the Appendix, Shakespeare used Warner's translation of the *Menaechmi*, written in 1594.

Shakespeare no doubt not only knew some Plautine comedies in the original, he will also have been familiar with Renaissance editions of Roman comedies and their humanist introductions and commentaries, especially those by Erasmus and Melanchthon. We have confirmation of this in the account by Beeston, a fellow actor in Shakespeare's company, to Aubrey, in which he mentions that Shakespeare, before coming to London, had worked for some time as a country schoolmaster.[3] Shakespeare further followed the humanist reception of Roman comedy by his inclusion of a satirical perspective. In a way comparable to Erasmus and More, Shakespeare's reception of classical comedy was coloured by his adoption of Lucian's satirical mode, and this was sometimes even made to serve subversive purposes. One major reason why Lucian became part of the humanist tradition is the fact that he blended a wide range of literary and cultural traditions, a fact which makes him an author of intertextuality *par excellence*.

Shakespeare's knowledge of the classical tradition mediated through Renaissance humanism has to be stressed because recent research has tended to overemphasize his indebtedness to the medieval popular tradition, so much so that even a play like the 'neo-classical' *Errors* has been interpreted in terms of the dramaturgy of the Mystery Plays; and the most recent survey of 'Shakespeare and the Traditions of Comedy' devotes no more than one or two sentences to Plautus, Terence and New Comedy. On the one hand, it is held that the University Wits like Lyly, Peele, Greene or Marlowe exerted a considerable influence on Shakespeare,[4] but at the same time the humanist tradition which they *represented* is played down almost to the point of insignificance.

Such a view is at variance with the facts. The well-known 'composite' quality of Shakespeare's art has to be considered more seriously, it is 'composite' not in the sense that only one tradition − the popular and medieval one − is predominant, but in the sense that classical comedy, with its rich potential of popular and mimic elements, is very powerfully present too. We have seen that Madeleine Doran was right with her conjecture that what seems to us typically 'romantic' or 'Italian' may have seemed quite Plautine to a contemporary audience. She appears to have been nearer the truth than critics who have laid too strong an emphasis on medieval romance. The romance framework in *Errors*, which at first sight appears to be of medieval origin, is firmly rooted in the tradition of New Comedy itself. The similar importance of the romance element in both New Comedy and the

---

[3] E.A.J. Honigmann has put forward new evidence in support of Beeston's information (*Shakespeare: The 'Lost Years'* [Manchester, 1986]).

[4] D. Daniell, 'Shakespeare and the traditions of comedy' in: *The Cambridge Companion to Shakespeare Studies*, ed. S.Wells (Cambridge, 1986), p.101 − 121.

medieval tradition is certainly a further major reason why the fusion of the two traditions was so readily possible. Shakespeare's 'romantic' comedy gains in depth if its links with the classical tradition are recognized; we need only remember the fact that *Two Gentlemen* was for a long time seriously misunderstood because its classical as well as humanist connections were not sufficiently appreciated.

The essential 'humanism' contained in the seemingly light *Errors* becomes crystal-clear once it is realized that no one in the Renaissance would have called a comedy of identity a farce. Rather, it was considered as a play which presented, as in a mirror, manners and morals and the need for self-knowledge. This picture is confirmed by the fact that in the Plautine *Amphitruo*, which has been so deplorably neglected by Shakespeare critics, the comic element is accompanied by serious situations. This play, called a *tragicomoedia* by Plautus himself and considered in recent scholarship as his masterly and most original creation, may have suggested to Shakespeare the possibility of evoking both comic and tragic emotions in one and the same play, thus presenting a more profound view of man than was possible in either tragedy or comedy alone. By refusing to make a clear distinction between tragedy and comedy, Shakespeare was again in line with the theory of drama followed by the Renaissance humanists.

The fact that *Errors* was performed at Gray's Inn is extremely important: here was an audience capable of appreciating Shakespeare's brilliant fusion of various traditions, because at Gray's Inn plays with a similarly composite character had been composed. This audience will certainly have appreciated not only the stunning brilliance of the fusion of two comedies of identity, *Menaechmi* and *Amphitruo*, but also the continuation and extension of the New Comedy structure that Shakespeare achieved with his 'classical' *Errors*.

Dorsch has convincingly shown how *Errors* might have been staged at the west end of Gray's Inn Hall, and the way in which the doors would most probably have been used in a production.[5] Walter Hodges's reconstruction of the first performance of *Twelfth Night* in Middle Temple Hall, a play which, as we have seen, is based on a remarkably 'Plautine' structure, looks very similar to a production at the Globe[6] and shows what a close resemblance there is between the two stage forms, the Halls being a variation upon the Renaissance Terentian stage and the popular playhouse.

We shall have to go a step further in order to draw a final conclusion. It appears that there was in fact an unbroken tradition of New Comedy in England. This has become evident from the results of recent research

[5] Op. cit., p.20 – 26; Dorsch's reconstruction of the Gray's Inn performance is far more convincing than that by M. Knapp and M. Kobialka ('The Prince of Purpoole: the 1594 production of *The Comedy of Errors* at Gray's Inn Hall', *Theatre History Studies*, 4 [1984], 71 – 81).

[6] Reprinted and therefore easily accessible in E. Story Donno, ed., *Twelfth Night*, The New Cambridge Shakespeare (Cambridge, 1985), p.2.

concerning the form of the comedies written in the Middle Ages. And it
is likely that in England this tradition also left its traces even on the
development of the stage. It is most striking that the many dramaturgic
resemblances between the plays of Plautus and of Shakespeare are also
paralleled in the basic similarity between the Elizabethan stage and what
we know of the stage of Plautus. The concept of the bare stage, with two
or three doors or houses at the back, is common to both. The acting area
is a neutral stage, and in Plautus it is usually defined by a character
entering the stage from one of the houses; it can, however, serve to
represent any place. One could claim that the two large doors on either
side of the Globe's back front were developed from the back houses of the
Plautine plays, and the arras in the middle position would then turn out
to be a 'transformation' of a third house; if required, it would have
served as an additional house, as, for example, when *Errors* was staged at
the Globe: then the Priory was certainly placed in front of the arras or
replaced it. Leslie Hotson concludes convincingly that 'small structural
units of frame and canvas called *mansions* or *houses* [...] with practical
doors, with curtains',[7] must have been in use on the public stage.

One might even claim that the native medieval stage of the Mystery
plays, too, was not an entirely new invention. The basic concept of the
neutral acting area and the defining quality of the houses confirms this
assumption. The clerical authors of the Mystery plays were most
probably familiar with Roman comedies, especially those of Terence. In
the plays of Plautus as well as of Terence, the term *platea* denotes the
indefinite acting space which is given individual significance by the action
of the plot and above all by the houses from which the actors enter the
stage or to which they return.[8] Do not the *domus* or *mansiones* of the
Mystery plays also resemble the houses of classical comedy, the difference
being, of course, that their number increased considerably?

In the case of Lyly's *Mother Bombie*, a play with a marked Plautine and
Terentian dramaturgy, the houses used have been interpreted as
descendants of the *mansiones* of the Mystery plays, and it has been claimed
that Lyly here adopted the older and native medieval dramaturgy of
'simultaneous staging'[9] or 'multiple staging'.[10] And more recently it has

---

[7] Quoted from Dorsch, op. cit., p.24.

[8] Cf. P. Harsh, 'Angiportum, Platea and Vicus', *CP*, 32 (1937), 44–58. P.
Theiner rightly claims that 'there is in fact a decided continuity and congruity
from the ancient Terence through the medieval Terence to the Renaissance
Terence'. ('The Medieval Terence', in: *The Learned and the Lewed. Studies in
Chaucer and Medieval Literature*, ed. L.D. Benson, Harvard English Studies, 5
(Cambridge, Mass., 1974), p.232.

[9] John Lyly, *The Humanist as Courtier* (London, 1962), p.107ff.

[10] P. Saccio, *The Court Comedies of John Lyly: A Study in Allegorical Dramaturgy*
(Princeton, 1969), p.11–25.

been suggested that the dramaturgy of the *platea* and the houses in *Errors* was also derived from this medieval theatrical tradition.[11] These assumptions are, however, rather absurd, for why should authors writing comedies in the classical tradition take dramaturgic suggestions from the Mystery plays? Does it not seem that the reverse of this theory makes sense and that the similarities can be explained by assuming an influence on the religious plays of the Middle Ages by Plautine and Terentian dramaturgy? Here we would have, then, the first instance of the fusion of native and classical traditions that reached its climax with Shakespeare.

These considerations contain a further implication: Robert Weimann's interpretation of the genesis of Shakespearean popular theatre becomes somewhat problematic. His distinction between a classical, humanist influence, manifesting itself in the relatively 'naturalistic' upstage *locus*, and the popular influence of ritual, burlesque and topsyturvydom acted downstage on the *platea*, is not really justified. Instead, it is far more reasonable to assume that the *entire* stage, with its 'dichotomy' of *locus* and *platea*, was familiar to the Elizabethans from the humanist tradition of New Comedy. Moreover, some dramaturgic aspects which appear to us so typical of the native tradition may have their roots in classical comedy. The authors of many pre-Shakespearean comedies, educated as 'humanists' but nevertheless aware of a very strong popular and mimetic element in Plautus, themselves contributed to the amalgamation of the dramaturgy of Plautine comedy and the native popular tradition.

Finally, Italy can serve to confirm our conclusion that the native popular tradition was not as exclusively important as is now generally held. There is the example of Angelo Beolco, called Ruzzante (1502 – 1542), the founder of a professional group of actors in Italy. His favourite *sujet* was the peasants, whom he presented from a critical and understanding perspective, and he was a major forerunner of the *commedia dell'arte*. We have an interesting draft from 1518/19 of one of his comedies showing a simultaneous stage with three houses (*mansiones*) and a *via publica* (1518/19). This draft, of course, has no direct connections with the English medieval stage, but clearly represents the Plautine stage. Although in his comedies Ruzzante is concerned with the peasants of his own time, he nevertheless makes use of the Plautine *Asinaria* and *Rudens*, because, as he puts it, he wants to 'cut jackets for the living from the shroud of a corpse'.[12]

---

[11] A.F. Kinney, 'Shakespeare's Comedy of Errors and the Nature of Kinds', *SP*, 85 (1988), 42.

[12] Quoted from H. Kindermann, *Theatergeschichte Europas* (Salzburg, 1959), II, 141.

12 A draft by Angelo Beolco (Ruzzante), MS It. XI, 66 (= 6730)

Our view is supported by the new insights resulting from research into the medieval 'theory of comedy'. We have seen that the common notion of the medieval concept of comedy as 'romantic' or 'epic' is most imprecise. Even in epic forms of comedy, dramaturgic elements from Terence were employed, and there was an awareness that Roman comedy set the standard for comedy.[13] Let us remember that in the tenth century Hrotsvita of Gandersheim used the Terentian dialogue in composing her Christian 'legends', in which she strove to out-Terence him by demonstrating the victory of chaste Christian virgins over pagan hetaerae and seducible women.[14] If Terence served Hrotsvita as a basis for her didactic and not at all comic *sujet*, then we cannot at all reject the idea that even in the Mystery plays some structural elements of Roman comedy – and this implies the *platea-locus*-opposition – may be alive. Does not Contemplation in the Hegge Plays announce that their subject matter 'may *profite*

---

[13] Cf. J. Suchomski, op. cit., p.142ff.

[14] H. Kuhn, 'Hrothsvits von Gandersheim dichterisches Programm' in: *Dichtung und Welt im Mittelalter* (Stuttgart, 1959), p.100. There is a new English translation of her plays by K.M. Wilson, *The Plays of Hrotsvit of Gandersheim* (London, 1989).

and plese eche persone present'?[15] This clear reference to Horace corresponds to the ideal of 'utilitas', which has been recognized as the basic
purpose of medieval comedy.[16] It is an ideal that did not essentially
change with the humanists, except that, after the discovery of more plays
by Plautus in the 15th century, Plautus soon acquired pride of place in
England. From whichever angle we view the impact of Roman comedy
on the English stage and in particular on Shakespeare, it turns out to be
far more interesting and important than has been assumed, and this
approach may still have some surprises in store for the student of
Shakespeare.

---

[15] *Ludus Coventriae or The Plaie Called Corpus Christi*, ed. K.S. Black, EETS ES,
   120 (1922), p.62, 56 (italics mine).
[16] Suchomski, op. cit.p.85.

APPENDIX

The Comedy of Errors *and*
William Warner's Translation of Menaechmi

One of the vexed questions in the criticism of *Errors* is whether Shakespeare did not know and consider William Warner's English translation of *Menaechmi*, completed in 1594. In a comprehensive study of Shakespeare's classical comedy this problem cannot be completely left aside, because clarity on this point would throw new light on how his imagination worked and because, in the case of positive evidence, it would prove that *Errors* is not a *very* early comedy and cannot have been written before 1594. There is no need to prove once more that Shakespeare could indeed have become acquainted with the manuscript of Warner's translation shortly after it was finished and before it was printed.[1]

For a scholar like Baldwin, it was an established fact that Shakespeare, because of his sufficient knowledge of Latin, had no need to use an English translation of *Menaechmi*.[2] To argue like this is, however, beside the point. There are enough Renaissance exemples testifying to the fact that translations of Plautus were made not only for readers unable to read Latin, but also for humanist readers. Indeed, some of the most scholarly editions contain complete translations of the Latin comedies.[3] Thus, if Shakespeare did use an English translation together with the original text, this would not have been in any way exceptional.[4]

One such translation was done by William Warner in 1594.[5] It is an interesting document for the study of the Elizabethan reception of Plautus. Several critics have considered it possible that Shakespeare may have used it,

---

[1] Cf., for example, Foakes, op. cit., p.xxv.

[2] This is the tenor of his study *On the Compositional Genetics of The Comedy of Errors* (Urbana, 1965).

[3] Suffice it to mention the interesting Terence edition (Leyden, 1560), which has not only extensive comments but also a complete French translation.

[4] Instead of listing all the translations of Roman comedies that were published in England in the 15th and 16th centuries, I merely refer to Pollard's *Short Title Catalogue of Books Printed in England, Scotland, and Ireland* (London, 1976), where we find a bilingual edition of Terence, published in Oxford in 1483; there were then six further editions, two of them printed by Wynkyn de Worde.

[5] It has been reprinted by E. Bullough, *Narrative and Dramatic Sources of Shakespeare* (London, 1957), I, 12 – 39. The critical edition by R.G. Brooks (*An Edition of W. Warner's 1595 Translation of Plautus' Menaechmi* [Diss. Univ. of Illinois, 1951]) has not been available to me.

on the strength of a number of important parallels which they have discovered. They have had to admit, however, that the influence may have been the other way round, namely that Warner wrote his translation under the fresh impression of Shakespeare's *Errors*.[6] I am convinced that Shakespeare did indeed use Warner; there is ample proof that the influence cannot be in the opposite direction. A close examination of this translation shows that Warner reinforces the romance element, which Shakespeare then goes on to amplify even more fully. I do not intend to assemble here all the evidence for Shakespeare's use of Warner, some of which may be circumstantial; I shall instead concentrate on the most salient points.

First, it appears that Shakespeare followed Warner in a small but significant detail. The Folio reads 'Epidamium' for the name of the city of 'Epidamnus' in which the action of *Menaechmi* takes place. Editors explain 'Epidamium' as a contamination of 'Epidamnum'. Warner always has 'Epidamnum' instead of the Plautine 'Epidamnus'. Furthermore, there is good reason to assume that Shakespeare followed Warner in his characterization of the Courtesan, although we have seen that he also was aware of the Italian 'cortigiana'. Warner goes so far as to call his courtesan a 'gentlewoman', and Menaechmus E visits her merely for 'entertainment' ('This woman entertained me most kindly' p. 39). When Antipholus E announces his intention of going to the Courtesan, he also characterizes her as a gentlewoman, using the same term as Warner does: 'Since mine own doors refuse to entertain me, / I'll knock elsewhere, to see if they'll disdain me' (III, i, 120 – 121). Yet whereas Warner obviously de-erotized the Plautine Erotium for reasons of respectability, this does not apply to Shakespeare's Courtesan as well, because there is enough coarse bawdy punning in the play.

Compared with Plautus, Warner in his translation increases the element of aggression, and Shakespeare by far outdoes Warner in this. In our context it is interesting that Shakespeare adopted the 'basting' (with a rope's end) (II, ii, 57) from Warner's adaptation (p.34), as Dromio E is expressly sent to buy a rope's end, with which his master intends to avenge himself on his wife for having shut him out from dinner. Furthermore, in Warner's version of the great scene V, ii, Menaechmus S, pretending to be mad, asks Phoebus whether he commands him 'to teare this dog (i.e. the Senex) in peeces with my nayles?' (p.32). It has often been pointed out that this is echoed in Antipholus E's threat to his wife: 'with these nails I'll pluck out these false eyes' (IV, iv, 102).

Although there are a number of other parallels between Warner and *Errors* for which there are no equivalents in the original Latin text, I shall confine myself to just one example. We have seen that the motif of Fortune was essential in the tradition of New Comedy, yet we have also seen that in Plautus this motif is much less directly present than in Menander. Particularly in

[6] Cf., for example, R.A. Foakes's comment on this problem, op. cit., p.xxvi.

Menaechmi we do not find this theme in any way expressed; it is only tacitly implied as the action unfolds with an uncompromising consistency. Warner, however, makes this theme much clearer and more prominent. In his attempt to furnish his translation with an Elizabethan touch, he makes Fortune part of the action, as it were. In the final recognition scene, Warner makes Menaechmus S exclaim: 'O Fortune!' when he begins to feel sure that the stranger he has met is indeed his twin brother (p. 38). Warner even needs an extra slave, not present in Plautus, to say that Messenio has had good fortune because his master has set him free (p. 35).

There are other occasions too where Warner introduces the theme of Fortune. Of special interest is the situation at the beginning of Act II. Baldwin has shown that II, i of *Menaechmi* provided Shakespeare with many suggestions for the development of his own *Errors*,[7] yet Warner must be considered as an *extra* link by which the romance frame of the comedy suggested itself even more strongly to Shakespeare. On first entering the stage, Warner's Menaechmus is a little more talkative even than his Plautine model: he says that it is a great joy for seafarers that, 'when they have been long tost and turmoyld in the wide seas' (p. 17), they, by good fortune, at last see land: 'they hap at last to ken land'. We may say that Menaechmus's narration of his having been 'tost [. . .] in the wild seas' was the dramatic nucleus out of which Shakespeare's romance-like frame was developed, for which he used material from the romance *Apollonius of Tyre*. And then, as we have seen, Shakespeare too introduced the goddess Fortune into his 'Roman' comedy, to an even greater extent than Warner. Egeon begins his tragic report by informing us that his 'hap' has been 'bad' (38). He describes the actual shipwreck on the open sea as an act of cruel Fortune which separated his family (105 – 106). He mentions the ship that rescued them and adds that its crew knew 'whom it was their hap to save' (112 – 113). This narration so touches the Duke that he responds with compassion: 'Hapless Egeon, whom the fates have mark'd / To bear the extremity of dire mishap' (140 – 141). In the final scene, hope suddenly begins to stir in Egeon's soul, although very tentatively, as we may infer from his way of talking: 'Haply I see a friend will save my life' (284). Aemilia indicates that her entering a convent and becoming an Abbess was a consequence of this same fortune' (361). We see that Fortune appears almost exclusively in the romance plot of the comedy.

It seems unnecessary to continue listing the series of correspondences between Warner and Shakespeare – with one exception. We have to consider the fact that the bracelet (*spinter*) which Menaechmus E presents to Erotium is replaced both in Warner and in *Errors* by a chain. Shakespeare took this suggestion from Warner because it served him for a specific dramatic purpose, but it is a purpose different from the one proposed by Baldwin who argued

---

[7] *Compositional Genetics*, p.159ff.

that a chain is better visible to the audience than a bracelet.[8] If this were a
valid argument, then the numerous scenes in European drama in which, for
example, rings have an important function would lack any dramatic effect.
The reason for Shakespeare's choice of the chain lies, I think, elsewhere.
When one produces the play on stage one begins to realize that in the last three
Acts Antipholus S, the quester, is often seen with the golden chain, which his
brother has ordered from the goldsmith. He is, however, not just carrying it,
but *wearing it round his neck*. If we bear in mind how very receptive the
Elizabethans were to the significance of visual signs, then we can hardly avoid
the conclusion that when Antipholus is seen wearing the golden chain this can
have an emblematic function.[9] He is singled out because he is preoccupied
with a specifically humanist pursuit: the finding of the self. Be that as it may, it
can no longer be argued that the replacement of the bracelet by a chain both in
Warner and in Shakespeare might be mere coincidence.

Yet still the old objection may be raised: cannot this obvious influence have
worked the other way round, so that Warner wrote his translation of
Menaechmi under the fresh impression of Shakespeare's classical play? After all,
Warner did not aim at a faithful translation but rather at an Elizabethan
adaptation. The assumption, however, that Warner may have been
influenced by the appearance of Shakespeare's *Errors* is unconvincing because
of cogent reasons. Warner is not a slavish translator, rather is he at pains to
transfer topical allusions to the world of ancient Rome into the everyday world
of the Elizabethans. Some of Warner's alterations have been inspired by his
sense of drama, and his prose version is highly theatrical. Yet he is so
meticulous that he announces to the reader that he will mark exactly all his
deviations from the original with an asterisk. We must therefore ask: Would a
translator of this kind take over suggestions from *Errors* without acknowledg-
ing them? Most certainly not. For if he had known *Errors* and had seen how
Shakespeare employed the belief in witchcraft and superstition in order to
make the confusions of identity more plausible, he would, no doubt, have
translated the *Menaechmi* in a more lively manner, especially in the dramatic
situation where the *Menaechmi* most resembles *Errors*. This is the soliloquy of
Menaechmus E in V, vii, in which he explains the series of confusions to
himself by saying that magical tricks have been played on him: 'nimia mira
mihi quidem hodie exorta sunt miris modis' ('Well, well, how strongly strange
things have happened to me today?' 1039), and thinks he has had a
miraculous dream: 'haec nihilo esse mihi videntur setius quam somnia' ('It
seems just like a dream' 1047). Here Menaechmus E approaches the

---

[8] Ibid., p.81.

[9] In Erasmus's *Praise of Folly* the gold chain is defined as a 'symbol of the concord
between all the virtues' (*Collected Works of Erasmus*, 27, Literary and Educational
Writings, 5, p.136). Mention should also be made of the fact that a gold chain
adorning the neck of a man is a frequent iconographic detail in Renaissance
portraits.

imaginative atmosphere created by Antipholus S in *Errors*; yet what do we find in Warner's translation of Menaechmus's soliloquy? Far from placing special emphasis on magic, Warner totally eliminates the original references to the supernatural. Here is his translation of the Plautine sentences quoted above: 'I was never thus perplext.' (p.36) '. . . who ever sawe such straunge demeanours?' (ibid.). This is a very weak rendering of the Latin text and shows that Warner takes no interest in a theme which is so essential to *Errors*. We may therefore safely conclude that Shakespeare not only used the original *Menaechmi* but also worked with Warner's English version when he wrote his *Errors*.

Bibliography

Selected Books and Articles on Plautus and New Comedy

CRITICAL BIBLIOGRAPHIES AND SURVEYS

Arnott, W.G., 'Menander, Plautus, Terence', *Greece and Rome. New Surveys in the Classics*, 9 (Oxford, 1975), 19ff.

Fogazza, D., 'Plauto 1935 – 1975', *Lustrum*, 19 (1979), 79 – 296

Hanson, T.A., 'Scholarship on Plautus since 1950', *Classical World*, 59 (1965 – 6), 126 – 129; 141 – 148

Hughes, J.D., *A Bibliography of Scholarship on Plautus* (Amsterdam, 1975)

Segal, E. 'Scholarship on Plautus 1965 – 1976', *Classical World*, 74 (1981), 252 – 433

Goldberg, S.M., 'Scholarship on Terence and the Fragments of Roman Comedy 1959 – 1980', *Classical World*, 75 (1981), 77 – 115

BOOKS AND ARTICLES

Abel, K., *Die Plautusprologe* (Mühlheim/R., 1955)

Arnaldi, F., *Da Plauto a Terenzio* (Naples, 1946/47), 2 vols.

Arnott, W.G., 'Time, Plot and Character in Menander', *Papers of the Liverpool Latin Seminar*, 2 (1979), 343ff.

Arnott, W.G., ed., *Menander*, Loeb Classical Library (Cambridge, Mass./ London, 1979), I

Bain, D., *Actors and Audience* (Oxford, 1977)

Barnes, H.E., 'The case of Sosia versus Sosia', *CJ*, 53 (1957 – 8), 19 – 23

Beare, W., *The Roman Stage* (New York, [3]1963)

Beare, W., 'Plautus, Terence and Seneca: A Comparison of Aims and Methods', (in:) M.J. Anderson, ed., *Classical Drama and its Influence. Essays Presented to H.D.F. Kitto* (London, 1965)

Bickford, J.D., *Soliloquy in Ancient Comedy* (Diss. Princeton, 1922)

Bieber, M., *The History of Greek and Roman Theatre* (Princeton, [2]1961)

Blänsdorf, J., 'Plautus', (in:) *Das römische Drama*, ed. E. Lefèvre (Darmstadt, 1978), 135 – 222

Blänsdorf, J., 'Voraussetzungen und Entstehung der römischen Komödie', in: *Das römische Drama*, ed. E. Lefèvre, 91 – 134

Blume, H.D., *Menanders 'Samia'. Eine Interpretation* (Darmstadt, 1974)

Blume, H.D., *Einführung in das antike Theaterwesen* (Darmstadt, 1978)

Blundell, J., *Menander and the Monologue* (Göttingen, 1980)

Bozanic, N., *Structure, Language and Action in the Comedies of Menander* (Diss. London, 1977)

Braun, L., 'Polymetrie bei Terenz und Plautus', *Wiener Studien*, 83 (1970), 66 – 83

Braun, L., *Die Cantica des Plautus* (Göttingen, 1970)

Brotherton, S., *The Vocabulary of Intrigue in Roman Comedy* (Diss. Menasha, 1926)

Büchner, K., *Das Theater des Terenz* (Heidelberg, 1974)

Charbonnier, C., 'La courtisane de Plaute à Ovide', *Bulletin Association G. Budé* (1969), 459 – 550

Colman-Norton, P.R., 'The Conception of Fortune in Roman Drama', (in:) *Classical Studies Presented to E. Capps* (Princeton, 1936)

Corbett, P.B., 'Vis comica in Plautus and Terence', *Eranos*, 62 (1964), 52 – 59

Curtius, E.R., *European Literature and the Latin Middle Ages*, transl. by W.R. Trask (London, 1953)

della Corte, F., *Da Sarsina a Roma* (Genova, ²1967)

della Corte, F., 'Maschere e personaggi in Plauto', *Dioniso*, 46 (1975), 163 – 193

Denzler, B., *Der Monolog bei Terenz* (Diss. Zürich, 1968)

Dessen, C.S., 'Plautus's Satiric comedy', *PQ*, 56 (1977), 145 – 68

Dorey, T.A. and Dudley, D.R., eds., *Roman Drama* (London, 1968)

Duckworth, G.E., 'The Structure of the ''Miles Gloriosus'' ', *CP*, 30 (1935), 228 – 46

Duckworth, G.E., 'Dramatic Suspense in Plautus', *Classical Weekly*, 1941 – 2

Duckworth, G.E., *The Nature of Roman Comedy* (Princeton, 1952)

Fields, D.E., *The Technique of Exposition in Roman Comedy* (Diss. Chicago, 1938)

Flury, P., *Liebe und Liebessprache bei Menander, Plautus und Terenz* (Heidelberg, 1968)

Forehand, W.E., 'Irony in Plautus' Amphitruo', *AJPh*, 92 (1971), 633 – 51

Fraenkel, E., *Plautinisches im Plautus* (Berlin, 1922); rev.ed.: *Elementi Plautini in Plauto*, transl. F. Munari (Firenze, 1961)

Friedrich, W.H., *Euripides und Diphilos* (München, 1953)

Fuhrmann, M., *Einführung in die antike Dichtungstheorie* (Darmstadt, 1973)

Fuhrmann, M., 'Plautus' in: *Der Kleine Pauly. Lexikon der Antike*, eds. K. Ziegler and W. Sontheimer (München, 1979), IV, 911 – 917

Gaiser, K., 'Zur Eigenart der römischen Komödie: Plautus und Terenz gegenüber ihren griechischen Vorbildern', (in:) *Aufstieg und Niedergang der römischen Welt*, ed. H. Temporieri, vol. I, 2 (Berlin/New York, 1972), p.1027 – 1113

Görler, W., 'Doppelhandlung, Intrige und Anagnorismos bei Terenz', *Poetica*, 5 (1972), 164 – 182

Görler, W., 'Über die Illusion in der antiken Komödie', *Antike und Abendland*, 18 (1973), 41 – 57

Goldberg, S.M., *The Making of Menander's Comedy* (Berkeley, 1980)

Gomme, A.W., *Essays in Greek History and Literature* (Oxford, 1937)

Gomme, A.W. and Sandbach, F.H., *Menander: A Commentary* (Oxford, 1973)

Grimal, P., et al., 'Le Théatre à Rome', *Association Guillaume Budé. Actes du IXe Congres 1973*, 9 (1975), 249 – 499

Grimal, P., 'Existe-t-il une "morale" de Plaute?', *Bulletin de l'Association Guillaume Budé* (1975), 485 – 98

Haberman, D., 'Menaechmi: A Serious Comedy', *Ramus*, 10 (1981), 129 – 139

Handley, E.W., *The Dyskolos of Menander* (London, 1965)

Handley, E.W., *Menander and Plautus: A Study in Comparison* (London, 1968)

Handley, E.W., 'Comedy' in: *The Cambridge History of Classical Literature* (Cambridge, 1985), I, 335 – 425 and 779 – 83

Harsh, P.W. *Studies in Dramatic 'Preparation' in Roman Comedy* (Diss. Chicago, 1935)

Hieatt, V.E., *Eavesdropping in Roman Comedy* (Diss. Chicago, 1946)

Holzberg, N., *Menander. Untersuchungen zur dramatischen Technik* (Nürnberg, 1974)

Hough, J.N., 'The Development of Plautus' Art', *CP*, 30 (1935), 43ff.

Hough, J.N., 'Link Monologues in Roman Comedy', *CP*, (1939), 123; 116 – 126

Hough, J.N., 'Exit Monologues in Roman Comedy', *CP*, (1942), 121

Hunter, R.L., *The New Comedy of Greece and Rome* (Cambridge, 1985)

Janko, R., *Aristotle on Comedy. Towards a Reconstruction of Poetics II* (Berkeley/ Los Angeles, 1984)

Jauss, H.R., 'Poetik und Problematik von Identität und Rolle in der Geschichte des Amphitryon' in: *Identität*, ed. D. Marquard and K. Stierle, Poetik und Hermeneutik, VIII (München, 1979)

Jens, W., *Zur Antike* (München, 1978)

Juniper, W.H., 'Character Portrayal in Plautus', *CJ*, 31 (1936), 276 – 88

Katsouris, A.G., *Tragic Patterns in Menander* (Athens, 1975)

Kistrup, I., *Die Liebe bei Plautus und den Elegikern* (Diss. Kiel, 1963)

Klien, E., *Aelius Donatus als Kritiker der Komödien des Terenz* (Diss. Innsbruck, 1948)

Knapp, C., 'References in Plautus and Terence to Plays, Players and Playscripts', *CP*, 14 (1919), 35 – 55

Konstan, D., *Roman Comedy* (Ithaca and London, 1983)

Lefèvre, E., *Die Expositionstechnik in den Komödien des Terenz* (Darmstadt, 1969)

Lefèvre, E., ed., *Die römische Komödie: Plautus und Terenz*, Wege der Forschung, 236 (Darmstadt, 1973)

Lefèvre, E., 'Römische Komödien', in: *Neues Handbuch der Literaturwissenschaft*, III, ed. M. Fuhrmann (Frankfurt/M., 1974), 33 – 62

Lefèvre, E., 'Theatrum Mundi: Götter, Gott und Spielleiter im antiken Drama', in: *Theatrum Mundi. Götter, Gott und Spielleiter im Drama von der Antike bis zur Gegenwart*, ed. F. Link und G. Niggl (Berlin, 1981), 49 – 91

Lefèvre, E., *Maccus Vortit Barbare. Vom tragischen Amphitryon zum tragikomischen Amphitruo*, Akademie der Wissenschaft und der Literatur, Geistes- und sozialwiss. Klasse, 5 (Mainz, 1982)

Lefèvre, E., E. Stärk, G. Vogt-Spira, *Plautus barbarus. Sechs Kapitel zur Originalität des Plautus* (Tübingen, 1990)

Leo, F., *Der Monolog im Drama* (Berlin, 1908)

Leo, F., *Plautinische Forschungen* (Berlin, 21912)

Levin, R., 'The double plots of Terence', *CJ*, 62 (1967), 301 – 305

Lodge, G., *Lexicon Plautinum* (Leipzig, 1933), 2 vols.

Loitold, E.G., *Untersuchungen zur Spieltechnik der plautinischen Komödie* (Diss. Wien, 1975)

Luck, G., 'Elemente der Umgangssprache bei Menander und Terenz', *RhM*, 108 (1965), 269 – 277

Marti, H., *Untersuchungen zur dramatischen Technik bei Plautus und Terenz* (Winterthur, 1959)

Miller, N., ed., *Menander. Plays and Fragments* (London, 1987)

Pauly, A.F.v., G. Wissowa, W. Kroll, K. Mittelhaus, eds., *Realencyklopädie der classischen Altertumswissenschaft* (Stuttgart, 1894 – 1972), 46 vols.

Pöschl, V., *Die neuen Menanderpapyri und die Originalität des Plautus* (Heidelberg, 1973)

Prescott, H.W., 'The Comedy of Errors', *CP*, 24 (1929), 32 – 41

Primmer, A., 'Die Handlung der Menaechmi', *Wiener Studien*, 100 (1987), 97 – 115; 101 (1988), 192 – 222

Questa, C., *Structure sceniche di Plauto e Menandro*, in: *Entretiens Hardt*, XVI, 205ff.

Rudolf, G., *The Theatrical Notation of Roman and Pre-Shakespearean Comedy*, Cooper Monographs, 29 (Bern, 1981)

Sandbach, F.H., *The Comic Theatre of Greece and Rome* (London, 1977)

Sandbach, F.H., 'Menander's Manipulation of Language for Dramatic Purposes', *Entretien Fondation Hardt*, 16 (Genève, 1970), 111 – 136

Schadewaldt, W., *Monolog und Selbstgespräch, Neue philologische Untersuchungen*, ed. W. Jaeger, Heft 2 (Berlin, 1926)

Schadewaldt, W., *Menander. Das Schiedsgericht. Der Menschenfeind* (Frankfurt/M., 1963)

Schmidt, W., *Die sprachlichen Mittel des Komischen bei Plautus* (Diss. Tübingen, 1960)

Sedgwick, W.B., 'Parody in Plautus', *CQ*, 21 (1927), 28 – 89

Sedgwick, W.B., ed. Plautus, *Amphitruo* (Manchester, 1960)

Segal, E., 'The Menaechmi: Roman Comedy of Errors', *Yale Classical Studies*, 21 (1963), 77 – 93

Segal, E., *Roman Laughter. The Comedy of Plautus* (Cambridge/Mass., 1968)

Slater, N.W., *Plautus in Performance. The Theatre of the Mind* (Princeton, 1985)

Steidle, W., 'Zur Komposition von Plautus' Menaechmi', *RhM*, 114 (1971), 247 – 261

Stoessl, F., 'Amphitryon. Wachstum und Wandlung eines poetischen Stoffes', *Trivium*, 2 (1944), 96ff.

Szondi, P., 'Fünfmal Amphitryon: Plautus, Molière, Kleist, Giraudoux, Kaiser', in *Schriften II* (Frankfurt/M., 1978), p.170 – 197

Taladoire, B.A., *Commentaires sur la Mimique et L'Espression Corporelle du Comédien Romain* (Paris, 1951)

Taladoire, B.A., *Essai Sur le Comique de Plaute* (Monaco, 1956)

Tobias, A.J., *Plautine Metrical Characterization* (Diss. Stanford, 1970)

Treu, M., 'Humane Handlungsmotive in der Samia Menanders', *RhM*, 112 (1969), 230 – 254

Webster, T.B.L., *Studies in Menander* (Manchester, 2‍1960)

Webster, T.B.L., *Greek Theatre Production* (London, 2‍1970)

Webster, T.B.L., *Later Greek Comedy* (New York, ²1970)
Webster, T.B.L., *An Introduction to Menander* (Manchester, 1974)
Williams, G., *Traditions and Originality in Roman Poetry* (Oxford, 1968)
Zagagi, N., *Tradition and Originality in Plautus* (Göttingen, 1980)

Literature on The Comedy of Errors *and selected works on Shakespearean Comedy*

RECENT EDITIONS OF *THE COMEDY OF ERRORS*

– ed. R.A. Foakes, The New Arden Shakespeare (London, 1962)
– ed. P.A. Jorgensen, The Pelican Shakespeare (Baltimore, 1969)
– ed. S. Wells, The Penguin Shakespeare (Harmondsworth, 1972)
– ed. H. Levin, The Signet Classical Shakespeare (New York, 1975)
– ed. K. Tetzeli v. Rosador, Englisch-deutsche Studienausgabe (Bern/ München, 1982)
– ed. T.S. Dorsch, The New Cambridge Shakespeare (Cambridge, 1988)

BOOKS AND ARTICLES

Babula, W., 'If I dream not: Unity in "The Comedy of Errors" ', *South Atlantic Bulletin*, 38 (1973), 26 – 33
Baldwin, T.W., *William Shakspere Adapts a Hanging* (Princeton, 1931)
Baldwin, T.W., 'Three Homilies in The Comedy of Errors' in: *Essays in Honor of Hardin Craig* (London, 1963), 137 – 147
Barber, C.L., *Shakespeare's Festive Comedy. A Study of Dramatic Form and its Relation to Social Custom* (Princeton, 1959)
Barber, C.L., 'Shakespearean Comedy in *The Comedy of Errors*', *CE*, 25 (1964), 493 – 497
Barber, C.L. and Wheeler, R.P., *The Whole Journey. Shakespeare's Power of Development* (Berkeley, Los Angeles, 1986)
Berry, R., *Shakespeare's Comedies. Explorations in Form* (Princeton, 1972)
Berry, R., *Shakespeare and the Awareness of the Audience* (London, 1985)
Bevington, D., *Action is Eloquence* (Cambridge, Mass./London, 1984)
Bland, D.S., 'The "Night of Errors" at Gray's Inn 1594', *N&Q*, 211 (1966), 127 – 128
Bonazza, B.O., *Shakespeare's Early Comedies. A Structural Analysis*, Studies in English Literature, 9 (London/The Hague/Paris, 1966)
Bond, R.W., 'The Framework of *The Comedy of Errors*' in: *Studia Otiosa. Some Attempts in Criticism* (London, 1938), p.43 – 50
Bradbrook, M.C., *The Growth and Structure of Elizabethan Comedy* (London, 1955)
Brooks, C., 'Shakespeare's Romantic Shrews', *SQ*, 11 (1960), 351 – 356
Brown, J.R., *Shakespeare and his Comedies* (London, 1957)
Carroll, W.C., *The Metamorphoses of Shakespearean Comedy* (Princeton, 1985)
Champion, L.S., *The Evolution of Shakespeare's Comedy. A Study in Dramatic Perspective* (Cambridge, Mass., 1970)
Charlton, H.B., *Shakespearean Comedy* (London, 1938)

Clemen, W., *English Tragedy Before Shakespeare. The Development of Dramatic Speech*, transl. T.S. Dorsch (London, 1961)

Clemen, W., *A Commentary on Shakespeare's Richard III*, transl. J. Bonheim (London, 1963)

Clemen, W., *Shakespeare's Dramatic Art. Collected Essays* (London, 1972)

Clemen, W., *The Development of Shakespeare's Imagery* (London, ²1977)

Clemen, W., *Shakespeare's Soliloquies*, transl. C. Scott-Stokes (London/New York, 1987)

Clubb, L.G., 'Italian Comedy and *The Comedy of Errors*', *CL*, 19 (1967), 240 – 251

Craig, H., *An Interpretation of Shakespeare* (Columbia, Miss., 1948)

Coghill, N., 'The Basis of Shakespearean Comedy', *E&S*, n.s. (1950), 1 – 28

Cutts, J.P., *The Shattered Glass: A Dramatic Pattern in Shakespeare's Early Plays* (Detroit, 1968)

Elliott, G.R., 'Weirdness in *The Comedy of Errors*', *UTQ*, 9 (1939), 95 – 106

Erickson, P. and Kahn, C., eds., *Shakespeare's 'Rough Magic'. Renaissance Essays in Honor of C.L. Barber* (Newark/London/ Toronto, 1985)

Evans, B., *Shakespeare's Comedies* (Oxford, 1960)

Felperin, H., *Shakespearean Romance* (Princeton, 1972)

Ferguson, F., '*The Comedy of Errors* and *Much Ado About Nothing*', *SR*, 62 (1954), 24 – 37

Freedman, B., 'Egeon's Debt: Self-Division and Self-Redemption in *The Comedy of Errors*', *ELR*, 10 (1980), 360 – 383

Fuzier, J, 'Shakespeare et la médecine mentale de son temps d'après *La Comédie des Erreurs*', *Etudes Anglaises*, 17 (1964), 421 – 33

Gesner, C., *Shakespeare and the Greek Romance* (Lexington, 1970)

Grivelet, M., 'Shakespeare, Molière, and the Comedy of Ambiguity', *ShS*, 22 (1969), 15 – 26

Hasler, J., *Shakespeare's Theatrical Notation: The Comedies* (Bern, 1974)

Hawkins, H., *Likenesses of Truth in Elizabethan and Restoration Drama* (Oxford, 1972)

Heilman, R.B., 'Shakespeare's Variations of Farcical Style' in: *Shakespeare's Craft. Eight Lectures*, ed. P.H. Highfill, Jr. (Carbondale, 1982), 94 – 112

Henze, R., '*The Comedy of Errors*: A Freely Binding Chain', *SQ*, 22 (1971), 35 – 41

Hunter, R.G., *Shakespeare and the Comedy of Forgiveness* (New York, 1965)

Huston, J.D., *Shakespeare's Comedies of Play* (New York, 1981)

Jones, E., *Scenic Form in Shakespeare* (Oxford, 1971)

Kahn, C., *Man's Estate. Masculine Identity in Shakespeare* (Berkeley, 1981)

Kinney, A.F., 'Shakespeare's *Comedy of Errors* and the Nature of Kinds', *SP*, 85 (1988), 29 – 52

Knapp, M. and Kobialka, M., 'Shakespeare and the Prince of Purpoole: The 1594 Production of *The Comedy of Errors* at Gray's Inn Hall', *Theatre History Studies*, 4 (1984), 71 – 81

Krieger, M., '*Measure for Measure* and Elizabethan Comedy', *PMLA*, 66 (1951), 775 – 784

Leech, C., 'Shakespeare's Comic Dukes', *REL*, 5 (1964), 101 – 114

Leggatt, A., *Shakespeare's Comedy of Love* (London, 1973)

Levin, H., *Shakespeare and the Revolution of the Times. Perspectives and Commentaries* (New York, 1976)

Levin, H., *Playboys and Killjoys. An Essay on the Theory and Practice of Comedy* (Oxford, 1987)

McCary, W.T., 'The Comedy of Errors: A Different Kind of Comedy', *NLH*, 9 (1977/78), 525 – 536

Mowat, B., *The Dramaturgy of Shakespeare's Romances* (Athens, Georgia, 1976)

Muir, K., *Shakespeare's Comic Sequence* (Liverpool, 1979)

Nevo, R., *Comic Transformations in Shakespeare* (London/New York, 1980)

Parrott, T.M., *Shakespearean Comedy* (New York, 1949)

Petronella, V.F., 'Structure and Theme Through Separation and Union in Shakespeare's "The Comedy of Errors" ', *MLR*, 69 (1974), 481 – 488

Pettet, E.C., *Shakespeare and the Romance Tradition* (London, 1949)

Pfister, M., *Studien zum Wandel der Perspektivenstruktur in elisabethanischen und jakobäischen Komödien* (München, 1974)

Phialas, P.G., *Shakespeare's Romantic Comedies. The Development of Their Form and Meaning* (Chapel Hill, 1966)

Riehle, W., *Das Beiseitesprechen bei Shakespeare. Ein Beitrag zur Dramaturgie des elisabethanischen Dramas* (Diss. München, 1964)

Riemer, A.P., *Antic Fables. Patterns of Evasion in Shakespeare's Comedies* (Manchester, 1980)

Salgado, G., ' "Time's deformed Hand": Sequence, Consequence, and Inconsequence in "The Comedy of Errors" ', *ShS*, 25 (1972), 81 – 91

Sanderson, J.L., 'Patience in *The Comedy of Errors*', *Texas Studies in Literature and Language*, 16 (1975), 603 – 618

Schloesser, A., 'Das Motiv der Entfremdung in der *Komödie der Irrungen*', *ShJ*, 100/1 (1964/65), 57 – 71

Sen Gupta, S.C., *Shakespearean Comedy* (London, 1950)

Snyder, S., *The Comic Matrix of Shakespeare's Tragedies* (Princeton, 1979)

Tetzeli v. Rosador, K., 'Plotting the Early Comedies: "The Comedy of Errors", "Love's Labour's Lost", "The Two Gentlemen of Verona" ', *ShS*, 37 (1984), 13 – 22

Thomas, S., 'The Date of *The Comedy of Errors*', *SQ*, 7 (1956), 377 – 384

Tillyard, E.M.W., *The Nature of Comedy and Shakespeare. Presidential Address to the English Association, 1958* (Oxford, 1958)

Tillyard, E.M.W., *Shakespeare's Early Comedies* (London, 1965)

Traversi, D., *William Shakespeare: The Early Comedies*, Writers and their Work, 129 (London, ²1964)

Traversi, D., *An Approach to Shakespeare* (London, 1938), 3rd. ed., revised and expanded (New York, 1969)

Turner, R.Y., *Shakespeare's Apprenticeship* (Chicago/London, 1974)

van Laan, T., *Role-Playing in Shakespeare* (Toronto/Buffalo/London, 1978)

Weimann, R., *Shakespeare and the Popular Tradition in the Theatre*, ed. R. Schwartz (Baltimore/London, 1978)

Weiss, T., *The Breath of Clowns and Kings. Shakespeare's Early Comedies and Histories* (London, 1971)

Weld, J., *Meaning in Comedy. Studies in Elizabethan Romantic Comedy* (Albany, 1975)

Wells, S., 'Reunion Scenes in *The Comedy of Errors* and *Twelfth Night*' in: *A Yearbook of Studies in English Language and Literature. Festschrift f.S. Korninger*, ed. O. Rauchbauer (Wien, 1986), 267 – 76

Williams, G., ' ''The Comedy of Errors'' Rescued from Tragedy', *REL*, 5 (1964), 63 – 71

Wilson, J.D., *Shakespeare's Happy Comedies* (London, 1962)

On Shakespeare's Classical Knowledge and the Influence of New Comedy, and Particularly of Plautus, on Shakespeare

Anson, J., *Dramatic Convention in Shakespeare's Middle Comedies* (Diss. Berkeley, 1964)

Arthos, J., 'Shakespeare's Transformations of Plautus', *CD*, I (1967/68), 239 – 253

Arthos, J., 'Shakespeare and the Ancient World', *Michigan Quarterly Review*, 10 (1971), 149 – 163

Baldwin, T.W., *William Shakspere's Small Latine and Lesse Greeke* (Urbana, 1944), 2 vols.

Baldwin, T.W., *Shakspere's Five-Act Structure* (Urbana, 1947)

Baldwin, T.W., *On the Compositional Genetics of The Comedy of Errors* (Urbana, 1965)

Barber, L.E., '*The Tempest* and New Comedy', *SQ*, 21 (1970), 207 – 212

Barton, A., 'The Comedy of Errors' in: *The Riverside Shakespeare*, ed. G.B. Evans (Boston, 1974), p.79 – 82

Bennett, A.L., 'The Sources of Shakespeare's *Merry Wives*', *RenQ*, 23 (1970), 429 – 33

Blume, H.D., 'Plautus und Shakespeare', *Antike und Abendland*, 15 (1969), 135 – 158

Boas, F.S., *Shakespeare and his Predecessors* (New York, n.d.)

Boesel, M.D., *Identitäts- und Rollenproblematik in den englischen Komödien der Amphitryon- und Menaechmi-Tradition* (Diss. Stuttgart, 1976)

Born, W., *Shakespeares Verhältnis zu seinen Quellen in 'The Comedy of Errors' und 'The Taming of the Shrew'* (Diss. Hamburg, 1955)

Bradbrook, M.C., 'Shakespeare and the Use of Disguise in Elizabethan Drama', *EC*, 2 (1952), 159 – 168

Bradbrook, M.C., *The Growth and Structure of Elizabethan Comedy* (London, 1955)

Brooks, H.F., 'Themes and Structure in ''The Comedy of Errors'' ', *Early Shakespeare*, Stratford-upon-Avon Studies, 3 (1961), 54 – 71

Charlton, H.B., *Shakespearean Comedy* (London, 1938)

Coulter, C.C., 'The Plautine Tradition in Shakespeare', *JEGP*, 19 (1920), 66 – 83

Curry, J.V. *Deception in Elizabethan Comedy* (Chicago, 1955)

Doran, M., *Endeavors of Art. A Study of Form in Elizabethan Drama* (Madison, 1954)

Draper, J.W., 'Mistaken Identity in Shakespeare's Comedies', *Revue Anglo-Américaine*, 11 (1933/34), 189 – 297

Draper, J.W., 'Falstaff and the Plautine Parasite', *CJ*, 33 (1937/38), 390 – 401

Forsythe, R.S., 'A Plautine Source of *The Merry Wives of Windsor*', *MP*, 18 (1920), 57 – 77

Freeburg, V.O., *Disguise Plots in Elizabethan Drama* (New York, 1915)

Frye, N., 'Characterization in Shakespearean Comedy', *SQ*, 4 (1953), 271 – 77

Garrett, J., ed., *Talking of Shakespeare* (London, 1954)

Gaw, A., 'The Evolution of *The Comedy of Errors*', *PMLA*, 41 (1926), 620-666

Gill, E., 'A Comparison of the Characters in *The Comedy of Errors* with those in the *Menaechmi*', *Univ. of Texas Bulletin, Studies in English*, 5 (1925), 79 – 95

Gill, E., 'The Plot-Structure of "The Comedy of Errors" in Relation to its Sources', *University of Texas Bulletin, Studies in English*, 10 (1930), 13 – 65

Heilman, R.B., 'Farce Transformed: Plautus, Shakespeare, and Unamuno', *CL*, 31 (1979), 113 – 123

Hosley, R., 'The Formal Influence of Plautus and Terence', in: J.R. Brown and B. Harris, eds., *Elizabethan Theatre*, Stratford-upon-Avon Studies, 9 (1966), 131 – 46

Hoy, C., *The Hyacinth Room. An Investigation Into the Nature of Comedy, Tragedy, and Tragicomedy* (London, 1964)

Isaac, H., 'Shakespeares Comedy of Errors und die Menächmen des Plautus', *Archiv*, 70 (1883), 1 – 28

Jones, E., *The Origins of Shakespeare* (Oxford, 1977)

Knox, B., '*The Tempest* and the Ancient Comic Tradition', *English Institute Essays 1954* (1955), 52 – 73

Labinski, M., *Shakespeares Komödie der Irrungen. Das Werk und seine Gestaltung auf der Bühne* (Diss. Breslau, 1934)

Levin, H., 'Two Comedies of Errors' in: *Refractions. Essays in Comparative Literature* (New York, 1966), 128 – 150

Long, T., 'The Calculus of Confusion: Cognitive and Associative Errors in Plautus's *Menaechmi* and Shakespeare's *Comedy of Errors*', *Classical Bulletin*, 53 (1976), 20 – 23

Mairhofer, H., *Der direkte Einfluss Plautus' auf die englische Komödie* (Diss. Wien, 1952)

Mehl, D., 'Zum Verständnis des Werkes', in: *Die Komödie der Irrungen*, Rowohlts Klassiker (Reinbek, 1969)

Newman, K., *Shakespeare's Rhetoric of Comic Character. Dramatic Convention in Classical and Renaissance Comedy* (New York/London, 1985)

Ornstein, R., *Shakespeare's Comedies. From Roman Farce to Romantic Mystery* (Newark/London/Toronto, 1986)

Pettet, E.C., *Shakespeare and the Romance Tradition* (London, 1949)

Reinhardstoettner, K.V., *Plautus. Spätere Bearbeitungen plautinischer Lustspiele* (Leipzig, 1886), 568 – 577

Riehle, W., 'Shakespeares monologische Redeformen dramaturgisch betrachtet', *ShJW*, 1985, 28 – 44

Righter, A., *Shakespeare and the Idea of the Play* (Harmondsworth, 1962)

Salingar, L.G., 'The Design of *Twelfth Night*', *SQ*, 9 (1958), 117 – 139

Salingar, L.G., *Shakespeare and the Traditions of Comedy* (Cambridge, 1974)

Salingar, L.G., *Dramatic Form in Shakespeare and the Jacobeans* (Cambridge, 1986)

Simpson, P., *Studies in Elizabethan Drama* (Oxford, 1955)

Svendsen, J.T. 'The Fusion of Comedy and Romance: Plautus' *Rudens* and Shakespeare's *The Tempest'* in: Hartigan, K.V., ed., *From Pen to Performance. Drama as Conceived and Performed* (Washington, D.C., 1983)

Taylor, G., *Reinventing Shakespeare. A Cultural History, From the Restoration to the Present* (London, 1989)

Thomson, J.A.K., *Shakespeare and the Classics* (London, 1962)

Vandiver, E.P., 'The Elizabethan Dramatic Parasite', *SP*, 32 (1935), 411 – 427

Velz, J.W., *Shakespeare and the Classical Tradition. A Critical Guide to Commentary, 1660 – 1960* (Minneapolis, 1968)

Velz, J.W., 'The Ancient World in Shakespeare: Authenticity or Anachronism? A Retrospect', *ShS*, 31 (1978), 1 – 12

Watt, H.A., 'Plautus and Shakespeare: Further comments on *Menaechmi* and *The Comedy of Errors*' *CJ*, 20 (1924 – 25), 401 – 7

Whitaker, V.K., *Shakespeare's Use of Learning* (San Marino, 1953)

Wickham, G., 'Small Latine and Lesse Greeke' in *Talking of Shakespeare*, ed. J. Garrett (London, 1954), 209 – 230

Selected Works on the Humanist Tradition

Bainton, R., *Erasmus of Christendom* (New York, 1969)

Baldwin, T.W., *Shakspere's Small Latine and Lesse Greeke* (Urbana, 1944), 2 vols.

Baratto, M., *La Commedia del Cinquecento* (Vicenza, 1975)

Baumann, U. and Heinrich, H.P., *Thomas Morus. Humanistische Schriften* (Darmstadt, 1986)

Boas, F.S., *University Drama in the Tudor Age* (Oxford, 1914)

Bradshaw, B., 'The Christian humanism of Erasmus', *Journal of theological studies*, n.s., 33 (1982), 411 – 47

Duncan, R., *Ben Jonson and the Lucianic Tradition* (Cambridge, 1979)

Gombrich, E.H., Tafuri, M. et al., *Giulio Romano* (Milano, 1989)

Greenblatt, S., *Renaissance Self-Fashioning. From More to Shakespeare* (Chicago/London, 1980)

Gutmann, E., *Die Colloquia Familiaria des Erasmus von Rotterdam*. Basler Beiträge zur Geschichtswissenschaft, 111 (Basel/Stuttgart, 1968)

Hassel, R.C., *Faith and Folly in Shakespeare's Romantic Comedies* (Athens, Georgia, 1980)

Heep, M., *Die Colloquia Familiaria des Erasmus und Lucian* (Halle, 1927)

Herrick, M.T., *Comic Theory in the Sixteenth Century* (Urbana, 1950)

Herrick, M.T., *Tragicomedy. Its Origin and Development in Italy, France, and England* (Urbana, 1955)

Huizinga, J., *Erasmus and the Age of Reformation*, transl. F. Hopman (Princeton, 1984)

Joseph, Sr M., *Shakespeare's Use of the Arts of Language* (New York, 1947)

Kaiser, W., *Praisers of Folly. Erasmus, Rabelais, Shakespeare* (Cambridge, Mass., 1963)

Kernodle, G.R., *From Art to Theatre. Form and Convention in the Renaissance* (Chicago, 1944)

Kindermann, H., *Das Theaterpublikum der Renaissance* (Salzburg, 1986), II

Kristeller, P.O., *The Humanist Movement, Renaissance Thought: The Classic, Scholastic and Humanist Strains* (New York, 1961)

Kristeller, P.O., *Renaissance Thought and its Sources*, ed. M. Mooney (New York, 1979)

Mansfield, B., *Phoenix of his Age. Interpretations of Erasmus 1550 – 1750* (Toronto/Buffalo/London, 1979)

Mattioli, E., *Luciano e l'Umanesimo* (Napoli, 1980)

McDonald, R., *Shakespeare and Jonson. Jonson and Shakespeare* (Brighton, 1988)

Motter, T.H.V., *The School Drama in England* (London, 1929)

Oreglia, G., *The Commedia dell'Arte* (London, 1968)

Radcliff-Umstead, D., *The Birth of Modern Comedy in Renaissance Italy* (Chicago/London, 1969)

Ristine, F.H., *English Tragicomedy. Its Origin and History* (New York, 1963)

Robinson, C., *Lucian and his Influence in Europe* (London, 1979)

Salzmann, W., *Molière und die lateinische Komödie* (Heidelberg, 1969)

Sargent, R.A., 'Sir Thomas Elyot and the Integrity of *The Two Gentlemen of Verona*', *PMLA*, 65 (1950), 1166 – 1180

Simon, J., *Education and Society in Tudor England* (Cambridge, 1966)

Southern, R.W., *Medieval Humanism and Other Studies* (Oxford, 1970)

Stäuble, A., *Commedia Umanistica del Quattrocento* (Firenze, 1968)

Suchomski, J., *'Delectatio' und 'Utilitas'* (Bern/München, 1975)

Thompson, C.R., *The Translations of Lucian by Erasmus and Thomas More* (Ithaca, 1940)

Tracy, J.D., *Erasmus. The Growth of a Mind* (Genève, 1972)

Trousdale, M., *Shakespeare and the Rhetoricians* (London, 1982)

Ullmann, W., *Medieval Foundations of Renaissance Humanism* (London, 1977)

Williams, K., ed., *Twentieth Century Interpretations of The Praise of Folly* (Englewood Cliffs, 1969)

Yates, F.A., *Theatre of the World* (London, 1969)

Zweig, S., *Erasmus*, transl. E. and C. Paul (London, 1934)

Index

(The Bibliography is not indexed)

Luciana argument (189-97)

Kinney's article attacked (198)

Sample of argument from "intentions" (253)

Giulio Romano & The greatness of
humanism, providing link to 8h. (259)
   see Pafford's Arden ed.